Studies on Chinese Discourse Grammar

This book extends the traditional research perspective of single sentences and contexts to the textual structure of real discourse materials.

Taking discourse functional grammar as its theoretical orientation, the book combines relevant theories with Chinese practice to work on a number of topics, including discourse phenomena and syntactic integration, the information status and discourse function of special syntactic structures, the emergence of discourse functions of metadiscourse components, and stylistic differences and their syntactic manifestations. Syntactic-semantic laws and discourse functions are examined in relation to each other, which better reveals their inner connection; a focus on the shaping of grammatical structures by interactional factors brings to light the functional motivations behind grammatical rules. In contrast to traditional Chinese grammar research, which takes individual simple or complex sentences as the object of study, this book mainly analyses grammatical phenomena that span sentences. By broadening the scope of research, it enables further exploration of issues that are difficult to address satisfactorily at the sentence level, thus enriching the study of Chinese grammar.

The book will be of great interest to students and scholars of interactional linguistics, Chinese linguistics and functional grammar.

FANG Mei is a Professor at the Institute of Linguistics, Chinese Academy of Social Sciences. She is currently the deputy editor-in-chief of *Studies of the Chinese Language* (中国语文) and the vice-president of Chinese Language Society. She has been working on Chinese grammar and discourse analysis with the functional approach, focusing on the emergent nature of grammatical patterns, pragmaticalization, and grammar in interaction.

China Perspectives

The *China Perspectives* series focuses on translating and publishing works by leading Chinese scholars, writing about both global topics and China-related themes. It covers Humanities & Social Sciences, Education, Media and Psychology, as well as many interdisciplinary themes.

This is the first time any of these books have been published in English for international readers. The series aims to put forward a Chinese perspective, give insights into cutting-edge academic thinking in China, and inspire researchers globally.

To submit proposals, please contact the Taylor & Francis Publisher for the China Publishing Programme, Lian Sun (Lian.Sun@informa.com)

Titles in linguistics currently include:

Cognitive Neural Mechanism of Semantic Rhetoric
Qiaoyun Liao, and Lijun Meng

Singapore Mandarin Grammar II
Lu Jianming

Automated Written Corrective Feedback in Research Paper Revision
The Good, The Bad, and The Missing
Qian Guo, Ruiling Feng, and Yuanfang Hua

The Chinese Rhyme Tables
Volume II
Pan Wenguo

The Cultural Turn in Translation Studies
Wang Ning

Studies on Chinese Discourse Grammar
FANG Mei

For more information, please visit https://www.routledge.com/China-Perspectives/book-series/CPH

Studies on Chinese Discourse Grammar

FANG Mei

Taylor & Francis Group
LONDON AND NEW YORK

Sponsored by the Chinese Fund for the Humanities and Social Sciences (No.20WYYB009).

First published 2024
by Routledge
4 Park Square, Milton Park, Abingdon, Oxon OX14 4RN

and by Routledge
605 Third Avenue, New York, NY 10158

Routledge is an imprint of the Taylor & Francis Group, an informa business

© 2024 FANG Mei
Translated by LIU Linjun

The right of FANG Mei to be identified as author of this work has been asserted in accordance with sections 77 and 78 of the Copyright, Designs and Patents Act 1988.

All rights reserved. No part of this book may be reprinted or reproduced or utilised in any form or by any electronic, mechanical, or other means, now known or hereafter invented, including photocopying and recording, or in any information storage or retrieval system, without permission in writing from the publishers.

Trademark notice: Product or corporate names may be trademarks or registered trademarks, and are used only for identification and explanation without intent to infringe.

English Version by Permission of Social Sciences Academic Press (China).

British Library Cataloguing-in-Publication Data
A catalogue record for this book is available from the British Library

ISBN: 978-1-032-58924-4 (hbk)
ISBN: 978-1-032-70066-3 (pbk)
ISBN: 978-1-032-70065-6 (ebk)

DOI: 10.4324/9781032700656

Typeset in Times New Roman
by SPi Technologies India Pvt Ltd (Straive)

Contents

List of illustrations	*vii*
Acknowledgements	*viii*
List of abbreviations	*ix*
1 Discourse grammar and studies on Chinese discourse grammar	1
2 Modes of clausal correlation and syntactic integration	30
3 Syntactic integration function of zero-subject clauses	44
4 Discourse functions of "indefinite-subject sentences"	71
5 Forms of action reference and their topic function	95
6 Discourse functions of verb-copying constructions	120
7 S-adverbs and their discourse functions	138
8 From quoting to hedging	157
9 Discourse function of speech verb metadiscourse	179
10 Discourse cohesion and orientation expression	197
11 Characteristics of traditional narratives and their impacts on Chinese grammar	204

Concluding remarks	235
Afterword to the Chinese Edition	237
Appendix	238
References	239
Index	266

Illustrations

Figures

2.1	Desententialization of Chinese clauses	41
6.1	Framework of Chinese NP anaphora (Xu Jiujiu, 2005a)	126

Tables

3.1	Transitivity features (adapted from Hopper and Thompson, 1980: 252)	59
5.1	Referential meaning differences between 这 (S) VP and S (这) VP	100
5.2	Distribution of different referential formats in discourse	104
5.3	Discourse distribution of 这 in front of VP and NP	107
5.4	Referential property of 这 before VP and NP	107
8.1	Usage of 说是	170
8.2	Expression function of "X是"	176
10.1	Frequency counts of 但见 and 单说 in Fresh Flavors	202

Acknowledgements

The research work of this book is supported by the Innovation Project of the Chinese Academy of Social Sciences (CASS), and is a phased achievement of "Syntax and Semantics of Modern Chinese", a key discipline construction project of the CASS.

Almost all the contents of this book have been presented at academic conferences, and have received comments and suggestions from the participating scholars. Special thanks to Wei-Tien Dylan Tsai, Chen Ping, Chen Yi, Feng Shengli, Guo Rui, Jin Lixin, Li Wei, Lee Hun Tak Thomas, Li Zongjiang, Li Xianyin, Liu Dawei, Liu Lening, Meichun Liu, Lu Bingfu, Kang Kwong Luke, Lu Jianming, Pan Haihua, Ren Ying, Shao Jingmin, Shen Jiaxuan, Shi Chunhong, Shi Dingxu, Shi Jinsheng, Tao Hongyin, Wan Quan, Wang Canlong, Wang Xiuli, Zhang Bojiang, Zhang Li, Zhang Wangxi, Zhang Yisheng, Zhu Qingzhi, Zhu Keyi, Xing Xin, Xu Liejiong, and Xu Yangchun.

Thanks are also due to Dr. Fang Di, Dr. Guan Yue, Dr. Tian Ting and Dr. Wang Wenying, for their reading and proofreading the full text of the manuscript. Finally, thanks to Prof. Liu Linjun at Beijing Language and Culture University and her work team for their translation of the book.

Abbreviations

·er	retroflex
ACH	achievement
aux.	auxiliary
CL	classifier
CM	complement marker 得 (*de*)
DUR	durative aspect marker
EXP	experiential 过 (-guò)
MP	modal particle
NM	noun marker 的 (*de*)
pass.	passive
PF	pause filler
PFV	perfective aspect marker
SFP	sentence final particle
SMP	sentence middle particle

1 Discourse grammar and studies on Chinese discourse grammar

Discourse grammatical analysis takes grammatical categories as the starting point to analyze grammatical phenomena in discourse, a level beyond individual sentences. It focuses on the status and functions of different grammatical categories and grammatical devices in discourse, and on the shaping of linguistic expressions and grammatical devices by interactional factors. Studies on Chinese discourse grammar adopt two distinct research orientations: one is top-down, taking the information structure and discourse phenomena as the entry point to discuss the choice of syntactic forms in terms of discourse needs; the other is bottom-up, starting from the syntactic roles or syntactic categories to explain the discourse-functional motivations for syntactic codes. With the progressive study of naturally occurring speech, discourse grammar has begun to focus on the influence and shaping of interpersonal factors on spoken discourse.

1.1 Introduction

An important task of linguistic research is to describe and explain the correlation between form and meaning, given that language components are unities of both form and meaning. In description, it is impossible to have a comprehensive understanding of discourse when it is taken as a static speech product in isolation. Analysis of discourse must take into account the external conditions of language use, including: 1) cognitive constraints, such as the way information is stored and extracted, cognitive strategies, memory constraints, and optimal procedures for information processing; 2) communicative context, which consists of the relationship between the two parties to conversation, the venue where the speech event occurs, and the purpose of communication; 3) cultural and ethnic contexts; that is, how cultural and ethnic differences or prejudices permeate into discourse.

Since the 1980s, there have been several important theoretical contributions to the study of discourse-functional linguistics.

The first one is Rhetorical Structure Theory (RST) (Mann and Thompson, 1987), whose main purpose is to analyze the logico-semantic connections of adjacent clauses. According to RST, there are more than 20 types of interclausal relations, which illustrate how clauses are hierarchically organized in discourse.

The second is the theoretical formulations of thematic structure (Givón, 1984/1990; Du Bois, 1980; Chen, 2004a; Luke, 2004a), which explain how people and things are introduced into discourse and how they recur in later discourse. The repeated occurrence of the same entity in the process of discourse unfolding constitutes a topic chain, an important aspect of the coherence of discourse structure, and the different strengths of topicality have different syntactic manifestations.

The third concerns the relationship between prosody and syntax. Noticing that intonation units does not correspond to syntactic nodes, Chafe (1987) has proposed the so-called one-new-concept constraint, i.e., only one new piece of information in one intonation unit (Chafe, 1987, 1994; Tao, 1996).

The fourth is about the variability of stylistic features. From the syntactic point of view, the core elements of stylistic variation can be summarized as differences in the degree of attention to temporal succession and agent orientation. Typical narratives exhibit both temporal succession and agent orientation; operational discourse shows temporal succession but not agent orientation; behavioral discourse does not have temporal succession but focuses on agent orientation; and expository discourse manifests neither temporal succession nor agent orientation. This variability results in a range of different syntactic choices (Longacre, 1983).

The fifth is the syntactic interaction of speech participants. During the process of communication, one participant's speech will enter into the syntactic structure of the other. For example, antecedent nouns and restrictive clauses can be produced jointly by both parties in conversation; increments independent of the clause structure provide a mechanism for turn-taking on the part of the participants; etc. (Ford, Fox and Thompson, 2002).

The sixth is "the syntax of sentences-in-progress", which interprets speech production in interactional communication from the perspective of online generation, giving emphasis to the fact that new information is superimposed over time. Word order is not only related to the status of the information conveyed by the syntactic constituent (old vs. new), but also suggests the relevant position for turn-taking in conversation (Lerner, 1991; Luke, 2000, 2002).

Discourse linguistics is a usage-oriented study that focuses on the influence of communicative-social factors on the process and product of speech events. When the focus is on the constraints of communicative-social factors on the process, Conversation Analysis emerges as a separate discipline; when the focus is on the effects of such factors on language product, the discipline Discourse Grammar comes into being.

Discourse Grammar is the analysis of grammatical phenomena across sentences, taking grammatical categories as the starting point. It focuses on the statuses and functions of different grammatical categories and grammatical devices in discourse, and on the way in which communicative interaction shapes linguistic expressions and grammatical devices. In some literature, especially around the 1980s, Discourse Analysis and Text Grammar are used interchangeably with Discourse Grammar, such as *Discourse Analysis* by Brown and Yule (1983) (Chen Ping, 1987b; Chu, 1998; Jiujiu Xu, 1995a).

Discourse-function oriented grammar research has two goals. One is description, showing how users use language forms. There are a large number of expressions in language that express the same "content" but take different "forms". For instance, when referring to an entity, one can use a noun phrase, a bare noun, or a pronoun. Then how does the speaker choose to use one form of expression over another? The second is explanation, which answers the question of "what shapes language structures". For example, what are the mechanisms that determine the universality of pronouns, a category that exists universally in human languages?

Functional grammarians generally seek explanations for the phenomena they describe in three ways, the cognitive perspective, the social or interactional perspective, and the perspective of diachronic evolution, which are in fact interrelated. Functional grammarians argue that the diversity of linguistic expressions derives from the different functional needs in communication, and that the competition between different needs shapes the structural forms of language (Du Bois, 1985).

An early monograph on Chinese Discourse Grammar is *A Discourse Grammar of Mandarin Chinese* by Chauncey Chu (1998/2006), which covers certain parts of clauses, compound sentences, and paragraphs, and maintains the following differences from Discourse Analysis: 1. Discourse Analysis generally focuses on communication, while Discourse Grammar focuses more on structure; 2. Discourse Analysis studies both spoken and written language, whereas Discourse Grammar in Chu's monograph mainly examines written language; 3. Discourse Grammar emphasizes structure at both the grammatical and discourse levels. Chu also argues that the syntax of pronominalization, reflexivization and aspect marking, which has not been sufficiently studied, can be better explained in Discourse Grammar. The book contains 11 chapters: 1. Introduction: between grammar and discourse; 2. Verbal affixes: aspect and discourse function; 3. Modality adverbs in discourse; 4. Sentence-final particles; 5. The structure of information; 6. Subordination and grounding structure; 7. Topicality, prototype and Chinese topic; 8. Anaphora in discourse; 9. Topic chain and Chinese sentence; 10. The paragraphs and beyond; and 11. Conclusion.

This book absorbs the main results of Chinese Discourse Grammar on the one hand, and summarizes the author's own research for many years on the other. The prototype approach to Chinese topic study, the relationship between the main–subordinate opposition and foregrounding structure in Chinese, the discourse function of aspect markers and the analysis of paragraphs and beyond can be particularly enlightening to linguistic research.

In the following, some major concepts in the study of Discourse Grammar are discussed, and the research ideas of functional linguists on the west coast of the United States are introduced and explained with relevant examples from Chinese with a view to facilitating the reader's understanding of the subsequent chapters.

1.2 Information flow

1.2.1 Nominal constituents and cognitive states

Information flow is a concept widely used by functionalist linguists who believe that the central and most basic function of language is to transmit information from the speaker/writer to the listener/reader. The ease with which information can be expressed or understood varies with both parties of communication. The speaker is responsible for deciding what aspect(s) to be put in to or out of focus of consciousness while the listener should attend to what the speaker says that is the same as or different from his or her own expectations and existing knowledge. In the process of communication, the cognitive states of different concepts in the human brain are different, and the communication of information necessarily involves the dynamic cognitive states of both the speaker and the listener. In order to focus the listener's attention on what is important, the speaker will code old information (i.e., information that the speaker believes is known to the listener) and new information (i.e., information that the speaker believes is unknown to the listener) differently. In general, old information is coded simply whereas new information is coded in a complex manner. The hierarchy from simple to complex coding can be represented as follows:

zero form > pronoun > bare noun > pronoun/demonstrative+noun > restrictive modifier+noun > descriptive modifier+noun > relative clause

When the speaker/writer believes that the listener/reader can distinguish the referent from other entities, he or she will use the minimal form, such as a pronoun or a zero form, or a more complex form otherwise, say a relative clause. The difference in the form of the referential structure reflects the speaker/writer's confirmation of the information status of the referent. Which referential form to use reflects the different verbal strategies of the language user.

In the process of communication, different concepts have different cognitive states in the human mind. Those that have been established in conversation are in an active state, thus known information (or old information) to the listener. Some concepts are not yet established at the moment of conversation, but can be inferred by the listener through background knowledge. Such semi-active information can be activated in interaction, which gives it the status of accessible information. When viewed from the opposition between "new" vs. "old" information or "known" vs. "unknown" information, accessible information lies in the middle of the continuum:

old information > accessible information > new information

The comprehension of accessible information relies on the knowledge system of the listener, which falls broadly into the following categories:

1) knowledge shared by the human species, e.g., kinship relations and the relationship between body and limbs;
2) knowledge specified by the speech scene, e.g., "Take down the clock.", which is licensed when there is only one clock in the scene;
3) knowledge shared by the speaker and the addressee, e.g., "The physics class in the afternoon has been canceled."

The degree of difficulty with which a nominal constituent is understood by the listener, which can be dubbed as accessibility, may vary with the coding form. The accessibility hierarchy is as follows:

> first person > second person > third person > anaphoric nominal > stated propositional content > situational context > shared knowledge > discourse revision

The first person is the most accessible while discourse revision is the least accessible. The more accessible element takes less time for the listener/reader to recognize in communication; conversely, it takes longer time. As introduced in Chen Ping (1987c), an experiment by Haviland and Clark (1974) shows that in "We got some beer out of the trunk. The beer was warm.", it takes less time to conclude that "some beer" and "the beer" are coreferential than to judge that "the beer" refers back to "the picnic supplies" in "We checked the picnic supplies. The beer was warm." The difference in the length of the judgment time illustrates from one perspective how different information statuses impact the process of comprehension.

Xu Yulong (2004) classifies Chinese referential expressions into three categories: high-accessibility marker, intermediate-accessibility marker, and low-accessibility marker. Zero-form pronouns, reflexive pronouns, and singular demonstratives are regarded as high-accessibility markers. When pronouns and demonstrative noun phrases act as grammatical objects, their referents are of intermediate accessibility.

If a constituent is highly accessible, it may very well take a zero form. Chen Ping (1987c) examines how referents are introduced into Chinese narratives from the perspective of discourse structure and how they are kept track of through various referential devices. The results show that the choice of zero-form and other referential forms relies heavily on discourse-pragmatic information.

1.2.2 *Light subject restriction and principle of linear increment*

The light subject restriction and the principle of linear increment concern sentence organization. The syntactic manifestations of information structure have been summarized by some scholars as "the principle of end weight" – complex structures are placed at the end of the sentence, and "the light subject restriction" – the subject of a sentence tends to take a light form. When it comes to nominal constituents, there is a continuum from the pronoun, which is relatively light in form, to the relative clause, which is a comparatively heavy form:

pronoun > bare noun > pronoun/demonstrative+noun > restrictive modifier+noun > descriptive modifier+noun > relative clause+noun

For a declarative sentence, the unmarked pattern (or the default order) is from old information to new information; that is, the subject normally expresses old information and the object conveys new information. Bolinger (1977) has summarized this tendency as the principle of linear increment, which means that the natural order of speech is to express old information before new information. With the progression of the sentence, the constituents that come later in the linear order provide more new information than those that come earlier. See (1) and (2).[1]

(1) a. *他们一看就懂上面两段古文
    *Tāmen yī kàn jiù dǒng shàngmiàn liǎng duàn gǔwén.
  b. 上面两段古文他们一看就懂
    Shàngmiàn liǎng duàn gǔwén tāmen yī kàn jiù dǒng.
    above two paragraph ancient.Chinese they once glance just understand
    'They understood the above two paragraphs of ancient Chinese at a glance.'
(2) a. ?一个老头走进储蓄所
    Yī gè lǎotóu zǒu jìn chúxùsuǒ.
  b. 储蓄所走进一个老头
    Chúxùsuǒ zǒu jìn yī gè lǎotóu.
    savings.house walk into one CL old.man
    'An old man walked into the savings house.'

When the referent of the head noun is indefinite, the modifying constituent is required to come after the head noun. For example, an adjective, when used as the modifier, usually occurs before the noun in English; but if the modified constituent is of generic reference, the adjective will occur after the modified constituent, such as *something new, something old, something blue, something borrowed*, etc., where this order is mandatory. A similar case in Chinese is seen in (3).

(3) a. 你们班里万一有谁吸毒的,谁这个瞎搞的,谁携枪的,这谁受得了啊!
Nǐmen bān lǐ wànyī yǒu shéi xīdú de,
your class in in.case have who take.drugs NM
shéi zhèige xiāgǎo de, shéi xié qiāng de,
who PF fool.around NM who carry gun NM
zhè shéi shòudeliǎo a!
this who able.to.stand SFP
'Should there be someone in your class that takes drugs, fools around, or carries a gun, who can stand it!'

b. *你们班里万一有吸毒的谁,这个瞎搞的谁,携枪的谁,这谁受得了啊!
*Nǐmen bān lǐ wànyī yǒu xīdú de shéi, zhège xiāgǎo de shéi, xié qiāng de shéi, zhè shéi shòudeliǎo a!

In (3), the referent of the head noun "谁" ('who') is indefinite, which renders it mandatory for the modifying constituent to come after it. The importance of the information increases from left to right of the sentence, which is in line with the principle of linear increment, with "你们班" ('your class') being the most definite and providing the least amount of new information, "谁" being something in between, and "吸毒的" ('that takes drugs') being the least definite. Therefore, it can be said that even in Chinese, whether the modifier precedes or follows the modified is closely related to the semantic certainty of the modified. The greater the amount of new information provided by the modifier, the more it tends to be placed after the modified.

Cross-linguistically, there is abundant evidence in support of this view. For example, Bernardo (1979) has drawn an enlightening conclusion from a study of The Pear Story told in English: two types of relative clauses can be distinguished based on the semantic relationship between the modifier and the modified: one is informative, and the other is non-informative but differentiating. Tao Hongyin (2002) examines the Chinese texts elicited also from the "Pear Story", finding that the main function of the relative clause encoded in the *de*-construction that occurs before the head noun is to refer back to, or to track a referent that has already appeared in the speech context. In other words, these constituents do not provide new information. Relative clauses that provide new information in spoken Chinese are generally postposed after the head noun (see Fang Mei, 2018, pp. 38–54).

(4) 你比如说你跟着那种水平不高的英语老师,他根本不知道那个纯正的英语发音,他英语语法也不怎么样,你就全完了。(Survey corpus)
Nǐ bǐrúshuō nǐ gēnzhe nà zhǒng shuǐpíng bù gāo
de Yīngyǔ lǎoshī,
you for.example you follow.DUR that kind level not high
NM English

tā   gēnběn   bù zhīdào   nàgè chúnzhèng de   Yīngyǔ
teacher he at.all   not know   that   pure   NM English
fāyīn, tā Yīngyǔ yǔfǎ yě bùzěnmeyàng, nǐ jiù quánwánle.
pronunciation he English grammar too not.good you just all finish.PFV

'For example, if you follow the kind of English teacher of a limited level, <u>who doesn't know pure English pronunciation at all</u>, and <u>who is not good at English grammar</u>, you would be all finished.'

In (4), the underlined are two relative clause, both modifying the preceding "英语老师" ('English teacher') with new information.

The light subject restriction and the principle of linear increment as discussed here apply to unmarked sentence types (mainly indicative sentences). Interrogative and imperative sentences, however, are more influenced by interactional communication patterns and may violate the principle of linear increment to place the important elements first under the influence of other discourse factors. "Transposition" of certain constituents in dialog represents a ready example (say 知道吗你? [Zhīdào ma nǐ?, 'Do you know?'], where "你" ('you') is transposed to follow its predicate and the sentence-final particle "吗"; 根本就不知道我们都 [Gēnběn jiù bù zhīdào wǒmen dōu, 'We don't know at all.', where "我们" ['we'] and "都" ['all'] are both transposed).

1.2.3 One-new-concept constraint and preferred argument structure

When a new message is to be conveyed in discourse, the speaker may use a more complete or elaborate structural form. Conversely, if the message is old information, a lighter form with a simpler structure will be used. This phenomenon is driven partly by the principle of economy, but more importantly by the limitations of human cognitive capacity as manifested in the restriction on the total amount of new information encoded in one intonation unit (IU).

In naturally occurring speech, continuous discourse consists not of an indivisible sequence of words, but of a sequence of prosodically patterned speech chunks. An intonation unit is a string of words within the framework of a natural intonation, a relatively independent prosodic unit, as well as a basic unit of expression. The amount and status of information conveyed by an intonation unit reflects the brain's processing of information, constituting an external manifestation of the thought process. Chafe (1994) argues that an intonation unit usually conveys no more than one new concept, i.e., "one new concept at a time", which is referred to as the one-new-concept constraint.

In terms of information presentation function, nominal constituents can be roughly grouped as follows (from old information to new information):

Old Info zero pronoun > pronoun > noun > nominal phrase **New Info**

In spoken Chinese, the one-new-concept constraint has great impact on the complexity of the unit of expression. If a speaker wants to convey two or more new concepts, he or she will split them up into their respective independent intonational units, which is the increment phenomenon commonly seen in spoken Chinese. That is, as speech progresses, the speaker keeps adding new information one piece at a time.

(5) 我刚买了辆车,日本原装进口的,越野,今年最流行的款式。
Wǒ   gāng   mǎile   liàng   chē,
I   just   buy.PFV CL   motor.vehicle
Rìběn   yuánzhuāng   jìnkǒu   de,   yuèyě,
Japan   original.packaging import   aux. off-road
jīnnián   zuì   liúxíng   de   kuǎnshì.
this.year most   popular   NM   model
'I've just bought a motor vehicle, imported from Japan, off-road, the most popular model of this year.'

In contrast, (5') is only marginally acceptable, in that the underlined modifying constituent is a bit too long.

(5') ?我刚买了辆<u>日本原装进口的今年最流行款式的越野</u>车。
?Wǒ gāng mǎile liàng <u>Rìběn yuánzhuāng jìnkǒu de jīnnián zuì liúxíng kuǎnshì de yuèyěchē</u>.

The one-new-concept constraint can be used to explain the information load that a clause can carry. Because there is generally no more than one piece of new information per intonation unit, a new intonation unit tends to be chosen over a long modifier with a complex structure when the information to be coded exceeds "one new concept". This pragmatic principle manifests itself in syntax by way of having only one lexical argument in a clausal argument structure. For instance, in "I am in love with a Shanghai girl", "I" is a pronoun and "a Shanghai girl" is the only lexical argument. Lexical arguments are usually associated with new information.

In speech, an intonation unit corresponds roughly to a clause. According to Du Bois' (1987) examination of Sacapultec, a clause tends to have only one lexical argument, which is dubbed as the "preferred argument structure": 1) there is at most one lexical argument in each clause; and 2) lexical arguments should be avoided in the subject slot of the transitive clause. Du Bois also proposes two pragmatic principles, namely: 1) at most one new information argument per clause; and 2) avoiding new information in the subject slot of a transitive clause.

Since the amount of new information that can be conveyed at a time (i.e., in one intonation unit) is limited, there are very few cases where two or more lexical arguments appear in the same intonation unit, a finding that can be seen as the syntactic manifestation of the one-new-concept constraint.

Drawing on Du Bois' research results, Tao (1996) has found that this pattern also applies to Chinese intonation units and syntactic patterns through a study of the clausal argument structure in corpora of Chinese oral narratives. In other words, Chinese clauses also prefer the pattern of one lexical argument at a time.

1.3 Discourse structure

1.3.1 Topic

"Topic" and "comment" make up a dichotomy of extensive use. From the perspective of communication, "topic" is "what is being talked about", while "comment" is "what is said about the topic". If a constituent X is called topic, it can answer the question "What about X?" In some languages, topics make up a pragmatic category, while in others, they enjoy an independent syntactic status (Xu Liejung, 2002).[2]

Either way, topic is a concept that spans different levels. It can be specific to a single utterance or cover a discourse stretch. In the former case, it is known as a sentence topic, and in the latter it makes a discourse topic.

The sentence topic is what the sentence is about, and the subject of the sentence in Chinese is also the default topic, a point that has been made in many works. It is, nonetheless, worth mentioning that some sentences fulfill the function of introducing the topic while the topic constituent is not in the position of the subject. In (6), for example, "几个男孩子" ('some boys') is in the object position of the verb "有" ('have'), but it is the constituent "being talked about". As a matter of fact, such "existential/presentational sentences" are often used to introduce topics in discourse.

(6) 这个时候在旁边有<u>几个男孩子</u>出来。有<u>一个男孩子</u>好像打着那个球,有个球跟那个拍子上面连着一条线,这样子哒!哒!哒!<u>其他的小孩子</u>过来帮他。(cited from Chen Peiling and Tao Hongyin, 1998)

Zhège shíhòu zài pángbiān yǒu <u>jǐgè nánháizi</u> chūlái.
this time at side have some boys come.out

Yǒu <u>yī gè nánháizi</u> hǎoxiàng dǎzhe nèigè qiú,
have one CL boy seem play.DUR PF ball

yǒu gè qiú gēn nàgè pāizi shàngmiàn liánzhe yī tiáo xiàn, zhèyàngzi dā! dā! dā!

<u>Qítā de xiǎo háizi</u> guòlái bāng tā.[3]
other NM little child come help him

'At this time, some boys came out from the side. One boy seemed to be playing a ball, which was attached to the racket with a line, making sounds of da-da-da. The other children came to help him.'

The discourse topic is what the discourse mainly talks about, usually the protagonist of the event. There are two different cases in which a concept can be mentioned in discourse. In one case, the concept is the topic, which, once introduced, will be tracked in different ways in subsequent discourse, such as "母亲" ('mother') in (7) below. In the other case, the concept appears only once, without being further mentioned, such as "袍罩" ('robe'), "炕" ('kang'), and "油盐店" ('oil and salt store') in the same example. If a concept is the major concern of discourse, more often than not it will appear many a time and is tracked in different ways, which is a sign of its topicality. The concept that appears only once is trivial information without topicality (see Tao Hongyin and Zhang Bojiang, 2000 for the syntactic manifestations of the protagonist of a speech event).

(7) **母亲**喝了茶,[1]脱了刚才上街穿的**袍罩**,[2]盘腿坐在**炕**上。她抓些铜钱当算盘用,大点的代表一吊,小点的代表一百。她先核计该还多少债,[3]口中念念有词,[4]手里捻动着几个铜钱,而后摆在左方。左方摆好,一看右方(过日子的钱)太少,[5]就又轻轻地从左方撤下几个钱,[6]心想:对**油盐店**多说几句好话,也许可以少还几个。[7]想着想着,她的手心上就出了汗,[8]很快地又把撤下的钱补还原位。(Lao She, *Under the Red Flag* [《正红旗下》])

Mǔqīn hēle chá, [1] tuōle gāngcái shàng jiē chuān de **páozhào**, [2] pántuǐ zuò zài **kàng** shàng. Tā zhuā xiē tóngqián dāng suànpán yòng, dà diǎn de dàibiǎo yī diào, xiǎo diǎn de dàibiǎo yībǎi. Tā xiān héjì gāi huán duōshǎo zhài, [3] kǒuzhōng niànniànyǒucí, [4] shǒulǐ niǎndòngzhe jǐ gè tóngqián, érhòu bǎi zài zuǒfāng. Zuǒfāng bǎihǎo, yī kàn yòufāng (guòrìzi de qián) tài shǎo, [5] jiù yòu qīngqīngde cóng zuǒfāng chèxià jǐ gè qián, [6] xīnxiǎng: Duì **yóuyándiàn** duō shuō jǐ jù hǎohuà, yěxǔ kěyǐ shǎo huán jǐ gè. [7] Xiǎngzhe~xiǎngzhe, tā de shǒuxīn shàng jiù chūle hàn, [8] hěn kuài de yòu bǎ chèxià de qián bǔhuán yuán wèi.

'Mother drank her tea, [1] took off the **robe** she had just worn on the street, [2] and sat cross-legged on the **kang**. She grabbed some copper coins and used them as an abacus, the larger ones representing a thousand each and the smaller ones a hundred each. She first calculated how much debt she should pay, [3] reciting the words under her breath. [4] (She) twirled a few coins in her hand, and then placed them on the left. When she noticed that the right side (the money to live on) was too little, [5] (she) gently removed some from the left side, [6] thinking: Maybe I could pay a bit less of the debt to **the oil and salt store** if I say some more good words to them. [7] As (she) thought about it, her palms became sweaty. [8] (She) then quickly put the money she had withdrawn back into place.'

The frequency and manner of anaphora can be used as important indicators of discourse topicality. For example, "母亲" ('mother') in (7) has two anaphoric forms, pronoun and zero-form. The pronoun "她" ('she') appears three times, and the zero-form eight times (as indicated by the bracketed numbers). Another concept, "铜钱" ('copper coin') also appears more than once in the passage, and after the first occurrence, it is mentioned in different ways, some in nominal phrases and others in numeral phrases (allomorphic anaphors: "大点的" ['the bigger'], "小点的" ['the smaller'], "几个" ['several']; homomorphic anaphor: "铜钱" ['copper coin']; and partial homomorphic anaphor: "钱" ['coin']). When the two concepts of "mother" and "copper coin" are compared, two distinctive features emerge for "mother": first, the frequency of anaphora is relatively high, and second, a large number of zero-forms are used for anaphoric purposes, both of which jointly grant "mother" the status as the default "object to be talked about". That is, in terms of frequency and manner of anaphora, "mother" is the discourse topic.

1.3.2 Topic continuity

Topic continuity, which refers to the strength and range of influence of a topic, is an important aspect of topic research. Topic continuity has three dimensions, 1) thematic continuity, 2) behavioral continuity, and 3) participant continuity, of which thematic continuity has the greatest range of influence. Topic continuity can be measured in three ways: look back, ambiguity, and decay (Givón, 1983)

Topic continuity manifests itself in different manners.

1) Syntactic position
The default position of topic is the subject position of the sentence, which usually has the dual identity of subject and topic, as well as the protagonist of the narrative. Therefore, the range of influence of the referent as denoted by the subject of a sentence can be limited to the hosting sentence or span multiple sentences, which is evidenced by the frequency of subject omission in later occurring sentences. The omission of the subject accounts for the vast majority of omissions, far exceeding that of other syntactic constituents. In Chinese, the syntactic possessor of the subject entity is second only to the subject in topic continuity, as shown by the fact that zero-forms are often seen in subsequent sentences to be coreferential with the possessor modifier of the subject of the preceding sentence (Fang Mei, 1985).
2) Syntactic and rhetorical structure
The higher the structural similarity between the neighboring sentences, the greater the possibility of continuing the same topic.

Chen Ping (1987c) argues that zero form anaphora requires the coreferential element to be as close as possible, with no complex constituent meddling in between. At the same time, the use of zero form is also constrained by the macro-structure of discourse.

Using Givón's (1983) measure to examine the continuity of the pronoun 他 'he', Xu Jiujiu (1990) has found that the (non)occurrence of 他 is constrained by a variety of factors – character constraint (single or multiple), plot constraint (beginning, development, or ending), temporal constraint (presence or absence), conjunction constraint (whether it is a post-conjunctive position), and structural constraint (whether the clause structure is the same).

Li and Thompson (1979) conducted a survey on the use of third-person pronoun by removing all 他 'he' from a passage in the narrative of *The Scholars* (《儒林外史》) and then asking native Chinese speakers to fill in the slots where they thought 他 should be found. The finding is as follows: no two people gave the same answer, and in the slots where 他 was removed, half of the respondents showed agreement on only two of all slots, leaving less than half of the respondents thinking that 他 should be used in the rest of the slots. This survey suggests that there is a certain degree of flexibility in the use of pronouns in Chinese, and that there are not many cases where the use of pronouns is strictly mandatory.

When it comes to anaphoric reference, the lighter the form, the more likely it is to continue the same topic: zero form > pronoun > homomorphic noun > demonstrative+noun > descriptive modifier+noun

(8) 马锐$_i$是来请求父亲$_j$批准出去玩一会儿的。但他$_i$没有直截了当地提出请求，而是在饭后0$_i$主动积极地去刷碗、扫地、擦桌子，0$_i$把一切归置完了，0$_i$像个有事要求主人的丫鬟把<u>一杯新沏的茶和一把扇子</u>递到正腆着肚子剔牙的马林生手里，自己站在一边不住地拿眼去找爸爸$_j$的视线，0$_i$磨磨蹭蹭地不肯走开，0$_i$没话找话地问：“还有什么要我干的么？”(Wang Shuo, *I'm Your Father* [《我是你爸爸》])

Mǎ Ruì$_i$ shì lái qǐngqiú fùqīn$_j$ pīzhǔn chūqù wán yīhuì·er de. Dàn tā$_i$ méiyǒu zhíjiéliǎodāng de tíchū qǐngqiú, érshì zài fàn hòu 0$_i$ zhǔdòng jījí de qù shuāwǎn, sǎodì, cā zhuōzi, 0$_i$ bǎ yīqiè guīzhì wán le, 0$_i$ xiàng gè yǒushì yào qiú zhǔrén de yāhuán <u>bǎ yī bēi xīn qī de chá hé yī bǎ shànzi</u> dì dào zhèng tiǎnzhe dùzi tīyá de Mǎ Línshēng shǒulǐ, zìjǐ$_i$ zhàn zài yībiān búzhù de ná yǎn qù zhǎo bàbà$_j$ de shìxiàn, 0$_i$ mómócèngcèng de bùkěn zǒukāi, 0$_i$ méihuàzhǎohuà de wèn: "Háiyǒu shénme yào wǒ gàn de me?"

'Ma Rui intended to ask for his father's approval of him going out to play for a while, but he did not make the request directly. Instead, (he) actively washed the dishes, swept the floor and cleaned the table after meal. When everything was done, (he), like a maid who had a favour to ask of her master, passed <u>a cup of freshly brewed tea and a fan</u> to Ma Linsheng, who was there bulging his belly and picking his teeth, and in the meantime kept trying to catch his father's attention, reluctant to go. (He) tried to start a conversation, "Is there anything else that I can do?"'

Different syntactic forms tend to reflect different degrees of topic continuity, which, from high to low, can be summarized as follows (as cited in Givón, 1983):

coding for most continuous/accessible topic
    zero anaphora
    unstressed/bound pronouns or grammatical agreement
    stressed/independent pronouns
    R-dislocated DEF-NP's
    neutral-ordered DEF-NP's
    L-dislocated DEF-NP's
    Y-moved NP's (contrastive topicalization)
    cleft/focus constructions
    referential indefinite NP's
coding for most discontinuous/inaccessible topic

Sun Chaofen's (1988) study shows that there is a close connection between the importance of theme in discourse and the use of quantifiers, in that a thematically important noun phrase tends to be introduced into discourse with a quantifier structure. Following a series of studies by Chen Ping on the referential properties and discourse functions of noun phrases, Xu Yulong (2005c) has further confirmed that topics in Chinese are often introduced into discourse by way of the object of an existential clause.

1.3.3 Foreground information and background information

Discourse displays different organizing principles. In the case of the narrative, whose basic function is to recount an event, its basic organization is the chronological sequence.

In a narrative discourse, there are always statements conveying information that makes up the mainline or backbone of the event. Such information is known as foreground information, which is used to directly describe the progression of events and to answer the question "What happened?" Other statements, in contrast, convey non-sequential information (e.g., the scene of the event, relevant factors, etc.) by laying out, setting up, or evaluating the main event. This type of information is called background information, to answer "why" or "how" questions. Foreground information and background information are presented in different ways at different levels.

At the discourse level, the main narrative line of the story makes up the foreground and the rest is the background. Accessible topics often represent the main characters of the narrative, spanning over a number of clauses or sentences to convey foreground information. Conversely, the statements concerning inaccessible topics constitute background information. A typical in accessible topic usually conveys trivial information. It is often a nominal phrase that neither refers back to an entity that has already occurred nor is referred back to by any subsequent expression. See (9) and (10) for illustration.

(9)　我$_i$从吴胖子家出来，0$_i$乘上地铁。地铁车厢很暖和，我手拉吊环几乎站着睡着了，列车到站0$_i$也没察觉，过了好几站0$_i$才猛然惊醒，0$_i$连忙下了车。

我跑上地面，0 站在街上拦出租车。来往的出租车很多，但没有一辆停下来。我走过两个街口，0 看到路边停着几辆出租车就上前问。几个司机是拉包月的，一位拉散座的说他要收外汇券。我说"知道知道"坐了上去从兜里拿出一沓外汇券给他看。(Wang Shuo, *Not Serious at All* [《一点正经没有》])

Wǒ$_i$ cóng Wú Pàngzi jiā chūlái, 0$_i$ chéng shàng dìtiě. Dìtiě chēxiāng hěn nuǎnhuo, wǒ shǒu lā diàohuán jīhū zhànzhe shuìzháole, lièchē dào zhàn 0$_i$ yě méi chájué, guòle hǎo jǐ zhàn 0$_i$ cái měngrán jǐngxǐng, 0$_i$ liánmáng xiàle chē. Wǒ pǎo shàng dìmiàn, 0$_i$ zhàn zài jiē shàng lán chūzūchē. Láiwǎng de chūzūchē hěnduō, dàn méi yī liàng tíng xiàlái. Wǒ zǒu guò liǎng gè jiēkǒu, 0$_i$ kàndào lùbiān tíngzhe jǐ liàng chūzūchē jiù shàng qián wèn, jǐ gè sījī shì lā bāoyuè de, wéiyī lā sǎnzuò de shuō tā yào shōu wàihuìquàn. Wǒ shuō "zhīdào zhīdào" zuòle shàngqù cóng dōu lǐ náchū yī dá wàihuìquàn gěi tā kàn.

'I came out from Fatty Wu's and got on the subway. The subway car was very warm. Holding the rings with the hand, I almost fell asleep, so that (I) didn't detect that the train had passed my station. It was not until quite a few stops later that (I) suddenly awakened and quickly got out of the subway car. I ran up to the ground, standing in the street to call a cab. Many a cab passed, but none stopped. I walked two blocks and saw a few cabs parked on the roadside. (I) went up, but was told by several drivers that they worked on monthly contracts. The only one who took individual passengers told me that he wanted foreign exchange certificates. I got in with the words "I know, I know", and took out a stack of foreign exchange certificates from my pocket to show him.'

(10) 平坦的柏油马路$_i$上铺着一层薄雪，0$_i$被街灯照得有点闪眼，偶尔过来一辆汽车，灯光远射，小雪粒$_j$在灯光里带着点黄，0$_j$像撒着万颗金砂。祥子……(Lao She, *Rickshaw Boy* [《骆驼祥子》])

Píngtǎn de bǎiyóu mǎlù$_i$ shàng pùzhe yī céng báoxuě, 0$_i$ bèi jiēdēng zhàode yǒudiǎn shǎnyǎn, ǒu'ěr guòlái liàng qìchē, dēngguāng yuǎn shè, xiǎo xuělì$_j$ zài dēngguāng lǐ dàizhe diǎn huáng liàng, 0$_j$ xiàng sǎzhe wàn kē jīn shā.

'The flat tarmac road was covered with a thin layer of snow, shining under the streetlights. The distant lights of occasional passing cars would stain the snow grains with yellowish brightness, turning (them) into thousands of gold sands.'

At the sentence level, the main clause is in the foreground, expressing the process of the event, with the subordinate clause in the background, representing elements other than the event process, such as time, conditions, accompanying states, etc. For example, the first clause in (11) indicates the reason for the first person narrator to be sleepy.

(11) 地铁车厢很暖和,我手拉吊环几乎站着睡着了,列车到站 0_i 也没察觉, 过了好几站 0_i 才猛然惊醒, 0_i 连忙下了车。(Wang Shuo, *Not Serious at All* [《一点正经没有》])

Dìtiě chēxiāng hěn nuǎnhuo, wǒ shǒu lā diàohuán jīhū zhànzhe shuìzháole, lièchē dào zhàn 0_i yě méi chájué, guòle hǎo jǐ zhàn 0_i cái měngrán jǐngxǐng, 0_i liánmáng xiàle chē.

'The subway car was very warm. Holding the rings with the hand, I almost fell asleep, so that (I) didn't detect that the train had passed my station. It was not until quite a few stops later that (I) suddenly awakened and quickly got out of the subway car.'

At the clause level, background information normally precedes foreground information in the serial verb construction (see also Zhang Bojiang, 2000).

(12) 我手拉吊环几乎站着睡着了。
Wǒ shǒu lā diàohuán jīhū zhànzhe shuìzháole.
I hand hold ring almost stand.DUR fall.asleep.PFV
'Holding the rings with the hand, I almost fell asleep.'

Since background information does not show the course of events, it cannot be negated by 没 'not'.

(13) a. 吃了饭看电影。
Chīle fàn kàn diànyǐng.
eat.PFV meal see movie
'Go to the movies after meal.'
b. *没吃了饭看电影。
*Méi chīle fàn kàn diànyǐng.

(14) a. 你什么时候去?
Nǐ shénme shíhòu qù?
you what time go
'When will you go?'
b. 吃了饭去。
Chīle fàn qù.
eat.PFV meal go
'(I'll) go after meal.'
c. *没吃了饭去。
*Méi chīle fàn qù.

Foreground information and background information are not only different at the semantic level of discourse, they also align with a series of syntactic-semantic factors, an issue that has already been addressed in depth by Hopper and Thompson (1980). In general, foreground information corresponds to a set of "high-transitivity" features, while background information corresponds to a set of "low-transitivity" features (Fang Mei, 2008).

When discussing background information in Chinese, Chu (1998) argues that syntactic correlate and information status are closely related, though each works at a different level. Background does not necessarily derive old information, and vice versa. Subordination is a common means of backgrounding. For example, 因为 (yīnwèi, 'because'), a subordinate conjunction, explicitly marks background information when the principle of background-to-foreground progression is violated. Nominalized clauses can function as both subjects and objects. When such a clause occurs as the subject, it imparts background information; if it is the object, its information status will be mainly determined by the nature of the main verb. Background generally consists of three mutually interactive pragmatic components: event-line, scene-setting and weight-reduction.

1.4 Interactional factors

1.4.1 Progressive speech

The process of speech is featured by dynamic on-line processing, whereby the participants introduce different characters and ideas into the discourse universe. Therefore, the phenomena that occur in the dynamic process of speech, especially in interactional communication, often reflect the psychological reality of language users.

The typical interactional discourse is conversation, the basic unit of which is "turn". Take (15) for example. A and B are having a conversation. When speaker A sends a message and hearer B receives it, the two utterances of A and B form two adjacent turns of speech.

(15)   A: What time is it?
       B: Five o'clock.

Conversation is conducted in alternating turns of speech (i.e., in A-B-A-B sequence). The alternation from the speaker to the hearer is called turn-taking. The mechanism responsible for turn-taking is called the "turn-taking mechanism", which allows participants to take turns in an orderly manner (i.e., to conduct conversation orderly) (Sacks, Schegloff and Jefferson, 1974).

In recent years, some scholars have drawn on Conversation Analysis to study the phenomenon of "extension" of utterances in actual discourse, considering the gradual production of sentences in the temporal axis as an important dynamic grammatical feature of naturally occurring speech.

Lerner (1991) has proposed the syntax of sentences-in-progress, suggesting that sentences should be examined in the context of alternating turns of speech.

Following Lerner's notion of sentences-in-progress, Brazil (1995) raises the notion of "linear grammar", emphasizing in particular that sentences unfold increment-by-increment in online discourse. Ford, Fox, and Thompson (2002) refer to increments that are syntactically difficult to classify as "extensional increment", which can be identified in terms of three scales:

1) syntactic scale: the constituent before an extensional increment has syntactic integrity and is self-sufficient;
2) prosodic scale: the preceding constituent has an independent intonation;
3) pragmatic scale: the increment can form the first part of an adjacent pair independently.

The parts in bold in (16) to (18) are instances of the so-called extensional increment.

(16) Have you been to New Orleans? **Ever?**
(17) We could'a used a little marijuana. **to get through the weekend.**
(18) An' how are you feeling? (0.4) **these days**.

Fox et al. argue that extensional increments have the following discourse features: 1) they occur in a transition-relevant position where there is no pickup; 2) they provide a transition point where the addressee can start a turn; and 3) they continue the speaker's conversation. From the above discussion, it is easy to see that grammarians' descriptions and explanations of the dynamic features are increasingly integrated into Conversational Analysis, with a view to re-examining the issues that traditional grammar does not care about or cannot explain and giving an explanation that is consistent with the communicative features of language.

For a long time, the phenomenon of extensional increment was regarded as "syntactic inversion" in the study of Chinese grammar (Li Jinxi, 1924). Chao (1968) also used the term "inverted sentence", and at the same time proposed the concept of "after-thought", addressed together with "unplanned sentences", with the finding that the preposed part must be a complete sentence and that the postposed should be articulated lightly and quickly. Zhu Dexi (1982) also used the notion "inversion", pointing out that the latter part was complementary in meaning, "This type of expression is only found in spoken Chinese. The preposed part is what the speaker is eager to express, while the latter part imparts a complementary flavor" (1982, pp. 221–2). Lu Jianming (1982b) discussed "transposed sentences" in depth, outlining four characteristics for this sentence type: 1) the stress is on the front part, and the latter part should be produced lightly; 2) the semantic focus is on the front part, and the latter part cannot be the object of emphasis; 3) the transposed constituent can be restored to its default slot without changing the meaning of the sentence; and 4) the sentence-final particle does not occur at the end of the latter part. Tai and Hu (1991) also discussed this issue in terms of after-thought; Zhang Bojiang and Fang Mei (1996/2014) regarded this kind of phenomenon as a means of important information fronting.

It is Luke (2000) that introduces the perspective of Conversation Analysis into his exploration of the relationship between postponing of Chinese sentence constituents and conversational turn-taking. He re-examined "inverted sentences" and "dislocated sentences" in terms of the syntax of sentences-in-progress and linear grammar, with the finding that the "dislocation" analysis has limitations (Luke, 2004a). Specifically, many constituents that are considered "dislocated" can by no means be restored to their respective original position, as illustrated in (19) and (20).

(19) 你不是有个游泳池的吗, 你家楼下?
Nǐ   bùshì yǒu gè yóuyǒngchí de   ma, nǐ   jiā
you not   have CL swimming.pool aux. MP your home
lóuxià?
downstairs
'Don't you have a swimming pool, downstairs your apartment building?'

(20) 我很敏感的, 我的鼻子。
Wǒ hěn mǐngǎn de, wǒ de   bízi.
I   very sensitive aux. I   NM   nose
'I'm very sensitive, (I mean) my nose.'

It is thus argued that a large number of "inverted" or "dislocated sentences" are actually "incremental sentences", the result of gradual increment of sentence constituents over time. Incremental sentences satisfy the following sentence-completing conditions: 1) the principal part must contain the core of the predicate (i.e., the predicate core) and be marked by the sentence-final intonation or the sentence-final particle; and 2) the increment cannot have the predicate core; nor can it bear the sentence-final intonation or the sentence-final particle. Luke believes that incremental sentences should be regarded as a regular syntactic structure in Chinese and that their sentence-completing issue should be addressed in terms of dynamic syntactic analysis.

Research on the dynamic characteristics of the speech process has been receiving ever-increasing attention. In early years, this line of research was mainly a focus of Conversation Analysis; in recent years, however, it has begun to gain attention from grammar researchers. The study of the dynamic characteristics of naturally occurring sentences has become a new feature of Discourse Grammar research, because the dynamic characteristics reflect the psychological reality of language in a multifaceted manner.

1.4.2 Functional differences of syntactic constituents

Narrative discourse and conversation, though both as unplanned, naturally occurring speech, show distinct characteristics. The differences between the two varieties are mainly manifested in the following two oppositions.

First, processivity vs. situativity: narrative discourse is processual and conversation is situationalized. In narrating events, the process is described in the chronological order, and the change of time often brings about the change of scenes and characters, which renders time considerably more important than other factors. The purpose of conversation, however, is to exchange information and opinions, and in naturally occurring conversation, the importance of the time factor recedes to a secondary position.

Second, eventfulness vs. commentariness: narrative discourse embodies eventfulness and conversation exhibits commentariness. Unlike narrative discourse that tells the course of events, conversation is oriented towards information and opinion exchange, with the focus on what is currently of mutual interest rather than on the course of events. Therefore, the major task of conversation participants is to describe or qualify things in various ways, and then name and characterize them.

Tao Hongyin (2002), and Fang Mei and Song Zhenhua (2004), both working on relative clauses sampled from transcriptions of unplanned naturally occurring speech and both taking an exhaustive statistical approach to the distribution of relative clauses, have, nonetheless, come up with results that differ with the variety of corpora. Firstly, Tao finds that the relative clauses occurring in narratives indicate most frequently time, followed by people, and then things. This is because the function of time-indicating clauses in narrative discourse is to mark plot transition, the most important in narratives. Fang and Song, on the other hand, find that the most frequent relative clauses in conversation denote in the foremost things, followed by time and people, which is predetermined by the locale authenticity and commentariness characteristics of conversational discourse. Secondly, relative clauses referring to people make up an important category in both narrative and conversation. Their primary function in the narrative discourse, according to Tao, is to track characters, followed by introducing them and naming them, whereas in conversation the primary function of relative clauses is to name characters, followed by tracking and introducing them. Thirdly, Fang and Song's investigation also shows that conversation is often characterized by the expression of non-realistic temporal states though it is not licensed in narrative discourse. All these differences can be attributed to the "processual" nature of narration and the "commentary" orientation of conversation.

1.4.3 Coding differences of syntactic constituents

The syntactic manifestations of information structure have been summarized by some scholars as the "principle of end weight" – placing complex structures at the end of the sentence (Leech, 1983), and the "light subject restriction" – the subject of a sentence tends to be a light form (Chafe, 1994).

Bernardo (1979) classifies relative clauses into two subcategories: the informative, which provides new information; and the non-informative, which plays only a differentiating role. In languages where modifiers follow head nouns, such as English, the latter subcategory tends to occur in simple forms while the former generally takes complex forms. Payne (1997, p. 326) has pointed out that although in general the position of the relative clause with respect to the head noun is the same with the descriptive modifier, the relative clause is seen in a large number of languages to follow the head noun. In other words, when the numeral and the descriptive modifiers precede the head noun, the relative clause still follows it. This strong tendency is perhaps due to the general pragmatic principle of placing heavy constituents later in the clause: that is, constituents that are highly descriptive and convey more new information are postposed.

In fact, the phenomenon as described by Payne (1997) also exists in Chinese. Although modifiers are usually put in front of the modified nominal constituent in Chinese, such as 蓝蓝的天 (lán~lán de tiān, 'blue sky'), 老李喜欢的曲子 (Lǎo Lǐ xǐhuān de qǔzi, 'the tune that Old Li likes'), the modifying constituents still tend to be postposed when they are complicated in structure and lengthy in linear sequence.

When complex modifiers are postposed, there are two coexisting syntactic configurations in Chinese. One is the direct postposition of the genitive *de*-construction, such as (21) and (22) below. The other is to use a clause with a conjunctive word to describe the nominal constituent, such as (23) and (24), where the clause beginning with 他 (tā, 'he') provides new information on, rather than restricting the scope of, the modified noun. In terms of semantics, the former configuration is "restrictive" and the latter "descriptive".

(21) 机动车驾驶人<u>不在现场或者虽在现场但拒绝立即驶离,妨碍其他车辆、行人通行的</u>,处二十元以上二百元以下罚款,并可以将该机动车拖移至不妨碍交通的地点或者公安机关交通管理部门指定的地点停放。(Road Traffic Safety Law of the People's Republic of China)

Jīdòngchē jiàshǐrén <u>bùzài xiànchǎng huòzhě suī zài xiànchǎng dàn jùjué lìjí shǐ lí, fáng'ài qítā chēliàng, xíngrén tōngxíng de</u>, chù èrshí yuán yǐshàng èrbǎi yuán yǐxià fákuǎn, bìng kěyǐ jiāng gāi jīdòngchē tuōyí zhì bù fáng'ài jiāotōng de dìdiǎn huòzhě gōng'ān jīguān jiāotōng guǎnlǐ bùmén zhǐdìng de dìdiǎn tíngfàng.

'The driver of a motor vehicle <u>who is not present or is present but refuses to drive away immediately so that the passage of other vehicles and pedestrians is obstructed</u> shall be fined not less than twenty yuan but not more than two hundred yuan, and the motor vehicle may be towed to a place where it does not obstruct traffic or a place designated by the traffic management department of the public security authorities to park.'

(22) 公安机关对举报人提供信息经查证属实的, 将给予一定数额的奖金。
(News report)

Gōng'ān jīguān duì jǔbàorén tígōng xìnxī jīng cházhèng shǔshí de, jiāng jǐyǔ yīdìng shù'é de jiǎngjīn.

'Public security organs will give a certain amount of bonus to whistle-blowers who provide information that is proven to be true.'

(23) a. 你比如说你跟着那种水平不高的英语老师,他根本不知道那个纯正的英语发音,他英语语法也不怎么样,你就全完了。

Nǐ bǐrúshuō nǐ gēnzhe nàzhǒng shuǐpíng bù gāo de Yīngyǔ lǎoshī, tā gēnběn bù zhīdào nàge chúnzhèng de Yīngyǔ fāyīn, tā Yīngyǔ yǔfǎ yě bù zěmeyàng, nǐ jiù quán wánle.

'For example, if you follow the kind of English teacher of a limited level, who doesn't know pure English pronunciation at all, and who is not good at English grammar, you would be all finished.'

b. ?你比如说你跟着那种水平不高的英语老师,根本不知道那个纯正的英语发音、⁴英语语法也不怎么样的,你就全完了。

Nǐ bǐrúshuō nǐ gēnzhe nàzhǒng shuǐpíng bù gāo de Yīngyǔ lǎoshī, gēnběn bù zhīdào nàge chúnzhèng de Yīngyǔ fāyīn(,) Yīngyǔ yǔfǎ yě bù zěmeyàng de, nǐ jiù quán wánle.

(24) a. 你站在大街上总能看见那种不管不顾的人,他看见红灯就跟不认得似的,照直往前骑,你当警察要爱生气得气死。

Nǐ zhàn zài dàjiē shàng zǒng néng kànjiàn nàzhǒng bùguǎnbùgù de rén, tā kànjiàn hóngdēng jiù gēn bù rènde shìde, zhàozhí wǎng qián qí, nǐ dāng jǐngchá yào ài shēngqì děi qì sǐ.

'Standing on the street, you can always see the kind of people who do not care at all when the lights are red and will ride straight ahead. If you are a policeman given to irritation, you would be angered to death.'

b. 你站在大街上总能看见那种不管不顾的人,看见红灯就跟不认得似的、照直往前骑的,你当警察要爱生气得气死。

Nǐ zhàn zài dàjiē shàng zǒng néng kànjiàn nàzhǒng bùguǎnbùgù de rén, kànjiàn hóngdēng jiù gēn bù rènde shìde(,) zhàozhí wǎng qián qí de, nǐ dāng jǐngchá yào ài shēngqì děi qì sǐ.

It is worth noting that examples (21) and (22) represent permissible syntactic configurations in written Chinese, which implies that they are rarely seen in spoken Chinese. Conversely, examples (23) and (24) are commonly seen sentence patterns in spoken Chinese, but they seldom occur in writing. This difference is particularly instructive, in that the latter is a manifestation of "the syntax of sentences-in-progress" in spoken language (Fang Mei, 2004).

1.4.4 Differences in semantic orientation

Interactional communication offers more possibilities for subjectivization and inter-subjectivization than non-interactional communication.

When a speaker produces a passage, he or she also indicates his or her stance, attitude, and feeling about the passage, thus leaving a mark of "self" in the discourse (Lyons, 1977, 1982; Finegan, 1995; Shen Jiaxuan, 2001), which is known as subjectivity. If this subjectivity is encoded in a specific structural form or a linguistic form evolves to acquire the expressive function of subjectivity, it is called subjectivization.

When the first person plural is used to refer to the speaker self, it expresses the subjective meaning of "self-effacement", as illustrated in (25).

(25) 我们认为这样做不够稳妥。

Wǒmen rènwéi zhèyàng zuò búgòu wěntuǒ.

'We think it is inappropriate to do so.'

Another case concerns the pronoun 人家, which is generally used to refer to a third party other than the speaker and the addressee. But in conversation, it can be used to refer to the speaker when his or her negative feelings are to be imparted. Compare (26a) with (26b).

(26) a. 你怎么才到啊!人家等了半个钟头了。

Nǐ zěnme cái dào a! Rénjiā děngle bàngè zhōngtóu le.

'What took you so long to get here? I've been waiting for half an hour.'

b. *你这么快就到了!人家等了半个钟头了。

*Nǐ zhème kuài jiù dàole! Rénjiā děngle bàngè zhōngtóu le.

'You're here so soon! I've been waiting for half an hour.'

Inter-subjectivity refers to the explicit linguistic expression of the speaker's concern for the addressee. This concern can manifest epistemically in terms of the addressee's attitude toward the content of the proposition, but more often in the social nature of communication, i.e., taking care of the addressee's "face" or "image" (Traugott, 1999). A linguistic form of inter-subjectivity must also show subjectivity. Likewise, inter-subjectivation always implies subjectivation, and a form cannot be inter-subjectivated without some degree of subjectivation. The difference between inter-subjectivation and subjectivation lies in the fact that subjectivation makes the meaning oriented more toward the speaker while inter-subjectivation makes the meaning oriented more towards the addressee.

The grammaticalization of pronouns is often accompanied by subjectivation and inter-subjectivation, as illustrated in (27) and (28) (Lü Shuxiang, 1985; Biq, 1990, 1991; Zhang Bojiang and Fang Mei, 1996/2014).

The inter-subjectivization of pronouns has two main dimensions.

First, it denotes psychological distance by focusing on the psychology of the addressee. For example, the first-person inclusive pronoun can be used to refer to the addressee alone so as to draw close the psychological distance.

(27) (Adult to child) 咱们都上学了,哪能跟他们小孩儿争玩具呀。

Zánmen dōu shàngxuéle, nǎ néng gēn tāmen xiǎo hái·ér zhēng wánjù ya.

"We are in school now, how can we compete with those small kids for toys?"

Second, it indicates the speaker's expectation of the addressee. For instance, the second person pronoun "你" ('you') in (28) does not refer to the addressee, but is used to prompt the addressee to pay attention to what the speaker is saying.

(28) 你老字号有什么了不起的,还不是吃全国,仗着在首都。

Nǐ lǎozìhao yǒu shénme liǎobùqǐ de, háibùshì chī quánguó, zhàngzhe zài shǒudū.

'What's the big deal about the old brand? It lives on the whole country, just because it's located in the capital city.'

Personal pronouns occur in different varieties, but their inter-subjectivization is unique to conversation. In comparison with non-interactional communication, speaker-oriented semantic interpretations are more favored in interactional communication.

From the 1970s to the 1980s, the analysis of Discourse Grammar was mostly focused on narratives, but since the 1990s, it has increasingly incorporated the results of Conversation Analysis, focusing on the influence of interaction on language structure (see Biq, Tai and Thompson, 1996 for a review of Chinese studies). Interactional linguistics has become a particularly interesting field of research ever since (for a review, see Lin Dajin and Xie Chaoqun, 2003).

1.5 Continuity

Functional linguists argue that syntactic phenomena are conditioned by discourse factors from their formation to their current shape, and that syntactic research without taking discourse factors into account is bound to yield no theoretically insightful interpretations. Grammar is gradually shaped in use and is constantly changing with the functional needs of discourse. In his article "Historical syntax and synchronic morphology", Givón (1971) suggests that the prefixes in Bantu as morphological devices originate from ancient Bantu pronouns, which prompts him to propose that today's morphology is yesterday's syntax. On the basis of a large amount of cross-linguistic material,

Givón's book *On Understanding Grammar* (Academia Press, 1979) further summarizes this idea as follows: grammar is the solidification of discourse, and syntacticization is the transformation from pragmatic patterns to syntactic patterns. Diagrammatically it can be represented as: discourse > syntax > morphology > morphophonology > zero form.

Some scholars even argue that there are no so-called syntactic constituents or syntactic rules that are independent of discourse. In 1987, Paul Hopper published his seminal article "Emergent Grammar" with the Berkeley Linguistic Society, which laid ever more emphasis on the dynamic nature of grammar. Hopper explicitly argues that structures and rules emerge from and are shaped by discourse, which is an ongoing process whereby grammar is constantly subject to change and fluidity. Consequently, the continuous changes exhibited by categories and meanings at the synchronic level should be the focus of grammaticalization research. This view represents the concern of functional linguists for the continuity feature between synchronic differences and diachronic evolution, leading grammaticalization research from a purely diachronic perspective onto the path of integrating synchronic with diachronic approaches. In the meantime, the different dimensions of synchronic differences have become a new hot spot of attention. A large number of studies starting from the examination of synchronic differences have turned to explore how the synchronic level interacts with the diachronic level.

De-categorization of linguistic elements constitutes an important stage of evolution. The so-called de-categorization refers to the phenomenon in which members of a syntactic category lose certain features of that category under certain circumstances. For example, *I think* is a frequently occurring form in English that can appear in different syntactic slots, but the syntactic performance of *think* varies with its linear position. When occurring in the predicate slot, it can appear in different tenses and collocate with different persons. However, if it appears at the end of a sentence, it will lose some of its grammatical features as a verb. The poor acceptability judgment of (29d) shows that *think* has been de-categorized.

(29) a. I think that the lock has been changed.
     b. She thought that the lock had been changed.
     c. The lock has been changed, I think.
     d. *The lock has been changed, she thought.

Existing cross-linguistic studies show that de-categorization has the following main features:

1) semantically, it presupposes semantic generalization or abstraction;
2) morphosyntactically, category members lose some typical distributional features of the category while acquiring the features of a new category;
3) the discourse function of the category will be expanded or transferred.

Compare the different uses of 又 in examples (30) to (34).

(30) 昨天迟到，今天又迟到了。(repetition)
 Zuótiān chídào, jīntiān yòu chídàole.
 yesterday be.late today again be.late.PFV
 'You were late yesterday; you're late again today.'

(31) 一年又一年 (twirling of time)
 Yī nián yòu yī nián
 one year again one year
 'Year after year.'

(32) 那是三伏的第一天，又潮湿，又没有风。(relevance)
 Nà shì sānfú de dìyī tiān,
 that be dog.days NM first day
 yòu cháoshī, yòu méiyǒu fēng.
 again humid again without wind
 'It was the first day of the dog days, and it was humid and without wind.'

(33) 又不是不努力，是条件太差了。(emphasizing speaker's stance)
 Yòu búshì bù nǔlì, shì tiáojiàn tài chà le.
 again not not work.hard be condition too bad aux.
 'It wasn't a lack of effort, but the conditions were too bad.'

(34) 看书呢，又。(telling the other person "I am concerned about you"; cf. 又看书哪, Yòu kànshū ne, '(You're) reading again.'
 Kànshū ne, yòu.
 read.books MP again
 '(You're) reading, again.'

The central meaning of 又 is "the same". The semantic interpretation of (30) is that something like "be late" happens repeatedly; that is, the same event repeats itself in the real world. The "sameness" encoded in (31), in contrast, is not entirely objective, because every "year" in the objective world is different. But it is not important whether it is "the same" in the real world, so long as it is "the same" in the world of mental awareness. In (32), "humid" and "without wind" are objectively two different states, and the use of 又 to put them together conveys the message of "sameness" in the speaker's cognition: both are the climate characteristics of "dog days", a connection established by the speaker's perception. If the word 又 is deleted, this subjective perception cannot be revealed. When it comes to (33), 又 has no direct objective correlation, but is entirely the speaker's evaluation. The use of 又 in (34) is still farther off "the same" reading, in that it expresses only the speaker's concern for the addressee.

The propositional meaning of the statement would remain intact when 又 is replaced with 你 'you' ("看书呢, 你。"). As a matter of fact, the word 又 in (33) and (34) may well be deleted without changing the semantics of the two sentences.

In examples (35) and (36) that follow, the third person pronoun "他" ('he') can refer to a certain kind of people, as it can be used interchangeably with its plural 他们 ('they').

(35) 但是路学长他们不同, 他不是翻译, 他就是做电影的一批人。他们是读电影长大的人, 或者说读影像更多, 对影像更有悟性的人, 他创作出来的东西会不一样。(Survey corpus)

Dànshì Lù Xuécháng tāmen bùtóng, tā bùshì fānyì, tā jiùshì zuò diànyǐng de yī pī rén. Tāmen shì dú diànyǐng zhǎngdà de rén, huòzhě shuō dú yǐngxiàng gèng duō, duì yǐngxiàng gèng yǒu wùxìng de rén, tā chuàngzuò chūlái de dōngxī huì bù yīyàng.

'But Lu Xuechang and his peers are different. They are not translators; they are a group of people who make movies. They are people who grew up reading movies, or people who read more images and have a better understanding of images. So what they create will be different.'

(36) 今天的演员在理论上他能知道四十年代、六十年代演员的基本感觉是什么, 但他有很多时候有露出马脚来的东西, 你要一点点去提示他。(Survey corpus)

Jīntiān de yǎnyuán zài lǐlùn shàng tā néng zhīdào sìshí niándài(,) liùshí niándài yǎnyuán de jīběn gǎnjué shì shénme, dàn tā yǒu hěnduō shíhòu yǒu lùchūmǎjiǎo lái de dōngxī, nǐ yào yīdiǎndiǎn qù tíshì tā.

'Today's actors can theoretically know what the basic feelings of actors in the 1940s and 1960s were, but they often give themselves away. You'll have to remind them bit by bit.'

For more related phenomena, see Tao (1999) and Fang Mei (2002).

De-categorization is an innovation on the part of language users, and this innovation has given rise to a large number of linguistic variations. Synchronically, these variations are often initially personal, informal, and created ad hoc out of certain pragmatic needs. Over time, what was once a personal, informal, and ad hoc form becomes a social, grammatical, formal, and rigorous rule, recognized by the majority of language users. Grammar is no more than the product of the conventionalization of language use patterns, the evolution of which spans four different levels (Givón, 1979, p. 208).[5]

a. Diachronic: Loose parataxis > Tight syntax
b. Ontogenetic: Early pragmatic mode > Later syntactic mode
c. Pidgins-Creoles: Nongrammar > Grammar
d. Register level: Unplanned-informal speech > Planned-formal speech

Thus, grammar is gradually formed in use and is subject to constant change, because it is shaped by the functional needs of discourse (for reviews of grammaticalization studies, see Shen Jiaxuan, 1994a, 1998; Sun Chaofen, 1994; and Wu Fuxiang, 2004).

1.6 Summary

The study of Chinese Discourse Grammar has gone through a development history of more than three decades. Generally speaking, there are roughly two different research orientations. One takes the discourse role (e.g. background information) or discourse phenomenon (e.g. anaphora) as the entry point to discuss the correlate syntactic expressions; and the other starts from the syntactic role (e.g. relative clause) or syntactic category (e.g. perfective/imperfective aspect) to discuss the functional motives of syntactic forms. The former focuses on discourse structure, and the latter on syntactic interpretation.

With the introduction of Conversation Analysis and the in-depth study of linguistic subjectivity in recent years, the research on Chinese Discourse Grammar has begun to attach importance to communicative participants' subjectivized means of expression as well as the influence and shaping effect of communicative factors on discourse structure. Given the overall picture of the study of Chinese Discourse Grammar, research on discourse structure enjoys a longer history, and the area of special interest is syntactic interpretation and the influence of communicative factors on the structure of discourse, given the fact that it remains relatively weak for the time being.

Taking the functional approach, this monograph represents an application of the theories of functional linguistics to Chinese linguistic practice. Specifically, syntactic integration, the information status and discourse function of special syntactic structures, and the emergence of metadiscourse constituents are explored in terms of information structure, topic chain, and discourse function.

Notes

1 Example sentences cited in this book come from three sources: books (bracketed post the examples), survey corpus (also bracketed post each example), and the author (with no bracketed notation).
2 For studies on Chinese topics, see Chao Yuen Ren, 1968/1979; Li and Thompson, 1981; Xu and Langendoen, 1985; Shen Jiaxuan, 1989; Shi Youwei, 1995; Zhang Bojiang and Fang Mei, 1996/2014; Xu Liejiong and Liu Danqing, 1998/2007; Shi, 1989, 2000; Chu, 2000; Yuan Yulin, 2002b; Xu Liejiong and Liu Danqing (eds.), 2003.
3 Given the discourse approach, many of the examples cited in this book are fairly long. To save space, word-by-word glosses are used sparingly for the key points under discussion only. Translator's note.
4 This punctuation mark as used in written Chinese is to mark a briefer pause than the comma, and hence transcribed as bracketed comma. Translator's note.

5 The revised version is as follows:
   a. Diachrony: loose, flat parataxis > tight, hierarchic syntaxis
   b. Ontogeny: pre-grammatical communication > grammatical communication
   c. Creology: pre-grammatical Pidgin > grammatical Creole
   d. Register: unplanned oral discourse > planned/edited written text

2 Modes of clausal correlation and syntactic integration

Unlike morphological languages, Chinese uses a large number of dependent clauses without explicitly marking their subordinate status with subordinate conjunctives. These syntactically unmarked clauses realize their dependency relation by way of low-transitivity features. The greater the transitivity difference between the clauses, the stronger the dependency of the low-transitivity clause on the high-transitivity clause. Since different registers require different degrees of syntactic integration, the contribution of the same syntactic means to syntactic integration may vary with the register.

2.1 Introduction

Chinese does not have the morphosyntactic changes that Indo-European languages have, which explains why Chinese has long been taken as a paradigmatic language (for a review, see Fang Mei and Zhu Qingxiang, 2015). In comparison with Indo-European languages, Chinese is relatively low in syntactic integration, as manifested in the following aspects:

1) Indo-European languages can clearly distinguish finite and non-finite clauses through the verb form, but Chinese cannot.
2) Indo-European languages have morphosyntactic markers for subject–predicate agreement while Chinese lacks such markers.
3) Indo-European languages make explicit use of conjunctives in compound and complex sentences and clear distinction between comma and period use. In contrast, Chinese compound and complex sentences do not rely on conjunctives for inter-clausal cohesion, and the use of comma vis-à-vis period is no more than a tendency.

Taken together, Indo-European languages are prominent in terms of morphosyntax while Chinese is not.

Then arises the question: is there syntactic integration between Chinese clauses? And, if so, by what form category? Traditional analyses have focused on conjunctives. Our discussion attempts to show that there are other form categories that can be referred to than conjunctives.

DOI: 10.4324/9781032700656-2

2.2 Two types of dependent clauses in typology

2.2.1 Clausal relations

In cross-linguistic study, the inter-clausal relationship can be subsumed under three syntactic levels by way of two parameters "dependency" and "embeddedness", "coordination", "cosubordination" and "subordination" (Foley and Van Valin, 1984: 241–2; Fang Mei, 2008: 291–2). Of the three, both cosubordination and subordination involve dependency.

coordination	cosubordination	subordination
-dependency	+dependency	+dependency
-embeddedness	-embeddedness	+embeddedness

The so-called independent clause is a syntactically self-sufficient clause that can enter discourse independently, and in morphologically developed languages, its predicate verb is fully inflected for finiteness. Conversely, the dependent clause refers to a syntactically non-self-sufficient clause that cannot enter discourse independently, the subject taking zero form, the verb being non-finite, and the various category information such as tense, aspect, and mood to be inferred with regard to the independent clause (Payne, 1997: 306; Fang Mei, 2008: 292).

(1) (a) He came in, (b) locking the door behind him. (cited from Payne, 1997: 306)

In the complex sentence of example (1), clause (b) is a dependent clause, whose subject is in the zero form and the verb is non-finite, whereas clause (a) is an independent clause with a finite verb. The understanding of the subject, tense, etc. of clause (b) must depend on clause (a).

There are two main types of dependent clauses: finite by way of addition of a qualifying conjunctive to a finite clause (such as "when" below), and non-finite by compressing a finite clause into a non-finite one (Halliday, 2000, p. 241).[1]

Dependent finite clause: <u>When</u> you reach the monument,…
Dependent non-finite clause: (On) reaching the monument,…

While the opposition between the finite and non-finite forms of the predicate verb is evident in morphologically developed languages, it is controversial whether there is such a distinction in isolating languages. Cristofaro (2005, pp. 53–5), based on a survey of 80 languages, points out that isolating languages, such as modern Chinese and the Tibetan-Burmese Nung, do not have the opposition between finite and non-finite verbs per se. Therefore, we should go beyond the finiteness of the verb in judging the status of the clause. So long as the verb of the clause and its related forms cannot occur independently, the verb should be taken as syntactically deranked, and the hosting clause as syntactically dependent.

The finite clause is independent in itself; to make it dependent requires the explicit use of a conjunctive word. The non-finite clause, in contrast, is syntactically dependent by nature, which renders explicit marking unnecessary. Deranked verb clauses can be used with conjunctives, as in (2) below.

(2)   He stared at me <u>as if seeing me for the first time</u>.

It is a general tendency in world languages that deranked verb clauses, with or without conjunctives, are less rich in morphosyntax than typical verb clauses (Halliday, 2000, pp. 239–40; Matthiessen and Thompson, 1988, p. 304).

(3)   Bare (Equatorial-Tucanoan: Columbia, from Aikhenvald, 1995)
      [ate   abeuka   nu-kása-ka]   nu-khawendya   beke   kuhú
      [until   when   1S-come-SEQ]   1S-pay   FUT   she
      'As soon as I come, I shall pay her.'

In example (3), "ate abeuka" is a conjunctive, equivalent to "as soon as" in English. The verb of the part inside the brackets does not have an independent tense marker, and the interpretation of its "tense" depends on the future tense marker "beke" of the main clause that follows.

Although there is no explicit morphological inflection to mark finite vis-à-vis non-finite verbs in Chinese, it does not mean that Chinese dependent clauses have no markers. Chinese language facts actually show that they can take two types of markers, conjunctives and non-self-sufficient predicate forms, to end up in three forms:

I. conjunctive + self-sufficient clause → dependent clause
    因为他已经到家了,……
    Yīnwèi   tā   yǐjīng   dào   jiā   le,
    because   he   already   arrive   home   PFV
    'Because he has arrived home, …'
    ("他已经到家了" is by itself a self-sufficient clause, but the occurrence of "因为" renders it dependent.)

II. Non-self-sufficient predicate → dependent clause
    到了家,…… (到了家 cannot stand alone.)
    Dàole   jiā, …
    arrive.PFV   home
    'Having arrived home, …'

III. conjunctive + non-self-sufficient predicate → dependent clause
因为拉着洋人，他们可以不穿号坎

Yīnwèi	lāzhe	yángrén,
because	pull.DUR	foreigner

tāmen	kěyǐ	bù	chuān	hàokǎn.
they	may	not	wear	numbered.vest

'Because they have foreigners on their rickshaws, they don't have to wear the numbered vests.'

("因为" is a conjunctive and in the meantime "拉着洋人" cannot be self-sufficient.)

The two devices have already been noted by scholars in Chinese studies, with Wen Lian observing that "it is common to predict the subsequent clause on hearing the originating clause", and that "the most obvious is that clauses with 因为 'because', 如果 'if', 虽然 'although' and the like must have a corresponding follow-up clause" (1992, pp. 261–2). Some syntactic configurations have also been found to be non-self-sufficient, such as 你通知一下他…… (Nǐ tōngzhī yīxià tā…, 'You inform him…'), 大家夸着你…… (Dàjiā kuāzhe nǐ…, 'Everyone boasting about you…'), 他从北京回来…… (Tā cóng Běijīng huílái…, 'He came back from Beijing…'), etc. However, due to the lack of inflection in Chinese, syntactic deranking is not directly reflected in verb morphology, which explains why the relationship between conjunctive words and complex sentences has been better studied for a long time whereas the dependent clauses formed by deranked verbs remain to be more adequately investigated. Some scholars noticed the importance of certain syntactic elements for sentence completion in the 1980s and 1990s (e.g., Hu Mingyang and Jin Song, 1989; Kong Lingda, 1994; Huang Nansong, 1994), and proposed the notion of "sentence-completing element". They also noted that clauses such as 到了家 (Dàole jiā, 'Having arrived home') cannot close up a sentence, but they seldom examined the syntactic behavior of "sentence-completing elements" in relation to inter-clausal association patterns.

2.2.2 *Conjunctive marked dependent clauses*

A conjunctive marked dependent clause is one that is formed by adding a conjunctive to an otherwise self-sufficient or finite clause. If the conjunctive is removed, such a clause can stand alone as an independent clause. In the case of conjunctives, English allows their occurrence either in the preceding clause or the ensuing clause, but rarely in both. Specifically, there are four possibilities, as illustrated in (4).

(4) a. <u>Because</u> he is ill, he is not present today. (conjunctive in the preceding clause)

b. He is ill, <u>so</u> he is not present today. (conjunctive in the ensuing clause)

c. He is not present today, <u>because</u> he is ill. (conjunctive in the ensuing clause)

d. *<u>Because</u> he is ill, <u>so</u> he is not present today. (conjunctives in both clauses)

In the example above, there is a difference between the conjunctive use in (4b) and (4c), though both have the conjunctive in the ensuing clause. In terms of logico-semantic relation, the conjunctive in (4b) is in the result clause, while that in (4c) is in the reason clause.

All three types of conjunctive uses are possible in Chinese; more importantly, Chinese licenses conjunctives to occur in both clauses.

(5) a. <u>因为</u>父亲病了,他要马上回家。(conjunctive in the preceding clause)
  <u>Yīnwèi</u> fùqīn bìngle, tā yào mǎshàng huíjiā.
  because father sick.PFV he need immediately go.home
  'Because his father is sick, he has to go home immediately.'

b. 父亲病了,<u>所以</u>他要马上回家。(conjunctive in the ensuing clause)
  Fùqīn bìngle, <u>suǒyǐ</u> tā yào mǎshàng huíjiā.
  father sick.PFV so he need immediately go.home
  'His father is sick, so he has to go home immediately.'

c. 他要马上回家,<u>因为</u>父亲病了。(conjunctive in the ensuing clause)
  Tā yào mǎshàng huíjiā, <u>yīnwèi</u> fùqīn bìngle.
  'He has to go home immediately, because his father is sick.'

d. <u>因为</u>父亲病了,<u>所以</u>他要马上回家。(conjunctive in both clauses)
  <u>Yīnwèi</u> fùqīn bìngle, <u>suǒyǐ</u> tā yào mǎshàng huíjiā.
  'Because his father is sick, so he has to go home immediately.'

Conjunctives are the hallmark of dependent clauses. An otherwise self-sufficient clause, once marked with a conjunctive, will become a dependent clause in a complex sentence. Even if the tense-aspect features are preserved, as in the English examples so far, the illocutionary force needed for self-sufficiency is still suppressed. Example (6) is cited from Foley and Van Valin (1984, pp. 239–40):

(6) a. Because Johann kicked the vase over, it broke into pieces.
  b. *Because did Johann kick the vase over, it broke into pieces.
  c. Because Johann kicked the vase over, did it break into pieces?

On its own, "Johann kicked the vase over." is self-sufficient, but with the conjunctive "because" it becomes (6a), which is no longer self-sufficient, as can be seen from the question test in (6b) and (6c). In (6b), the dependent clause is interrogative, the main clause is declarative, and the sentence as a whole is unacceptable; in (6c), the dependent clause is declarative, the main clause is interrogative, and the sentence as a whole is acceptable. Foley and Van Valin (1984, pp. 239–40) point out that, in general, the embedded clause is in a part–whole relationship with the main clause, and that the embedded clause should maintain its unmarked declarative status, generally occurring as a presupposed, backgrounded component.

2.2.3 *Dependent clauses marked by non-self-sufficient predicates*

This type of dependent clause is formed by reducing sentence-completing devices so that a clause becomes dependent on a self-sufficient one. Examples (7) and (8) below are from Halliday (2000, p. 240).

(7) Having said goodbye, John went home.
(8) Alice walked on in silence, puzzling over the idea.

Typologically, the so-called clause-chaining language is featured by the contribution of dependent clauses to the formation of complex sentences. The complex sentence pattern of clause-chaining languages can be portrayed as: medial clause$_1$ + medial clause$_2$ +... final clause.

Complex sentences in clause-chaining languages consist of multiple clauses, which necessitates the distinction between final clauses and non-final clauses: only final clauses have all the components that an independent clause should have, the predicate fully developed in terms of tense-aspect morphology; non-final clauses are often referred to as medial clauses, which are dependent on the final clause and cannot stand alone syntactically (Payne, 1997, p. 321; Longacre, 2007, pp. 398–401).

(9) Kanite (spoken in Papua New Guinea, a clause-chaining language, see Longacre, 2007, p. 401):
    a. his-u'a-ke-'ka,
       do-we-DS-you
    b. naki   a'nemo-ka   hoya   ali-'ka,
       so   women-you   garden work-you
    c. naki   ali   ha'noma   hu-neatale-ka,
       so   work   finish   do-COMPL-you
    d. popo hu-ka,
       hoe   do-you
    e. inuna kae-ka,
       weeds burn-you

f. naki   hano   hu-talete-ke-taa,
   so   finish   do-COMPL-DS-you

g. naki   viemoka-ta'a   keki'yamo'ma   ha'noma   ne-his-i-ana.
   so   men-we   fence   finish   FUT-do-it-1PL

'If we do this, you women work the garden, when it is finished hoe and burn the weeds, when that is finished we men will finish making the fence.'

Typical clause-chaining languages do not use conjunctives. In the example above, the verbs in clauses (9a) to (9f) are not tense-marked; neither can the two clauses stand independently. Only the final clause (9g) is tense-marked and self-sufficient.

There are few clause-chaining languages as typical as some spoken languages in Papua New Guinea and Irian Jaya. Languages with syntactic configurations similar to clause chains, however, can be found from Colombia, Ecuador, and Peru in South America to the American Southwest in North America. Clause chaining can also be found in some Central Asian languages, as well as in Korean and Japanese in East Asia (Longacre, 2007, p. 399). English, an Indo-European language, also has this phenomenon, where the final clause is finite and the preceding ones non-finite. In other words, the medial clauses are dependent. See (10) for illustration.

(10) Sitting down, taking out a pencil, he began to write. (cited from Myhill and Hibiya, 1988, p. 363)

In summary, the two types of dependent clauses, given their different modes of formation, predetermine the nature of their hosting sentences. Indeed, some languages do not or rarely use conjunctives, but it is difficult to find complex sentences that do not use dependent clauses at all. Therefore, the study of dependent clauses without conjunctives is indispensable to reveal the syntactic landscape of language, and it is especially important for languages, which lack syntactic morphology, such as Chinese.

2.3 Internal cohesion of complex sentences without conjunctives

The use of dependent clauses as an association pattern of complex sentences is widespread in world languages. From the point of view of discourse cohesion, dependent clauses cannot stand on their own; instead, they require either the co-occurrence of other clauses or a special context as the condition for them to constitute independent clauses. Therefore, a comprehensive depiction of the syntactic features of dependent clauses without conjunctives is indispensable for a full account of the syntax of a language.

2.3.1 *Flowing sentences*

The phenomenon of "flowing sentences" was first proposed by Lü Shuxiang, who found that "there are many flowing sentences in spoken Chinese, one clause following another, and in many places the clauses can be either separated or connected" (1979, p. 27). Hu Mingyang and Jin Song argue that "the frequency of such complex sentences is quite high in both spoken and written Chinese", pointing out that "flowing sentences are a kind of complex sentence where the non-sentence-ending clause can take sentence-ending intonation, and the member clauses are semantically loosely linked, without explicit use of conjunctives" (1989, pp. 42–54). From the above analysis, two characteristics emerge of Chinese flowing sentences: 1) flowing sentences are complex sentences, but generally do not use conjunctive words; and 2) flowing sentences frequently occur not only in spoken Chinese but also in written Chinese.

The term "flowing sentences" is in fact no more than an analogy, because the status and nature of the clauses within a flowing sentence are not exactly the same. Hu Mingyang and Jin Song (1989, p. 48) have keenly noted that within a flowing sentence, there are "independent segments" and "non-independent segments". In our view, the so-called "independent segments" are clauses that are syntactically self-sufficient, while the "non-independent segments" are clauses that are not syntactically self-sufficient.

(11) a. 山朗润起来了, b. 水涨起来了, c. 太阳的脸红起来了。(Zhu Ziqing, Spring [《春》], quoted from Deng Lingyun, 2005)

a. Shān lǎngrùn qǐlái le, b. shuǐ zhǎng qǐlái le, c. tàiyáng de liǎn hóng qǐlái le.

'a. The mountains take on a luster, b. the water starts to rise, c. and there's a blush on the face of the sun.'

(12) a. 说完, b. 岳拓夫忿忿地把手提包往胳肢窝里一夹, c. 带着一副殉道者的模样快步地走出了家门。(Zhang Jie, The Conditions Are Not Mature Yet [《条件尚未成熟》], quoted from Wu Jingcun and Liang Boshu, 1992)

a. Shuō wán, b. Yuè Tuòfū fènfèn de bǎ shǒutíbāo wǎng gāzhīwō li yī jiā, c. dàizhe yīfù xùndàozhě de múyàng kuàibù de zǒuchū le jiāmén.

'a. With these words, b. Yue Tuofu angrily put the handbag under his arm, c. and walked out of the house quickly as if he were a martyr.'

In the two examples above, the nature of the clauses forming the flowing sentences is different: the three clauses in (11) are self-sufficient and can each stand alone; in contrast, the three clauses in (12) are not self-sufficient, none of them forming an independent clause. See (11') and (12').

(11') a. 山朗润起来了。b. 水涨起来了。c. 太阳的脸红起来了。

a. Shān lǎngrùn qǐlái le. b. Shuǐ zhǎng qǐlái le. c. Tàiyáng de liǎn hóng qǐlái le.

'a. The mountains take on a luster. b. The water starts to rise. c. There's a blush on the face of the sun.'

(12') a*说完。

b*岳拓夫忿忿地把手提包往胳肢窝里一夹。

c?带着一副殉道者的模样快步地走出了家门。

a *Shuō wán.

b*Yuè Tuòfū fènfèn de bǎ shǒutíbāo wǎng gāzhīwō li yī jiā.

c? Dàizhe yīfù xùndàozhě de múyàng kuàibù de zǒuchū le jiāmén.

'a* With these words.

b*Yue Tuofu angrily put the handbag under his armpit.

c? (He) walked out of the house quickly as if he were a martyr.'

The three clauses in (12') are not self-sufficient, but the nature of their non-self-sufficiency varies. (12'c) is not self-sufficient in that it lacks a grammatical subject; otherwise, it can occur independently. Conversely, (12'b) has a subject of its own, but it is not self-sufficient, nonetheless. (12'a) has no subject, either, and it would remain non-self-sufficient even with the addition of a subject.

From the above analysis, it can be seen that the sentences traditionally known as "flowing sentences" can be divided into at least three categories:

1) The constituent clauses are each syntactically self-sufficient;
2) The constituent clauses are each syntactically non-self-sufficient;
3) The constituent clauses consist of both self-sufficient and non-self-sufficient clauses.

Of the three categories, the first makes up the truly "breakable" flowing sentences, which have their own particular stylistic requirements to be discussed in more detail below. The latter two categories deserve special in-depth exploration. Kong Lingda (1994) and Huang Nansong (1994) in their studies on sentence-completing elements have made it clear that dependent clauses "can be constituent clauses in a complex sentence although they cannot form sentences on their own", and that "these configurations cannot stand as self-sufficient sentences... but only as clauses in sentences of coordination or subordination." We believe that one important feature of Chinese flowing sentences is the use of "dependent clauses" to form dependent complex sentences.

2.3.2 Grouping patterns of dependent clauses

In Chinese, as in English, the dependent clause is not necessarily an originating clause; it can also be a subsequent clause, which gives rise to two types of grouping patterns, "backward-oriented dependent clause" and "forward-oriented dependent clause", the former illustrated in (13) and (14) and the latter in (15) and (16).

(13) <u>Having told a few bad jokes</u>, Harvey introduced the speaker. (cited from Payne, 1997, p. 320)

(14) <u>抱着厚厚的一摞书</u>,他晃晃悠悠地走了出去。
<u>Bàozhe hòu~hòu de yī luò shū</u>, tā huànghuàngyōuyōu de zǒule chūqù.
'<u>Holding a thick stack of books</u>, he staggered out.'

(15) He went out to run <u>to get help</u>.

(16) 他进来了,<u>抱着厚厚的一摞书</u>。
Tā jìnlái le, <u>bàozhe hòu~hòu de yī luò shū</u>.
'He came in, <u>holding a thick stack of books</u>.'

The backward-oriented dependent clause is highly cohesive and predictive, requiring the occurrence of a subsequent clause. However, when the dependent clause occurs later in a complex sentence, it is dependent on the preceding independent clause, not necessarily requiring a subsequent clause thereafter.

Chen Ping (1987c) correlates the phenomenon of zero-subject cataphora in Chinese with inter-clausal association.

(17) 0$_i$ <u>能在天亮的时候赶到</u>,0$_i$ <u>把骆驼出了手</u>,他$_i$可以一进城就买上一辆车。(Lao She, *Rickshaw Boy* [《骆驼祥子》])
0$_i$ <u>Néng zài tiānliàng de shíhòu gǎndào</u>, 0$_i$ <u>bǎ luòtuó chūle shǒu</u>, tā$_i$ kěyǐ yī jìnchéng jiù mǎishàng yī liàng chē.
'If (he) could make it at dawn and sell the camels, he would be able to buy a rickshaw as soon as he entered the city.'

Example (17) is a case of zero-subject cataphora, where neither of the two early occurring clauses can function appropriately as an independent clause.

Fang Mei (2008, p. 293) emphasizes, in particular, the dependency of the cataphoric zero-subject clause, arguing that: 1) the cataphoric zero-subject of a dependent clause is coreferential with the explicit subject of the subsequent clause; and 2) the clause with a cataphoric zero-subject has no tense or mood elements.

There are also clauses whose subjects are neither zero-form anaphor nor zero-form cataphor, and such clauses are equally inappropriate to stand alone in modern Chinese. But their acceptability as independent clauses can be improved by the addition of sentence-final particles, modal adverbs, negative adverbs, and complements of location, as in (18").

(18) <u>老头儿立住</u>,呆呆的看着那四匹牲口。(Lao She, *Rickshaw Boy*)
<u>Lǎotóu·er lìzhù</u>, dāidāide kànzhe nà sìpǐ shēngkǒu.

old.man   stand.still

'The old man stood still, staring blankly at the four animals.'

(18') ?老头儿立住

?Lǎotóu·er lìzhù.

'The old man stood still.'

(18") 老头儿立住了/老头儿慢慢地立住/老头儿没有立住。

Lǎotóu·er lìzhù le/Lǎotóu·er mànman de lìzhù/Lǎotóu·er méiyǒu lìzhù.

'The old man stood still. / The old man slowly stood still. / The old man didn't stand still.'

In (18"), 了 is a sentence-final particle, 慢慢地 is a modal adverb, and 没有 is a negative adverb.

It was Hu Mingyang and Jin Song (1989, p. 48) who proposed the notion of a "sentence-completing element" to distinguish independent clauses from dependent clauses. In the 1990s, the study of sentence completion and sentence-completing elements became a matter of great interest (Kong Lingda, 1994; Huang Nansong, 1994, etc.). But at that time, scholars were more concerned with the influence of the grammatical categories with regard to the predicate verb (e.g., tense, complement, sentence-final particle, etc.) on sentence completion. It is only studies from the discourse perspective that have linked the (non)occurrence of the clausal subject to the syntactic properties of the hosting clause (e.g., Chen Ping, 1987c; Fang Mei, 2008). It can be argued here that the full picture remains to be depicted of inter-clausal association of complex sentences without explicit use of conjunctives in Chinese. What matters more is that such depiction must be conducted in the context of distinguishing between different text styles.

2.4 Syntactic properties of dependent clauses

2.4.1 Hierarchical nature of dependent clauses

Dependent clauses are the results of desentialization, a process whereby a clause, when integrating with other clauses, loses the properties that an independent clause should have, and is gradually reduced from a clause to a syntactic constituent. The desentialization of the clause first reduces the outermost component, and from outside to inside, a clause can be reduced to a nominality verbal noun, which represents the highest degree of desentialization.[2] According to Lehmann (1988, p. 193), the pattern of outside-in layer-by-layer reduction is as follows:

> no illocutionary force > constraints on illocutionary elements > constraints on/loss of modal elements and mood > constraints on/loss of tense and aspect > dispensability of complements > loss of personal conjugation >

conversion of subject into oblique slot > no polarity > conversion of verbal into nominal government > dispensability of subject > constraints on complements

This hierarchical formulation suggests that there is also a matter of degree of self-sufficiency on the part of the dependent clause itself. The above categories are not found in all languages, and based on Lehmann (1988, p. 200), Gao Zengxia (2003; 2006, p. 118) has adapted them to Chinese, proposing that at one end of the continuum is the sentence with a fully declarative function, and at the other end is the nominality verbal noun or adverbial constituent, with each node along the continuum corresponding to different internal and external features, as represented in Figure 2.1.

Reduction, as discussed above, is sequential and hierarchical, which implies that, if a certain node along the continuum is reduced, the component(s) to its left must be reduced. Take the subject argument and T (time)/A (aspect)/M (mood) for example. The hierarchy goes as follows: actant reduced → T/A/M reduced; that is, if the subject is reduced, then T/A/M must be reduced; conversely, if T/A/M is reduced, the subject argument may or may not be reduced.

The above law of hierarchical reduction seems to be unobjectionable, but Cristofaro (2005, pp. 287–8), after surveying 80 languages including Chinese, points out that there are a large number of counterexamples in which T/A/M can be coded in the relative clause without being reduced while the subject of the clause is reduced to zero form. Cristofaro (2005, p. 288) argues that it is the principle of syntagmatic economy that is at work: the relative clause shares the same subject with the main clause, and given the fact that the relative clause is next to the main clause, it is not necessary to express the subject in its full form. So the zero subject of the relative clause is not the outcome of the same reduction mechanism as works on T/A/M in syntactic integration.

Another example is the integration of multiple clauses in discourse. When the subject is the same in different clauses, what is first integrated may not be the tense/aspect features; instead, it is the subject of the subsequent clause(s) that is reduced in priority, to become the so-called "zero form." This is often the case with "topic-prominent" languages. The following is an example of a flowing sentence cited from Hu Mingyang and Jin Song (1989).

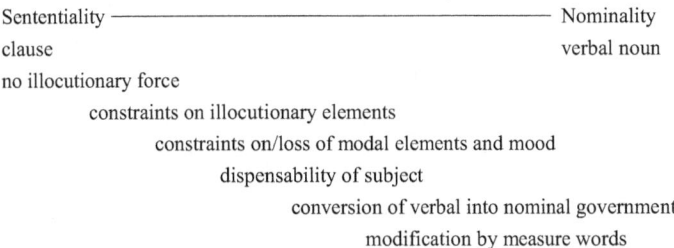

Figure 2.1 Desententialization of Chinese clauses

(19) 现而今, a. 那臭水沟埋了, b. [ ]修上条大马路了。(*5A Auspicious Lane* [《吉祥胡同甲五号》])

Xiàn'érjīn, (a) nà chòushuǐgōu máile, (b) [ ] xiūshàng tiáo dàmǎlù le.

'Nowadays, (a) the stinky water ditch has been buried up, (b) [ ] a main road has been built (in its place).'

In this example, the tense/aspect feature of both clauses a and b has been retained, in that both have the aspect marker -*le* in the final slot. But the subject of clause b is reduced to zero form because it is associated with the subject of clause a: it is on top of the buried ditch that the main road has been built.

When the tense/aspect features are concerned, tense lies outside aspect. If the tense feature is reduced, the aspect feature is more often than not reduced as well. This is, however, an overall tendency, not an compulsory law. See (20).

(20) 穷苦人出身的朱德, 已经确立救国救民之志, 他不再为高官厚禄去打伤害平民百姓的"混"仗。(*The Ten Marshals of the Communist Party of China* [《中共十大元帅》])

Qióngkǔrén chūshēn de Zhū Dé, yǐjīng quèlì jiùguójiùmín zhī zhì, tā bùzài wèi gāoguānhòulù qù dǎ shānghài píngmínbǎixìng de "hùn" zhàng.

'Zhu De was born into a poor family. Having set as his life goal to save his country and his people, he would no longer fight for power and wealth at the cost of the interest of the common people.'

In example (20), the word "已经" ('already') clearly denotes tense, but the clause lacks aspect marker le_{1+2} needed for self-sufficiency, which renders the clause non-self-sufficient.

2.4.2 *Reduction process of dependent clauses*

Desententialization actually consists of two processes, namely, the process of reduction and the process of addition. In the process of reduction, the clause keeps losing sentence properties, such as mood, speech act forces, specific spatio-temporal restrictions, and elements of specific reference. At the same time, it is accompanied by a process of addition, with the constant addition of non-sententialization feature markers and distributional functions.

When a clause is reduced to a modifying element, conjunctives can be added; when it is reduced to a nominal element, the addition of prepositions and case markers can be licensed (Lehmann, 1988, p. 193).

(21) 去年八月, 他在新雅餐厅当临时工时, 结识了一位顾客。 (quoted from Chen Ping, 1987c: 81)

Qùnián bāyuè, tā zài Xīnyǎ Cāntīng dāng línshígōng shí, jiéshìle yī wèi gùkè.

'In August last year, he met a customer <u>while</u> working as a temporary employee at Xinya Restaurant.'

(22) <u>这一顿</u>好打，直把卢云打得晕倒在地，待他醒<u>后</u>，只见四下一片黑暗，自己已倒在柴房中。(*Heroes* [《英雄志》], Chapter 5)

<u>Zhè yī dùn</u> hǎodǎ, zhí bǎ Lú Yún dǎ de yūndǎo zàidì, dài tā xǐng <u>hòu</u>, zhǐjiàn sìxià yīpiàn hēi'àn, zìjǐ yǐ dàozài cháifáng zhōng.

'<u>Such a good thrashing</u> knocked Lu Yun out on the ground. <u>After</u> he woke up, he found himself in the woodshed, shrouded in darkness.'

Although there are both additions and reductions, the nature of the added and reduced is different: the reduced are the sentence-completing elements while the added are often features of nominal elements.

2.5 Summary

To recap, dependent clauses are clauses that need to depend on other clauses to be integrated into discourse. In languages with syntactic morphology, they represent themselves in non-finite forms.

Since Chinese is an isolating language, the conditions that determine clause dependency and self-sufficiency are different from those of languages with syntactic inflection. The status of the clause in Chinese is not only reflected in lexical means (e.g., use of conjunctives or not) and sentence-completing elements (such as tense, mood, and intonation), but also in the configuration of the clausal subject (e.g., cataphoric zero-subject) and in the structural complexity of the object.

On top of this, dependent clauses also vary with the text style in terms of their syntactic features and linking patterns, which is to be detailed in later chapters.

Notes

1 Halliday (2000, p. 223) also suggests a more special case, i.e., the embedded: "Picture, <u>if you can</u>, a winkle." Cases like this are left aside for the moment and the focus is on the more conventional types.
2 The strongest reduction occurs when a clause is reduced to a nominality verbal noun, but it does not mean that reduction always operates in the direction of nominality. For instance, a clause can be reduced to an adverbial, which can by no means be further reduced to a nominal. In comparison with reduction to an adverbial, reduction to nominality, nonetheless, is of a higher degree. In this manner, reduction to a nominality verbal noun represents the end of the process.

3 Syntactic integration function of zero-subject clauses

The zero-subject clause is a syntactic device to manifest not only topic continuation, but also the information property and syntactic status of the clause. When used for topic continuity, such a clause exhibits the following properties: a. the zero-subject is coreferential with the subject of the preceding clause; b. the zero-subject is coreferential with the possessor modifier of the subject of the preceding clause when the referent of the possessor modifier is a discourse topic; c. the use of a conjunctive is required. Conversely, cataphoric zero-subject clauses are used to express background information in writing, which explains why there is a great deal of subject omission in written Chinese. The absence of the subject is in essence a means of syntactic integration.

3.1 Introduction

There are three main lines of research on zero-subject clauses in Chinese discourse. The first one is in terms of anaphoric relations and referential choices, where the coding form of the clausal subject, be it a noun, a pronoun or a zero form, is taken as a function of discourse factors and cognitive laws (e.g., Fang Mei, 1985; Liao Qiuzhong, 1986a; Chen Ping, 1987c; Xu Jiujiu, 2010; Xu Yulong, 1996, 2005; etc.). The second is from the perspective of topic continuity, whereby zero-subject clauses are examined to see how they function to introduce and continue topics (e.g., Li and Thompson, 1981; Chen Ping, 1987c; Chu, 1998; Xu Yulong, 2005c; Fang Mei, 2005a; Song Rou, 2013; etc.). And the third line focuses on the information properties of zero-subject clauses and their role in syntactic integration (e.g., Fang Mei, 2008, 2016b; Chen Manhua, 2010).

In narrative discourse, three main categories of zero-subjects are identified (Fang Mei, 1985; Chen Ping, 1987c; Fang Mei, 2008; Chen Manhua, 2010; Xu Jiujiu, 2010; etc.):

1) anaphoric zero-subject, which is known as anaphoric subject omission in traditional grammatical description;
2) cataphoric zero-subject, traditionally called cataphoric subject omission;
3) zero-subject with no antecedent, traditionally described as subject-made-implicit.

In terms of frequency of use, the majority of the zero-subject clauses in Chinese discourse have the subject of the preceding clause as the antecedent (about 80%, see Fang Mei, 1985), followed by the object of the preceding clause, or the possessive modifier of the subject of the preceding clause. The above pattern can be largely explained by the accessibility and topicality of the subject referent.

The zero-subject can also be coreferential with other syntactic constituents in the preceding clause, a phenomenon that can hardly be explained in terms of accessibility or topic continuity. According to Fang Mei's (1985) investigation, the syntactic distribution of the antecedent of the zero-subject can be summarized as follows.

1) Syntactic constituents in the main clause: a. main clause subject; b. main clause object; c. indirect object in the double-object construction; d. "pivot" in the pivotal construction; e. possessive modifier.
2) Syntactic constituents in the embedded clause: a. subject of the subject-predicate construction functioning as predicate; b. subject of the subject-predicate construction serving as object; c. subject of the subject-predicate construction used as the complement of 得 (*de*); d. possessive modifier.

Unlike political discourse, narrative discourse does not depend on logico-semantic devices for cohesion, which renders it difficult to rely on conjunctions to determine whether the clauses are related by way of subordination or coordination. For Chinese, a language lacking syntactic morphology, it is also difficult to identify the syntactic status of a clause by referring to the finiteness of its predicate, as is the normal practice in morphological languages.

This study has found that the zero-subject clause in Chinese plays a unique role in syntactic integration, and the coreferentiality of the zero-subject with other constituents in the sentence reflects not only topic continuity in discourse, but also the syntactic status and informational properties of the hosting clause in complex sentences.

3.2 Main types of zero-subject clauses

3.2.1 *Anaphoric zero-subject clauses*

There are two main types of zero-subject clauses in terms of their coreferentiality with the antecedent. In one type, the zero-subject is coreferential with the subject of the preceding clause; and in the other, the zero-subject is coreferential with syntactic constituents other than the subject of the preceding clause.

3.2.1.1 Zero-subject coreferential with the subject of the preceding clause

See examples (1) to (3) for illustration.

(1) 他ᵢ扛起铺盖,0ᵢ灭了灯,0ᵢ进了后院。(Lao She, *Rickshaw Boy* [《骆驼祥子》])
    Tāᵢ kángqǐ pùgài, 0ᵢ mièle   dēng, 0ᵢ jìnle
    he   pick.up bedding   put.out.PFV light   enter.PFV
    hòuyuàn.
    backyard
    'He picked up the bedding, put out the light, and went into the backyard.'

(2) 她ᵢ没理我ⱼ,0ᵢ贴着游泳池的边上了岸。(Wang Shuo, *Half Flame, Half Seawater* [《一半是火焰,一半是海水》])
    Tāᵢ méi lǐ   wǒⱼ, 0ᵢ tiēzhe   yóuyǒngchí   de biān
    she not attend.to me   against swimming.pool NM edge
    shàngle   àn.
    up.PFV   bank
    'She ignored me, and went ashore against the edge of the swimming pool.'

(3) 她ᵢ看了我ⱼ一眼,0ᵢ扭头走了。(Wang Shuo, *Half Flame, Half Seawater*)
    Tāᵢ kànle   wǒⱼ yī   yǎn, 0ᵢ niǔtóu   zǒule.
    she look.PFV me   one look   turn.round walk.PFV
    'She took a look at me, turned round and walked away.'

When more than one zero-subject clause is juxtaposed, the later occurring clause(s) can be supplemented by the continuative adverb 又 (yòu), whereby (1) can be reproduced as (1') and (1").

(1') 他ᵢ扛起铺盖,0ᵢ**又**灭了灯,0ᵢ进了后院。
(1") 他ᵢ扛起铺盖,0ᵢ灭了灯,0ᵢ**又**进了后院。

In terms of syntactic status, strong eventfulness correlates with independent clauses and weak eventfulness correlates with dependent clauses.

In addition to the above-mentioned cases that express serial action, the zero-subject of the subsequent clause can also be understood as having the same referent with the subject of the preceding clause even when the preceding clause is a passive one. Compare (4) with (4') and (4"), where 被 is a passive marker.

(4) 妹妹ᵢ被哥哥ⱼ拿走三支笔,0ᵢ急得到处找。
    Mèimèiᵢ bèi   gēgēⱼ   názǒu   sān   zhī bǐ,
    sister   pass. brother take.away three CL   pen
    0ᵢ jíde   dàochù   zhǎo.
        worry.CM   everywhere look.for
    'Sister had three pens taken away by brother, and went looking for them everywhere in a hurry.'

(4') *妹妹ᵢ被哥哥j拿走三支笔, 0ᵢ 急得到处找。
(4") *妹妹ᵢ被哥哥j拿走三支笔, 0ᵢ+0ⱼ急得到处找。

3.2.1.2 Zero-subject not coreferential with the subject of the preceding clause

There are two main categories of zero-subjects whose antecedents are syntactic constituents other than the subject of the preceding clause. First, the zero-subject may have the same reference with the possessive modifier of the subject of the preceding clause.

(5) 祥子ᵢ的心中很乱, 0ᵢ 末了听到太太说怕血, 0ᵢ 似乎找到了一件可以安慰她的事。(Lao She, *Rickshaw Boy*)

| Xiángziᵢ | de | xīnzhōng | hěn | luàn, |
| Xiangzi | NM | heart | very | in.turmoil |

0ᵢ mòliǎo tīngdào tàitài shuō pà xuè,
   at.last hear madame say be.afraid blood

0ᵢ sìhū zhǎodàole yī jiàn kěyǐ ānwèi tā de shì.
   seem find.PFV one CL may comfort her NM thing

'Xiangziᵢ's heart was in turmoil. When (he) at last heard that madame was afraid of blood, (he) seemed to have found something to comfort her about.'

(6) 那时, 我ᵢ的酒量很小, 0ᵢ 喝了几口葡萄酒就晕乎乎的。(Wang Shuo, *Half Flame, Half Seawater*)

Nàshí, wǒᵢ de jiǔliàng hěn xiǎo,
then I NM drinking.capacity very small

0ᵢ hēle jǐ kǒu pútáojiǔ jiù yūnhūhū de.
  drink.PFV several CL wine just dizzy aux.

'At that time, I was not a good drinker. A few sips of wine made me dizzy.'

(7) 她ᵢ搭在我肩上的手夹着烟, 0ᵢ 不时歪着头吸上一口。(Wang Shuo, *Half Flame, Half Seawater*)

Tāᵢ dā zài wǒ jiān shàng de shǒu jiāzhe yān,
she put on my shoulder on NM hand hold.DUR cigarette

0ᵢ bùshí wāizhe tóu xīshàng yī kǒu.
  from.time.to.time tilt.DUR head smoke.ACH one puff

'Her hand on my shoulder holding a cigarette, from time to time (she) would tilt her head to take a puff.'

It is especially worth noting that if the zero-subject of the subsequent clause is coreferential with the possessive modifier of the preceding clause, such as "祥子" ('Xiangzi') in example (5), "我" ('I') in example (6) and "她" ('she') in example (7), the referent of the possessive modifier must be the same as the discourse topic on the topic chain.

In the second category, the zero-subject has the same reference with the object of the preceding clause. See example (8).

(8) 我ᵢ见过他女朋友ⱼ, 0ⱼ 长得特别漂亮。
Wǒᵢ jiànguò tā nǚpéngyǒuⱼ, 0ⱼ zhǎngde tèbié piàoliàng.
I see.EXP his girlfriend grow.CM particularly good-looking
'I have seen his girlfriend, who is particularly good-looking.'

Unlike the previous category, this type of zero-subject clause does not express a successive act; instead, it only describes the referent of the object in the preceding clause, i.e., "他女朋友" ('his girlfriend') in (8).

In terms of frequency of use, when there is more than one nominal constituent in the preceding clause, the zero-subject of the subsequent clause is in most cases coreferential with the subject of the preceding clause. It has been found that the zero-subject referring to other constituents than the subject of the preceding clause accounts for about 20% of the total of zero-subjects. The syntactic distribution of the antecedent can be very complex when the subject of the subsequent clause refers to syntactic constituents other than the subject of the preceding clause (see Fang Mei, 1985 for details).

When the semantic relation is considered, the zero-subject clause and its preceding clause express two successive actions of the same event. The conditions that license non-coreferential zero-subjects in the succeeding clauses are to be discussed in detail below.

3.2.2 Cataphoric zero-subjects

This category refers to the case where the zero-subject clause precedes a clause with an explicit subject, in which case the zero-subject can be coreferential with the subject of the subsequent clause, as illustrated in example (9), or with the possessive modifier of the subject of the subsequent clause, as in example (10). The expressive function of such zero-subject clauses is similar to that of non-finite verb clauses in morphological languages.

(9) 0ᵢ看着父亲痛苦的样子, 她ᵢ不禁泪流满面。
0ᵢ kànzhe fùqīn tòngkǔ de yàngzi, tāᵢ bújìn lèiliúmǎnmiàn.
look.DUR father pain NM look she can't.help shed.tears
'Looking at her father in pain, she couldn't help but shed tears.'

(10) 0ᵢ到了曹宅门外,他ᵢ的手哆嗦着去按门。(Lao She, *Rickshaw Boy*)

    0ᵢ dàole   Cáozhái   mén   wài,
    reach.PFV   Cao's.house   gate   outside

    tāᵢ de   shǒu   duōsuōzhe   qù   àn   mén.
    he   NM   hand tremble.DUR go   press door

    'Reaching the gate of Cao's house, he pressed the knocker with a trembling hand.'

Chen Ping (1987c) has pointed out that such zero-subject clauses are syntactically subordinate, and Fang Mei (2008) has observed the following syntactic restrictions on cataphoric zero-subject clauses:

1) the cataphoric zero-subject is coreferential only with the subject of the subsequent clause;
2) the cataphoric zero-subject clause has no tense or mood components, and the configuration of its verb predicate is rather constrained, the high-frequency types including:
    a. verb + *le* + noun: 丢了车 (diūle chē, 'lost the cart')
    b. verb + *zhe* + noun: 红着脸 (hóngzhe liǎn, 'red-faced')
    c. verb + direction verb (+ noun): 扛起铺盖 (kángqǐ pùgài, 'carry up the bedding')
    d. verb + location: 坐在胡同口 (zuò zài hútóngkǒu, 'sitting at the entrance to the alley')
    e. verb + wan ('finish') (+ noun): 吃完(饭) (chīwán (fàn), 'finish eating [a meal]')

More importantly, the cataphoric zero-subject is obligatory under certain circumstances, which is manifested by the fact that the stronger the syntactic contrast between the main and the subordinate clause, the stronger the requirement of the zero-subject (for details, see Fang Mei, 2008). Examine (11) to (13).

(11) 0ᵢ坐在床沿上,0ᵢ呆呆的看着这个瓦器,他ᵢ打算什么也不去想。(Lao She, *Rickshaw Boy*)

    0ᵢ zuò zài chuángyán shàng, 0ᵢ dāidāide kànzhe zhège wǎqì, tāᵢ dǎsuàn shénme yě bù qù xiǎng.

    'Sitting on the edge of the bed, staring blankly at the earthenware, he intended to think about nothing.'

(12) 0ᵢ能在天亮的时候赶到,0ᵢ把骆驼出了手,他ᵢ可以一进城就买上一辆车。(Lao She, *Rickshaw Boy*)

    0ᵢ néng zài tiānliàng de shíhòu gǎndào, 0ᵢ bǎ luòtuó chūle shǒu, tāᵢ kěyǐ yī jìnchéng jiù mǎishàng yīliàng chē.

'If (he) could arrive at dawn and get the camel off his hands, he would be able to buy a rickshaw as soon as he got into town.'

(13) 0$_i$ 无缘无故的丢了车, 0$_i$ 无缘无故的又来了这层缠绕, 他$_i$觉得他$_i$这一辈子大概就这么完了, 无论自己怎么要强, 全算白饶。(Lao She, *Rickshaw Boy*)

0$_i$ wúyuánwúgù de diūle chē, 0$_i$ wúyuánwúgù de yòu láile zhè céng chánrào, tā$_i$ juéde tā$_i$ zhè yībèizi dàgài jiù zhème wánle, wúlùn zìjǐ zěnme yàoqiáng, quán suàn báiráo.

'Having lost the rickshaw for no reason, which was complemented by this undeserved trouble, he felt that his life is probably over. No matter how strong he intended to be, all counted for nothing.'

In sequences containing cataphoric zero-subject clauses, when the main clause has an explicit subject, the zero-subject clauses are mostly adverbial. For example, the two zero-subject clauses in (11) indicate the accompanying states, those in (12) are conditional, and the two in (13) denote the causes.

Cataphoric zero-subject clauses and clauses containing explicit subjects cannot be interleaved. Example (11) is reproduced as (14a) below. Compare the different versions where the subject is made explicit in clauses of varying sequencing order.

(14) a. 坐在床沿上, 呆呆的看着这个瓦器, **他**打算什么也不去想。
 b. **他**坐在床沿上, 呆呆的看着这个瓦器, 打算什么也不去想。
 c. ?坐在床沿上, **他**呆呆的看着这个瓦器, **他**打算什么也不去想。
 d. *__他__坐在床沿上, **他**呆呆的看着这个瓦器, 打算什么也不去想。
 e. #**他**坐在床沿上, **他**呆呆的看着这个瓦器, **他**打算什么也不去想。

In the sentence group above, (14c) is of marginal acceptability; (14d) is not acceptable; and (14e) can only be interpreted as rhetorical in prose style, licensed when a certain state is emphasized in particular.

The clause containing an explicit subject is "primary" and the clause containing a zero-subject is "secondary", which makes the zero-subject clause a means of indicating the relation between the main clause and the subclause. In contexts where the syntactico-semantic relationship is clear, it is not even possible to fill in the subject of the zero-subject clause. See (15).

(15) a. 0$_i$ 病了, 他$_i$ 舍不得钱去买药, 自己硬挺着。(Lao She, *Rickshaw Boy*)

 0$_i$ bìngle, tā$_i$ shěbudé qián qù mǎi yào, zìjǐ yìng tǐngzhe.

 'When sick, he wouldn't spare the money to buy medicine, trying to hold himself together.'

 b. 0$_i$ **即使**病了, 他$_i$ **也**舍不得钱去买药, 自己硬挺着。

 0$_i$ **jíshǐ** bìngle, tā$_i$ **yě** shěbudé qián qù mǎi yào, zìjǐyìng tǐngzhe.

'Even when sick, he wouldn't spare the money to buy medicine, trying to hold himself together.'

c. ?他$_i$病了, 他$_i$舍不得钱去买药, 自己硬挺着。
   Tā$_i$ bìngle, tā$_i$ yě shěbudé qián qù mǎi yào, zìjǐ yìng tǐngzhe.

The zero-subject clause in example (15a) indicates a condition, and the use of the conditional conjunctive (即使…也) turns it into (15b). However, if the subject of the zero-subject clause is added, as in (15c), the sentence becomes ungrammatical, because the implicit presence of the conjunctive reflects, to some extent, the respective strength of the eventfulness of the clauses (Reinhart, 1984).

In Chinese, one syntactic deranking device is characterized by the mandatory use of cataphoric zero-subjects, which can be understood as a compensation for the lack of morphological markers in the morphosyntactic system. The use of cataphoric zero-subjects turns syntactic relations between clauses from coordination to subordination. Cataphoric zero-subject clauses package background information, such as cause or condition. If the syntactic relation is coordination, the default principle is for the clause with an explicit subject to precede the zero-subject clause. Once this default principle is violated and the clause uses a cataphoric zero-subject, its syntactic status is deranked. In Chinese, the implicit-or-explicit use of conjunctives governs the strength of eventfulness and syntactic self-sufficiency. The explicit use of a conjunctive implies what the hosting clause conveys is part of the event process (Fang Mei, 2008).

3.2.3 *Zero-subject clauses without antecedents*

There are two main types of zero-subject clauses that fall in this category.

In the first type, the subject of the zero-subject clause refers back to the subject of the preceding sentence. See (16).

(16) 有一天, 我$_i$打车去现代城。0$_i$ 刚说出地名, 的哥一脸茫然:"这儿不就是吗?" (cited from Chen Manhua, 2010)

Yǒuyītiān, wǒ$_i$ dǎchē qù Xiàndàichéng. 0$_i$ gāng shuōchū dìmíng, dīgē yīliǎn mángrán: "Zhè·er bú jiùshì ma?"

'One day, I took a taxi to the Modern City. (I) just said the name of the place, and the taxi driver looked confused, "Isn't this the place?"'

In example (16), the zero-subject of the clause "刚说出地名" ('just said the name of the place') is coreferential with the subject "我" ('I') of the preceding sentence, instead of referring cataphorically to the subject of the following clause "的哥" ('taxi driver'). This is a common phenomenon in narrative discourse, where the zero-subject is often the main character of discourse.

In the second type, the referent of the zero-subject of the clause is uncertain, and it is difficult to be established in the context. See examples (17) to (19), where the explicit subjects are marked by bold font.

(17) <u>也不知怎么的</u>，**她**说着说着就哭起来了。

Yě bùzhī zěnme de, **tā** shuōzhe~shuōzhe jiù kūqǐlái le.

'<u>Somehow,</u> **she** started to cry as she talked.'

(18) **天台**见无法回家，急得团团转，不由地把斧子往地上一摔，<u>只听"哗啦"一声闪开一个山门</u>，门里走出一个道姑……

Tiāntái jiàn wúfǎ huíjiā, jíde tuántuánzhuàn, bùyóude bǎ fǔzi wǎng dìshàng yī shuāi, <u>zhǐ tīng "huālā" yī shēng shǎnkāi yīgè shānmén</u>, ménli zǒuchū yī gè dàogū …

'Seeing that he could not go home, **Tiantai** paced about in such anxiety that he dropped the axe to the ground, <u>only to hear a "crack", and a mountain gate appeared, out of which</u> walked a Taoist nun…'

(19) **那银鳗**在月光下不停地闪腰，盘舞，旋转……速度越来越快，节奏越来越紧，突然银光一闪，**鳗儿**不见了，<u>只见月影中站立着一个天仙般的龙女</u>，柳叶眉，杏花脸，玉笋手，细柳腰，金纱披身，莲花镶裙。

Nà yínmán zài yuèguāng xià bùtíng de shǎnyāo, pánwǔ, xuánzhuǎn … sùdù yuèláiyuè kuài, jiézòu yuèláiyuè jǐn, tūrán yínguāng yī shǎn, **mán·er** bú jiàn le, <u>zhǐjiàn yuèyǐng zhōng zhànlìzhe yīgè tiānxiān bān de lóngnǚ</u>, liǔyè méi, xìnghuā liǎn, yùsǔn shǒu, xìliǔ yāo, jīnshā pī shēn, liánhuā xiāng qún.

'In the moonlight **the silver eel** kept flashing its waist, dancing, rotating… faster and faster in speed, tighter and tighter in rhythm. Suddenly in a silver flash, **the eel** disappeared, <u>only to see a heavenly dragon lady standing in the moonlight</u>, with arched eyebrows like willow leaves, face like apricot blossom, hands like bamboo shoots, waist like thin willow, body draped in a golden veil, and skirt set with lotus flowers.'

In (17) to (19) above, the three underlined clauses are all subjectless, and none of the subjects can be recovered. "也不知怎的" (literally 'not knowing how') in (17) is a highly colloquial adverbial clause; "只听" in (18) leads an adverbial clause indicating the accompanying state; and "只见" in (19) has grammaticalized into a discourse conjunctive in modern Chinese to introduce topical elements (see Fang Mei, 2017b).

3.3 Zero-subject clauses and topic continuity

3.3.1 Topic continuity

The topic of the sentence is the entity (person, object, etc.) about which specifications are made, and the specifications about this entity are called comment (Crystal, 1997/2008).

The dichotomy of "topic" and "comment" is widely used, and in terms of interaction, "topic" is "what is being talked about" and "comment" is "what is said about the topic". If a constituent X is called topic, it can answer the question "What about X?" In some languages, topic is no more than a pragmatic category, while in others it enjoys an independent syntactic status (Xu Liejung, 2002).[1]

Chao (1968/1979), in his discussion of the Grammatical Meaning of Subject and Predicate (Section 2.4), proposes that the grammatical meaning of subject and predicate in Chinese is topic and comment, rather than actor and action.

Topicality is not a property acquired by the referent based on the hosting clause, but based on the discourse (Givón, 1984/1990).

Topic continuity[2] refers to the strength and range of influence of a topic, and it makes up an important aspect of topic study. In a variety of languages, anaphoric clausal zero-subjects are syntactic manifestations of strong topic continuity.[3]

3.3.2 *Sentence topics and discourse topics*

From the perspective of discourse, topics should first be categorized into sentence topics and discourse topics. A sentence topic is what the sentence is about, and the subject of a sentence in Chinese is usually also a topic at the same time, a point which has been discussed in many works. In Chinese discourse, the topic occurring in the subject slot can become the antecedent of a number of subsequent zero-subjects. See (20), for example.

(20) 那是一个下午,我们$_i$按照王朔$_j$模糊的记忆摸到葛优$_k$住的那幢楼,0$_i$到那儿才发现原来就在我曾经住过的楼的隔壁。因为0$_i$不知道具体门牌号码,0$_i$也没有葛优的电话。0$_i$在楼里几经打听才找到他$_k$住的单元。0$_i$敲门,没人应。0$_i$再敲门,隔壁单元走出一位女士$_l$,0$_l$是葛优媳妇的嫂子。0$_l$说明来意后,嫂子$_l$告诉我们,葛优外出,估计0$_k$快回来了。(Feng Xiaogang, *Saving No Worry* [《不省心》])

Nà shì yīgè xiàwǔ, wǒmen$_i$ ànzhào Wáng Shuò$_j$ móhú de jìyì mō dào Gě Yōu$_k$ zhù de nà zhuàng lóu, 0$_i$ dào nà·er cái fāxiàn yuánlái jiù zài wǒ céngjīng zhùguò de lóu de gébì. Yīnwèi 0$_i$ bù zhīdào jùtǐ ménpáihàomǎ, 0$_i$ yě méiyǒu Gě Yōu de diànhuà. 0$_i$ zài lóu lǐ jǐ jīng dǎtīng cái zhǎodào tā$_k$ zhù de dānyuán. 0$_i$ qiāo mén, méi rén yīng. 0$_i$ zài qiāo mén, gébì dānyuán zǒu chū yī wèi nǚshì$_l$, 0$_l$ shì Gě Yōu xífù de sǎozi. 0$_l$ shuōmíng láiyì hòu, sǎozi$_l$ gàosù wǒmen, Gě Yōu wàichū, gūjì 0$_k$ kuài huílái le.

'It was an afternoon when we followed Wang Shuo's vague memory to the building where Ge You lived, only to find that it was next door to the building where I used to live. (We) didn't know the exact number of his unit, neither did (we) have his phone number. It was after (we) asked about for a while in the building that (we) finally found his unit. (We) knocked on the door, but no one answered. (We) knocked again, and a woman came out of the neighboring unit. (She) was Ge You's wife's sister-in-law. (We) explained the reason for the visit, and the sister-in-law told us that Ge You was out and that he would probably be back soon.'

Discourse topics can be observed mainly along two dimensions, frequency and manner of anaphora,[4] which are also important factors in determining discourse topics. The topic referred back to in the form of zero-subject or pronoun is a most accessible topic, such as "我们" ('we') in the above example.

A discourse topic is what a discourse mainly talks about, usually the main character of the speech event. There are two different cases in which a concept is mentioned in a discourse. In one case, the topic, once introduced into the discourse, can be tracked in different manners in the subsequent discourse, as is the case of "我们" in (20). In the other case, the concept appears only once, without being mentioned again, such as "长途车司机" ('coach driver'), "交通监理人员" ('traffic supervisors'), and "汽车喇叭" ('car horns') in (21).

(21) 那天上午,在靠近保山的山间公路发生了一场车祸,一辆载货卡车和一辆长途汽车在转弯处迎头相撞。所幸两车速度不高未翻到崖下,也未造成严重伤亡,只是两车车头损坏,长途车司机受了轻伤,但相撞的两车横直,道路堵塞了交通达四小时。待交通监理人员从保山赶来勘查了现场判定了肇事责任,这才开来一辆吊车将损坏的两车吊至路旁恢复了公路畅通。这期间有数百辆各型客货车堵在山间公路上连绵十余公里,汽车喇叭此伏彼起响成一片,车上的人纷纷下来站在公路上互相聊天到处走动。(Wang Shuo, *Playing It for the Thrill* [《玩儿的就是心跳》])

Nàtiān shàngwǔ, zài kàojìn Bǎoshān de shānjiān gōnglù fāshēngle yī chǎng chēhuò, yī liàng zài huò kǎchē hé yī liàng chángtú qìchē zài zhuǎn-wān chù yíngtóu xiāngzhuàng. Suǒxìng liǎng chē sùdù bù gāo wèi fān dào yá xià, yě wèi zàochéng yánzhòng shāngwáng, zhǐshì liǎng chē chētóu sǔn-huài, chángtúchē sījī shòule qīng shāng, dàn xiāngzhuàng de liǎng chē héngzhí, dàolù dǔsèle jiāotōng dá sì xiǎoshí. Dài jiāotōng jiānlǐ rényuán cóng Bǎoshān gǎnlái kānchále xiànchǎng pàndìngle zhàoshì zérèn, zhè cái kāi lái yī liàng diàochē jiāng sǔnhuài de liǎng chē diào zhì lùpáng huīfùle gōnglù chàngtōng. Zhè qījiān yǒu shù bǎi liàng gè xíng kè-huòchē dǔ zài shānjiān gōnglù shàng liánmián shí yú gōnglǐ, qìchē lǎbā cǐfúbǐqǐ xiǎng-chéng yīpiàn, chē shàng de rén fēnfēn xiàlái zhàn zài gōnglù shàng hùxiāng liáotiān dàochù zǒudòng.

'That morning, there was a traffic accident on the mountain highway near Baoshan, where a truck carrying goods and a coach collided head-on at a turn. Fortunately, the speed of the two vehicles was not high. So there was no tumbling of vehicles off the cliff or serious casualties. Only the front of the two vehicles were damaged, and the driver of the coach was slightly injured. But the collision caused the two vehicles to stay across the highway, blocking the traffic for four hours. It was not until the traffic supervisors from Baoshan came to investigate the scene and determine the responsibility of the accident that a crane came to lift the two damaged vehicles to the roadside to restore the highway traffic. During this period, there were hundreds of various types of coaches and trucks blocked on the mountain highway, stretching more than 10 kilometers. Car horns were sounding one after another, and the passengers came down to stand on the highway chatting with each other and walking around.'

When a concept is the discourse protagonist, it often appears many a time in the discourse and is tracked in different ways, both being the manifestations of its topicality. The concepts that appear only once are trivial information with no topicality (see Tao Hongyin and Zhang Bojiang, 2000 for the syntactic representations of discourse protagonists).

3.3.3 Syntactic means of topic introduction

Subject zero anaphora is a commonly seen means of topic continuation in topic management. The strong coding choice is for the zero-subject to be coreferential with the subject of the preceding clause. Chen Ping (1987c) has identified two main patterns of zero-subject clause sequencing. The first one is the so-called parallel progression pattern, in which the theme of the preceding clause is resumed as the theme of the present clause, as in (22).

(22) 他$_i$擦车, 0$_i$ 打气, 0$_i$ 晒雨布, 0$_i$ 抹油。(cited from Chen Ping, 1987c)
Tā$_i$ cā chē, 0$_i$ dǎ qì, 0$_i$ shài yǔbù, 0$_i$ mǒ yóu.
'He wiped the car, pumped up the tires, aired the rain cloth, and greased the surface.'

The second is known as the cascading progression pattern, where a new information element in the preceding clause is picked up as the theme of the present clause. See (23) and (24) for illustration (cited from Chen Ping, 1987c).

(23) 他$_i$必定也看见了那些老弱的车夫$_j$, 0$_j$ 穿着薄薄的破衣$_k$, 0$_k$ 根本抵御不住冬日的风寒。
Tā$_i$ bìdìng yě kànjiànle nàxiē lǎo ruò de chēfū$_j$, 0$_j$ chuānzhe báo~báo de pò yī$_k$, 0$_k$ gēnběn dǐyù-bú-zhù dōngrì de fēnghán.
'He must have also seen the old and weak cart pullers, who wore thin rags that could not withstand the winter wind chill.'

(24) 村上有一个扶着水平仪三脚架的工人$_i$, 0$_i$ 在观察着, 远处还有个打红小旗的工人$_j$, 0$_j$ 跟他$_i$遥相呼应。
Cūnshàng yǒu yī gè fúzhe shuǐpíngyí sānjiǎojià de gōngrén$_i$, 0$_i$ zài guāncházhe, yuǎnchù hái yǒu gè dǎ hóng xiǎo qí de gōngrén$_j$, 0$_j$ gēn tā$_i$ yáoxiānghūyìng.

'There in the village is <u>a worker holding a level gauge tripod</u>, busy watching, and in the distance <u>a worker with a small red flag in hand</u> echoes him.'

In (23) and (24) above, the new information encoded in the theme or comment is most likely to become the theme of the subsequent clause, and is therefore strong in ushering in new discourse.

In Chinese, certain sentence patterns have the function of topic introduction, irrespective of the fact that the topic element does not occur in the subject slot. One specific case is the so-called existential construction, whose predicate can be of the following semantic types[5]:

1) the existential verb 有 ('have'):

从前<u>有</u>个泥水匠叫刘善,……
Cóngqián   <u>yǒu</u>   ge   níshuǐjiàng   jiào   Liú Shàn,…
once.upon.a.time   have   CL   plasterer   named   Liu Shan
'Once upon a time there was a plasterer named Liu Shan,…'

2) verbs that indicate the appearance or disappearance of someone or something:

正在这时候,<u>出</u>了个汉子叫二郎,……
Zhèngzài zhè shíhòu,   <u>chū</u>le   ge   hànzi   jiào   Èrláng,…
right   this moment appear.PFV   CL   man   named   Erlang
'At this very moment, out came a man named Erlang,…'

3) verb constructions that indicates where someone or something is located:

台上<u>坐着</u>主席团。
Tái   shàng   <u>zuòzhe</u>   zhǔxítuán.
stage   on   sit.DUR   presidium
'On the stage sits the presidium.'

4) verbs indicating the result of a certain experience:

从前有个泥水匠叫刘善,他<u>养了</u>一只八哥。
Cóngqián   yǒu   ge   níshuǐjiàng   jiào   Liú Shàn,…
once.upon.a.time   have   CL   plasterer   named   Liu.Shan
tā   <u>yǎngle</u>   yī   zhī   bāgē.
he   raise.PFV   one   CL   myna
'Once upon a time there was a plasterer named Liu Shan, who raised a myna.'

The existential construction is often used in discourse to introduce topics (Li and Thompson, 1981; Chen Ping, 1987c; Xu Yulong, 2004, 2007).

Sun Chaofen's (1988) study has shown that there is a close link between the importance of a topic in discourse and the use of quantifiers, with a thematically more important noun phrase tending to be introduced into discourse by way of a quantifier construction.

The findings of Chen Ping (1987c) and Sun Chaofen (1988) are in general agreement with the study of Li and Thompson (1981). Xu Yulong's (2004, 2005) studies further confirm that the most important means of marking a newly introduced entity as a potential discourse topic are the existential construction and the indefinite noun phrase. Xu (2007) even suggests that in Chinese, the indefinite noun phrase in the existential construction seems to be the only syntactic means to introduce an important discourse topic.

A topic, once established, is maintained mainly by means of zero-subject or pronoun anaphora. For topic switching (i.e., the topic is switched from one entity to another), the definite descriptor denoting the new topic entity generally needs to be repeated once in the subject position (Xu Yulong, 2004, p. 173).

(25) [大土霸]ᵢ气势汹汹地对老渔翁j说:"……"老渔翁j听了, 0j 知道是土霸故意刁难他, 0j 又怒又恨,…… (topic shifting from 大土霸 to 老渔翁)

[Dà tǔbà]ᵢ qìshìxiōngxiōng de duì lǎo yúwēngⱼ shuō: "…" Lǎo yúwēngⱼ tīngle, 0ⱼ zhīdào shì tǔbà gùyì diāonàn tā, 0ⱼ yòu nù yòu hèn,…

'[The big bully] said to the old fisherman in an aggressive manner, "…" When the old fisherman heard this, (he) knew that the bully had deliberately made things difficult for him, which made him both angry and hateful,…'

The above observation of Xu Yulong (2004) is somewhat different from the cascading progression pattern as proposed by Chen Ping (1987c). In our view, the phenomenon outlined by the cascading progression pattern occurs roughly in the cases where the preceding clause indicates the existence or emergence of an entity. In such cases, the post-verbal constituent tends to be a quantifier construction, which becomes the topic of the subsequent clause(s), as illustrated in examples (23) and (24). It is true that the subject in Chinese is also the topic (Chao, 1968, pp. 69–70; Zhu Dexi, 1982, p. 96), but the subject in such subsequent clauses does not initiate a new topic chain, and thus may not be the discourse topic. If the subject of the subsequent clause indeed starts a new topic chain, the topic noun still has to be repeated once in the subject position of the clause, as in example (25), even though the noun has already appeared in the previous clause.

3.4 Zero-subject clauses with subjects of transferred reference

3.4.1 Topic continuity of zero-subject clauses

In earlier literature, zero-subject clauses and topic continuation are approached from the grammatical perspective by examining the types of omitted subjects in compound and complex sentences (Fang Mei, 1985). Topic continuity of event participants is believed to manifest in two main ways: (1) the zero-subject of the clause is coreferential with the subject of the preceding clause (anaphoric subject omission); (2) the zero-subject of the clause is coreferential with the possessive modifier of the subject of the preceding clause (anaphoric modifier omission).

Xu Yulong (1996) has proposed the principle of sentence topic identification in Chinese discourse: any preverbal noun phrase that indicates a participant (i.e., some concrete or abstract cognitive entity) in the course of the action described in the sentence is a sentence topic. However, as mentioned above, the case of zero-subjects pointing to elements other than the subject of the preceding clause is very complex. It is not uncommon in Chinese for the zero-subject of a clause to be non-coreferential with the subject of the preceding clause when the preceding clause is not an existential construction, as is the case of (26).

(26) 一位好心的教授ᵢ把他的一份原版 Word 安装盘借给我ⱼ用。0ⱼ 拿回自己办公室不过半个小时，他ᵢ就打电话过来问"装完了吗？"(调查语料)

Yīwèi hǎoxīn de jiàoshòuᵢ bǎ tā de yī fèn yuánbǎn Word ānzhuāngpán jiègěi wǒⱼ yòng. 0ⱼ ná huí zìjǐ bàngōngshì búguò bàngè xiǎoshí, tāᵢ jiù dǎdiànhuà guòlái wèn "Zhuāng wán le ma?"

'A kind professor lent me a copy of his original Word installation disk. It was no more than half an hour since (I) took it back to my office that he called to ask, "Is it done?"'

In the example above, the zero-subject of the clause "拿回自己办公室不过半个小时" can only be "我"('I'), rather than the subject of the preceding clause "一位好心的教授" ('a kind professor'). How to explain this kind of phenomenon? The zero-subject of the subsequent clause does not refer to the subject of the preceding clause, which makes it deviate from the parallel progression pattern. If the criterion "taking a new information component in the comment part of the preceding clause as the subject" is referred to, it seems that the example follows the cascading progression pattern. But the typical cascading progression pattern is to introduce a topic component, whereas the referent of the zero-subject in this clause is obviously not a topic, because "他" ('he') in the following clause refers anaphorically to the kind professor.

Reference transfer of zero-subjects, in fact, often suggests a discontinuity in the topic chain.

3.4.2 Reference transfer of zero-subjects and clause transitivity

On the whole, it is a high-frequency phenomenon for the zero-subject to refer anaphorically to the subject of the preceding clause. When the zero-subject is coreferential with other syntactic constituents in the preceding clause, some of the lexical choices do not have competing referents.

(27) 小王给我买了三个饼，都是肉馅儿的。
   Xiǎo Wáng gěi wǒ mǎile sān gè bǐng, dōu shì ròuxiàn·er de.
   'Wang bought me three pies, all filled with meat.'
(28) 她喜欢穿平底鞋，没跟儿。
   Tā xǐhuān chuān píngdǐ xié, méi gēn·er.
   'She likes to wear flat shoes with no heels.'

In these two cases, the later occurring zero-subject clauses are not likely to be used to describe people, but such cases are not the focus of discussion for now.

As mentioned above, zero-subjects coreferential with constituents other than the subject of the preceding clause often suggest discontinuity in the topic chain. This phenomenon can be accounted for in terms of syntactico-semantic behavior, in that the zero-subject clause and its preceding clause are of significant difference in transitivity.

Here transitivity is used in the sense as proposed by Hopper and Thompson (1980), which is predetermined by a set of features (10 in total). The transitivity of a clause depends on the number of syntactico-semantic features embodied in the clause, as listed in Table 3.1.

In Chinese, low transitivity shows the following features:

Participants: 1 (e.g., subject only, or object only)
Kinesis: non-action (e.g., 有 [yǒu, 'have'], 存在 [cúnzài, 'exist'])
Aspect: atelic (e.g., V着/V起来 [V zhe /V qǐlái]), where the former is durative and the latter inchoactive
Punctuality: non-punctual (e.g., 睡 [shuì, 'sleep'], 躺 [tǎng, 'lie'])
Volitional: non-volitional (e.g., 死 [sǐ, 'die'], 存在 [cúnzài, 'exist'])
Mode: irrealis (e.g., supposition clauses, conditional clauses, time clauses)
Agency: low in potency (e.g., 认为 [rènwéi, 'think'], 判断 [pànduàn, 'judge'])
Affectedness of object: not affected (e.g., mental verb 喜欢 [xǐhuān, 'like'])

Table 3.1 Transitivity features

Feature	High transitivity	Low transitivity
Participants[a]	2	1
Kinesis	action	non-action
Aspect	telic	atelic
Punctuality	punctual	continuous
Volitionality	volitional	non-volitional
Affirmation	affirmative	negative
Mode	realis	irrealis
Agency	high in potency	low in potency
Affectedness of object	totally affected	not affected
Individuation of object	highly individuated	non-individuated

Source: Adapted from Hopper and Thompson, 1980, p. 252.

Note:
[a] The original reads as "2 or more participants, A and O" and "1 participant."

Individuation of object: non-individuated (e.g., non-referential nominal object, such as 大碗 in 吃大碗 [chī dà wǎn, 'eat (with) big bowls']).

In general, foreground information corresponds to high-transitivity features, while background information corresponds to low-transitivity features. When it comes to zero-subject clauses, the absence of the subject renders them characterized by only "one participant". The main behavior differences of the variety of zero-subject clauses are predetermined by the performance of the rest of the features in Table 3.1. Take (26), for example. In the zero-subject clause "拿回自己办公室不过半个小时", neither the agent (subject) nor the patient (object) occurs. Moreover, the clause is an adverbial that provides temporal information. Bearing three low transitivity features as enumerated above, the clause is low in transitivity.

3.4.3 Subsequent zero-subject clauses as low-transitivity clauses

When the preceding clause is an existential construction, the zero-subject refers to the post-verbal nominal constituent of the hosting clause. The typical existential construction is the *you*-clause, such as (24) above, which has received intensive attention in existing studies. Low-transitivity clauses actually constitute a cline, with *you*-clauses being a prototypical category. In what follows, the focus is on three other types of low-transitivity clauses that occur before zero-subject clauses: emergence-denoting clauses, clauses of evidential verbs, and clauses of psycho-epistemic verbs.

3.4.3.1 Emergence-denoting clause as preceding clause

The so-called "emergence-denoting clause" is a verbal clause in which the predicate verb indicates the emergence/appearance of someone or something. This type of clause is characterized by the fact that the grammatical subject is in the post-verb object position. See (29) and (30).

(29) 首先是政治上, 美国i出了个里根总统j, 0j开始重塑美国人的信仰, 0j重塑人民对国家的信任。他j是一个非常有主义的总统,……(Gao Xiaosong, *Morning Call* (《晓说》))

Shǒuxiān shi zhèngzhìshàng,

Měiguói chūle gè Lǐgēn zǒngtǒng$_j$,
America emerge.PFV CL Reagan president

0$_j$ kāishǐ chóngsù Měiguórén de xìnyǎng, 0$_j$ chóngsù rénmíng duì guójiā de xìnrèn. Tā$_j$ shì yī gè fēicháng yǒu zhǔyì de zǒngtǒng,…

'First of all, politically, there emerged in America President Reagan, (who) began to reshape the faith of Americans and the people's trust in the country. He was a president with his own ism,…'

(30) ......敲门,没人应。再敲门,隔壁单元走出一位女士$_i$,0$_i$ 是葛优媳妇的嫂子。说明来意后,嫂子$_i$告诉我们,葛优外出,估计快回来了。 (Feng Xiaogang, *Saving No Worry*)[6]

Qiāo mén, méi rén yīng. Zài qiāo mén,
<u>gébì   dānyuán zǒu   chū   yī   wèi   nǚshì</u>$_i$,
next.door   unit   walk   out   one   CL   woman

0$_i$ shì Gě Yōu xífù de sǎozi$_i$. Shuōmíng láiyì hòu, sǎozi$_i$ gàosù wǒmen, Gě Yōu wàichū, gūjì kuài huílái le.

'(We) knocked on the door, but no one answered. (We) knocked again, and <u>a woman came out of the neighboring unit</u>. (She) was Ge You's wife's sister-in-law. (We) explained the reason for the visit, and the sister-in-law told us that Ge You was out and that (he) would probably be back soon.'

Since the emergence-denoting clause has the actor in the object position, its topic-introducing function, when preceding a zero-subject clause, is similar to that of the *you*-clause, though the topic continuity of the actor would be much weaker. Specifically, the immediate subsequent clause can have a zero-subject, but the still later occurring clauses will require a pronoun or noun subject: in (29), third person pronoun "他" is used anaphorically to refer to President Reagan, and in (30), "嫂子" ('sister-in-law') refers anaphorically to "一位女士" ('a woman').

3.4.3.2 Evidential verb clause as preceding clause

The so-called evidential verbs are all sensory verbs in lexical semantics, such as 看 ('see') and 听 ('hear'). In terms of transitivity, their objects are not as much affected by the actions they denote as the patient objects of typical action verbs such as 打 ('hit'), 扔 ('throw'), etc.

(31) 我$_i$有一次在街上,0$_i$一抬头看见树杈上停着一只孔雀$_j$,0$_j$ 拖着大尾巴。(Gao Xiaosong, *Morning Call*)

Wǒ$_i$ yǒuyīcì zài jiēshàng, 0$_i$ yī táitóu <u>kànjiàn</u> shùchà shàng tíngzhe yī zhī kǒngquè$_j$, 0$_j$ tuōzhe dà wěibā.

'I was once on the street. (When I) looked up, (I) saw a peacock resting on a tree branch, dragging its big tail.'

When there is a grammatical element expressing the perfective aspect in the preceding clause, such as the clause final "了" in the following example, the referent of the zero-subject of the subsequent clause will change. Compare the two versions in (32).

(32) a. 我$_i$见过你们处长$_j$,0$_j$ 昨天还来过一趟呢。

Wǒ$_i$ jiànguò nǐmen chùzhǎng$_j$, 0$_j$ zuótiān hái láiguò yī tàng ne.

'I have met your director. (He) even came yesterday.'

b. 我ᵢ见过你们处长ⱼ了, 0ᵢ/*0ⱼ 昨天还来了一趟呢。

Wǒᵢ jiànguò nǐmen chùzhǎngⱼ le, 0ᵢ/*0ⱼ zuótiān hái láile yī tàng ne.

'I have met your director. (I/*He) even came yesterday.'

The difference between (32a) and (32b) is whether or not the first clause has the clause-final particle "了", which expresses the completion of the action. When the particle does not occur, the zero-subject of the subsequent clause is coreferential with the object of the previous clause; when it occurs, the zero-subject refers to the subject of the previous clause.

3.4.3.3 Psycho-epistemic verb clause as preceding clause

When the preceding clause is a psycho-epistemic verb clause, the interpretation of the reference of the zero-subject of the subsequent clause depends to a large extent on the transitivity of the predicate of the clause. See (33) and (34).

(33) a. 她ᵢ一眼就认出了老张ⱼ, 0ᵢ二话不说跪下了。

Tāᵢ yīyǎn jiù rènchūle Lǎo Zhāngⱼ, 0ᵢ èrhuà bù shuō guìxiàle.

'She recognized Old Zhang at once, and knelt down without saying a word.'

b. 她ᵢ一眼就认出了老张ⱼ, 0ⱼ圆脸、高鼻梁, 嘴角边总带着一丝微笑。

Tāᵢ yīyǎn jiù rènchūle Lǎo Zhāngⱼ, 0ⱼ yuán liǎn(,) gāo bíliáng, zuǐjiǎo biān zǒng dàizhe yī sī wéixiào.

'She immediately recognized Old Zhang, who had a round face, a high nose, always with a smile at the corners of his mouth.'

(34) 他ᵢ喜欢那些刚来工作的学生ⱼ, 0ⱼ随叫随到。

Tāᵢ xǐhuān nàxiē gāng lái gōngzuò de xuéshēngⱼ, 0ⱼ suíjiàosuídào.

'He likes those students who have just come to work; (they) are on call at any hour.'

In example (33a), the zero-subject clause "二话不说跪下了" ('knelt down without saying a word') uses a punctual action verb in the telic aspect, which makes the clause highly transitive and the zero-subject coreferential with the subject of the preceding clause. In (33b), the zero-subject is coreferential with the object of the preceding clause. The subsequent clause "嘴角边总带着一丝微笑" contains the verb (带, 'wear'), one that does not express an individuated event, but a habitual state, which renders a state description just the same as "round face" and "high nose". In example (34), the subsequent clause "随叫随到" does not express a specific event, either. Although it denotes an act, it is no more than a certain normative characteristic of the said entities. Therefore, its zero-subject also refers to the object of the preceding clause.

When there is reference competition in the context and the predicate of the subsequent clause is the same, the reference of the zero-subject will depend on the causativity of the preceding clause. The stronger the causativity of the preceding clause, the more likely the zero-subject of the subsequent clause refers to the object – the affected entity.

(35) 他ᵢ拉进来一头毛驴ⱼ, 0ⱼ 浑身湿淋淋的, 0ⱼ 哆嗦个不停。
Tāᵢ lā jìnlái yī tóu máolǔⱼ, 0ⱼ húnshēn shīlínlín de, 0ⱼ duōsuō gè bù tíng.
'He pulled in a donkey, all wet and shivering incessantly.'

In this example, the predicate "拉进来" ('pulled in a donkey') in the preceding clause already contains the result of the action, so the referent of the zero-subject in the subsequent clause is interpreted as coreferential with "a donkey" in the preceding clause.

If the predicate of the preceding clause is slightly changed to make it denote a durative state, the zero-subject of the subsequent clause would be understood as coreferential with the subject of the preceding clause; that is, all three clauses would be describing the state of "他".

(36) 他ᵢ手里牵着一头毛驴ⱼ, 0ᵢ 浑身湿淋淋的, 0ᵢ哆嗦个不停。 (cited from Chen Ping, 1987c, where "着" is the durative aspect marker)
Tāᵢ shǒulǐ <u>qiānzhe</u> yītóu máolǔⱼ, 0ᵢ húnshēn shīlínlín de, 0ᵢ duōsuō gè bù tíng.
'<u>Holding</u> a donkey in hand, he was all wet and shivering incessantly.'

In other words, when the transitivity of the zero-subject clause is significantly lower than that of the preceding clause, the object of the preceding clause (the affected entity) is understood to be the referent of the zero-subject; when the transitivity of the zero-subject clause is not significantly different from that of the preceding clause, the subject of the preceding clause will enjoy priority and the zero-subject is understood to be coreferential with it. Also see (37).

(37) 我ᵢ认识一个二十出头的长得很帅的小伙子ⱼ, 0ⱼ 开始还是个助理, 0ᵢ 几年没见他, 人家ⱼ已经是好莱坞排名前几名的那种大型经纪公司的亚太区总裁, 0ⱼ 才三十岁不到。(Gao Xiaosong, *Morning Call*)
Wǒᵢ rènshí yī gè èrshí chūtóu de chángde hěn shuài de xiǎohuǒziⱼ, 0ⱼ kāishǐ háishì gè zhùlǐ, 0ᵢ jǐ nián méi jiàn tā, rénjiāⱼ yǐjīng shì Hǎoláiwū páimíng qián jǐ míng de nàzhǒng dàxíng jīngjì gōngsī de yàtài qū zǒngcái, 0ⱼ cái sānshí suì bú dào.
'I came to know a very handsome young man when he was in his early twenties. (He) started as an assistant. (I) hadn't met him for a few years. (Now) he is already president of the Asia-Pacific region of a top ranking Hollywood brokerage company. (He) is not thirty yet.'

In the complex sentence above, there are three zero-subject clauses, among which two ("开始还是个助理" and "才三十岁不到") are not action–verb clauses, which makes them lower in transitivity than that of the preceding clause "我认识一个二十出头的长得很帅的小伙子". Thus the zero-subject of these two low-transitivity clauses is both coreferential with the object of the preceding clause. The other zero-subject clause, "几年没见他", expresses an act, whose transitivity is thus higher than that of the judgement clause headed by "是" (clause 2). Therefore, the zero-subject refers anaphorically to the subject "我" of the preceding clause, though intercepted by another zero-subject clause whose subject refers to a different entity (i.e., "开始还是个助理").

In summary, when the preceding clause is low in transitivity (e.g., the predicate verb being an epistemic, emergent, or existential verb), the zero-subject of the subsequent clause will refer to an entity different from the subject of the preceding clause. And the subsequent zero-subject clause is adverbial by nature, lying outside the main event-line by providing background information only.

3.4.4 Preceding clause as a high-transitivity clause

The causative, double-object, and verb-complement constructions are all of high transitivity in terms of the number of participants, aspect, and the degree of affectedness of the object.

When the preceding clause is a strong causative construction, the zero-subject of the subsequent clause may refer anaphorically to a syntactic constituent other than the subject of the preceding clause, in which case we would argue that the two consecutive clauses are in a coordinating relationship.

3.4.4.1 Antecedent being the object of causation

The object of causation, which is strong in ushering in later discourse, is the preferred referent of the zero-subject of the subsequent clause. Such an object can be either the object of causative verbs such as 使 ('make'), 让 ('let'), or the subject of the complement clause.

3.4.4.1.1 OBJECTS IN CLAUSES USING CAUSATIVE VERBS 使/让

Clauses using causative verbs 使/让 are high in transitivity. The zero-subject of the subsequent clause often refers anaphorically to the object of the preceding causative clause.

(38) 她$_i$这一哭使那个警察$_j$很反感, 0$_j$ 轻蔑地看着我, "就你这样儿还打算在我们王府井一带称霸呢?……" (Wang Shuo, *Fierce Animals* [《动物凶猛》])

Tā$_i$ zhè yī kū shǐ nàgè jǐngchá$_j$ hěn fǎngǎn, 0$_j$ qīngmiè de kànzhe wǒ, "Jiù nǐ zhèyàng·er hái dǎsuàn zài wǒmen Wángfǔjǐng yīdài chēngbà ne? …"

'Her cry made the police officer very disgusted. (He) looked at me contemptuously, "Someone like you still intends to dominate in our Wangfujing area?...."'

In the example above, the zero-subject is anaphoric to the object "the police officer" in the preceding clause.

If the preceding clause uses a causative verb as the predicator, the zero-subject of the subsequent clause refers back to the object of causation, as illustrated in (39a); but it will be otherwise when a causative object occurs in the zero-subject clause, as in (39b).

(39) a. 他$_i$叫我$_j$做一个语料库, 0$_j$写一个用法说明。

Tā$_i$ jiào wǒ$_j$ zuò yī gè yǔliàokù, 0$_j$ xiě yī gè yòngfǎ shuōmíng.

'He asked me to build a corpus and write a usage note.'

b. 他$_i$叫我$_j$做一个语料库, 0$_i$给我算工作成绩。

Tā$_i$ jiào wǒ$_j$ zuò yīgè yǔliàokù, 0$_i$ gěi wǒ suàn gōngzuò chéngjī.

'He asked me to build a corpus and (he) would count it as my task achievement.'

The object of the causative verb is in the meanwhile the semantic agent of the verb that follows it, such as "那个警察" ('the police officer') in example (38) and "我" ('I') in example (39).

In the case of successive zero-subject clauses, the reference interpretation of the zero-subjects relies on the one hand on the conjunction to determine topic continuity, and on the other on the syntactic relationship between the clauses as reflected in the strength of transitivity.

(40) "二战"的时候, 150万美军在诺曼底登陆, 横扫欧洲。德国$_i$最后想不出办法来了, 于是0$_i$就弄了一大批英文说得好并且接受过美国历史和地理培训的自己人$_j$, 0$_j$穿着美军军装——反正德国人跟美国人长得也差不多, 0$_j$就这么混入了美军队伍里。(Gao Xiaosong, *Morning Call*)

"Èrzhàn" de shíhòu, 150 wàn měijūn zài Nuòmàndǐ dēnglù, héngsǎo Ōuzhōu. Déguó$_i$ zuìhòu xiǎngbùchū bànfǎ lái le, yúshì 0$_i$ jiù nòngle yī dà pī Yīngwén shuōdehǎo bìngqiě jiēshòu guò Měiguó lìshǐ hé dìlǐ péixùn de zìjǐ rén$_j$, 0$_j$ chuānzhe měijūn jūnzhuāng – fǎnzhèng Déguórén gēn Měiguórén zhǎngde yě chàbùduō, 0$_j$ jiù zhème hùnrùle měijūn duìwǔ lǐ.

'In World War II, 1.5 million American troops landed in Normandy and swept through Europe. Germany couldn't think of a way out, so in the end (it) got a large number of its own people who spoke good English and had received training in American history and geography to wear the U.S. army uniforms – the Germans looked similar to the Americans anyway – and in this manner (they) blended into the American army.'

In the example above, the conjunction "于是" ('then') conjoins two clauses, "德国最后想不出办法来" ('Germany couldn't think of a way out') and "弄了一大批英文说得好并且接受过美国历史和地理培训的自己人" (the underlined), by indicating the chronological sequence of the two clausal events as well as their coordinating syntactic relation. The subsequent clause "穿着美军军装" ('wearing the U.S. army uniforms') is of low transitivity, in that "着" is an atelic marker and "美军军装" does not denote an individuated object. Overall, the clause is descriptive by nature, providing background information. As mentioned above, the zero-subject of such clauses refers anaphorically to the object of the preceding clause.

3.4.4.1.2 CAUSATIVE OBJECTS IN COMPLEMENT CLAUSES

That the causative object is strong in ushering in ensuing discourse is also manifested in the fact that the subject of the complement construction, if it is a causative object at the same time, is also good at introducing later discourse. Compare (41) and (42), where the underlined are complement clauses.

(41) 她ᵢ这么一说倒说得<u>我ⱼ怪舒服的</u>, 0ⱼ 不禁大笑起来, "当着他们的面, 我哪好意思跟你多说话呀。" (Wang Shuo, *Fierce Animals*)

Tāᵢ zhème yī shuō dào shuō de <u>wǒⱼ guài shūfú de</u>, 0ⱼ bùjīn dà xiào qǐlái, "Dāngzhe tāmen de miàn, wǒ nǎ hǎoyìsi gēn nǐ duō shuōhuà ya."

'Hearing her say so, <u>I felt so comfortable</u> that I couldn't help but laugh, "In front of them, I don't have the heart to talk to you more."'

(42) 她ᵢ由一进门, 嘴便开了河, 直说得<u>李太太ⱼ的脑子里像转疯了的留声机片</u>, 0ⱼ只剩了张着嘴大口的咽气。 (Lao She, *Divorce* [《离婚》])

Tāᵢ yóu yī jìnmén, zuǐ biàn kāile hé, zhí shuō de <u>Lǐ tàitàiⱼ de nǎozi lǐ xiàng zhuǎn fēng le de liúshēngjī piàn</u>, 0ⱼ zhǐ shèngle zhāngzhe zuǐ dàkǒu de yànqì.

'The moment she entered, she began talking with such volubility that <u>Mrs. Li's brain was driven to work like a crazily spinning gramophone disk</u> – Mrs. Li could do nothing but gulp for breath with an open mouth.'

In example (41), the causative object "我" ('I') is the subject of the complement clause; and in example (42), the causative object "李太太" ('Mrs. Li') is the subject modifier in the complement clause. Irrespective of their different syntactic status, they are both directly affected by the action denoted by the predicate of the main clause.

3.4.4.2 Ditransitive construction

The ditransitive construction consists of two types, the double-object construction and the construction with the beneficiary object, both highly transitive.

We first examine the case where the preceding clause is a double-object construction. The double-object construction is highly transitive: the predicate verb is both volitional and telic; the verb carries three nominal arguments, of which the direct object denotes a thing and the indirect object, nominal or pronominal, refers to a person. When the preceding clause of a zero-subject clause is a double-object construction, the referent of the zero-subject is the affected entity of the preceding clause. Compare the pair of sentences in (43).

(43) a. 我$_i$买了老王$_j$一辆车，0$_i$没过几天后悔了。
　　　　Wǒ$_i$ mǎile Lǎo Wáng$_j$ yīliàng chē, 0$_i$ méi guò jǐ tiān hòuhuǐle.
　　　　'I bought a car from Old Wang, and regretted it a few days later.'
　　 b. 我$_i$卖了老王$_j$一辆车，0$_i$没过几天后悔了。
　　　　Wǒ$_i$ màile Lǎo Wáng$_j$ yīliàng chē, 0$_i$ méi guò jǐ tiān hòuhuǐle.
　　　　'I sold Old Wang a car, and regretted it a few days later.'

In (43), the subject of the latter occurring zero-subject clause is coreferential with the subject "我" ('I') in the preceding clause. Whether it is "buy" or "sell", "I" is the volitional actor. The two clauses in (43a) and (43b) tend to be taken as expressing two successive actions in time, though the predicate verb in the subsequent clause is psychological in semantics, thus not as transitive as the preceding ditransitive construction.

When the volitionality of the verb is weakened, the zero-subject of the subsequent clause will be obviously biased toward the beneficiary of the preceding clause. For example, the Chinese word "借" can be either "borrow" or "lend". When contextualized, its interpretation will affect how to establish the referent of the zero-subject of the subsequent clause. In the following example, the referent of the zero-subject can only be understood as the party who "gets" the new car.

(44) a. 我$_i$借$_{[借进]}$了老王$_j$一辆新车，0$_i$没过几天出车祸了。
　　　　Wǒ$_i$ jiè $_{[jiè jìn]}$le Lǎo Wáng$_j$ yī liàng xīn chē, 0$_i$ méi guò jǐ tiān chū chēhuò le.
　　　　'I borrowed a new car from Old Wang, and had an accident within a few days.'
　　 b. 我$_i$借$_{[借出]}$了老王$_j$一辆新车，0$_j$没过几天出车祸了。
　　　　Wǒ$_i$ jiè $_{[jiè chū]}$le Lǎo Wáng$_j$ yī liàng xīn chē, 0$_j$ méi guò jǐ tiān chū chēhuò le.
　　　　'I lent Old Wang a new car, and (he) had an accident within a few days.'
　　 c. 我$_i$借了老王$_j$一辆新车$_k$，0$_k$没过几天丢了。
　　　　Wǒ$_i$ jièle Lǎo Wáng$_j$ yī liàng xīn chē$_k$, 0$_k$ méi guò jǐ tiān chū chēhuò le.
　　　　'I borrowed a new car from Old Wang/lent Old Wang a new car; (it) was lost within a few days.'

If the predicate of the subsequent zero-subject clause in (44a) and (44b) is slightly changed but without changing the "borrowing" or "lending" relation, the reference of the zero-subject will remain unchanged.

(44') a. 我$_i$借来老王$_j$一辆新车,0$_i$没过几天病了。
Wǒ$_i$ jièlái Lǎo Wáng$_j$ yī liàng xīn chē, 0$_i$ méi guò jǐ tiān bìngle.
'I borrowed a new car from Old Wang and got sick within a few days.'
b. 我$_i$借给老王$_j$一辆新车,0$_j$没过几天病了。
Wǒ$_i$ jiègěi Lǎo Wáng$_j$ yī liàng xīn chē, 0$_j$ méi guò jǐ tiān bìngle.
'I lent Old Wang a new car, and (he) got sick within a few days.'

In fact, whether the zero-subject refers anaphorically to the subject or the object of the preceding clause, it is semantically the beneficiary – the affected object – of the action of "借". This strategy of giving priority to the beneficiary has the same rationale as the phenomenon of the prepositional object becoming the antecedent of the zero-subject.

(45) 老李$_i$送给我$_j$的电脑没几天就坏了,0$_j$只好到处托人修。(Survey corpus)
Lǎo Lǐ$_i$ sòng gěi wǒ$_j$ de diànnǎo méi jǐ tiān jiù huàile, 0$_j$ zhǐhǎo dàochù tuō rén xiū.
'The computer that Old Li gave me broke down within a few days, and (I) had to ask someone to fix it.'

In (45) above, the agent (subject) of the clause "只好到处托人修" ('had to ask someone to fix it') is the prepositional object of the preceding clause – the beneficiary "我" ('me'). This interpretation strategy is the same as in the case where the preceding clause is a passive construction.

When the subject of the subsequent clause is coreferential with the subject of the preceding clause, the reflexive pronoun 自己 will be used as the subject instead of the zero-subject.

(46) 她$_i$拿出一本影集扔给我$_j$,自己$_i$/*0$_j$在桌前坐下,端详着镜子里的自己。(Survey corpus)
Tā$_i$ ná chū yī běn yǐngjí rēng gěi wǒ$_j$, zìjǐ$_i$/*0$_j$ zài zhuō qián zuòxià, duānxiángzhe jìngzi lǐ de zìjǐ.
'She took out a photo book and threw it to me. She then sat down at the table and examined herself in the mirror.'

In the example above, the subject of the second clause "自己" can be neither replaced with the third-person pronoun 她 nor omitted. This use of reflexive pronouns reflects their unique contribution to topic continuity.

3.5 Summary

The zero-subject clause is an important device to maintain topic continuity, and in Chinese it is also a means to reflect the syntactic status and informational properties of its hosting clauses.

As a device of topic continuation, there are three ways for the zero-subject clause to be presented in discourse. First, the zero-subject corefers with the subject of the preceding clause. Second, the zero-subject refers anaphorically to the possessive modifier of the subject of the preceding clause, on condition that the referent of the possessive modifier is the discourse topic. Third, conjunctive words, such as 又 (yòu, 'also'), 还 (hái, 'still'), etc., can be used to indicate the logical relation between clauses.

The zero-subject clause is also a backgrounding device. It may occur first, with its zero-subject coreferential with the subject or the possessive modifier of the subject of the subsequent clause, which results in zero-subject cataphora.

A small number of zero-subject clauses have antecedents that are not discourse topics, as in the following cases. First, when the preceding clause is of high transitivity (e.g., the causative construction, the ditransitive construction, the verb-complement construction, etc.) and the zero-subject is not coreferential with the subject of the preceding clause, the two clauses are syntactically in coordination, both of which presenting foreground information.

Second, when the preceding clause is of low transitivity (i.e., the predicate verb denoting epistemic, emergent, or existential meaning) and the zero-subject refers to an entity other than the subject of the preceding clause, the subsequent clause is a modifying clause that expresses background information.

Notes

1 For the relationship between topics and zero-subjects in Chinese discourse, see Chao (1968), Li and Thompson (1981), Chen Ping (1987), Shen Jiaxuan (1989), Zhang Bojiang and Fang Mei (1996/2014), Xu Liejiong and Liu Danqing (1998/2007), Shi Dingxu (1999), Shi (2000), Chu (1998), Xu Yulong (2003, 2004, 2005c), and Chu (2006).
2 Continuity involves three aspects (Givón, 1983): (1) thematic continuity, (2) behavioral continuity, and (3) participant continuity. Of the three, thematic continuity has the greatest range of influence. Continuity can be measured in terms of look back, ambiguity, and decay.
3 Syntactic representations of accessible vs. inaccessible topics (Givón, 1983).

Most Accessible Topics
Zero anaphora
Unstressed/bound pronouns or grammatical agreement
Stressed or non-adhesive pronouns (stressed/independent pronouns)
Rightwardly dislocated qualitative noun phrases (R-dislocated DEF-NP's)
Qualitative noun phrases in regular order (neutral-ordered DEF-NP's)
Qualitative nouns (noun phrases) with leftward excursion (L-dislocated DEF-NP's)
Contrastive topicalization of displaced nouns (Y-moved NP's)
Split/focus constructions (cleft/focus constructions)
Referential indefinite NP's (referential noun phrases)
Most Inaccessible Topics

4 For studies on Chinese pronominal anaphora, see Xu Jiujiu (1990, 2010) and Wang Canlong (2000).
5 For the internal variation of the existential construction, see Li Linding (1986, pp. 73–91; pp. 92–103) and Huang Nansong (1996a).
6 For a fuller context, see example (20). Translator's note.

4 Discourse functions of "indefinite-subject sentences"

In Chinese studies, the so-called "indefinite-subject sentence" refers to a sentence in which the subject is of the "*yi*+CL+NP" configuration. There are two types of "indefinite subjects" in Chinese: one is of individual reference and the other of generic reference. The former is found in event clauses which convey background information of the event and are descriptive in nature, while the predicate of the latter type is featured by a habitual-aspect predicate which does not express a specific event, and is thus evaluative in essence. The occurrence of the "indefinite-subject sentence" in the habitual aspect marks the shift from narration to evaluation. Although the "indefinite-subject sentence" can be transformed into the *you*-sentence, no such transformation can be licensed when contextualized, which reveals that this syntactic pattern has its own independent discourse value.

4.1 Introduction

Subject in Chinese has topic attributes, and in general occurs in the form of definite NPs (Chao, 1968; Lü Shuxiang, 1979; Zhu Dexi, 1982). But there are some sentences where the subject is encoded in the configuration "*yi* (一, 'one')+CL+NP", which gives them the name of "indefinite-subject sentences." Since the 1980s, "indefinite-subject sentences" have attracted much academic attention (see Li Linding, 1986; Uchida, 1989; Wang Hongqi, 2001; Liu Anchun and Zhang Bojiang, 2004; Wang Canlong, 2003; Zhang Xinhua, 2007; Xiong Zhongru, 2008; Li Jinrong, 2016; Zhou Shihong and Li Shen, 2017; among others).

With regard to the special encoding of "indefinite-subject sentences", Fan Jiyan (1985) points out that most of such sentences can be preceded by *you* (有, literally 'have') at the very beginning, an observation which suggests that "indefinite-subject sentences" have similar expressive functions with *you*-sentences.

Researchers of discourse functional linguistics have noted for long that *you*-sentences function to introduce discourse topics, in that the post-*you* nominal element is more often than not a concept that is newly introduced into discourse (see Li and Thompson, 1981; Chen Ping, 1987c; Chu, 1998; Xu Yulong, 2005c; etc.).

Conversely, other studies have found that the addition of *you* is subject to some constraints. By examining the "indefinite-subject sentences" in *Miao Folk Stories* and the examples cited in Fan Jiyan (1985), Wang Hongqi (2001, 2014) finds that whether *you* can occur to precede an "indefinite-subject sentence" is mainly restricted by the pragmatic conditions as detailed below.

1) When the meaning of "existence" is already indicated by the context, *you* cannot be added to precede the indefinite subject.

(1) "救命啦!救命啦!"
一阵阵凄厉的喊声,[1]在寂静的山谷里发出雷鸣般的震响,送来一阵阵回音。(cited from Wang Hongqi, 2001)

"Jiùmìng la! Jiùmìng la!"

Yī	zhèn~zhèn	qīlì	de	hǎnshēng,
one	CL.redup.	mournful	NM	shout

zài jìjìng de shāngǔ lǐ fāchū léimíng bān de zhènxiǎng, sònglái yī zhèn~zhèn huíyīn.

'"Help! Help!"
Waves of mournful shouts resonated thunderously in the silent valley, sending waves of echo.'

According to Wang, the underlined indefinite subject cannot be preceded by *you*, in that the earlier occurring shouts themselves already indicate the existence of sound.

2) Avoidance of repetition inhibits the addition of *you*.

(2) ……那官府的老爷就把胡氏提来审问:"你这小女子,为何要毒死你家老爷呀!""回父母官,老爷是吃粑粑死的呀!""乱说!打!"一伙差役举起板子围着胡氏就是一顿狠打。(cited from Wang Hongqi, 2001)

Nà guānfǔ de lǎoyé jiù bǎ Hú shì tílái shěnwèn: "Nǐ zhè xiǎo nǚzǐ, wèihé yào dúsǐ nǐjiā lǎoyé ya!" "Huí fùmǔguān, lǎoyé shì chī bābā sǐ de ya!" "Luànshuō! Dǎ!" Yī huǒ chāiyì jǔqǐ bǎnzi wéizhe Hú shì jiùshì yī dùn hěn dǎ.

'The magistrate of the government brought Mrs. Hu to interrogate, "You little woman, why did you poison your master?" "Mr. Magistrate, my master died from eating a rice cake!" "Nonsense! Spank her!" A group of runners raised their boards around Mrs. Hu and gave her a fierce beating.'

To Wang, the underlined NP cannot be preceded by *you*, because there must be runners in a feudal government; that is, the two notions are conceptually associated. There are also examples in Wang (2001) where a later occurring NP indicates part of the referent of an earlier occurring NP. In (3), for example, the sentence initial "他们" ('they') is for collective reference while the subsequent "一路" ('one group') and "另一路" ('the other group') are for partial reference.

(3) 他们用重金买通了起义军中的一些软骨头，就派出比起义军多好几倍的人，分兵两路攻打猫山。<u>一路</u>正面硬攻，这一路一次又一次被打败了。可<u>另一路</u>却在起义军全力对付正面硬攻的时候，迂回到后寨…… (cited from Wang Hongqi, 2001)

Tāmen yòng zhòngjīn mǎitōng le qǐyìjūn zhōng de yīxiē ruǎngǔtou, jiù pàichū bǐ qǐyìjūn duō hǎojǐ bèi de rén, fēnbīng liǎng lù gōngdǎ Māoshān. <u>Yīlù</u> zhèngmiàn yìng gōng, zhè yīlù yīcì yòu yīcì bèi dǎbài le. Kě <u>lìngyīlù</u> què zài qǐyìjūn quánlì duìfù zhèngmiàn yìnggōng de shíhòu, yūhuí dào hòuzhài

'**They** used a lot of money to buy out some of the weak-kneed in the rebel army, and then sent out several times more people than the rebel army to attack the Cat Mountain in two groups. <u>One group</u> launched frontal attacks but was defeated time and again. But <u>the other group</u> had made a detour to the back of the camp of the rebel army when they were doing their utmost to resist the frontal attacks…'

As a matter of fact, not all "*yi*+CL+NP" subjects are indefinite in modern Chinese. Their being dubbed as "indefinite subjects" is mainly prompted by the structural formulation of the noun phrase. Take the above sentences from Wang (2001), for example. Only (1) is a typical "indefinite-subject sentence"; that is, there is an alignment between the referential function and the syntactic form. In other cases, there is either a conceptual association between the referent of the "*yi*+CL+NP" phrase and a nominal concept already existing in discourse, which renders the referent identifiable in the situational context, as in (2), or a part-whole relationship between the "*yi*+CL+NP" and an already established nominal concept in discourse, as in (3), where "一路" ('one group') and "另一路" ('the other group') are both members of "他们" ('they') in earlier discourse, a case referred to in Wang Canlong (2003) as "anaphoric contrast". In a word, there is no strict correlation between "*yi*+CL+NP" and indefinite reference in Chinese discourse. Although it has been noted that "*yi*+CL+NP" in Chinese is no counterpart to indefinite NPs in morphological languages in terms of grammatical function (e.g. Lü Shuxiang, 1979; Chen Ping, 1987a; Yang Suying, 2000; etc.), this phenomenon has not received due attention in earlier discussions on the discourse functions of "indefinite-subject sentences".

Some other studies have raised the view that the Chinese "indefinite-subject sentence" features a salient sense of on-siteness and liveliness of narration and that the emphasis of the "indefinite-subject sentence" is not to express what an entity really does, but to describe a situation, prompt a scene-setting, or narrate the emergence of a fact (Uchida, 1989/1993). Lü Jining (2004) also accounts for this sentence pattern in terms of orientation taking, making the point that the use or non-use of *you* before the indefinite NP depends on how the event is observed: when *you* is used at the beginning of the sentence, an off-site interpretation is preferred.

(4) 她"噢"了一声，看了眼窗外的街景。<u>一辆越野吉普车</u>在马路上猛地刹住，稍顷，<u>一个长发男子</u>从车顶杠下飞出，一骨碌面对面坐在车前马路上，两手抱着右膝神态痛苦地向一侧倒下。(Wang Shuo, *Death after Addiction* [《过把瘾就死》])

Tā "ō" le yī shēng, kànle yǎn chuāngwài de jiējǐng. <u>Yī liàng yuèyějípǔchē</u> zài mǎlùshàng měng de shāzhù, shāoqǐng, <u>yī gè chángfà nánzǐ</u> cóng chēdǐnggàng xià fēi chū, yīgūlu miànduìmiàn zuò zài chē qián mǎlù shàng, liǎng shǒu bàozhe yòu xī shéntài tòngkǔ de xiàng yī cè dǎoxià.

'**She** gave an "Oh" and looked at the street view outside the window. <u>An SUV</u> suddenly stopped on the road. A second later, <u>a long-haired man</u> flew out from below the bumper, and with a spring sat on the road, face to face with the vehicle, before he fell painfully to one side, holding his right knee in both hands.'

In (4), the subject of the first sentence is "她" ('she'), which suggests that the description is not from the orientation of a narrator inside the event. When the observer is outside the event process, *you* can be used; when the observer is part of the event, *you* need not be used. Both (5) and (6) below narrate in the first person, which renders unnecessary the use of *you*.

(5) 银光闪闪的杨树叶在我头顶倾斜小雨般地沙沙响,透出蒙蒙灯光的窗内人语呢喃,脚下长满青苔的土地踩上去滑溜溜的,**我**的脚步悄无声息,前面大殿的屋脊上,<u>一只黑猫</u>蹑手蹑脚地走过。(Wang Shuo, *Ferocious Animal* [《动物凶猛》])

Yínguāngshǎnshǎn de yángshùyè zài wǒ tóudǐng qīngxié xiǎoyǔ bān de shā~shā xiǎng, tòuchū méng~méng dēngguāng de chuāngnèi rén yǔ nínán, jiǎoxià zhǎng mǎn qīngtái de tǔdì cǎi shàngqù huáliuliū de, **wǒ** de jiǎobù qiāowúshēngxī, qiánmiàn dàdiàn de wūjí shàng, <u>yī zhī hēimāo</u> nièshǒunièjiǎo de zǒuguò.

'The silver-shimmering poplar leaves rustled over my head. There were whispers inside the dimly lit windows. The mossy land was very slippery under my feet. **My** footsteps were all silent. <u>A black cat</u> crept past the ridge of the main hall ahead.'

(6) 我心情绝望,又站了一会儿,不知该沿哪条路追下去。<u>一个牧羊人</u>赶着一群口外羊从东边过来,羊群挤挤挨挨胖胖叫着从我身边走过。(Wang Shuo, *Death after Addiction*)

Wǒ xīnqíng juéwàng, yòu zhànle yīhuǐ·er, bùzhī gāi yán nǎ tiáo lù zhuī xiàqù. <u>Yī gè mùyángrén</u> gǎnzhe yīqún kǒuwài yáng cóng dōngbian guòlái, yángqún jǐjǐāiāi zāng~zāng jiàozhe cóng wǒ shēnbiān zǒuguò.

'In despair, **I** stood another while, wondering which way to go, when <u>a shepherd</u> drove a flock of sheep coming from the east. The sheep bleated past me, bumping against one another.'

Wang Canlong (2003) finds that "indefinite-subject sentences" are poor in syntactic self-sufficiency. To Wang, they are highly context-dependent and rarely occur independently. And according to the position of occurrence, "indefinite-subject sentences" are divided into two groups, those as discourse openers and those as discourse continuations. It is also found that some "indefinite-subject sentences" with only marginal acceptability can be accepted in specific contexts.

Liu Anchun and Zhang Bojiang (2004) note that "indefinite-subject sentences" focus on introducing the occurrence of new events. There are often time-indicating expressions in front of them; otherwise, such expressions can be added. So the NP, though indicating new information, need not be precisely positioned. "*Yi*+CL+NP" can often be interpreted as "any one of the NP", which explains why some scholars tend to think that the indefinite NP at the beginning of an "indefinite-subject sentence" is inclined to indicate generic reference.

To sum up, the existing studies seem to have come up with the following findings:

1) Some "indefinite-subject sentences" can be preceded by *you* (Fan Jiyan, 1985).
2) The indefinite NP, when preceded by *you*, can form the existential construction, performing the function of setting a new course for the forthcoming discourse. The "indefinite-subject sentence", in contrast, fulfills a different discourse function: it introduces a new character into discourse, marking a transition in plot.
3) The indefinite subject can be preceded by you, unless there is already a hint of "existence" in context.
4) Whether *you* can occur to precede the indefinite subject is predetermined by pragmatic factors, such as the narrative orientation (inside vs. outside the event).

We note, however, that the "sense of on-siteness and liveliness" interpretation has great limitations: it does not explain why some allow the addition of *you* at the beginning of the sentence while others do not, given the same narrative orientation. As in example (4), where two "indefinite-subject sentences" occur consecutively, the former rejects the addition of *you* whereas its occurrence can be licensed in the latter. When (5) and (6) are examined, *you* is used in neither of them, but a shift of the narrative orientation (say substituting the third person "he" for the first person "I") seems to make no difference in licensing the addition of *you*. Moreover, frequency counts have shown that "indefinite-subject sentences" are used more frequently in political and narrative discourses (Wang Hongqi, 2014), a finding which can barely claim any inherent correlation with the "sense of on-siteness and liveliness" interpretation. Therefore, it is necessary to further sort out the language facts and disclose the usage characteristics and related constraints on this syntactic configuration.

For the purpose of this research, we refer to three sources of data on colloquial Beijing dialect: 1) *This Is Beijing* (《这里是北京》), a live narrative program broadcast by Beijing TV, A Long being the on-site narrator, about 980,000 characters in size; 2) *Morning Call* (《晓说》), a talk show program, Gao Xiaosong as the off-site narrator, about 200,000 characters; 3) Feng Tang's novels and essays, about 830,000 characters; and Feng Xiaogang's essay collection *Saving No Worry* (《不省心》), about 60,000 characters.

4.2 Referentiality of subject

The referentiality of the subject of the "indefinite-subject sentence" falls into two categories: individual reference and generic reference.

Earlier discussions of the "indefinite-subject sentence" mainly focus on the configuration of the subject, i.e., "*yi*+CL+NP." In terms of referentiality, this syntactic configuration is not confined to referring to indefinite referents (for the referential characteristics of Chinese reference nouns, see Chen Ping, 1987a).

First of all, the interpretation of "*yi*+CL+NP", quantitative or indefinite, depends on whether the predicate has a quantity indicating component part.

(7) a. 其实说来,明朝已经够黑暗了。当时,有一种刑法叫"连坐"。就是,<u>一个人</u>犯了罪,街坊邻居都得受牵连。(*This Is Beijing*)

Qíshí shuōlái, Míngcháo yǐjīng gòu hēi'àn le. Dāngshí, yǒu yī zhǒng xíngfǎ jiào "liánzuò". Jiùshì, <u>yī gè rén</u> fànle zuì, jiēfāng línjū dōu děi shòu qiānlián.

'In fact, the Ming Dynasty was dark enough. At that time, there was a criminal law named "implication". That is, if a person committed a crime, all the neighbors would be implicated.'

b. 我还是偏执地认为,<u>一个男人</u>四十岁再写诗和三十岁再尿床一样,是个很二的行为。(Feng Tang, *36 Puzzles in Life* [《三十六大》])

Wǒ háishì piānzhí de rènwéi, <u>yī gè nánrén</u> sìshí suì zài xiě shī hé sānshí suì zài niàochuáng yīyàng, shì gè hěn èr de xíngwéi.

'I'm still paranoid that a man writing poetry at forty is like a man wetting his bed at thirty, which is very stupid behavior.'

In (6a), if the subject "一个人" ('one person') in the clause "一个人犯了罪" ('a person committed a crime') is stressed, adverb "都" ('all') will subject "街坊四邻" ('neighbors') in the subsequent clause to universal quantification reading. "一个人" is then a quantitative expression, contrasting with the following clause that hosts "都". In (6b), "都" can be added to the last part to come up with "都是很二的行为" ('both are stupid behavior'), but the meaning will be different from the original. Sentences of "*yi*+CL+NP" subjects which express quantity (such as [6a]) are not within the scope of our discussion.

Secondly, the "*yi*+CL+NP" subject may refer to a newly introduced discourse entity which can be identified by way of association with information provided in the context. Such a subject may be related to an existing entity in different manners, such as part-whole, superordinate concept-subordinate concept, "frame-pane" (Liao Qiuzhong, 1986c), or associative anaphora (Xu Jiujiu, 2005b). This kind of "y*i*+CL+NP" subject can be characterized as follows: although the information it conveys is accessible information, the nominal concept contributes to topic progression, which makes it possible to be referred back to in subsequent discourse, as in (2) above. In terms of referentiality, it shares nothing in common with indefinite NPs irrespective of the same coding form.

4.2.1 "Yi+CL+NP" subject of indefinite reference

The "y*i*+CL+NP" subject can refer to a newly introduced entity when the referent is indefinite, such as "一只黑猫" ('a black cat') in (5) and "一个牧羊人" ('a shepherd') in (6) above. But it would be easier to see the actual function of sentences containing such subjects in discourse.

(8) 当年,洪承畴那边,在东北打了败仗,这边崇祯皇帝,以为爱将已经殉国。于是在前门外的这座关帝庙里,给洪承畴,建了座塑像,供老百姓瞻仰纪念。只可惜,多情总被无情伤。<u>一个太监把洪承畴降清的消息带回了京城</u>。这回崇祯可是伤透了心。一赌气,砸了塑像,大卸八块儿。还命人把碎块,扔到了厕所的茅坑里。眨眼的工夫,洪承畴在荣辱之间,飞快转换。(*This Is Beijing*)

Dāngnián, Hóng Chéngchóu nàbiān, zài dōngběi dǎle bàizhàng, zhèbiān Chóngzhēn huángdì, yǐwéi àijiàng yǐjīng xùnguó. Yúshì zài Qiánmén wài de zhè zuò Guāndìmiào lǐ, gěi Hóng Chéngchóu, jiànle zuò sùxiàng, gōng lǎobǎixìng zhānyǎng jìniàn. Zhǐ kěxí, duōqíng zǒng bèi wúqíng shāng. <u>Yī gè tàijiàn</u> bǎ Hóng Chéngchóu xiáng qīng de xiāoxī dàihuíle jīngchéng. Zhèhuí Chóngzhēn kěshì shāng tòu le xīn. Yī dǔqì, zále sùxiàng, dàxièbākuài·er. Hái mìng rén bǎ suìkuài, rēng dào le cèsuǒ de máokēng lǐ. Zhǎyǎn de gōngfū, Hóng Chéngchóu zài róngrǔ zhījiān, fēikuài zhuǎnhuàn.

'At that time, Hong Chengchou was defeated in the northeast, but here (in the capital city) Emperor Chongzhen thought that his favorite general had died for his motherland. So in the Temple of Guan Yu outside Qianmen, a statue was built for Hong Chengchou so that the ordinary people could pay tribute to him. Unfortunately, love is always mercilessly hurt. <u>A eunuch</u> brought the news of Hong Chengchou's downfall to the Qing Dynasty back to the capital city. Emperor Chongzhen was so hurt that he ordered in fury to smash the statue into eight pieces, which were then thrown into the toilet pit. In the blink of an eye, Hong Chengchou shifted from honor to disgrace.'

In this example, "一个太监" ('a eunuch'), the subject of its hosting clause, conveys new information, and its referent is indefinite in discourse. Furthermore, this nominal concept is not re-mentioned in subsequent discourse, which makes it trivial information. According to Wang Canlong (2003), it is the norm for "indefinite-subject sentences" to represent trivial information.[2]

4.2.2 *"Yi+CL+NP" subject of generic reference*

As far as referentiality is concerned, some "*yi*+CL+NP" subjects are generic. A characteristic of this kind of subject is that it can be encoded in the form of a bare noun without the classifier modifier, as in (9).

(9) <u>一个人</u>关键是要有理想，循序渐进并且持之以恒。比如练轻功，从一尺深的坑里往上跳，每天加一寸，一点也不难，三个月之后，就能飞檐走壁了。(Feng Tang, *Give Me a Girl at Eighteen* [《十八岁给我一个姑娘》])

<u>Yī gè rén</u> guānjiàn shì yào yǒu lǐxiǎng, xúnxùjiànjìn bìngqiě chízhīyǐhéng. Bǐrú liàn qīnggōng, cóng yī chǐ shēn de kēng lǐ wǎng shàng tiào, měitiān jiā yī cùn, yīdiǎn yě bù nán, sān gè yuè zhīhòu, jiù néng fēiyánzǒubì le.

'The key to <u>a person</u> is to have ideals, make progress gradually and persevere. Take practicing flying skills in Chinese martial arts for example. You jump up from a one-foot-deep pit, and it is not difficult at all if you add one inch a day. But in three months, you will be able to leap from the ground to the roof and walk upon walls.'

Here, the subject "一个人" ('one CL person') can be replaced by the bare noun "人" ('person').

The referent of the "*yi*+CL+NP" subject cannot be interpreted as an individuated entity, because it is generic in reference. Not only can such subjects be rewritten as bare nouns, they can also be preceded by "作为" ('as'). See (10) for illustration.

(10) 像往常一样，他打了两壶开水，为自己泡了一杯茶，九点钟玻璃板上会有今天的报纸，可以就着茶学习。那些都是很重要的东西，<u>一个教师</u>需要仔细研究以明确塑造学生灵魂的方向。(Feng Tang, *Give Me a Girl at Eighteen*)

Xiàng wǎngcháng yīyàng, tā dǎle liǎng hú kāishuǐ, wèi zìjǐ pàole yī bēi chá, jiǔdiǎnzhōng bōlíbǎn shàng huì yǒu jīntiān de bàozhǐ, kěyǐ jiùzhe chá xuéxí. Nàxiē dōushì hěn zhòngyào de dōngxī, <u>yī gè jiàoshī</u> xūyào zǐxì yánjiū yǐ míngquè sùzào xuéshēng línghún de fāngxiàng.

'As usual, he draws two pots of boiling water and makes a cup of tea for himself. At nine o'clock, there will come on to the glass board the day's newspapers that he can study with tea. The newspapers are very important, and <u>a teacher</u> needs to study them carefully so as to make clear the direction in which to shape the students' soul.'

In (10), "一个" in the underlined "*yi*+CL+NP" subject does not refer to any specific person. In this case, "*you*" cannot be added to the beginning of the sentence, because the topic of this discourse stretch is a specific person – "他" ('he'). But the sentence can be rephrased as "作为一个教师需要仔细研究以明确塑造学生灵魂的方向" ('<u>As a teacher</u>, (he) needs to study them carefully so as to make clear the direction in which to shape the students' soul.').

Liu Anchun and Zhang Bojiang (2004) are of the view that the "indefinite-subject sentence" is mainly used to introduce the occurrence of a new event. So the NP in it does not need to be accurately positioned, which makes it compatible with the new information status. "一个NP" ('one CL NP') can often be understood as "any NP", which explains why some scholars tend to think that the sentence initial indefinite NP is for generic reference. However, this analysis has failed to take into consideration the different predicates corresponding to the two types of "*yi*+CL+NP"-subject sentences as delineated here, as well as their respective function in discourse: providing background information or making evaluation, which are elaborated separately in Sections 4.3 and 4.4.

4.3 Background information status

As mentioned above, narration takes the event process as the main line, and the narrative discourse progresses following the time order of the event and the behavior of the event participants. Therefore, information on the main line of narration makes up foreground information. Conversely, background information is information outside the main line of events, which includes condition, cause, time, place, accompanying state, etc.

4.3.1 Indicating condition and cause

Clauses of "*yi*+CL+NP" subjects can function as adverbial clauses to indicate condition or cause.

(11) **这袁崇焕啊**, 从进大牢, 到被处决, 前后八个月。可您知道, **他**在大牢里干什么了吗?写了一封长信。就是劝那些, 已经归顺了大清朝的, 祖大寿这些人哪, 继续效忠大明朝。**这袁崇焕**自己都混到这份上了, 还劝别人忠君爱国, 可见啊, **这人**是绝对够仗义。就算是这崇祯皇帝真的铁石心肠, 也应该被感动了吧。但是, 哎, 重要的就是这"但是", 人家是皇上。咱们平时都说啊, 大丈夫一言既出驷马难追, 更何况是皇上, 没那么轻易认错。所以呢, 只能是将错就错, 把袁崇焕给杀了。**话说袁崇焕**被杀了之后啊, 愣是被老百姓给分了吃了。后来呢, <u>一位义士夜晚盗取了袁崇焕的头颅</u>, <u>埋在了东花市</u>, 这才有了咱们下一个地点, 袁崇焕祠堂。(This Is Beijing)

Zhè Yuán Chónghuàn a, cóng jìn dàláo, dào bèi chǔjué, qiánhòu bā gè yuè. Kě nín zhīdào, **tā** zài dàláo lǐ gàn shénme le ma? Xiěle yī fēng cháng xìn. Jiùshì quàn nàxiē, yǐjīng guīshùnle dà Qīngcháo de, Zǔ Dàshòu zhèxiē rén na, jìxù xiàozhōng dà Míngcháo. **Zhè Yuán Chónghuàn** zìjǐ dōu hùn dào zhè fèn shàng le, hái quàn biérén zhōngjūnàiguó, kějiàn a, **zhè rén** shì juéduì gòu zhàngyì. Jiùsuàn shì zhè Chóngzhēn huángdì zhēnde tiěshíxīncháng, yě yīnggāi bèi gǎndòngle ba. Dànshì, āi, zhòngyào de jiùshì zhè "dànshì", rénjiā shì huángshàng. Zánmen píngshí dōu shuō a, dàzhàngfū yīyánjìchū sìmǎnánzhuī, gèng hékuàng shì huángshàng, méi nàme qīngyì rèncuò. Suǒyǐ ne, zhǐnéng shì jiāngcuòjiùcuò, bǎ Yuán Chónghuàn gěi shāle. **Huàshuō Yuán Chónghuàn** bèi shāle zhīhòu a, lèng shì bèi lǎobǎixìng gěi fēnle chīle. Hòulái ne, <u>yī wèi yìshì yèwǎn dàoqǔ le Yuán Chónghuàn de tóulú, mái zài le Dōnghuāshì</u>, zhè cái yǒule zánmen xiàyīgè dìdiǎn, Yuán Chónghuàn cítáng.

'**Yuan Chonghuan** spent eight months in prison before he was executed. But do you know what **he** did in prison? **He** wrote a long letter, trying to persuade those who had surrendered to the Qing Dynasty, such as Zu Dashou, to continue to serve the Ming Dynasty. **Yuan Chonghuan** was in such a miserable situation himself, but he still attempted to persuade others to be loyal to the emperor and the country. So it can be seen that **he** was absolutely a righteous person. Stone-hearted as he might be, Emperor Chongzhen should have been moved. But, ah, what matters is this "but". Chongzhen was the emperor. We usually say that a real man never goes back on his words, let alone the emperor, who would not admit mistakes easily. So the mistake was left uncorrected and Yuan Chonghuan was executed. On top of that, his remains was even eaten by the common people. It was later on that <u>a righteous man stole Yuan's head at night and buried it at Donghuashi</u>. This is the story behind the Temple of Yuan Chonghuan, our next resort.'

In this example, the protagonist is Yuan Chonghuan, anaphorically referred to respectively as "他" ('he'), "这袁崇焕" ('this Yuan Chonghuan'), and "这人" ('this person') in later discourse. The underlined "indefinite-subject sentence" fulfills the function of a conditional clause, indicating the precondition for the establishment of the Temple of Yuan Chonghuan. The subject "一位义士" ('a righteous man') is trivial information, and the character is narrated no more in subsequent discourse.

If the status of the sentence as a clause of condition is changed by deleting "才", an adverb indicating the condition relation, the subject can no longer take the configuration of "yi+CL+NP", as illustrated by (11'a). Neither can the sentence be rewritten as a *you*-sentence, as in (11'b).

(11') a.* 后来呢,一位义士夜晚盗取了袁崇焕的头颅,埋在了东花市,这()有了咱们下一个地点,袁崇焕祠堂。("才" is deleted.)
  b.* 后来呢,(有)一位义士夜晚盗取了袁崇焕的头颅,埋在了东花市,这()有了咱们下一个地点,袁崇焕祠堂。(The addition of "有" before the indefinite subject turns the sentence into a *you*-sentence.)

  Below is an example where the "*yi*+CL+NP"-subject sentence is used as a clause of cause.

(12) 这个井口是后加的。为什么说后加的呢?因为第二年,**珍妃**被她姐姐瑾妃从井里捞了出来。按说,<u>一个死人</u>被井水泡了一年,应该泡得腐烂了,没想到面目栩栩如生。(*This Is Beijing*)

Zhège jǐngkǒu shì hòu jiā de. Wèishéme shuō hòu jiā de ne? Yīnwèi dì'èr nián, **Zhēnfēi** bèi tā jiějie Jǐnfēi cóng jǐnglǐ lāole chūlái. Ànshuō, **yī gè sǐrén bèi jǐngshuǐ pàole yī nián**, yīnggāi pào de fǔlànle, méi xiǎngdào miànmù xǔxǔrúshēng.

'The wellhead is a later addition. Why can I say so? Because **Concubine Zhen** was brought out of the well by her sister Concubine Jin the next year. Normally **a dead person** would be rotten after being soaked in well water for a year. But unexpectedly the face of Concubine Zhen looked lifelike.'

In (12) above, "being soaked in well water" is a possible cause for getting "rotten." "A dead person" refers to "Concubine Zhen," a character that has been introduced into discourse, but the example has refrained from using a proper noun or a personal pronoun for anaphora. This kind of "*yi*+CL+NP" subject sentence, when used to indicate cause, cannot become a *you*-sentence in the context of occurrence.

4.3.2 *Indicating time*

"*Yi*+CL+NP"-subject sentences can also be used as adverbials of time. The referent of the "*yi*+CL+NP" subject does not have topic continuity; neither can "*you*" be added to the very beginning of the sentence. The "*yi*+CL+NP"-subject sentence is the only option for such use, as illustrated in (13).

(13) 当年,**洪承畴**那边,在东北打了败仗,这边**崇祯皇帝**以为**爱将**已经殉国。于是在前门外的这座关帝庙里,给**洪承畴**建了座塑像,供老百姓瞻仰纪念。只可惜,多情总被无情伤。一个太监把洪承畴降清的消息带回了京城。这回**崇祯**可是伤透了心。一赌气,砸了塑像,大卸八块ㄦ。还命人把碎块,扔到了厕所的茅坑里。眨眼的工夫,**洪承畴**在荣辱之间,飞快转换。
(*This Is Beijing*)

Dāngnián, **Hóng Chéngchóu** nàbiān, zài dōngběi dǎle bàizhàng, zhèbiān **Chóngzhēn huángdì** yǐwéi **àijiàng** yǐjīng xùnguó. Yúshì zài Qiánmén wài de zhè zuò Guāndìmiào lǐ, gěi **Hóng Chéngchóu** jiànle zuò sùxiàng, gōng lǎobǎixìng zhānyǎng jìniàn. Zhǐkěxī, duōqíng zǒng bèi wúqíng shāng. Yī gè tàijiàn bǎ Hóng Chéngchóu xiáng qīng de xiāoxī dàihuíle Jīngchéng. Zhèhuí **Chóngzhēn** kěshì shāng tòu le xīn. Yīdǔqì, zále sùxiàng, dàxièbākuài-er. Hái mìng rén bǎ suìkuài, rēng dào le cèsuǒ de máokēng lǐ. Zhǎyǎn de gōngfū, **Hóng Chéngchóu** zài róngrǔ zhījiān, fēikuài zhuǎnhuàn.

'At that time, **Hong Chengchou** was defeated in the northeast, but here (in the capital city) **Emperor Chongzhen** thought that his **favorite general** had died for his motherland. So in the Temple of Guan Yu outside Qianmen, a statue was built for **Hong Chengchou** so that the ordinary people could pay tribute to him. Unfortunately, love is always mercilessly hurt. A eunuch brought the news of Hong Chengchou's downfall to the

Qing Dynasty back to the capital city. **Emperor Chongzhen** was so hurt that he ordered in fury to smash the statue into eight pieces, which were then thrown into the toilet pit. In the blink of an eye, **Hong Chengchou** shifted from honor to disgrace.'

In (13), it was when "a eunuch brought the news of Hong Chengchou's downfall to the Qing Dynasty back to the capital city" that Emperor Chongzhen began to feel hurt. Liu Anchun and Zhang Bojiang (2004) notice that, although there are no time-indicating expressions such as 这时/此时(zhèshí/cǐshí, 'at this time') before "indefinite-subject sentences," the meaning can be clearly seen from the context. Moreover, expressions such as 此时 can occur sentence initially. And it seems acceptable to add "*you*" before the "*yi*+CL+NP" subject when such a sentence occurs independently; it will be inappropriate, however, when the sentence is used in context, such as in (13), because the eunuch is not the main character of the story, irrespective of the fact that it is new information in discourse. Many of the examples cited in Wang Canlong (2003) fall into this category of adverbial clauses, in that they are illegitimate as sentences when standing alone, but acceptable when contextualized.

From the perspective of discourse organization, we are of the view that "*yi*+CL+NP" subjects convey trivial information which is off the main narrative line. They are used not to introduce new entities of topicality, but to provide background information together with other sentence component parts. Although the NP in the "*yi*+CL+NP" subject is a carrier of new information, it is of low topicality. Unlike its counterpart in the *you*-sentence, the referent of the subject NP lies outside the main line of narration and is not in the topic chain of discourse.

4.3.3 Indicating accompanying state

As mentioned above, the NP in the "*yi*+CL+NP"-subject sentence is the carrier of new information, and its referent is not a link of the topic chain. For instance, both "一只黑猫蹑手蹑脚地走过" ('a black cat crept past') in (5) and "一个牧羊人赶着一群口外羊从东边过来" ('a shepherd drove a flock of sheep coming from the east') in (6) describe the setting of the event.

We note that some examples in Wang Hongqi (2001) also fall into this category; that is, they also provide background information, such as (14):

(14) 走啊走啊,他们来到一个山坡上,忽然一头野猪从他们身边跑过,一群小鸟唱着歌儿从他们头上飞过…… (cited from Wang Hongqi, 2001)

Zǒu a zǒu a, tāmen lái dào yī gè shānpō shàng, hūrán yī tóu yězhū cóng tāmen shēnbiān pǎoguò, yī qún xiǎo niǎo chàngzhe gē·er cóng tāmen tóu shàng fēiguò…

'Walking and walking, they came to a hillside. Suddenly a wild boar ran past them, a flock of birds flew over them, singing songs…'

We do not think that 有('have') can occur in front of "一头野猪" ('a wild boar') or "一群小鸟" ('a flock of birds') in (14), because the subject of the preceding clause is "他们" ('they'), the referents of which are repeatedly mentioned in discourse. In contrast, the activities of the wild boar and the birds only make up the background events in the plot. See also (15):

(15) a. 当官兵铺天盖地冲到坟前时,(*有)<u>一阵狂风</u>吹来,坟自动裂开一条口子……

Dāng guānbīng pūtiāngàidì chōng dào fén qián shí, (*yǒu) <u>yī zhèn kuángfēng</u> chuī lái, fén zìdòng lièkāi yī tiáo kǒuzi...

'When the soldiers rushed to the grave, (*there was) <u>a gust of wind</u> blew over, and the grave automatically split a hole...'

b. 他飞上九天一看,(*有)<u>一口仙水</u>在空中飞来飞去,他晓得定是它在作怪……

Tā fēi shàng jiǔtiān yī kàn, (*yǒu) <u>yī kǒu xiānshuǐ</u> zài kōngzhōng fēiláifēiqù, tā xiǎodé dìngshì tā zài zuòguài...

'He flew up to the Ninth Heaven and saw (*there was) <u>a mouthful of fairy water</u> flying around in the air. He knew that it must be it at work...'

In (15a) and (15b), the two clauses hosting the underlined indefinite subjects are accompanying states, both subjects expressing trivial information, neither of them being the discourse topic. If *"you"* is added, they would become a syntactic configuration that introduces the discourse topic, which renders the addition unacceptable in their respective context.

According to Liu Anchun and Zhang Bojiang (2004), the function of the "indefinite-subject sentence" is to divert the plot of a narrative text by introducing a new participant and a new event. Examine (16) and (17) (both cited from Liu and Zhang [2004]):

(16) 唐僧正在发愁,恰好<u>一只小船</u>从上游撑来。八戒赶紧招呼摆渡。

Tánggēng zhèngzài fāchóu, <u>qiàhǎo yī zhǐ xiǎochuán</u> cóng shàngyóu chēng lái. Bājiè gǎnjǐn zhāohū bǎidù.

'The Tang Monk was worrying when <u>a boat</u> came from the upstream. Pigsy hurriedly asked for ferry.'

(17) 她打开收音机,照例收听每日新闻,突然<u>一个十分熟悉的声音</u>从收音机里传出,她凝神细听,这不是毛泽东在说话吗?是他……砰的一声,她昏倒在沙发上。

Tā dǎkāi shōuyīnjī, zhàolì shōutīng měirì xīnwén, <u>túrán, yī gè shífēn shúxī de shēngyīn</u> cóng shōuyīnjī lǐ chuán chū, tā níngshén xì tīng, zhè búshì Máo Zédōng zài shuōhuà ma? Shì tā... Pēng de yī shēng, tā hūndǎo zài shāfā shàng.

'She turned on the radio and listened to the daily news as usual. Suddenly, <u>a very familiar voice</u> came out of the radio. She listened attentively. Isn't that Mao Zedong talking? It is him... With a bang, she fainted into the sofa.'

To us, the "*yi*+CL+NP" subjects in (16) and (17) have indeed disrupted the topic chains, but their referents are not discourse topics when the hosting clauses are taken as a whole. What both clauses convey is nothing but background information. The protagonists of (16) are the Tang Monk and his disciples, and the main character of (17) is "she".

In other words, in narrative discourse, the subject of an "indefinite-subject sentence" can introduce new information, but "*yi*+CL+NP" is not the preferred formulation for introducing discourse topics. According to our observation of a corpus of 50 hours of naturally occurring oral discourse, the "*yi*+CL+NP"-subject sentence, when indicating the accompanying state, is a syntactic configuration that bears characteristics of written narratives.

4.4 Evaluative "*yi*+CL+NP"-subject sentences

4.4.1 Tense-aspect characteristics

When used for evaluation, the predicate of the "*yi*+CL+NP"-subject sentence does not represent the event process.[3] It may be coded in the form of an adjective; when it is a verb, it occurs in the habitual aspect. And if the subject is "一个人" ('a person'), it can be replaced by the bare noun "人". See (18):

(18) 文绣离婚以后回到了北京, 0_i 找到了一所小学当老师。但总有人跟踪骚扰她。0_i 无奈之下, 文绣只好辞职。于是, 她$_i$ 用离婚时得到的青春补偿费, 0_i 在德胜门内的刘海胡同安了家, 0_i 雇了几个丫头老妈子, 0_i 过起了大门不出、二门不迈, 0_i 看书学画的清闲日子。在兵荒马乱的年月里, <u>一个离了婚的单身女人想过安生日子并不容易</u>。文绣曾经是皇帝的老婆, 再加上又年轻又有点钱, 难免令一些男人垂涎。上到高官, 下到地痞, 各种各样的男人, 不断地到刘海胡同来骚扰文绣, 令她不胜其烦, 毫无安全感可言。(*This Is Beijing*)

Wénxiù líhūn yǐhòu huídàole Běijīng, 0_i zhǎodàole yī suǒ xiǎoxué dāng lǎoshī. Dàn zǒng yǒurén gēnzōng sāorǎo tā$_i$. 0_i wúnài zhīxià, **Wénxiù** zhǐhǎo cízhí. Yúshì, tā$_i$ yòng líhūn shí dédào de qīngchūn bǔcháng fèi, 0_i zài Déshèngmén nèi de Liú Hǎi Hútòng ānle jiā, 0_i gùle jǐgè yātou lǎomāzi, 0_i guò qǐ le dàmén bù chū(,) èrmén bú mài, 0_i kànshū xuéhuà de qīngxián rìzi. Zài bīnghuāngmǎluàn de niányuè lǐ, <u>yī gè líle hūn de dānshēn nǚrén xiǎng guò ānshēng rìzi bìngbù róngyì</u>. **Wénxiù** céngjīng shì huángdì de lǎopó, zàijiāshàng yòu niánqīng yòu yǒudiǎn qián, nánmiǎn lìng yīxiē nánrén chuíxián. Shàng dào gāoguān, xià dào dìpǐ, gèzhǒnggèyàng de nánrén, búduàn de dào Liú Hǎi Hútòng lái sāorǎo Wénxiù, lìng tā bùshēngqífán, háo wú ānquán gǎn kě yán.

'After divorce, **Wenxiu** returned to Beijing and found a teaching job at a primary school. But there were always people stalking her. Helpless, **she** had to resign. With the compensation money **she** got from divorce, (**she**) settled down in Liu Hai Hutong inside Deshengmen. (**She**) hired a few maidservants and began to live a leisure life, staying home, reading and painting. <u>It's not easy for a divorced single woman to live a restful life during the years of war</u>. **Wenxiu** used to be the emperor's wife, and on top of that (**she**) was young and had some money. So inevitably (**she**) was coveted by men of all walks, up to senior officials, down to local ruffians. (**They**) came constantly to Liu Hai Hutong to harass Wenxiu, so that she was too bothered to feel any security at all.'

In (18) above, the main character is Wenxiu, who is anaphorically referred to in the subsequent clauses in the form of proper noun, pronoun, and zero pronoun. In the underlined sentence, however, "一个离了婚的单身女人" ('a divorced single woman') does not refer specifically to Wenxiu, and the predicate "想过安生日子并不容易" ('not easy to live a restful life') does not represent an event that has a temporal structure. The sentence, instead, expresses a constant proposition.

The predicate nucleus of (18) is "不容易" ('not easy'), which is adjectival. When the predicate is verbal, it expresses no individuated event, either.

(19) 只可惜,此次承德消暑游,对于咸丰来说,只能用四个字概括,叫做"有去无回"。咸丰十一年七月十七,慈安、慈禧成了寡妇了。<u>一个男人倒下去,两个女人站起来</u>。从此以后,慈安、慈禧手拉手,肩并肩,联合恭亲王,灭了八大辅臣。怀揣"同道堂""御赏"两枚大印,抱着孩子,走上了清末政治舞台。(*This Is Beijing*)

Zhǐ kěxí, cǐ cì Chéngdé xiāoshǔ yóu, duìyú Xiánfēng láishuō, zhǐnéng yòng sì gè zì gàikuò, jiàozuò "yǒuqùwúhuí". Xiánfēng shíyī nián qī yuè shíqī, Cí'ān(,) Cíxǐ chéngle guǎfù le. <u>Yī gè nánrén dào xiàqù, liǎng gè nǚrén zhàn qǐlái</u>. Cóngcǐ yǐhòu, Cí'ān(,) Cíxǐ shǒu-lā-shǒu, jiān-bìng-jiān, liánhé Gōngqīnwáng, mièle bā dà fǔchén. Huáichuāi "Tóngdàotáng" "Yùshǎng" liǎng méi dàyìn, bàozhe háizi, zǒushàngle qīngmò zhèngzhì wǔtái.

'Unfortunately, the summer tour to Chengde, for Xianfeng, can only be summed up in a single expression – "there is no return". On July 17, 11th year of Xianfeng, Ci'an and Cixi were widowed. <u>When one man falls down, two women stand up</u>. From then on, Ci'an and Cixi, hand in hand, shoulder to shoulder, defeated the eight auxiliary officials by uniting with Prince Gong. In possession of two seals respectively engraved with "Tong Dao Tang" and "Yu Shang", and with a child in arms, Ci'an and Cixi stepped onto the political stage of the late Qing Dynasty.'

In terms of reference, it seems that "一个男人" ('one man') refers to Emperor Xianfeng while "两个女人" ('two women') refers to Ci'an and Cixi (see the underlined sentence). The context, however, would prevent the two indefinite subjects from being replaced by Emperor Xianfeng, and Ci'an and Cixi. Moreover, the context has also ruled out the possibility of adding the perfective aspect marker "了" (*le*) to come up with expressions such as "一个男人倒了下去" or "一个男人倒了下去了". The same applies to "两个女人站起来". Moreover, the two clauses can only occur in symmetry. Deleting one while keeping the other would be unacceptable. In other words, the habitual aspect of the predicate shows that this sentence does not have an internal temporal structure and that it is not narrating the event. Here, the "*yi*+CL+NP"-subject clause constitutes a syntactic configuration for speaker-exposure.

4.4.2 Speech acts

Clauses of the habitual aspect do not represent event processes; neither do they introduce discourse topics. Therefore, they cannot transform into *you*-sentences. More importantly, in a longer narrative discourse, the occurrence of the "*yi*+CL+NP"-subject sentence means the termination of the narrative action of story-telling by making assessment of what has been narrated.

(20) 清史稿上说,**张廷玉**ᵢ,仗着自己是三朝元老,要这要那,患得患失。却也有**人**说,乾隆心胸狭窄,嫉贤妒能。君臣的事情,自古就没有对错。**张廷玉**ᵢ为大清朝贡献了一辈子,不可能因为乾隆朝的官方评价,就葬送了**他**ᵢ一世的清白。即便如史书记载,**0**ᵢ真是倚老卖老,**0**ᵢ患得患失了,转过头来想一想,<u>一个年近古稀之人奉献了一辈子,也谨慎了一辈子;好不容易鼓起勇气,想为自己争取点什么,又有何罪过呢</u>。(*This Is Beijing*)

Qīngshǐ gǎo shàng shuō, **Zhāng Tíngyù**ᵢ, zhàngzhe zìjǐ shì sāncháo yuánlǎo, yào zhè yào nà, huàndéhuànshī. Què yěyǒu rén shuō, Qiánlóng xīnxiōng xiázhǎi, jíxiándùnéng. Jūnchén de shìqíng, zìgǔ jiù méiyǒu duìcuò. **Zhāng Tíngyù**ᵢ wèi dà Qīngcháo gòngxiànle yībèizi, bù kěnéng yīnwèi Qiánlóng cháo de guānfāng píngjià, jiù zàngsòngle **tā**ᵢ yīshì de qīngbái. Jíbiàn rú shǐshū jìzǎi, **0**ᵢ zhēnshi yǐlǎomàilǎo, **0**ᵢ huàndéhuànshīle, zhuǎn guò tóu lái xiǎng-yī-xiǎng, <u>yī gè nián jìn gǔxī zhī rén fèngxiànle yībèizi, yě jǐnshènle yībèizi; hǎobùróngyì gǔqǐyǒngqì, xiǎng wèi zìjǐ zhēngqǔ diǎn shénme, yòu yǒu hé zuìguo ne</u>.

'According to the Qing history manuscripts, **Zhang Tingyu**, taking advantage of being minister to three emperors, wanted a whole lot of things and worried about personal gains and losses. But there are also people saying that Emperor Qianlong was narrow-minded and jealous of the talented. There has been no right or wrong in matters of the emperor and ministers since ancient times. **Zhang Tingyu** devoted his entire life to the Qing Dynasty. It was impossible to ruin his innocence because of the official evaluation of the Qianlong Period. What if **he** had prided himself on being a veteran and cared much about his personal gains and losses? If you give it a second thought, <u>what sin is there in a person's finally summoning up courage to win something for himself at an age approaching 70, when he has dedicated his entire life and has been cautious all along?</u>'

The topic of this example is Zhang Tingyu. After its introduction into discourse, it is referred back to respectively with proper noun, third-person pronoun and zero pronoun. The "*yi*+CL+NP"-subject sentence (the underlined) is used when the speaker begins to make assessment. "转过头来想一想" ('give it a second thought') is not the behavior of the character described, but an insertion that leads to the narrator's assessment. Although "一个年近古稀之人" ('a man approaching 70 years old') can be understood as Zhang Tingyu – an entity that has been introduced in earlier discourse, the following clauses are no longer narration of the event process, but the speaker's assessment of the narrated.

See also (21):

(21) 1)我们今天所说的<u>贤良祠</u>,和曾经介绍过的贤良寺,可不是一码事儿。贤良寺,现在的遗址,在石景山虎头峰下。而<u>贤良祠</u>位于地安门西大街103号。<u>这座祠堂</u>,聚集了自雍正八年,也就是1730年以来的99位劳动模范的牌位。其中当然少不了刘统勋。据史料记载,刘统勋死后,只留下一个儿子,也就是,我们所熟悉的宰相刘罗锅刘墉,还有一个孙子。至于财产,仅有田数十亩,茅舍一处。 据说刘统勋的官服,50年没变过尺寸,**可见**他生活的节俭和朴素。刘统勋死后,排位入贤良祠。据说刘墉在朝中得到认可,还是沾了老爸刘统勋的光。<u>一个忠良之后的头衔儿足以让刘墉少奋斗十年。如果说,刘统勋一辈子,没给子孙留下过什么遗产,但这"名声"二字,可算是千金难买的财富了</u>。(*This Is Beijing*)

Wǒmen jīntiān suǒ shuō de <u>Xiánliáng Cí</u>, hé céngjīng jièshàoguò de Xiánliáng Sì, kě búshì yī mǎ shì·er. Xiánliáng Sì, xiànzài de yízhǐ, zài Shíjǐngshān Hǔtóu Fēng xià. Ér <u>Xiánliáng Cí</u> wèiyú Dì'ānmén Xīdàjiē 103 hào. <u>Zhè zuò cítáng</u>, jùjíle zì Yōngzhèng bā nián, yějiùshì 1730 nián yǐlái de 99 wèi láodòng mófàn de páiwèi. Qízhōng dāngrán shǎobùliǎo Liú Tǒngxūn. Jù shǐliào jìzǎi, Liú Tǒngxūn sǐ hòu, zhǐ liúxià yī gè érzi, yě jiùshì, wǒmen suǒ shúxī de zǎixiàng Liú Luóguo Liú Yōng, háiyǒu yī gè sūnzi. Zhìyú cáichǎn, jǐnyǒu tián shù shí mǔ, máoshè yī chù. Jùshuō Liú Tǒngxūn de guānfú, 50 nián méi biànguò chǐcùn, **kějiàn** tā shēnghuó de jiéjiǎn hé pǔsù. Liú Tǒngxūn sǐ hòu, páiwèi rù Xiánliáng Cí. Jùshuō Liú Yōng zài cháozhōng dédào rènkě, háishì zhānle lǎobà Liú Tǒngxūn de guāng. <u>Yī gè zhōngliáng zhīhòu de tóuxián·er zúyǐ ràng Liú Yōng shǎo fèndòu shí nián. Rúguǒ shuō, Liú Tǒngxūn yībèizi, méi gěi zǐsūn liúxiàguò shénme yíchǎn, dàn zhè "míngshēng" èr zì, kě suànshì qiānjīn nán mǎi de cáifù le.</u>

'Xianliang Shrine that we are to talk about today is not the same thing as Xianliang Temple that we have introduced. Xianliang Temple is located at the foot of Hutou Peak of Shijingshan District. Xianliang Shrine, however, is located at 103 Di'anmen West Street. This shrine has gathered the memorial tablets of 99 model workers since the eighth year of Yongzheng, that is, 1730. Of course, Liu Tongxun's is a must here. According to historical records, Liu Tongxun left behind only a son, the familiar prime minister Liu Yong, nicknamed Hunchback Liu. He also had a grandson. As for property, there were only dozens of acres of farmland and one hut. It is said that Liu Tongxun's official uniform had not changed size in 50 years, **which attests to** the frugality and simplicity of his life. After Liu Tongxun's death, his tablet entered Xianliang Shrine. It is said that it was due to the father-son relationship that Liu Yong was recognized at the court. The title "descendant of a loyal" is enough to save Liu Yong ten years of struggle. If Liu Tongxun did not left much legacy to his descendants in his entire life, "reputation" can be regarded as an asset that is hard to buy.'

In (21) above, the discourse topic is Xianliang Shrine, its location and the story behind its name being introduced. The first sentence of the underlined part is an "indefinite-subject sentence", where the "*yi*+CL+NP" subject "一个忠良之后的头衔儿" ('the title "descendant of a loyal"') is a newly introduced concept. Although there is "可见" ('it can be seen') in earlier discourse to lead in the commentary "他生活的节俭和朴素" ('the frugality and simplicity of his life'), it is the "*yi*+CL+NP"-subject sentence that marks the overall division: the preceding discourse is narrative while the following is speaker's assessment of what has been narrated. Further assessment is introduced by "如果说"[4] in the subsequent sentence.

All in all, the so-called "indefinite-subject sentence" has its specific discourse functions. In the narrative genre, the "*yi*+CL+NP"-subject sentence is a marked sentence pattern that disrupts topic continuity. From the point of view of information packaging, this marked pattern highlights a shift in speech act type. Accordingly, it can be argued that the so-called "indefinite-subject sentence," as a marked syntactic configuration, is used in discourse to distinguish two different speech acts: narration vs. non-narration.

4.5 Mandatory use of "*yi*+CL+NP"-subject sentences

It seems that "*you*" can be added to precede a "*yi*+CL+NP"-subject sentence when the sentence stands in isolation, as previous literature has pointed out (Fan Jiyan, 1985). In actual contexts, however, it is not necessarily the case. Whether "*you*" can occur is in fact sensitive to two discourse considerations: its topicality and likelihood to be the main clause.

4.5.1 Weak topicality

You-sentences are known to have the function of introducing discourse topics. Because of their strength in ushering in subsequent discourse, they constitute the only option in such contexts.

(22) 话说呢,在这个明朝嘉靖年间,<u>有一个落迫的书生</u>。有一天啊,**0**ᵢ溜溜达达,**0**ᵢ就到了鹤年堂药铺的门口了。掌柜的一看啊,<u>这书生</u>ᵢ挺可怜的,叫进来,留宿一宿吧。<u>这书生</u>ᵢ呢,为了表达感激之情,**0**ᵢ就给这药铺啊,题了一块匾,上书三个大字,鹤年堂。等到几十年过去了,有人啊,一看这匾,说这匾上啊,字里行间带着奸气儿。这匾为什么带着奸气儿呢?这就得说到题匾的人了。这题匾的人啊,就是今天节目的主角儿,明朝的奸相,严嵩。(*This Is Beijing*)

Huàshuō ne, zài zhège Míngcháo Jiājìng niánjiān, <u>yǒu yī gè luòpò de shūshēng</u>. Yǒu yītiān a, **0**ᵢ liūliūdādā, **0**ᵢ jiù dàole Hèniántáng yàopù de ménkǒu le. Zhǎngguìde yīkàn a, <u>zhè shūshēng</u>ᵢ tǐng kělián de, jiào jìnlái, liúsù yī xiǔ ba. <u>Zhè shūshēng</u>ᵢ ne, wèile biǎodá gǎnjī zhī qíng, **0**ᵢ jiù gěi zhè yàopù a, tíle yī kuài biǎn, shàng shū sān gè dàzì, hè nián táng. Děngdào jǐ shí nián guòqùle, yǒurén a, yīkàn zhè biǎn, shuō zhè biǎn shàng a, zìlǐhángjiān dàizhe jiānqì·er. Zhè biǎn wèishénme dàizhe jiānqì·er ne? Zhè jiù děi shuōdào tí biǎn de rén le. Zhè tí biǎn de rén a, jiùshì jīntiān jiémù de zhǔjiǎo·er, Míngcháo de jiān xiāng, Yán Sōng.

'Say, during the Jiajing period of the Ming Dynasty, <u>there was a scholar who fell into desolation</u>. One day, (he) wandered to the gate of Heniantang medicine shop. The shopkeeper noticed that <u>the scholar</u> was very pitiable. So he asked him in and allowed him to stay for the night. To express his gratitude, <u>the scholar</u> wrote on the plaque to the drugstore three characters, *he nian tang* (鹤年堂). Several decades later, a person took a look at the plaque and said that there was an evil spirit between the strokes of the characters. Why is the plaque so treacherous? We have to talk about the person who wrote the plaque. The person is the protagonist of today's program, Yan Song, the traitor of the Ming Dynasty.'

In (22), the concept encoded in the post-*you* "*yi*+CL+NP" configuration is introduced into discourse for the first time, and repeatedly referred to in different ways (reduced NP and zero anaphor) in subsequent discourse.

"*Yi*+CL+NP" is a marked syntactic configuration that serves a double function: on the one hand, it disrupts topic continuity; and on the other, it terminates the temporal structure of the narrative. See (23):

(23) 说起宣武区的菜市口,给人印象最深的,就得数清朝时候的刑场了。但今天,我们要给您念叨的,是菜市口另外一个身份,**奸相严嵩**的户口所在地,丞相胡同。菜市口菜市口,指的就是这个路口。路口南边的菜市口胡同,便是**明朝大奸臣严嵩**住的地方。过去,这儿叫丞相胡同。有人说,因为**严嵩**当年住在胡同里,而**他**官至丞相,所以这条胡同,被老百姓称为丞相胡同了。但也有人说,是因为明朝的时候,有个绳匠住在胡同里,所以最早,这儿叫绳匠胡同。后来老百姓叫顺了嘴了,就叫成"丞相"胡同了。绳匠也好,丞相也罢。反正**严嵩**当年住在这儿,是无可质疑的。**严嵩**住的宅子,究竟有多大呢?您琢磨琢磨吧。现在的菜市口南大街,就是过去的丞相胡同。就算当年的胡同没有现在的大马路这么宽,那咱就按照单向车道的宽窄算。甭管是占地面积,还是使用面积,也都不算小了吧。<u>一个丞相住在半条菜市口大街上,这倒也是无可厚非的事儿</u>。所以咱也没有必要,追究人家不明财产的来历。(*This Is Beijing*)

Shuōqǐ Xuānwǔqū de Càishìkǒu, gěi rén yìnxiàng zuì shēn de, jiù děi shǔ Qīngcháo shíhòu de xíngchǎng le. Dàn jīntiān, wǒmen yào gěi nín niàndao de, shì Càishìkǒu lìngwài yī gè shēnfèn, **jiān xiāng Yán Sōng** de hùkǒu suǒzàidì, Chéngxiàng hútòng. Càishìkǒu Càishìkǒu, zhǐ de jiùshì zhège lùkǒu. Lùkǒu nánbian de Càishìkǒu hútòng, biàn shì **Míngcháo dà jiānchén Yán Sōng** zhù de dìfāng. Guòqù, zhè·er jiào Chéngxiàng hútòng. Yǒurén shuō, yīnwèi **Yán Sōng** dāngnián zhù zài hútòng lǐ, ér **tā** guān zhì chéngxiàng, suǒyǐ zhè tiáo hútòng, bèi lǎobǎixìng chēngwéi Chéngxiàng hútòng le. Dàn yě yǒurén shuō, shì yīnwèi Míngcháo de shíhòu, yǒu gè shéngjiàng zhù zài hútòng lǐ, suǒyǐ zuìzǎo, zhè·er jiào Shéngjiàng hútòng. Hòulái lǎobǎixìng jiào shùn le zuǐ le, jiù jiào chéng "Chéngxiàng" hútòng le. Shéngjiàng yěhǎo, Chéngxiàng yěbà. Fǎnzhèng **Yán Sōng** dāngnián zhù zài zhè·er, shì wúkězhìyí de. **Yán Sōng** zhù de zháizi, jiūjìng yǒu duōdà ne? Nín zhuómó~zhuómó ba. Xiànzài de Càishìkǒu Nándàjiē, jiùshì guòqù de Chéngxiàng hútòng. Jiùsuàn dāngnián de hútòng méiyǒu xiànzài de dàmǎlù zhème kuān, nà zán jiù ànzhào dānxiàng chēdào de kuānzhǎi suàn. Béngguǎn shì zhàndìmiànjī, háishi shǐyòng miànjī, yě dōu bú suàn xiǎo le ba. <u>Yī gè chéngxiàng zhù zài bàn tiáo Càishìkǒu dàjiē shàng, zhè dào yěshì wúkěhòufēi de shì·er</u>. Suǒyǐ zán yě méiyǒu bìyào, zhuījiū rénjiā bùmíng cáichǎn de láilì.

'Speaking of Caishikou in Xuanwu District, the most impressive thing about it should be the execution grounds in the Qing Dynasty. But today, what we want to introduce to you is another identity of Caishikou. It used to be the residence of **the traitor Yan Song**, so it is also known as Prime Minister Hutong. The so-called Caishikou refers to this intersection. To the south of the intersection is Caishikou Hutong. That's where **Yan Song, a traitor of the Ming Dynasty**, once lived. In the past, this place was called Prime Minister Hutong. According to some people, that was because **Yan Song** lived here. Since he was an official as high as prime minister, the public called the hutong Prime Minister Hutong. However, other people seem to have a different story about the name of the hutong. They say that it was because there used to be a rope maker living in the hutong in the Ming Dynasty. So it was originally called Rope Maker Hutong. Later, for the convenience of articulation,[5] people began to call it "Prime Minister" Hutong. Whether it is Rope Maker or Prime

Minister, there is no doubt that **Yan Song** lived here back then. How big was **Yan Song**'s residence? Think about it. The current Caishikou South Street is the old Prime Minister Hutong. Given that the hutong back then was not as wide as the current main road, let's calculate according to the width of a one-way lane. It was far from small whether it was in terms of floor area or usable area. <u>There is nothing wrong with a prime minister living in a residence taking up half of Caishikou Street.</u> So there is no need for us to investigate the origin of his unknown property.'

In this example, Prime Minister Yan Song has already been mentioned in the context preceding the "*yi*+CL+NP"-subject sentence (underlined) as a topic of strong topic continuity. So the subjects of the subsequent sentences may very well be coded in definite forms (such as proper noun or pronoun) to refer back to Yan Song. But the underlined sentence has chosen to use "一个丞相", an indefinite form taking the configuration of "*yi*+CL+NP". The topic chain is thus terminated.

Furthermore, an essential feature of the narrative genre is to report events with intrinsic temporality (Labov, 1972; Longacre, 1983; Schiffrin, 1994).[6] When the coding occurs in the habitual aspect, the narrated will jump out of the temporal structure of an individual event.

4.5.2 *Small likelihood to be the main clause*

Most "*yi*+CL+NP"-subject sentences can be transformed into *you*-sentences when standing alone, but when contextualized, they seem to defy such transformation.

First of all, "*yi*+CL+NP"-subject sentences are adverbial by nature, indicating condition (see [11]), cause (e.g. [12]), time (e.g. [13]), and accompanying state (e.g. [14] and [15]). From the perspective of syntactic integration, they all bear characteristics of subordinate clauses.

If a "*yi*+CL+NP"-subject sentence occurs as the main clause, it needs to be preceded by adverbials of time or place, as in (24).

(24)　一天,<u>一个老者</u>讨饭到她家来了。
　　　Yītiān, <u>yī gè lǎozhě</u> tǎofàn dào tājiā lái le.
　　　'One day, an old man came to her house to beg for food.'

In this example, the "*yi*+CL+NP"-subject sentence is preceded by "一天" ('one day'), an adverbial of time, and ends with "了", a sentence-completing element.

In fact, an adverbial of time or place is often used before the "*yi*+CL+NP"-subject sentence to mark the starting point of a new plot. This kind of occurrence often requires the subject of the subsequent sentence to be coreferential with the preceding "*yi*+CL+NP"-subject, and to be reproduced in the form of a noun (not a pronoun). See 25, where "老人" (lǎorén, 'old man') is a nominal expression.

(25) 一天,<u>一个老者</u>讨饭到她家来了。<u>老人</u>看上去已经很久没有吃东西了,……

Yītiān, <u>yī gè lǎozhě</u> tǎofàn dào tājiā lái le. <u>Lǎorén</u> kànshàngqù yǐjīng hěnjiǔ méiyǒu chī dōngxī le, …

'One day, an old man came to her house to beg for food. The old man seemed to have eaten no food for a long time.'

We have also discovered that the coding form marking the start/end point of a plot is not limited to time or place adverbials that occur at the beginning of the sentence. As a marked syntactic configuration, the so-called "indefinite-subject sentence" can also fulfill the function.

Secondly, "*yi*+CL+NP"-subject sentences can stand alone as independent sentences when occurring in the habitual aspect. Such sentences cannot be transformed into *you*-sentences, as is the case in (18), (19), and (20); when transformed, they would perform a very different function, as illustrated by (23).

Some "*yi*+CL+NP"-subject sentences can be embedded into other sentences, in which case they would resist *you*-transformation even more strongly. See (26), where the said syntactic configuration is a subject clause.

(26) 五次来北京,康有为一共七次上书,请求变法。起初根本没人搭理他。俗话说"人微言轻",<u>一个老百姓</u>想跟皇上说上话太难了。更何况那会儿主事儿的,是光绪皇帝的大姨妈,慈禧太后。重重障碍。康有为除了跟那些权贵,混了个脸儿熟之外,没有任何收获。北京留给他的,除了郁闷,还是郁闷。(*This Is Beijing*)

Wǔ cì lái Běijīng, Kāng Yǒuwéi yīgòng qī cì shàngshū, qǐngqiú biànfǎ. Qǐchū gēnběn méi rén dāli tā. Súhuà shuō "rénwēiyánqīng", <u>yī gè lǎobǎixìng xiǎng gēn huángshàng shuō shàng huà</u> tài nán le. Gèng hékuàng nàhui·er zhǔshì·er de, shì Guāngxù huángdì de dàyímā, Cíxǐ tàihòu. Chóng~chóng zhàng'ài. Kāng Yǒuwéi chúle gēn nàxiē quánguì, hùnle gè liǎn·ershú zhīwài, méiyǒu rènhé shōuhuò. Běijīng liúgěi tā de, chúle yùmèn, háishì yùmèn.

'Kang Youwei came to Beijing five times and wrote seven letters in total to request reform. No one paid any attention to him at first. As the saying goes, "the words of the lowly carry little weight". <u>It is too difficult for an ordinary man to talk to the emperor</u>. What's more, it was Emperor Guangxu's aunt, Empress Dowager Cixi, who was in power at that time. Too many obstacles. Apart from getting familiar with those powerful, Kang Youwei gained nothing. Beijing left him nothing but depression.'

In comparison with adverbial clauses, the "*yi*+CL+NP"-subject sentence, when embedded, is even more unlikely to function as the main clause (see also Fang Mei, 2008, 2018).

You-sentences introduce discourse topics and represent foreground information, but it is not necessarily the case with the so-called "indefinite-subject sentence". Its syntactic status and discourse function are closely related to its position in syntactic integration.

In written narratives, the "indefinite-subject sentence" embodies background information, unless it is preceded by a time or place adverbial to mark a turning point in the plot and accordingly change its background information status.

When it is to express the speaker's assessment that lies outside the event-line or to provide background information, it is mandatory to use "indefinite-subject sentences". And in such circumstances they cannot be transformed into *you*-sentences.

4.6 Summary

The "*yi*+CL+NP" subject in the so-called "indefinite-subject sentence" actually represents two kinds of noun phrases with diametrically different referentiality: specific reference vs. generic reference. The hosting clause of the former reports a specific event and has a temporal structure; that of the latter, by contrast, requires the predicate to occur in the habitual aspect or to be adjectival, not representing the event process. The former is descriptive, and the latter is evaluative. Although previous studies have argued that "indefinite-subject sentences" can be transformed into *you*-sentences, this study has demonstrated that "*yi*+CL+NP"-subject sentences have different discourse functions from *you*-sentences and that they are carriers of different speech acts. Only in very limited circumstances can a "*yi*+CL+NP"-subject sentence be replaced by a *you*-sentence. In narrative discourse, the use of a "*yi*+CL+NP"-subject sentence in the habitual aspect marks the transition from narration to assessment. It is also a means to make the speaker visible. To sum up, the so-called "indefinite-subject sentence" has its specific discourse functions.

Notes

1 Unless otherwise noted, the underlined parts of the examples cited in this chapter are either "indefinite subjects" of the configuration "*yi*+CL+NP" or "indefinite-subject sentences" hosting such subjects. To save space, word-by-word glosses are provided only when absolutely necessary. Translator's note.
2 This observation of Wang (2003) is very accurate, but his paper makes another argument: the indefinite subject sentence provides foreground information. To us, these two points cannot attest to each other. Of the five examples cited in Wang (2003), the indefinite subjects are of different uses although they all represent newly introduced referents. In one example, the indefinite subject contains a relative clause ("一个穿蓝棉衣的黑大个男人" [yī gè chuān lán miányī de hēi dà gè nánrén, 'a big black man that wears a blue cotton coat']); in another example (i.e., his example

[9]), the hosting clause can be interpreted as expressing background information, while the subject of the clause in the foreground is a proper noun ("牟其中", 'Mu Qizhong'); in his example 6, the subject of the indefinite-subject clause is new information and the subject of the subsequent clause is coreferential with it, but again it is not the main focus of discussion.

3 For studies in this line, see Fang Mei and Yue Yao (2017, pp. 1–63).
4 For the usage difference between 如果 (rúguǒ, 'if') and 如果说 (rúguǒshuō, literally 'if say'), see Dong Xiufang (2003a), and Li Jinxia and Liu Yun (2003).
5 As can be seen from the pinyin transcription, "丞相" (chéngxiàng, 'Prime Minister') and "绳匠" (shéngjiàng, 'rope maker') are fairly close in pronunciation. Translator's note.
6 Labov (1972) proposes that narration contains factors of four categories: temporal, descriptial, evaluative and interpersonal, which are presented alternately in discourse. When comparing narration with listing, Schiffrin (1994) proposes that the temporal structure be an important feature of narration.

5 Forms of action reference and their topic function

In Chinese, verb phrases can be used as subjects and objects without changing their syntactic coding to refer to actions. In the meantime, there do exist structures that change their syntactic configurations for the purpose of action reference, such as "N *de* V" in written Chinese. In Beijing dialect, there are two forms of action reference, "*zhe* (S) VP" and "S *zhe* VP", which have different referential properties: the former is for generic reference and the latter is for individual reference. In terms of discourse function, "*zhe* (S) VP" is used to establish a topic whereas "S *zhe* VP" occurs mainly to refer anaphorically to an action of information accessibility in the context. Although the subject can occur in the form of a verb phrase in Chinese, the syntactically transformed subject makes an important contribution to topic establishment and management.

5.1 Introduction

It is well known that verbs in Chinese can play the syntactic roles of subject and object typically fulfilled by nouns without changing their morphosyntactic form; that is, verbs can be used directly in the subject or object position for reference purposes. In the meantime, Chinese does have constructions for action reference by changing the morphosyntactic form of the verb, such as the so-called "N *de* V" construction.

As a matter of fact, "N *de* V" is the most extensively discussed nominalization construction in Chinese. Although grammarians are divided as to whether "N *de* V" is a case of the so-called syntactic operation "nominalization" or not, all agree that as a whole it is a noun phrase that is used for reference (see Fang Mei and Zhu Qingxiang, 2015).

In Chinese, verbs can serve directly as subjects without any syntactic change, but it does not mean that discourse makes no syntactic wrapping for the topical element that refers to an action.

It is known that a concept is understood by the addressee with different levels of difficulty. The difficulty level can be referred to as accessibility, which is stronger when the concept is easy to understand, and weaker when

DOI: 10.4324/9781032700656-5

it is not. The accessibility hierarchy of concepts in discourse can be represented as follows:

personal pronoun > anaphoric noun > stated proposition > situational context > shared knowledge > speech modification

Such a perspective can be used not only to observe the accessibility of nominal concepts, but also to examine the expression and understanding of actions.

The following discussion of action reference in both spoken and written Chinese shows that topic properties have preferential requirements for syntactic forms. The seemingly special syntactic configurations are actually motivated by discourse functions. In terms of structural choice, the establishment of a discourse topic differs from that of a sentence topic which is normally the subject of the sentence.

5.2 Action reference in spoken Chinese and its topic function

5.2.1 Reference form

When demonstrative 这 (zhè, 'this') is used together with a VP for reference, there are two main formats in colloquial Beijing dialect. One is to put 这 directly before the VP or the clause with its subject, to act as subject or object, hereinafter called format A.

Format A: 这 (S) VP

(1) 我怎么不知道?我打小学一年级就开始装病都装到现在啦!**这装病**有几个窍门儿我教给教给你,开始你得假装疼得满地打滚儿…… (*I Love My Family* [《我爱我家》])

Wǒ zěnme bù zhīdào? Wǒ dǎ xiǎoxué yī niánjí jiù kāishǐ <u>zhuāngbìng</u> dōu zhuāng dào xiànzài la! **Zhè zhuāngbìng** yǒu jǐge qiàomén·er wǒ jiàogěi~jiàogěi nǐ, kāishǐ nǐ děi jiǎzhuāng téngde mǎndì dǎgǔn·er…

'How come I don't know? I started <u>pretending to be sick</u> when I was in Grade One and I'm still doing so now! **Pretending to be sick** needs a few tricks that I'll teach you. At first you have to pretend to roll around in pain…'

(2) 结果是,曾国藩诬陷满族官员,<u>削职自省</u>。说到这儿,您还没明白吗。曾国藩这折子,道光皇帝到底看见了没有,别人又在皇帝面前垫了什么话儿,**这处置**又是怎么来的,您就撒开了想去吧。(*This is Beijing* [《这里是北京》])

Jiéguǒ shì, Zēng Guófān wúxiàn mǎnzú guānyuán, <u>xuèzhí zìxǐng</u>. Shuōdào zhè·er, nín hái méi míngbái ma. Zēng Guófān zhè zhézi, Dàoguāng huángdì dàodǐ kànjiànle méiyǒu, biérén yòu zài huángdì miànqián diànle shénme huà·er, **zhè chǔzhì** yòushì zěnme lái de, nín jiù sākāile xiǎngqù ba.

'The result is that Zeng Guofan <u>was deprived of office to introspect</u> for falsely accusing the Manchu officials. Speaking of this, you still don't get it? Had Zeng Guofan's memorial ever reached Emperor Daoguang? What had others said about Zeng in front of the emperor? And how come **this sanction**? You may just use your imagination to answer these questions.'

(3) 衣食住行这四件事,对咱们百姓和对人家皇室完全不一样。今天咱们说"食"。**这吃**在宫廷里可是不那么简单。(*This Is Beijing*)

Yīshízhùxíng zhè sì jiàn shì, duì zánmen bǎixìng hé duì rénjiā huángshì wánquán bù yīyàng. Jīntiān zánmen shuō "shí". **Zhè chī** zài gōngtíng lǐ kěshì bú nàme jiǎndān.

'What the four things, clothing, eating, housing, and transportation, mean for us ordinary people is completely different from that for the imperial family. Let's talk about "eating" today. **This eating** is not so simple in the palace.'

(4) **这头脑有毛病**是不是有遗传啊?咱们换人吧。(*I Love My Family*)

Zhè tóunǎo yǒu máobìng shìbùshì yǒu yíchuán a? Zánmen huàn rén ba.

'Is it hereditary when **the brain has problems**? Let's change the person.'

The second format is to insert 这 between the subject and the predicate to function as subject or object, hereinafter called format B.

Format B: S这VP

(5) 我跟你说,今晚上**中国队这发挥**太失常了。(*I Love My Family*)

Wǒ gēn nǐ shuō, jīn wǎnshàng **Zhōngguódùi zhè fāhuī** tài shīcháng le.

'I'm telling you, **the performance of the Chinese team** was too bad tonight.'

(6) 我就佩服他**这吃**,他可是太能吃了。(*I Love My Family*)

Wǒ jiù pèifú tā **zhè chī**, tā kěshì tài néng chī le.

'I admire him for **his eating**, he is so good at it.'

The question then is whether there are differences in meaning and function between the two reference forms. To us, the major difference between format A and format B is reflected in two aspects, referential property and topic continuity, which are discussed separately below.

5.2.2 *Referential property*

Generic reference means to refer to the category as a whole, without referring to an individual entity in the context, such as "鲸" in 7, "研究生" and "本科生" in 8.

(7) 鲸是哺乳动物。

Jīng	shì	bǔrǔdòngwù.
whale	be	mammal

'Whales are mammals.'

(8) 研究生都很难找到理想的工作,更不用说本科生了。
Yánjiūshēng dōu hěn nán zhǎodào lǐxiǎng de gōngzuò,
graduate.student even very difficult find ideal NM job
gèng bùyòngshuō běnkēshēng le.
still not.to.mention undergraduate student aux.
'It is difficult even for a graduate student to find a good job, let alone an undergraduate.'

Individual reference refers to individual entities, such as "他", "客人" and "一支香烟" in 9 and "门口" and "一辆宝马" in 10.

(9) 他递给客人一支香烟。
Tā dìgěi kèrén yī zhī xiāngyān.
he hand guest one CL cigarette
'He handed the guest a cigarette.'

(10) 门口停着一辆宝马。
Ménkǒu tíngzhe yī liàng bǎomǎ.
door park.DUR one CL BMW
'At the door parked a BMW.'

Like NPs, VPs can also make the distinction between generic vs. individual reference, with the former referring to a category of action and the latter to a specific action. In colloquial Beijing dialect, format A can be used for generic reference, as in examples (1) and (3), or for individual reference, as in examples (2) and (4). Conversely, format B is used only for individual reference, as in examples (5) and (6).

When a VP plus 这 is used for generic reference, it can be referred back to in the form "这种 (zhè zhǒng, 'this kind') + superordinate noun", as illustrated by 11.

(11) 原本是大伙儿受慈禧的牵连,才遭此劫数。最终幸免于难了,却还要山呼着,托老佛爷的福,多亏了老佛爷的庇佑。看来**这口不对心**呐也算是大臣们练就的一种本事了。(*This Is Beijing*)
→看来(口不对心)**这种事儿**呐也算是大臣们练就的一种本事了。

Yuánběn shì dàhuǒ·er shòu Cíxǐ de qiānlián, cái zāo cǐ jiéshù. Zuìzhōng xìngmiǎnyúnànle, què háiyào shānhū zhe, tuō lǎofóyé de fú, duōkuīle lǎofóyé de biyòu. Kànlái **zhè kǒubúduìxīn** na yě suànshì dàchénmen liànjiù de yī zhǒng běnshì le.

→Kànlái (kǒubúduìxīn) **zhè zhǒng shì·er** na yě suànshì dàchénmen liànjiù de yī zhǒng běnshì le.

'Originally, the group was implicated by Cixi and suffered this calamity. But when they finally had a narrow escape, they called all out to thank

Cixi for her Buddha-like blessing. It seems that it was a practiced skill for the ministers to **be not true to their heart**.'

→It seems that **this kind of thing** (as being not true to one's heart) was a skill that the ministers had practiced.'

When it is used for individual reference, this rewriting would be unacceptable for anaphoric use. For instance, both (2') and (5') are inappropriate.

(2') 结果是,曾国藩诬陷满族官员,削职自省。说到这儿,您还没明白吗?曾国藩这折子,道光皇帝到底看见了没有,别人又在皇帝面前垫了什么话儿,**这处置**又是怎么来的,您就撒开了想去吧。

→*(处置)**这种事儿**又是怎么来的,您就撒开了想去吧。

(5') 我跟你说,今晚上中国队这发挥太失常了。

→*我跟你说,今晚上(中国队这发挥)**这种事儿**太失常了。

Nonetheless, 这次 (zhè cì, 'this time') can be used to replace 这 in format A when it is used for individual reference, as in (2″).

(2″) 结果是,曾国藩诬陷满族官员,削职自省。说到这儿,您还没明白吗?曾国藩这折子,道光皇帝到底看见了没有,别人又在皇帝面前垫了什么话儿,**这处置/这次处置**又是怎么来的,您就撒开了想去吧。

It is worth noting that format A can be used for either generic or individual reference. Format B, unlike format A, when used for individual reference, often indicates a specific meaning, a function that is the same as that of 这 when inserted between the possessive modifier and the possessed noun in colloquial Beijing dialect, both of which refer to things at the scene of conversation. See (12) and (13) for illustration.

(12) **我这头**疼得我想死的心都有。

Wǒ zhè tóu téng dé wǒ xiǎng sǐ de xīn dōu yǒu.

'I have a headache that makes me want to die.'

(13) 今儿这肘子啊,差点意思。不是我不成啊,**您这肉**不成。这您家里预备的肉不成。(*The Courtyard of Love* [《情满四合院》])

Jīn·er zhè zhǒuzi a, chà diǎn yìsi. Búshì wǒ bùchéng a, **nín zhè ròu** bùchéng. Zhè nín jiālǐ yùbèi de ròu bùchéng.

'This pork hock today is not so good. It's not that I can't do it well, but that **your meat** is not good. The meat you prepared is no good.'

Therefore, this syntactic means of action reference in colloquial Beijing dialect can be regarded as an analogy of the means of entity reference, which is to be discussed in detail in Section 5.3.

Table 5.1 Referential meaning differences between 这 (S) VP and S (这) VP

	Generic reference	Individual reference
这 (S) VP	+	-
S (这) VP	-	+

In summary, the distribution of the referential meanings of the two formats can be tabulated in Table 5.1.

When Wang Li's *Lectures on the History of the Chinese Language* (《汉语史稿》) (1980), Lü Shuxiang's *Pronouns in Pre-modern Chinese* (《近代汉语指代词》) (1985), Tatsuo Ohta's *A Historical Grammar of Modern Chinese* (《中国语历史文法》) (1958) and *A General Examination of the History of the Chinese Language* (《汉语史通考》) (1988) are referred to, neither of the two formats of action reference introduced above is discussed.

We have also referred to the often-cited literature on colloquial Beijing dialect, such as *A Collection of Chinese Language Characters* (《语言字迹集》), *Yanjing Women's Language* (《燕京妇语》), and *Little E* (《小额》), finding no such formats either. Thus, it can be claimed with some certainty that neither of the two formats of action reference appeared before the nineteenth century. The addition of 这 before or in between the predicate should be a relatively recent phenomenon.

We believe that the main mechanism of attaching 这 to a VP or a clause for action reference is analogy: format A is an analogy of "这+noun" for nominal reference while format B is an analogy of "personal pronoun + demonstrative pronoun + noun".

Format A is parallel to "这+noun" in distribution and function, in that both can serve to establish a topic. Format B is used to refer to an action occurring at the scene of speech or an action described in the preceding context, but is not used to establish discourse topics, which makes it similar in distribution and function to the "personal pronoun + demonstrative pronoun + noun" configuration already existent in the grammar system.

5.3 Topic continuity

When referring to things by nominals, the choice of different forms (e.g. pronoun or noun, bare noun or noun phrase, general modifying construction or relative clause) depends on the discourse needs. Similarly, when referring to an action, the different forms also reflect the relationship between the action referred to and the action(s) already described in the context.

5.3.1 *Referential property*

In terms of context dependency, there are basically two types of action reference formed by the addition of 这: exophoric reference and endophoric reference.

5.3.1.1 Exophoric reference

Exophoric reference is used to refer directly to an act at the speech scene. See (14) and (15) for illustration.

(14) A: 总让您一趟一趟跑怪不落忍的。
B: **我这还钱**不也是应该的嘛!
A: Zǒng ràng nín yī tàng yī tàng pǎo guài bùlàorěn de.
B: **Wǒ zhè huái qián** bù yěshì yīnggāi de ma!
'A: It's not easy for you to make the trip again and again.
B: It's my duty to **pay back the money**!'

(15) 我都上车了, **你这不拉我**是不是拒载啊!
Wǒ dōu shàngchē le, **nǐ zhè bù lā wǒ** shìbushì jùzài a!
'I'm already in your car. If **you don't carry me**, isn't it ignoring the passenger!'

In this kind of usage, the act described by the post-这 verb has not appeared in the previous context, but it is what actually happens at the scene of the conversation.

It is worth noting that topics of "S这VP" format can be referred to anaphorically by way of demonstrative 这, such as in (16).

(16) 秦淮茹,冷静啊,咱冷静冷静,不能这么着。**你这半夜三更打架**,这真快离了婚了这个,我跟你说呀。(*The Courtyard of Love*)
Qín Huáirú, lěngjìng a, zán lěngjìng~lěngjìng, bùnéng zhème zhe. **Nǐ zhè bànyèsāngēng dǎjià**, zhè zhēn kuài líle hūn le zhège, wǒ gēn nǐ shuō ya.
'Qin Huairu, calm down, let's calm down. You can't do this. **You're fighting in the middle of the night**, and **this** is really close to divorce, I'm telling you.'

In the example above, "半夜三更打架" ('fighting in the middle of the night') is a statement of what is going on at the scene of speech, but "你这半夜三更打架" is a case of reference, which is anaphorically referred to with "这' in the ensuing clause.

5.3.1.2 Endophoric reference

Endophoric reference consists of two subcategories: one refers back to an act discussed in previous discourse, and the other to an act associated with one discussed in previous discourse.

1) Anaphoric reference, which can be achieved by attaching 这 to the same verb as occurred in previous discourse.

(17) A: 过去这个想法就不对,净想发财,这叫什么思想呢!
　　B: 就是嘛!
　　A: 发财的思想我可没有。
　　B: 你比他们强。
　　A: 提起**这发财**来有个笑话。(from a crosstalk)

　　A: Guòqù zhège xiǎngfǎ jiù búduì, jìng xiǎng <u>fācái</u>, zhè jiào shénme sīxiǎng ne!
　　B: Jiùshì ma!
　　A: Fācái de sīxiǎng wǒ kě méiyǒu.
　　B: Nǐ bǐ tāmen qiáng.
　　A: Tíqǐ **zhè fācái** lái yǒu gè xiàohuà.

　　'A: It was not right to think that way in the past. Only wanting to <u>make a fortune</u>. What kind of thinking was that?
　　B: That's right!
　　A: The idea of making a fortune, I don't have.
　　B: You are better than them.
　　A: Speaking of **making a fortune**, there is a joke about it.'

(18) 你瞧<u>你生什么气</u>呀,**这生气**能管什么用啊……(*The Courtyard of Love*)
　　Nǐ qiáo <u>nǐ shēng-shénme-qì</u> ya, **zhè shēngqì** néng guǎn shénme yòng a...
　　'Look, why <u>are you getting angry</u>? Any use in **getting angry**?...'

In this kind of usage, the verb post 这 has already occurred in previous discourse, and the verb for anaphoric use can take the same form as the verb that has already appeared in previous discourse, as in example (17), or it can take partially the same form, as in example (18). "这+verb", like "这+noun", also exhibits topic continuity.

2) Associative reference. The verb that follows 这 does not appear in previous discourse, but the act to which the verb refers has been implied already. See (19).

(19) 康六:<u>宫里当差的人家谁要个乡下丫头</u>?
　　刘麻子:这不你女儿命好吗?
　　康六:谁呀?
　　刘麻子:大太监,庞总管!你也听说过庞总管吧?伺候着太后,红得不得了哇!人家家里头,打醋那瓶子都是玛瑙的!
　　康六:**这要孩子给太监做老婆**,我怎么对得起女儿呀? (Lao She, *Teahouse* [《茶馆》])

　　Kāng Liù: <u>Gōng lǐ dāngchāide rénjiā shéi yào gè xiāngxià yātou</u>?
　　Liú Mázi: Zhè bù nǐ nǚ'ér mìng hǎo ma?

Kāng Liù: Shéi ya?

Liú Mázi: Dà tàijiàn, Páng zǒngguǎn! Nǐ yě tīngshuōguò Páng zǒngguǎn ba? Cìhòuzhe tàihòu, hóng de bùdeliǎo wa! Rénjiā jiālǐtou, dǎ cù nà píngzi dōushì mǎnǎo de!

Kāng Liù: **Zhè yào háizi gěi tàijiàn zuò lǎopó**, wǒ zěnme duìdeqǐ nǚ'ér ya?

'Kang Liu: Who working in the palace would want to marry a country maid?

Pockmark Liu: It's your daughter's good fortune, isn't it?

Kang Liu: Who is that?

Pockmark Liu: The eunuch, Chief Steward Pang! You've heard of him, right? Serving the Empress Dowager, very popular! In his household, the bottle of vinegar is made of onyx!

Kang Liu: **Asking my daughter to be a eunuch's wife**, how can I face her?'

In the example above, "要孩子给太监做老婆" is associated with the aforementioned "宫里当差的人家谁要个乡下丫头", but takes only a different orientation of narration: the early occurring one is from the male's orientation, while the later occurring takes the female's orientation in the event of marriage. In terms of information status, "要孩子给太监做老婆" belongs to the category of activatable information. See (20) for another example.

(20) A: 您说您这一下午嗑那么些瓜子儿您不怕咸着啊?

B: <u>抽烟不咸你们让我抽吗</u>?志新呐,你那儿还有没有富余的香烟呐?上次我给你的那包云烟,你看现在,真家里没有人,天知地知你知我知......

A: 破坏**您这戒烟**这责任我可担当不起。(*I Love My Family*)

A: Nín shuō nín zhè yī xiàwǔ kè nàme xiē guāzǐ·er nín búpà xiánzhe a?

B: <u>Chōuyān bù xián nǐmen ràng wǒ chōu ma</u>? Zhìxīn na, nǐ nà·er hái yǒu-méiyǒu fùyú de xiāngyān na? Shàngcì wǒ gěi nǐ de nà bāo yúnyān, nǐ kàn xiànzài, zhēn jiālǐ méiyǒu rén, tiān zhī dì zhī nǐ zhī wǒ zhī...

A: Pòhuài **nín zhè jièyān** zhè zérèn wǒ kě dāndāng bùqǐ.

'A: You've been cracking sunflower seeds the whole afternoon. Don't you feel salty?

B: <u>Smoking is not salty, but would you allow me to smoke</u>? Zhixin, still have spare cigarettes there? That pack of Yunyan cigarettes I gave you last time. You see now, really no one's at home, only God and you and I know...

A: Disrupting **your effort to quit smoking**, I can't shoulder the responsibility.'

Table 5.2 Distribution of different referential formats in discourse

	这(S)VP	S这VP
On-site & first occurrence	+	+
Off-site & first occurrence	+	(+)
Verb in fully or partially identical form with statement	+	+
Associated with known concepts or shared knowledge	+	+

Although "戒烟" does not occur directly in the preceding utterances in 20, speaker B's rhetorical question implies that he is restricted from smoking. Therefore, in terms of information status, "戒烟" is also activatable information.

5.3.2 *Discourse distribution*

The distribution of format A "这(S)VP" and format B "S这VP" in discourse can be summarized in Table 5.2.

Obviously, the difference in the position of 这 attests to the status difference of the action referred to in discourse. Comparatively speaking, format B with embedded 这 is more context-dependent than format A with 这 preceding (S) VP, in that format B requires that the referent act occur in the speech scene or is already mentioned in previous discourse.

The verb in format A can be identical with what has occurred in the preceding discourse, as in examples 1 and 11, or partially identical, as in example 18, both of which can be regarded as anaphoric. The verb can also denote knowledge associated with the earlier discourse, as in example 21, or it can be an act that has not been stated in the preceding conversation, as in example 4. Format B, by contrast, when appearing for the first time, has to satisfy the condition that the act has actually occurred at the scene of speech. The "(+)" in the above table indicates that the distribution is relatively rare. In fact, we find only one case of it, i.e., example 28 below.

Format A, which is anaphoric in reference, has the effect of marking a statement as the topic, as in 17 and 18 above. When 这 is not used in such examples, they can be interpreted as a subsequent act or a conditional clause. When 这 is added, topicality is highlighted, and "这+VP" as a whole establishes its topic status.

Format A can also be used for the first mention of a certain type of action. See (21).

(21) 看我说什么来着,**这妈把傻爸推出去**,有人正巴不得呢。这回好了,咱妈做了一件全天下最傻的事儿。(*The Courtyard of Love*)

Kàn wǒ shuō shénme láizhe, **zhè mā bǎ shǎ bà tuī chūqù**, yǒurén zhèng bābudé ne. Zhèhuí hǎo le, zán mā zuòle yī jiàn quán tiānxià zuì shǎ de shì·er.

'See what I've said, **mom has pushed Stupid Dad out**, and someone is just dying for it. This time, our mom has done the stupidest thing in the world.'

In the above example, the clause under examination would still be acceptable without "这" at the beginning of it. When "这" is used, it is to highlight the topic status of "妈把傻爸推出去", so as to make the following comment ("咱妈做了一件全天下最傻的事儿") on this act of the mother.

As illustrated in (21), there can be a pause after "这(S)VP", to make it topical. Moreover, 这 can also be added to precede a conditional clause, wrapping it up as a topic, as in (22) and (23).

(22) 槐花:三大爷爷, 要照您这么说, **这女人要是嫁给哪个男人**, 她就像哪个男人啊?

三大爷:那是, 这就叫潜移默化。(*The Courtyard of Love*)

Huáihuā: Sāndàyéyé, yào zhào nín zhème shuō, **zhè nǚrén yàoshi jiàgěi năge nánrén**, tā jiù xiàng năge nánrén a?

Sāndàye: Nàshì, zhè jiù jiào qiányímòhuà.

'Huaihua: Grandpa Three, according to what you've said, **if a woman marries a man**, she will be like the man ah?

Grandpa Three: Of course, it's called subliminal transformation.'

(23) 工作是开玩笑的事情吗?投资这么大, 你以为钱是用气吹来的吗?你不来, **这菜品马上下来了**, 客人怎么说, 没有客人来怎么办? (*The Courtyard of Love*)

Gōngzuò shì kāiwánxiào de shìqíng ma? Tóuzī zhème dà, nǐ yǐwéi qián shì yòng qì chuī lái de ma? Nǐ bù lái, **zhè càipǐn mǎshàng xiàláile**, kèrén zěnme shuō, méiyǒu kèrén lái zěnme bàn?

'Is work a matter of joking? The investment is so big, do you think the money is blown in by the air? When you do not come, **the quality of the dishes immediately drops**. What do the guests say? What if no guests come?'

This type of "这SVP" makes up the clausal topic, and the subsequent comment can be a single clause, as in (22), or a series of clauses, as in (23).

The usage discussed above is parallel to nominal topics that express new information in colloquial Beijing dialect, in that both contribute to topic establishment.

这 in colloquial Beijing dialect can be used as a topic marker, introducing NPs that express new information and in the meantime making such new information "like" old information (see Fang Mei, 2002).

(24) 你知道吗, 就**这外国人**呐说话都跟感冒了似的, 没四声。

Nǐ zhīdào ma, jiù **zhè wàiguórén** na shuōhuà dōu gēn gǎnmàole shì de, méi sì shēng.

'You know, **foreigners speak Chinese** as if they have a cold, (because they speak) without the falling tone.'

When referring to things, different nominal forms often reflect different referential properties (Chen Ping, 1987a). In Chinese, a bare noun may be nonreferential, i.e., without referring to any entity in the context, such as "食堂" ('canteen') in "我习惯吃食堂" (wǒ xíguàn chī shítáng, 'I am used to eating at the canteen.'). It may also be referential, referring to an entity in the context, such as "食堂" in "我在去图书馆的路上看到一个食堂" (wǒ zài qù túshūguǎn de lùshàng kàndào yī gè shítáng, 'I saw a canteen on my way to the library.'). Still, it can be used for definite reference, such as "食堂" in "今天食堂有节日加餐" (jīntiān shítáng yǒu jiērì jiācān, 'There is an extra dish for holiday in the canteen today.'). It may be generic in reference as well, such as "食堂" in "食堂也就是个让人填饱肚子的地方, 怎么能满足特色口味呢?" (shítáng yějiù shì gè ràng rén tiánbǎo dùzi de dìfāng, zěnme néng mǎnzú tèsè kǒuwèi ne? 'The canteen is no more than a place to fill your stomach; how can it satisfy special tastes?').

When (24) is concerned, removal of "这" does not change the generic referencing feature of "外国人", as in (25).

(25) 你知道吗, 就**外国人**呐说话都跟感冒了似的, 没四声。

It seems that 这 plays a role greater than securing the generic reference property. We would argue that it is mainly used for topic establishment. As a form of reference, it is necessary to satisfy the need for discourse coherence and topic continuity. 这 has a strong function of topic continuation, so it can be used to package a brand new concept as one of definite reference (Fang Mei, 2002).

Format B "S这VP" is more context-dependent, and mostly used to refer to an act that occurs in the speech scene or one that has been described in the previous context. There is only one case in our corpora where format B is used to refer to an action that appears for the first time.

(26) 重要的在于参与啊, 还有三等奖, 三等奖, 三等奖也非同小可, 香港七日游。这还真麻烦, 麻烦啦, 麻烦了, 还得现学广东话。你到了香港, 像**我嫂子这跑丢了**, 跟香港警察叔叔你说不清楚。(*I Love My Family*)

Zhòngyào de zàiyú cānyù a, háiyǒu sānděngjiǎng, sānděngjiǎng, sānděngjiǎng yě fēitóngxiǎokě, Xiānggǎng qī rì yóu. Zhè hái zhēn máfan, máfan la, máfan le, hái děi xiàn xué guǎngdōnghuà. Nǐ dào le Xiānggǎng, xiàng **wǒ sǎozi zhè pǎo diū le**, gēn Xiānggǎng jǐngchá shūshu nǐ shuō-bu-qīngchǔ.

'What matters is participation, and there is the third prize. The third prize, the third prize is also non-trivial, a seven-day trip to Hong Kong. But it is really troublesome, troublesome, troublesome, (because you'll) have to learn Cantonese now. When you get to Hong Kong, say **my sister-in-law gets lost**, you wouldn't be able to tell (what the matter is) clearly to the Hong Kong police.'

Unlike format A, format B here codes no more than trivial information, though it is mentioned for the first time in discourse. Such information will not be tracked in subsequent discourse; neither does it occur to establish a topic.

Format B is parallel in distribution and function to "personal pronoun + demonstrative pronoun + noun", such as "我这胳臂" (wǒ zhè gēbì, 'this arm of mine'), a configuration already existent in the grammar system, which is also used to refer to something that is available at the speech scene or to keep track of something that has been mentioned in the previous context, but not to establish a topic.

5.3.3 Commonalities with topic NPs

Format A is used for action reference, which is an analog of NPs referring to entities. There is consistency between the two in terms of referential property, discourse distribution, and function.

First, 这 occurs before VP or NP, which gives parallelism to the discourse distribution of these two types of reference forms (Table 5.3).

In terms of referential properties, as with pre-NP 这, "这+(S)VP" can be used for individual reference (e.g., example [21]) or generic reference (e.g., example [11]). See Table 5.4 for summary.

The consistency in referential property and discourse function can be used as evidence for analogy in the synchronic system of the Chinese language. When historical materials are referred to, the early format for individual reference is "这+一+VP", rather than "这+ (S)VP".

Table 5.3 Discourse distribution of 这 in front of VP and NP

	这+(S)VP	这+NP
On-site & first occurrence	+	+
Off-site & first occurrence	+	+
Fully or partially identical form with statement	+	+
Associated with known concepts or shared knowledge	+	+

Table 5.4 Referential property of 这 before VP and NP

	individual reference	generic reference
这+NP	+	+
这+(S)VP	+	+

(27) ......那知道钱能通神,这个姓王的,又请喽一个律师,不是怎么啾咕的,会又**发回原审**啦。**这一发回原审**,又不定得多会儿才能完呢,你说这事多们麻烦,够多们教人可气呀!(*Pekingese Conversation* [《京语会话》])¹

Nà zhīdào qián néng tōng shén, zhège xìng Wáng de, yòu qǐng lou yī gè lǜshī, búshì zěnme dígū de, huì yòu fā huí yuánshěn la. **Zhè yī fā huí yuánshěn**, yòu búdìng děi duōhui·er cáinéng wán ne, nǐ shuō zhè shì duōmen máfan, gòu duōmen jiào rén kěqì ya!

'... Who knows that money can be a master of God? This Wang hired another lawyer. I don't know how they plotted, the case has been sent back to the original judge. **Once the case is sent back to the original judge**, no one can tell how much more time it will take. You see how troublesome it is, how irritating!'

(28) **胎里坏告辞**,额大奶奶又说了这个好话。胎里坏连说,应当尽心,同着李顺笑嘻嘻的去了。**胎里坏这一去**,应了一句俗语儿啦,真是羊肉包子打狗,从此就永不回头了。(*Little E* [《小额》])

Tāilǐhuài gàocí, É dà nǎinai yòu shuōle xiēge hǎohuà. Tāilǐhuài lián shuō, yīngdāng jìnxīn, tóngzhe Lǐ Shùn xiàoxīxī de qùle. **Tāilǐhuài zhè yī qù**, yīngle yī jù súyǔ·er la, zhēnshi yángròu bāozi dǎ gǒu, cóngcǐ jiù yǒng bù huítóu le.

'When Born Bad took leave, Grandma E said some more good words. Born Bad responded that he would do his best, and went away with Li Shun all smiling. **Born Bad's leaving** fits the saying perfectly: Hit a dog with a mutton bun, and there is no return.'

In terms of distribution, however, "这+一+VP" is mostly used as an adverbial of time or condition, a usage that has continued to this day and is fairly distant from "这+(S)VP" in contemporary colloquial Beijing dialect. Therefore, we tend to argue that "这+(S)VP" is derived from the noun phrase "这+NP" by means of analogy.

5.4 Topic function of "N *de* V"² in written Chinese

The most well-discussed nominalization construction in Chinese is "N *de* V", which is commonly seen in the written variety.

(29) 据阿Q说,他的回来,似乎也由于不满意城里人。(Lu Xun, *The True Story of Ah Q* [《阿Q正传》])

Jù Ā Q shuō, tā de huílái, sìhū yě yóuyú bù mǎnyì chénglǐrén.

'According to Ah Q, it seems that his return was also due to his dissatisfaction with the city dwellers.'

(30) 你实在是邋遢,头发乱如茅草,胡子不刮,衣服发皱,但现在你是名人,名人的不修边幅是别一种的潇洒呀! (Jia Pingwa, *Celebrities* [《名人》])

Nǐ shízài shì lātà, tóufà luàn rú máocǎo, húzi bù guā, yīfú fā zhòu, dàn xiànzài nǐ shì míngrén, míngrén de bùxiūbiānfú shì bié yī zhǒng de xiāosǎ ya!

'You are really unkempt, your hair as messy as thatch, your beard unshaven, your clothes wrinkled. But now you are a celebrity, and the unkemptness of a celebrity is a different kind of dashing!'

Zhan Weidong (1998) has found that the "N *de* V" construction is mainly used to refer to an event that has already happened, or to a previous statement. "N *de* V"s of modifier-head configuration, when functioning as subjects, all refer anaphorically to earlier discourse. When they are used as objects, 20 out of 59 instantiations are of definite anaphoric reference, and the non-anaphoric uses are not strictly new information from the communicative point of view.

Zhan's findings suggest that the occurrence of "N *de* V" requires a certain context. Our investigation also reveals that "N *de* V" is characterized by high accessibility in terms of referential property, which is evidenced by the following:

1) the verb in "N *de* V" has already appeared as a predicate in the preceding context, which renders it no new information;
2) the verb does not appear directly in the prior context, but is related to a certain concept in the prior context.

In what follows, the instantiations of "N *de* V" as discussed in earlier studies are reexamined in their respective hosting discourse to see how it is used.

5.4.1 *"N* de *V" preceded by a topic sentence*

The "N *de* V" structure is preceded by a topic sentence, which introduces the theme of the discourse, such as (31).

(31) **我要离开吉兆胡同**，在这里是异样的空虚和寂寞。我想，只要离开这里，子君便如还在我的身边；至少，也如还在城中，有一天，将要出乎意表地访我，像住在会馆时候似的。

然而一切请托和书信，都是一无反响；我不得已，只好访问一个久不问候的世交去了。他是我伯父的幼年的同窗，以正经出名的拔贡，寓京很久，交游也广阔的。

(10个自然段)

我的离开吉兆胡同，也不单是为了房主人们和他家女工的冷眼，大半就为着这阿随。(Lu Xun, *Sadness* [《伤逝》])

Wǒ yào líkāi Jízhào hútòng, zài zhèlǐ shì yìyàng de kōngxū hé jìmò. Wǒ xiǎng, zhǐyào líkāi zhèlǐ, Zijūn biàn rú hái zài wǒ de shēnbiān; zhìshǎo, yě rú hái zài chéngzhōng, yǒuyītiān, jiāngyào chūhūyìbiǎo de fǎng wǒ, xiàng zhù zài huìguǎn shíhòu shìde.

Rán'ér yīqiè qǐngtuō hé shūxìn, dōushì yīwúfǎnxiǎng; wǒ bùdéyǐ, zhǐhǎo fǎngwèn yī gè jiǔ bù wènhòu de shìjiāo qùle. Tā shì wǒ bófù de yòunián de tóngchuāng, yǐ zhèngjǐng chūmíng de bágòng, yù jīng hěnjiǔ, jiāoyóu yě guǎngkuò de.

(10 gè zìrán duàn)

Wǒ de líkāi Jízhào hútòng, yě bùdān shì wèile fángzhǔ rénmen hé tā jiā nǚgōng de lěngyǎn, dàbàn jiù wèizhe zhè Ā Suí.

'**I wanted to leave Jizhao Hutong**, which was a strange emptiness and loneliness to me. As soon as I left here, I thought, Zijun would still be with me. At least, she would seem to be still be in the city, and one day she would pay me an unexpected visit, as she had done when she lived in the Hall.

However, none of my requests and letters was answered. I had no choice but to visit a long-lost family friend. He was my uncle's classmate in his childhood, and was known for being a decent scholar. He had lived in Beijing for a long time, with a wide range of contacts.

(ten paragraphs omitted)

My leaving Jizhao Hutong was not only because of the cold eyes of the house owners and their female workers, but mostly because of this Ah Sui.'

In example (31), the "N *de* V" structure appears after the topic sentence "我要离开吉兆胡同" ('I wanted to leave Jizhao Hutong') in the preceding context. The use of "N *de* V" changes a central event from a statement to a referent, thus establishing the event as a topic in discourse.

In "N *de* V", the semantic relationship between the noun and the verb can be agent-action, as in (31), where it is "I" that "wanted to leave Jizhao Hutong", or patient-action, such as in "这个问题的提出" in (32), where "the question" is the patient of the act "raise". In either case, "N *de* V" refers to the central discourse event.

(32) **这个问题的提出**，远在作品发表不久的一九二六年。这年十一月六日出版的《文学周报》上，发表了西谛的文章《呐喊》，提出"**像阿Q那样的一个人，终于要做起革命党来**，终于受到那样大团圆的结局，似乎连作者他自己在最初写作时也是料不到的。至少在人格上似乎是两个"。对此，鲁迅在同年十二月写的《阿Q正传的成因》中作了回答。他说："据我的意思，**中国倘不革命，阿Q便不做，既然革命，就会做的**。我的阿Q的命运，也只能如此，人格也恐怕并不是两个。"这话说得很明确，也很肯定，但问题并没有解决，或者说没有被人们接受和理解。到五、六十年代，阿Q典型的问题又引起了争论。在讨论中，理论家们仍在"试图回答为什么阿Q是个农民但阿Q精神胜利法却是一种消极的可耻的现象这样一个难题"（何其芳：《文学艺术的春天·序》)这就是说，阿Q是个农民，受尽了压迫和凌辱，**他的要求革命**是理所当然的，但为什么又有那么严重落后的精神胜利法呢？反过来说，既然有那么严重落后的精神胜利法，还能要求革命么？问题似乎仍在三十年前原来的地方漫步。 (Qu Zhengping, *On the Characters in Lu Xun's Novels* [《论鲁迅小说中的人物》])

Zhège wèntí de tíchū, yuǎn zài zuòpǐn fābiǎo bùjiǔ de yījiǔ'èrliù nián. Zhè nián shíyī yuè liù rì chūbǎn de "Wénxué Zhōubào" shàng, fābiǎole Xī Dì de wénzhāng "Nàhǎn", tíchū **"xiàng Ā Q nàyàng de yī gè rén, zhōngyú yào zuòqǐ gémìng dǎng lái,** zhōngyú shòudào nàyàng dà tuányuán de jiéjú, sìhū lián zuòzhě tā zìjǐ zài zuìchū xiězuò shí yěshì liào bù dào de. Zhìshǎo zài réngé shàng sìhū shì liǎng gè". Duì cǐ, Lǔ Xùn zài tóngnián shí'èr yuè xiě de "Ā Q Zhèngzhuàn de Chéngyīn" zhōng zuòle huídá. Tā shuō: "Jù wǒ de yìsi, **Zhōngguó tǎng bù gémìng, Ā Q biàn bù zuò, jìrán gémìng, jiù huì zuò de.** Wǒ de Ā Q de mìngyùn, yě zhǐnéng rúcǐ, réngé yě kǒngpà bìng bùshì liǎng gè." Zhè huà shuōde hěn míngquè, yě hěn kěndìng, dàn wèntí bìng méiyǒu jiějué, huòzhě shuō méiyǒu bèi rénmen jiēshòu hé lǐjiě. Dào wǔ(,)liùshí niándài, Ā Q diǎnxíng de wèntí yòu yǐnqǐle zhēnglùn. Zài tǎolùn zhōng, lǐlùnjiāmen réng zài "shìtú huídá wèishénme Ā Q shìgè nóngmín dàn Ā Q jīngshén shènglì fǎ què shì yī zhǒng xiāojí de kěchǐ de xiànxiàng zhèyàng yī gè nántí". (Hé Qífāng: Wénxué Yìshù de Chūntiān·Xù) Zhè jiùshì shuō, Ā Q shì gè nóngmín, shòujǐnle yāpò hé língrù, **tā de yāoqiú gémìng** shì lǐsuǒdāngrán de, dàn wèishénme yòu yǒu nàme yánzhòng luòhòu de jīngshén shènglì fǎ ne? Fǎnguòlái shuō, jìrán yǒu nàme yánzhòng luòhòu de jīngshén shènglì fǎ, hái néng yāoqiú gémìng me? Wèntí sìhū réng zài sānshí nián qián yuánlái de dìfāng mànbù.

'**The raise of this question** was as early as 1926, shortly after the publication of the work. In Literary Weekly issued on November 6 of that year, an article entitled "Call to Arms" by Xi Di was published, suggesting that **"a man like Ah Q, who finally became a revolutionary party member** and finally received such a happy ending, seemed to be unexpected even by the author himself when he first wrote. It seems that even the author himself could not have expected this kind of happy ending when he first wrote it. At least in terms of personality, it seems that there were two Ah Q." To this, Lu Xun made a reply in "The Genesis of Ah Q" written in December of the same year. He said, "According to me, **if China had not been revolutionary, Ah Q would not have done it, but since it was revolutionary, he would.** This is the fate of my Ah Q. And I am afraid that there are not two personalities." These words were clear and unambiguous, but the problem was not solved, or the reply was not accepted or understood. By the 1950s and 1960s, the question of Ah Q's archetype was debated again. In the debate, theorists were still "trying to answer the difficult question of why the peasant Ah Q could embrace the negative and shameful spiritual triumph (He Qifang, *The Spring of Literature and Art* – Preface). That is, Ah Q, as a peasant, suffered a lot of oppression and humiliation, which justified **his demand for revolution**. But why was there such a serious backwardness his spiritual triumph? Conversely, since there was such a seriously backward method of spiritual triumph, would one still ask for revolution? It seemed that the problem was still strolling in the same place as it had been thirty years before.'

112 *Forms of action reference and their topic function*

In the above example, "Ah Q wanted a revolution" is the core event of the entire paragraph. The "N *de* V" construction "他的要求革命" ('his demand for revolution') has as its antecedent the forerunning proposition that Ah Q wanted to join the revolutionary party, where this demand is made known information.

5.4.2 *Antecedent being a high transitive clause*

As we know, the main event is presented in discourse as foreground information, which is featured by high transitivity.

(33) 但未庄也不能说是无改革。几天之后,**将辫子盘在顶上的**逐渐增加起来了,早经说过,最先自然是茂才公,其次便是赵司晨和赵白眼,后来是阿Q。倘在夏天,**大家将辫子盘在头顶上**或者打一个结,本不算什么稀奇事,但现在是暮秋,所以这"秋行夏令"的情形,在盘辫家不能不说是万分的英断,而在未庄也不能说无关于改革了。
   ……
   阿Q听到了很羡慕。他虽然早知道**秀才盘辫的大新闻**,但总没有想到自己可以照样做,现在看见赵司晨也如此,才有了学样的意思,定下实行的决心。**他用一支竹筷将辫子盘在头顶上**,迟疑多时,这才放胆的走去。
   ……(11段)
   ……他对于**自己的盘辫子**,仿佛也觉得无意味,要侮蔑;为报仇起见,很想立刻放下辫子来,但也没有竟放。…… (Lu Xun, *The True Story of Ah Q*)

Dàn Wèizhuāng yě bùnéng shuō shì wú gǎigé. Jǐ tiān zhīhòu, **jiāng biànzi pán zài dǐng shàng de** zhújiàn zēngjiā qǐlái le, zǎojīng shuōguò, zuì xiān zìrán shì Màocái gōng, qícì biàn shì Zhào Sīchén hé Zhào Báiyǎn, hòulái shì Ā Q. Tǎng zài xiàtiān, **dàjiā jiāng biànzi pán zài tóudǐng shàng huòzhě dǎ yī gè jié**, běn bù suàn shénme xīqí shì, dàn xiànzài shì mùqiū, suǒyǐ zhè "qiū xíng xià lìng" de qíngxíng, zài pán biàn jiā bùnéng bù shuō shì wànfēn de yīngduàn, ér zài Wèi zhuāng yě bùnéng shuō wú guānyú gǎigé le.
   …
   Ā Q tīngdàole hěn xiànmù. Tā suīrán zǎo zhīdào **xiùcái pán biàn de dà xīnwén**, dàn zǒng méiyǒu xiǎngdào zìjǐ kěyǐ zhàoyàng zuò, xiànzài kànjiàn Zhào Sīchén yě rúcǐ, cái yǒule xué yàng de yìsi, dìng xià shíxíng de juéxīn. **Tā yòng yī zhī zhú kuài jiāng biànzi pán zài tóudǐng shàng**, chíyí duōshí, zhè cái fàngdǎn de zǒu qù.…
   (11 duàn)
   … Tā duìyú **zìjǐ de pán biànzi**, fǎngfú yě juédé wú yìwèi, yào wǔmiè; wèi bàochóu qǐjiàn, hěn xiǎng lìkè fàngxià biànzi lái, dàn yě méiyǒu jìng fàng.…

'But it could not be said that there was no reform at Wei Village. A few days later, there were more people **who coiled their braids on top of the**

head. As mentioned earlier, the first one was Maocai, the scholar, followed by Zhao Sichen and Zhao Baiye, and later by Ah Q. If in summer, it would not be unusual **for people to coil their braids on top of their heads or tie a knot**, but now it was late autumn. So this "observing summer practices in autumn" was no less than a wise decision on the part of the braid-coiling practitioners, and a manifestation of reform at Wei Village.

...

Ah Q was very envious of this deed. Although he had learned **the big news of the scholar's coiling his braid**, it never occurred to him that he himself could follow suit. See Zhao Sichen had done so, he came up with the idea and decided to practice it as well. **He used a bamboo chopstick to coil his braid on top of his head**, and hesitated a long while before he boldly went out....

(11 paragraphs omitted)

... As for **his coiling of the braid**, he felt as if it was meaningless and insulting. He wanted to put down his braid immediately for revenge, but he did not do so in any case....'

In 33 above, the whole excerpt is devoted to a novel phenomenon, coiling the braid, which, as the central event, occurs in this part in different forms: "将辫子盘在顶上的" ('who coiled their braids on top of the head') refers to people; "大家将辫子盘在头顶上" ('for people to coil their braids on top of their heads or tie a knot') is a high-transitivity clause; then it occurs as a noun modifier in "秀才盘辫的大新闻" ('the big news of the scholar's coiling his braid'); next is another high-transitivity clause "他用一支竹筷将辫子盘在头顶上" ('He used a bamboo chopstick to coil his braid on top of his head,'); and in its final occurrence, it takes the form of "N *de* V" preceded the topic introducing preposition "对于" ('as for').

5.4.3 *Association by way of shared knowledge*

Some instantiations of "N *de* V" do not have the verb occur in the preceding text. Instead, they are associated with the topic sentence by way of shared knowledge, which renders the referent accessible.

(34) **你成了名人,你的一切令人们都刮目相看**。你本来是很丑的,但总有人在你的丑貌里寻出美的部分。
比如你的眼睛没有双眼皮,缺乏光彩,总是灰浊,而"单眼皮是人类进化的特征呀",灰浊是你熬夜的结果呀!
......
于是你又有了通宵工作的佳话,甚至还会有那长河中的轮船以你那长夜不熄的窗灯作航示灯的故事。
你实在是邋遢,头发乱如茅草,胡子不刮,衣服发皱,但现在你是名人,**名人的不修边幅**是别一种的潇洒呀! (Jia Pingwa, *Celebrities*)

Nǐ chéngle míngrén, nǐ de yīqiè lìng rénmen dōu guāmùxiāngkàn. Nǐ běnlái shì hěn chǒu de, dàn zǒng yǒurén zài nǐ de chǒu mào lǐ xún chū měi de bùfèn.

Bǐrú nǐ de yǎnjīng méiyǒu shuāngyǎnpí, quēfá guāngcǎi, zǒngshì huī zhuó, ér "dānyǎnpí shì rénlèi jìnhuà de tèzhēng ya", huī zhuó shì nǐ áoyè de jiéguǒ ya!

……

Yúshì nǐ yòu yǒule tōngxiāo gōngzuò de jiāhuà, shènzhì hái huì yǒu nà chánghé zhōng de lúnchuán yǐ nǐ nà chángyè bù xī de chuāng dēng zuò hángshìdēng de gùshì.

Nǐ shízài shì lātà, tóufǎ luàn rú máocǎo, húzi bù guā, yīfú fā zhòu, dàn xiànzài nǐ shì míngrén, **míngrén de bùxiūbiānfú** shì bié yī zhǒng de xiāosǎ ya!

'**You have become a celebrity, and people are impressed by everything about you**. You are ugly, but someone can always find the beauty in your ugly appearance.

For example, your eyes do not have double eyelids, and lack luster, always looking grayish, but people would say, "Single eyelid is a feature of human evolution," and (your eyes looking) grayish is the result of your staying up late at night!

……

Then you have a good story of working all night; even the ships in the long river would take your window lamp as their navigation light.

You are really unkempt, your hair as messy as thatch, your beard unshaven, your clothes wrinkled. But now you are a celebrity, and **the unkemptness of a celebrity** is a different kind of dashing!'

In example 34 above, the topic sentence "你成了名人" ('You have become a celebrity,') is followed by several paragraphs describing what happens when one become a celebrity. The "V *de* N" construction "名人的不修边幅" is licensed by the context of the central event "becoming a celebrity".

In short, from the point of view of the accessibility of the concept referred to, "N *de* V" indicates an action that has already been stated in discourse. This construction, therefore, is an important means of expressing the central event.

5.5 Reference form and topic continuity

As mentioned above, the subject of a Chinese sentence is also the topic. But a topic noun may not be an argument, in which case the hosting sentence cannot be reduced to a subject–predicate sentence. Such Chinese sentences can then be taken as the outcome of left-dislocation or some other syntactic operations, as is the case in English. Take (35) for example.

(35) 那场大火,幸亏消防队来得早。
 Nà chǎng dàhuǒ, xìngkuī xiāofáng duì láide zǎo.
 'That fire, fortunately the fire department arrived early.'

We have also noticed that non-argument topics are different from other topic categories, in that they are incompatible with the coding form of bare noun. See (36) for illustration.

(36) a. 那场大火,幸亏消防队来得早。
 Nà chǎng dàhuǒ, xìngkuī xiāofángduì láide zǎo.
 'That fire, fortunately the fire department arrived early.'
 b. 这场大火,幸亏消防队来得早。
 Zhè chǎng dàhuǒ, xìngkuī xiāofángduì láide zǎo.
 'This fire, fortunately the fire department arrived early.'
 c. *大火,幸亏消防队来得早。
 *Dàhuǒ, xìngkuī xiāofángduì láide zǎo.
 '*Fire, fortunately the fire department arrived early.'

This syntactic restriction suggests that non-argument topics are subject to certain discourse requirements. They are either anaphoric, coreferential with noun constituents already present in discourse, or cataphoric, with its referent continuing to be topical in the ensuing text. If such a topic serves as the opener of an event, it can be topic marked with 说起 (shuōqǐ, 'speaking of'), 要说 (yàoshuō, 'to speak of'), etc., such as (37).

(37) 说起/要说那场大火啊,幸亏消防队来得早。
 Shuōqǐ/yàoshuō nà chǎng dàhuǒ a, xìngkuī xiāofángduì láidé zǎo.
 'Speaking of/To speak of that fire, fortunately the fire department arrived early.'

Our survey of such topic sentences confirms the above analysis, in that none of the topics is coded in the form of bare noun. Example (38) presents some sentences from an online search that are used to open or close a story.

(38) a. 高速上发生的二次事故,幸亏车上人员都撤离到护栏之外。
 Gāosù shàng fāshēng de èr cì shìgù, xìngkuī chē shàng rényuán dōu chèlí dào hùlán zhī wài.
 'A secondary accident happened on the highway. Fortunately the people on board the car had been evacuated outside the guardrail.'
 b. 某高速发生7连撞车事故,场面惊心动魄,幸亏救援人员来得及时。

Mǒu gāosù fāshēng 7 lián zhuàngchē shìgù, chǎngmiàn jīngxīndòngpò, <u>xìngkuī</u> jiùyuán rényuán láidé jíshí.

'Seven cars crashed consecutively into each other on a highway. The scene was shocking, but <u>fortunately</u> the rescuers came in time.'

c. 这么倒霉的车祸,<u>幸亏</u>有记录仪!

Zhème dǎoméi de chēhuò, <u>xìngkuī</u> yǒu jìlù yí!

'Such an unlucky car accident; fortunately there was the drive recorder!'

d. 惨烈的车祸,<u>幸亏</u>戴了头盔,只是脑震荡。

Cǎnliè de chēhuò, <u>xìngkuī</u> dàile tóukuī, zhǐshì nǎo zhèndàng.

'A tragic car accident. <u>Fortunately</u>, (the driver) was wearing the helmet, just concussion.'

The above sentences are all used in accident reporting. Sentences (38a) and (38b) appear at the beginning of the narrative, while sentences (38c) and (38d) are used to end the reporting. (38c) and (38d) differ from (38a) and (38b) in that the clause containing "幸亏" ('fortunately') has chosen zero-subject, but the reference to the zero-subject is definite in discourse.

Further observation shows that these topic sentences, even if the clause containing "幸亏" is a verbal predicate, have the overall function of making comments rather than narration, as in example (35).

When the topic nouns are examined, they have a commonality; that is, they are all event nouns, such as "大火" ('fire'), "事故" ('incident'), "车祸" ('car accident'), etc. In discourse, the main function of a non-argument topic sentence is to comment on an event, and the event being commented on is the referent of the sentence-initial topic. When the event being commented on is not expressed in the noun form, the following usage emerges.

(39) 菜市口,说大不大,说小也不小。跟老辈儿人一打听,这地界儿的历史,十有八九都会提到当年杀人砍头的刑场。往深了,还能跟您絮叨絮叨,在这儿英勇就义的戊戌六君子。<u>但是一说到道光年间著名的缉毒大队长林则徐,就全都一问三不知了</u>。<u>幸亏</u>我们的编导提前查阅了大量的资料,在一本名叫《北京名居》的书上,找到了相关的信息。"贾家胡同"第一次引起了我们的注意。(*This Is Beijing*)

Càishìkǒu, shuō dà bú dà, shuō xiǎo yě bù xiǎo. Gēn lǎobèi·er rén yī dǎtīng, zhè dìjiè·er de lìshǐ, shíyǒubājiǔ dōu huì tídào dāngnián shārén kǎntóu de xíngchǎng. Wǎng shēn le, hái néng gēn nín xùdāo~xùdāo, zài zhè·er yīngyǒng jiùyì de Wùxū Liùjūnzǐ. <u>Dànshì yī shuō dào Dàoguāng niánjiān zhùmíng de jīdú dàduìzhǎng Lín Zéxú, jiù quándōu yīwènsānbùzhī le</u>. **Xìngkuī** wǒmen de biāndǎo tíqián cháyuèle dàliàng de zīliào, zài yī běn míng jiào "Běijīng Míngjū" de shū shàng, zhǎodàole xiāngguān de xìnxī. "Jiǎjiā hútòng" dìyīcì yǐnqǐle wǒmen de zhùyì.

'Caishikou is not big, but it is not small either. When you inquire with the older generation about the history of this area, nine times out of ten, they will mention it as the torture ground where the people were killed and beheaded. To go deeper, they can also talk to you about the Six Gentlemen of Wuxu who bravely died here. But when it comes to Lin Zexu, the famous anti-drug leader during the Daoguang period, they will shake their heads in answer to all questions. Fortunately, our director has consulted a lot of information in advance and found the relevant information in a book entitled *Famous Residences in Beijing*. Jiajia Hutong comes to our attention for the first time.'

In this example, the commentary led by "幸亏" ('fortunately') is directed at the fact stated in the preceding sentence.

5.6 Summary

As discussed above, "N *de* V" is mainly used to refer to actions, and most of them are pre-existing already, which gives the construction a clear anaphoric feature in discourse. In terms of information expression, it does not convey new information in its strict sense.

In ancient Chinese, "subject *zhi* (之) predicate" shares similar functional properties to "N *de* V". According to Lü Shuxiang (1985) and Wang Li (1980), the function of 之 is to turn a sentence into a phrase by canceling the independent status of the sentence. Zhu Dexi (1983) maintains that 之 is a nominalization marker, transforming the predicative subject–predicate construction into a modifier–head construction. Wang Li (1989) rejects the original "phraseization" theory by adopting the "nominalization" theory instead.

Song Shaonian and Zhang Yan (1997) argue that 之 is a self-referencing marker, and accordingly the *zhi*-construction is a self-referencing subject–predicate construction. Li Zuofeng (1994) also upholds the characterization of "referentialization". Hong Bo (2008) finds that, in addition to the cancellation of syntactic independence, the "subject *zhi* predicate" construction conveys exclusively information of high accessibility. It is not difficult to see that this information property is essential of the thematic structure.

The syntactic variation of embedding a demonstrative in a subject-predicate clause has been existent for long, and its ancient form is "subject *zhi* predicate", which can be used either as subject, as in (40a), or as object, as in (40b).

(40) a. 人之爱其子也,亦如余乎? (*The Spring and Autumn Annals · Year 13 of Chao* [《左传·昭公十三年》])
　　　Rén　zhī　ài　　qí　　zi　　yě,　yì　　rú　　yú　　hū?
　　　people zhi love their son SMP too like me SFP
　　　'Do people love their sons just as I do mine?'

b. 不患人之不己知,患不知人也。(*Analects* ·*Xue Er* [《论语·学而》])
Bù huàn rén zhī bù jǐ zhī, huàn bù zhī
not worry one zhi not self know worry not know
rén yě.
other SFP

'It is not worrying if one does not know himself; what is worrying is that one does not know others.'

Although there is no direct inheritance between "S这VP" in contemporary colloquial Beijing dialect and "subject *zhi* predicate" in ancient Chinese, we can see how the functional needs of discourse directly contribute to the shaping of syntactic structures.

It is worth noting that the "event" represented by "subject *zhi* predicate" in ancient Chinese is either known to both parties or can be inferred by the addressee based on the "speech context", "physical context", or his own "encyclopedic context" (Li Zuofeng, 1994; Hong Bo, 2008).[3] This construction has some commonalities with "S这VP" in contemporary colloquial Beijing dialect in terms of discourse distribution, in that both are used to express known or activatable information.

Regarding the "subject *zhi* predicate" construction, Wang Li (1980, p. 397) argues that the construction gradually phased out from speech post Middle Chinese, leaving only writers to imitate the ancient style prose. It became extinct in speech after the creation of the word 的 (底) in the spoken variety. It is also argued that the construction declined dramatically in the early years of the Western Han Dynasty and disappeared from the popular speech in the early Northern and Southern Dynasties (Wang Hongjun, 1987). In any case, the existence of "subject *zhi* predicate" at least indicates that the syntactic device of demonstrative embedding is inherent in the Chinese language.

Although the Chinese grammatical system allows verbs to be used directly for reference from ancient times to the present, the means to refer to actions by changing the syntactic form exist in both ancient and modern times. Whether it is 之 in ancient Chinese or 的 in modern written Chinese,[4] or 这 in contemporary colloquial Beijing dialect, this syntactic transformation has been consistent in terms of discourse function.

Notes

1 *Pekingese Conversation* is a textbook of the Chinese language in the late Qing Dynasty and the early Republic of China. The relevant historical background can be found in Zhang Meilan and Chen Siming (2006).
2 "N *de* V" is actually the simplified rendition of "NP *de* VP". Translator's note.
3 Hong Bo (2008) proposes that such constructions refer to actions with high accessibility. Hong's explanation is as follows: what I know, you most likely also know, then it is information of high accessibility, which licenses the addition of 之; what I have heard, you most likely have not heard, then it is information of low

accessibility, so 之 is not added. The word 之, to Hong, is a modifier marker. Shen Jiaxuan and Wan Quan (2009), however, have argued that 之 in this kind of construction is still a demonstrative, which functions to promote the "degree of differentiation".

4 Zhang Min (2003a) proposes that "NP *zhi* VP" appeared in the bronze inscriptions of the Warring States, *Book of Documents* (《尚书》), and *Book of Poetry* (《诗经》); that is, it already existed in the Spring and Autumn and Warring States Periods. When this 之 was created and put to popular use, its modifier marker usage was not yet mature, which justified its demonstrative interpretation.

6 Discourse functions of verb-copying constructions

The composition and syntactic interpretation of verb-copying constructions constitute an important topic in Chinese grammatical analysis. Previous studies have confined their scope of discussion to single utterances. When examined in discourse, however, they are found to occur in specific contexts. The early occurring verb–object structure of this syntactic format expresses old information or information with relatively high accessibility, while the subsequent verb-complement structure conveys new information. The verb-copying construction indicates action continuity and is thus a means of topic continuity. It is only that the topic is an action, rather than an entity.

6.1 Introduction

The so-called verb-coping construction consists of a "verb-object" followed by a "verb-complement". The simplest verb-copying construction is illustrated in (I):

(I) 看书看累了。
    Kàn shū kàn lèi le.
    read book read tired aux.
    '(Someone) has got tired from reading a book.'

Sentences made up of the verb-copying construction are called verb-copying sentences, whose composition can be more complex. See (II):

(II) a. 他看书看累了。
    Tā kàn shū kàn lèi le.
    he read book read tired aux.
    'He's got tired from reading a book.'
  b. 他做数学题做得头晕脑胀。
    Tā zuò shùxué tí zuòde tóuyūnnǎozhàng.
    he do maths question do.CM dizzy
    'He got dizzy from doing math questions.'

(III) 她切菜切破了手指。

Tā	qiē	cài	qiē	pò	le	shǒuzhǐ.
she	cut	vegetables	cut	torn	PFV	finger

'She cut her finger (when) cutting vegetables.'

A verb-copying sentence can be a sentence without an agent subject, such as (I); it may very well have the agent as the subject, e.g. (II) and (III). The object of the first part (i.e., "verb-object") can be a complex noun phrase, as in (IIa); the complement of the "verb-complement" part can be a phrase containing the auxiliary 得 (*de*), such as (IIb); it may even contain an object of its own, i.e., "手指" ('finger') in (III).

The syntactico-semantic interpretation of the verb-copying construction is extremely well documented by different schools of research. The more representative ones are as follows.

- First, Huang (1989) proposes that Chinese syntax is subject to the restriction of phrase structure rules; that is, only one immediate constituent is allowed to the right of the predicate head. Huang Yueyuan (1996b) and others also hold this view, arguing that "one verb, one complement" is the case requirement of the Chinese language, and that the existence of the verb-copying construction is the result of this syntactic requirement.
- Second, the description of the syntactic constraint of the verb-copying construction is closely related to its semantic interpretation. Some scholars suggest that the second verb (the verb in "verb-complement") is the semantic focus of the verb-copying construction, while the forerunning "verb-object" is not a typical predicate because the nominal object in it does not have a discourse referent (see Zhong Xiaoyong, 2010 among others). In other words, the focus of the expression "他看书看累了" is "看累" (see [IIa]). Chinese lacks syntactic morphology, and the syntactic coding does not directly distinguish the main predicate verb (or the finite verb) from others. In terms of linguistic contrast, this semantic interpretation is of great importance: although there is no syntactic marker to indicate the difference between "看书" and "看累", there is indeed the distinction between primary vs. secondary information.
- Nie Renfa (2001) argues that syntactic structure is the result of grammaticalization of discourse structure. The verb-copying sentence then derives from the discourse structure of "context-purpose", where VP1 introduces the contextual event and VP2 constitutes the focus of the clause by stating the purpose of discourse. The pragmatic value of the verb-copying sentence lies in its introduction of VP1, rather than the simultaneous introduction of the object and the complement of the verb. The "context-purpose" relation is universally attested in Chinese.
- Third, the verb-copying construction has been noted to have a special expressive function, highlighting the supernormal aspects of things and actions, or

expressing events that seem to the speaker to have unexpected, supernormal results (Xiang Kaixi, 1997). For example, "她等丈夫等了十年" (Tā děng zhàngfū děngle shí nián, 'She waited for his husband for ten years.') is a sentence not only stating the event but also expressing that, in the speaker's opinion, "waiting for ten years" is beyond the normal case. Shi Chunhong (2010) further summarizes this as the conventionalization of the causative event (the early occurring verb–object phrase in the verb-copying construction) and the caused event (the later occurring verb-complement phrase). The supernormal and unexpectedness readings are both derived from the degree of conventionalization.

The pragmatic explanation above can partly show that some unacceptable sentences are, in many cases, not on account of syntactic constraints, but due to pragmatic reasons. See (1).

(1) a. 她切菜切破了手指。
    Tā   qiē   cài   qiē   pò   le   shǒuzhǐ.
    she   cut   vegetables cut   torn   PFV   finger
    'She cut her finger while cutting the vegetables.'
  b. ?她切菜没切破手指。
    Tā   qiē   cài   méi   qiē   pò   shǒuzhǐ.
    she   cut   vegetables not   cut   torn   finger
    '?She didn't cut her finger while cutting the vegetables.'

Example (1a) above is an acceptable sentence, but (1b) is not because it is inappropriate in pragmatics. The cutting of a finger when cutting vegetables is an accident, not expected by the speaker, which renders the addition of the negator "没" weird.

Nonetheless, the depiction and interpretation of a construction as it stands is of very limited use in enhancing language learners' understanding. For instance, Wang Canlong (1999) has pointed out that, in isolation, it is difficult to tell which of the two VPs is the semantic focus of the verb-copying construction. When the preceding context has already indicated the action denoted by the verb, such as "走路" (zǒ lù, 'walk'), it is not necessary to use the verb-copying construction "他走路走岔了" (tā zǒu lù zǒu chà le, 'He walked the wrong way when walking.'); instead, people can simply say "他走岔了" (tā zǒu chà le, 'He walked the wrong way.'). In what follows, we will cite examples from authentic discourse to show that such introspection-based conclusions may not be in line with linguistic reality.

In addition, Wang (1999) also argues that some cases can hardly be explained in terms of "supernormal". "他抽大烟抽上了瘾" (Tā chōu dàyān chōu shàngle yǐn, 'He got addicted to opium smoking.') and "他说相声每次都说得台下哄堂大笑" (Tā shuō xiàngshēng měicì dōu shuōde táixià hǒngtángdàxiào, 'He made the audience laugh every time he did his comedy.') are two of

Discourse functions of verb-copying constructions 123

such cases, in that it is natural to get addicted to opium smoking and to do comedy is supposed to make the audience laugh. It can then be seen that the "supernatural" account may not be able to capture the pragmatic features of the verb-copying construction.

To recapitulate, earlier studies have explored the grammar of the constituents of the verb-copying construction, its syntactic constraints and expressive features in Chinese. There remain, however, some questions that have not been satisfactorily answered, including:

1. when to use the verb-copying construction?
2. is the person referencing noun (or pronoun) at the beginning of the construction the topic or the subject?
3. what is the relationship between the two verbs in this construction?

These questions will be discussed one by one in what follows. The approach is to restore the verb-copying constructions cited in the published literature to their original discourse contexts, so as to reveal patterns that are difficult to see when the constructions are examined in isolation.

6.1.1 Information structure

In the process of communication, different concepts are in different cognitive states in the human brain. Those concepts that have been established during the course of speech are in the active state, which make up known information (or old information) to the listener. Some concepts are not yet established at the current stage of communication, but the addressee can infer their meaning through background knowledge. Such concepts are semi-active and can be activated in the speech event, which gives them the status of accessible information. When viewed from the perspective of "new" vs. "old" or "known" vs. "unknown", accessible information lies in the middle of the continuum: old information > accessible information > new information.

The ease or difficulty with which a concept can be understood by the addressee varies, and this degree of ease or difficulty is called accessibility. Accessibility is higher when a concept is easy to understand, and lower when it is difficult to understand. The levels of accessibility of concepts in discourse are as follows:

personal pronoun > anaphoric noun > stated proposition > situational context > shared knowledge > speech modification

In fact, such a perspective can be used not only to observe the accessibility of nominal concepts, but also to examine the expression and understanding of actions. In the following, we will examine the discourse contexts in which verb-copying constructions occur.

6.1.1.1 Anaphora

In discourse, NP elements can be referred to in homomorphic anaphora, partial homomorphic anaphora, and heteromorphic anaphora. When it comes to actions, reference can also be made in homomorphism and partial homomorphism of the verb.

1) Verb homomorphism

The action expressed by the first verb in the verb-copying sentence is already present in the preceding context. The first occurrence of the verb can be in the immediately preceding clause, as in (2).

(2) 她出了办公室去**找厕所**，**找了几圈没找到**，又不敢问，做贼似的。后来总算找到了，厕所里又有公务员在清扫。(Wang Anyi, *The Song of Everlasting Sorrow* [《长恨歌》])

Tā chūle bàngōngshì qù **zhǎo cèsuǒ**, **zhǎole jǐ quān méi zhǎo dào**, yòu bù gǎn wèn, zuò zéi sìde. Hòulái zǒngsuàn zhǎo dào le, cèsuǒ lǐ yòu yǒu gōngwùyuán zài qīngsǎo.

'She went out of the office to **look for the toilet**. (She) **looked around a few times but found none**. She was afraid to ask, as if she were a thief. When she finally found one, there was a civil servant doing the cleaning.'

The first occurrence of the action denoted by the first verb in the verb-copying sentence may also be in the preceding sentence, or even in the forerunning paragraph, as in (3).

(3) 杨妈在正厅里给金一趟的扣碗茶续了开水，立刻端进东内室去。她惟恐老爷子**找完了书**又跑出来找金枝的麻烦。
杜逢时见母亲进来，便捧着几本线装的医书溜了。金一趟**找书找累了**，靠在一把藤椅上闭着眼喘息。(Chen Jiangong and Zhao Danian, *The Roots of the Imperial City* [《皇城根》])

Yángmā zài zhèngtīng lǐ gěi Jīn Yītàng de kòuwǎnchá xùle kāishuǐ, lìkè duān jìn dōng nèishì qù. Tā wéikǒng lǎoyézi **zhǎo wán le shū** yòu pǎo chūlái zhǎo Jīn Zhī de máfan.

Dù Féngshí jiàn mǔqīn jìnlái, biàn pěngzhe jǐ běn xiànzhuāng de yīshū liūle. Jīn Yītàng **zhǎo shū zhǎo lèi le**, kào zài yī bǎ téngyǐ shàng bìzhe yǎn chuǎnxī.

'After refilling boiling water for Jin Yitang's covered teacup in the main hall, Amah Yang immediately brought it into the east inner room, fearing that the old man would come out to find trouble with Jin Zhi once he **finished looking for his books**.
When Du Fengshi saw his mother come in, he slipped away with a few threadbare medical books. Jin Yitang **got tired from looking for books** and leaned back into a rattan chair with his eyes closed to catch breath.'

2) Partial homomorphism of verbs

As a recurring form, the noun in the verb–object construction may be fully homomorphic or partially homomorphic to its first occurrence. In this usage, the action expressed by the first verb in the verb-copying sentence may not be completely the same with what is stated in the preceding context, but the event expressed will still be coreferential with the aforementioned, as in (4).

(4) 我在好些年以前**写过一些史论专著**，记得曾有几位记者在报纸上说我**写书写得轻松潇洒**，其实完全不是如此。(Yu Qiuyu, *Cultural Odyssey* [《文化苦旅》])

Wǒ zài hǎoxiē nián yǐqián **xiě guò yīxiē shǐ lùn zhuānzhù**, jìdé céng yǒu jǐ wèi jìzhě zài bàozhǐ shàng shuō wǒ **xiě shū xiě de qīngsōng xiāosǎ**, qíshí wánquán búshì rúcǐ.

'**I wrote some monographs on history** some years ago, and I remember that several journalists once said in the newspapers that **I wrote books with ease and grace**, which was not at all the case.'

In (4), VP1 in the verb-copying construction is "写书" ('write books'), though not homomorphic to "写过一些史论专著" ('wrote some monographs on history') in the preceding clause, indicates a coreferential event. For further illustration, see (5).

(5) 一连几天，公婆都在谈论小孙子，又高了，又胖了，更懂事了，**还学着钢琴**，将来一定大有出息。亦秋还听见他们在偷偷算着日期，又是周末了，罗雷不知会不会来，一定要告诉景昆，不要让他**学琴学得太累了**，小孩子，正长身子，时间坐长了不好。(Zhang Lin, *Love Desolation* [《爱意荒凉》])

Yīlián jǐ tiān, gōngpó dōu zài tánlùn xiǎo sūnzi, yòu gāole, yòu pàngle, gèng dǒngshìle, **hái xué zhe gāngqín**, jiānglái yīdìng dà yǒu chūxī. Yìqiū hái tīngjiàn tāmen zài tōutōu suànzhe rìqī, yòu shì zhōumò le, Luō Léi bùzhī hui-bú-huì lái, yīdìng yào gàosù Jǐngkūn, búyào ràng tā **xué qín xué de tài lèi le**, xiǎo háizi, zhèng zhǎng shēnzi, shíjiān zuò cháng le bù hǎo.

'For several days in a row, the parents-in-law were talking about their little grandson, taller, stouter, more knowledgeable, and **learning the piano**, so he must be a great success in the future. Yiqiu also heard them secretly calculating the date. It was weekend again. They did not know if Luo Lei would come, but they had made up their mind to tell Jingkun not to let Lei to **learn the piano too hard**. He was just a kid and he was growing. Sitting long hours would do him no good.'

In (5), the first occurring coding form is "学着钢琴" ('learning the piano'), and in the verb-copying construction it takes the form "学琴". Even though the noun in the verb–object construction is different, "琴" being a more general term than "钢琴", the events expressed by the two segments are the same.

126 *Discourse functions of verb-copying constructions*

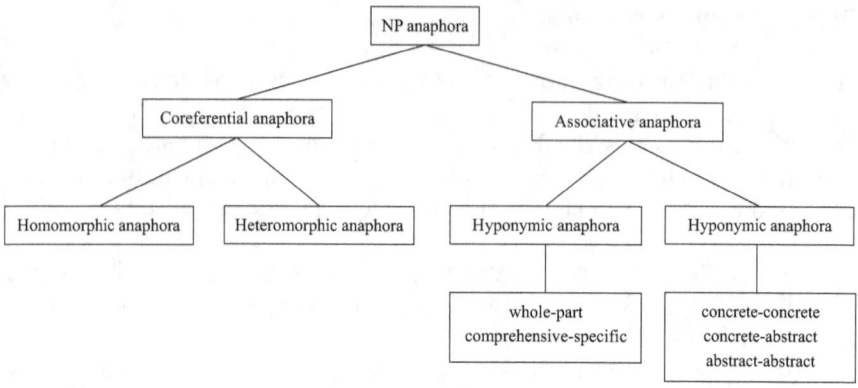

Figure 6.1 Framework of Chinese NP anaphora (Xu Jiujiu, 2005a)

6.1.1.2 Conceptual association

In discourse, NP constituents are tracked by way of homomorphic anaphora, partial homomorphic anaphora, and heteromorphic anaphora. In addition, there is still another type of anaphora, associative anaphora, where an anaphor does not have an explicit antecedent. The categories of NP anaphora in discourse can be roughly diagrammed as follows.

Examples (6) and (7) below are from Xu Jiujiu (2005a).

(6) 就在此时,有一名男子从隔离带跳了下来,直奔奥迪车冲过来,另几名男子将车围住,一人拉开**(驾驶室的)门**和徐先生争抢**方向盘**,趁徐先生惊愕之时,另一人拉开**副驾驶室门**盗走了徐先生装有一万多元的书包。(*Beijing Times* [《京华时报》], November 23, 2003)

Jiù zài cǐshí, yǒu yī míng nánzǐ cóng gélídài tiàole xiàlái, zhí bēn Àodí chē chōng guòlái, lìng jǐ míng nánzǐ jiāng <u>chē</u> wéizhù, yī rén lā kāi **(jiàshǐshì de) mén** hé Xú xiānshēng zhēngqiǎng **fāngxiàngpán**, chèn Xú xiānshēng jīng'è zhī shí, lìng yī rén lā kāi **fùjiàshǐshì mén** dàozǒule Xú xiānshēng zhuāng yǒu yī wàn duō yuán de shūbāo.

'Just then, a man jumped from the median and rushed straight to the Audi. Several other men surrounded the <u>car</u>. One pulled open **the door (on the driver's side)** to scramble for **the steering wheel** with Mr. Xu. While Mr. Xu was stunned, another person pulled open **the co-driver's door** and stole Mr. Xu's bag containing more than 10,000 yuan.'

(7) 儿子自不用说,那小眼睛早盯上了**家里**的统治权,恨不得把**老爸老妈**永远踩在脚下,所以极力赞成。[*Beijing Times*, November 22, 2003]

<u>Érzi</u> zì búyòng shuō, nà xiǎo yǎnjīng zǎo dīngshàngle **jiā** lǐ de tǒngzhìquán, hènbudé bǎ **lǎobà lǎomā** yǒngyuǎn cǎi zài jiǎoxià, suǒyǐ jílì zànchéng.

'<u>The son</u>, needless to say, has long had his eyes on the ruling power of **the family**, and can't wait to step (his) **father and mother** down forever. So he strongly approves.'

We find that associative anaphora of NPs also has impact on the referential relations of action expressions.

(8) 小冷饮店里已经没几个顾客了，我们**要的饮料**也都喝光了。从下午5点起，我们吃了一顿好饭，看了一场好电影，又在这个冷饮店里坐了几个小时，吃遍了这家店所有品种的冰激凌，花光了我们俩身上的所有钱，**再要一瓶汽水也要不起了**。可是我感到幸福，像好天气好酒一样让人周身舒坦。(Wang Shuo, *Death by Addiction* [《过把瘾就死》])

Xiǎo lěngyǐn diàn lǐ yǐjīng méi jǐ gè gùkè le, wǒmen **yào de yǐnliào** yě dōu hē guāng le. Cóng xiàwǔ 5 diǎn qǐ, wǒmen chīle yī dùn hǎo fàn, kànle yī chǎng hǎo diànyǐng, yòu zài zhègè lěngyǐn diàn lǐ zuòle jǐ gè xiǎoshí, chī biàn le zhè jiā diàn suǒyǒu pǐnzhǒng de bīngjīlíng, huā guāng le wǒmen liǎ shēnshang de suǒyǒu qián, **zài yào yī píng qìshuǐ yě yào-bù-qǐ le**. Kěshì wǒ gǎndào xìngfú, xiàng hǎo tiānqì hào jiǔ yīyàng ràng rén zhōushēn shūtan.

'There weren't many customers left in the small cold drink store, and we had run out of **the drinks we ordered**. Since 5 p.m., we had a good meal, watched a good movie, and sat in this cold drink store for several hours, having eaten all the varieties of ice creams in the store. We had spent all the money we had, and **couldn't even afford another bottle of soda water**. But I felt happy, like good weather and good wine, which can make people feel good all around.'

In this example, the action expressed by the first VP in the verb-copying sentence "要一瓶汽水" ('order another bottle of soda water') does not appear explicitly in the preceding context, but it has a direct conceptual association with the early occurring "饮料" ('drinks'), though not in the predicate slot. From the point of view of concept introduction, this VP is not new information. See also (9).

(9) 审判员拿过厚厚一沓笔迹不一的证人证词看了两眼，从第一份证词看了两眼，从第一份证词提供的情况开始问："你母亲方面的证人说你父亲在日常生活中对你照顾得很不够，经常给你**吃挂面**，即便在节假日也怎么省事怎么来，基本一天主要的两顿饭都是**面条**，早饭则断断续续，时有时无，这情况属实么？"

"差不多。"马锐眼睛看着保险柜回答。

"我想问你，你们家**吃面条吃得复杂**么?我是说是否需要很复杂的配料和制作像山西人那样？" (Wang Shuo, *I Am Your Father* [《我是你爸爸》])

Shěnpànyuán náguò hòu~hòu yī dá bǐjì bù yī de zhèngrén zhèngcí kànle liǎng yǎn, cóng dìyī fèn zhèngcí kànle liǎng yǎn, cóng dìyī fèn zhèngcí tígōng de qíngkuàng kāishǐ wèn: "Nǐ mǔqīn fāngmiàn de zhèngrén shuō nǐ fùqīn zài rìcháng shēnghuó zhōng duì nǐ zhàogù de hěn búgòu, jīngcháng gěi nǐ **chī guàmiàn**, jíbiàn zài jiéjiàrì yě zěnme shěngshì zěnme lái, jīběn yī tiān zhǔyào de liǎng dùn fàn dōu shì **miàntiáo**, zǎofàn zé duànduànxùxù, shíyǒushíwú, zhè qíngkuàng shǔshí me?"

"Chàbùduō." Mǎ Ruì yǎnjīng kànzhe bǎoxiǎnguì huídá.

"Wǒ xiǎng wèn nǐ, nǐmen jiā **chī miàntiáo chī de fùzá** me? Wǒ shìshuō shìfǒu xūyào hěn fùzá de pèiliào hé zhìzuò xiàng Shānxī rén nàyàng?"

'The judge took over a thick pile of witness statements in different handwriting styles, and had a look at them. Glancing over the first testimony, the judge began to ask from the beginning of it, "The witness on your mother's side claims that your father does not take enough care of you in daily life, often making you **eat noodles**, even on holidays, just to save trouble. Basically the two main meals of the day are both **noodles**, with irregular breakfasts. Is it true?"

"More or less." Ma Rui answered, his eyes on the safe.

"I want to ask you, does your family **eat noodles in a complex way**? I mean, do you have very complicated ingredients and preparations like the Shanxi people do?"'

Although the first VP in the verb-copying construction "吃面条" ('eat noodles') does not appear directly in the preceding context in (9), there are such expressions as "你吃挂面" ('you eat noodles') and "基本一天主要的两顿饭都是面条" ('Basically the two main meals of the day are both noodles'), which makes "吃面条" in the verb-copying construction anything but new information.

In this usage, the action expressed by VP1 of the verb-copying construction is not present in the preceding context verbatim, but there is a conceptual association between the preceding and ensuing actions, which bears similarity to associative anaphora between NPs.

6.1.1.3 Shared knowledge association

The comprehension of accessible information depends on the knowledge system of the addressee, which roughly includes the following: 1) knowledge shared by human beings, e.g., kinship, the relationship between limbs and human body; 2) knowledge specified by the speech scene; that is, when there is only one clock in the speech scene, one is licensed to say "Bring down the clock."; 3) knowledge shared by the speaker and the addressee, e.g., "I won't go to the afternoon physics class."

Some knowledge entertains certain accessibility, and this property makes the referent not exactly equivalent to a brand new concept. The same is true for action expressions in discourse. See (10) for example.

(10) "蒜苔"就有这个本事，在你对他意见最大的时候，能以最天真无邪的表情，来赢得你的谅解。记得老曹"**官复原职**"以后，他既不是痛哭流涕，也不是满脸羞愧，而是走到老曹面前，肩膀一耸，以天真到烂漫程度的表情、语气说："**我过去斗你斗错啦**，上当受骗嘛！这么大个运动，我这算个什么问题呢?"老曹能说什么呢?自然是:"算不了什么问题......" (Liu Xinwu, *Representative Works of Liu Xinwu* [《刘心武代表作》])

"Suàntái" jiù yǒu zhège běnshì, zài nǐ duì tā yìjiàn zuì dà de shíhòu, néng yǐ zuì tiānzhēnwúxié de biǎoqíng, lái yíngdé nǐ de liàngjiě. Jìdé Lǎo Cáo **guānfùyuánzhí** yǐhòu, tā jì búshì tòngkūliútì, yě búshì mǎn liǎn xiūkuì, érshì zǒu dào Lǎo Cáo miànqián, jiānbǎng yī sǒng, yǐ tiānzhēn dào lànmàn chéngdù de biǎoqíng(,) yǔqì shuō: "**Wǒ guòqù dòu nǐ dòu cuò la**, shàngdàngshòupiàn ma! Zhème dà gè yùndòng, wǒ zhè suàn gè shénme wèntí ne?" Lǎo Cáo néng shuō shénme ne? Zìrán shì: "Suàn-bù-liǎo shénme wèntí..."

"'Garlic Sprout' has this ability: when you are most dissatisfied with him, he can wear the most innocent expression to win your pardon. When Old Cao **was reinstated**, he was neither crying, nor full of shame, but went to Old Cao, shrugged the shoulders, tuned his expression and voice to the most naive and innocent, "**I made a mistake criticizing and denouncing you in the past**. I was duped! In such a big movement, my mistake seems to be nothing." What could Old Cao say? Naturally it was, "It's nothing...""

In this example, "斗" in "我过去斗你斗错啦" means to "批斗" (pīdòu, 'criticize and denounce'). The basis for this interpretation is the shared knowledge of modern Chinese people that some persons can be removed from office during political movements, and that a significant number of those removed from office are also subject to criticism and denouncement. This shared knowledge between the characters in the story and between the author and the reader helps establish a conceptual association between "斗" in "我过去斗你斗错啦" and "官复原职 ('be re-instated')", which in turn makes "斗" activatable information.

Another example is (11) below, where "当农民" ('be a farmer') as VP1 of the verb-copying construction appears also for the first time in discourse. The basis for the understanding of the entire construction is that, in people's general knowledge, being a farmer is the least difficult job because there is no technical threshold for it.

(11) 你是个大学生,有知识,我相信你在任何工作岗位上都能发挥出你的聪明才智来。你不像有些同志,除了有一点公安工作的经验之外,就没有别的知识了,这些同志换什么工作都很难。以前我们转移出去的个别同志,**不要说干别的工作,当农民都当不了**。我们帮他安排的工作,干几天就干不下去了,最后自己的生活都成问题了。你的情况跟那些同志完全不同。(Hai Yan, *Jade Goddess of Mercy* [《玉观音》])

Nǐ shì gè dàxuéshēng, yǒu zhīshì, wǒ xiāngxìn nǐ zài rènhé gōngzuò gǎngwèi shàng dōu néng fāhuī chū nǐ de cōngmíngcáizhì lái. Nǐ bú xiàng yǒuxiē tóngzhì, chúle yǒu yīdiǎn gōng'ān gōngzuò de jīngyàn zhīwài, jiù méiyǒu bié de zhīshì le, zhèxiē tóngzhì huàn shénme gōngzuò dōu hěn nán. Yǐqián wǒmen zhuǎnyí chūqù de gèbié tóngzhì, **búyàoshuō gàn biéde**

gōngzuò, dāng nóngmín dōu dāng-bù-liǎo. Wǒmen bāng tā ānpái de gōngzuò, gàn jǐ tiān jiù gān-bù-xiàqù le, zuìhòu zìjǐ de shēnghuó dōu chéng wèntí le. Nǐ de qíngkuàng gēn nàxiē tóngzhì wánquán bùtóng.

'You are a college graduate, and you have knowledge. I believe you can use your intelligence in any job. You are not like some comrades, who, except for a little experience in public security work, have no other knowledge, and it is difficult for them to change to any other job. In the past, we transferred out a few comrades. **Not to mention doing other work, they couldn't even work as farmers**. They stayed only a couple of days on the positions that we helped arrange for them. Finally their own living became a problem. You are completely different from those comrades.'

It is not difficult to see that there are contextual conditions for the occurrence of verb-copying sentences: the action described in the verb–object part, i.e. VP1 of the verb-copying sentence, is generally what has been stated in early discourse or is already in the shared knowledge of the communicative parties, which gives it a high degree of accessibility.

6.1.2 Functioning as topics

6.1.2.1 Topic and subject

In *A Grammar of Spoken Chinese*, Chao (1968, Section 2.4) makes the statement that the grammatical meaning of subject and predicate in Chinese is that of topic and comment.

Li and Thompson (1981) suggest that Chinese is a topic-prominent language. In contrast to languages such as English, which are subject-prominent, the syntax of topic-prominent languages, such as Korean and Japanese, emphasizes the "topic-comment" structure of the sentence.

Li and Thompson (1981, pp. 85–7) characterize Chinese topics as follows: 1) they occur in sentence-initial position; 2) they are often followed by a pause particle; 3) they are definite or generic in reference; and 4) they are typically noun phrases or verb phrases. Usually, the subject of a simple sentence is also the topic, such as "我" in "我喜欢吃苹果" (wǒ xǐhuān chī píngguǒ, 'I like eating apples.']. In Chinese, the difference between subject and topic is usually found in sentences where subject and topic co-occur, such as "那只狗我已经看过了"(nà zhī gǒu wǒ yǐjīng kàn guò le, 'That dog I have seen.'), where "那只狗" ('that dog') is topic and "我" ('I') is subject.

On basis of this, Cao Fengfu (1990/2005, p. 48) proposes the following features of Chinese topics: 1) topics always occupy the sentence-initial position; 2) topics can be separated from the rest of the sentence by pause particles such as 啊(呀)([y]a), 呢 (ne), 么 (me), and 吧 (ba); 3) topics are always definite; 4) the topic is a discourse notion, which can and often does extend its semantic jurisdiction to multiple sentences; 5) the topic controls the deletion of all the pronouns or coreferential NPs in the topic chain; and 6) the topic, unless it is also the subject, is not involved in syntactic operations such as reflexivization, NP deletion, or imperativization.

Cao (1990/2005, p. 45) argues that subject is different from topic in Chinese. In contrast with topic, the Chinese subject can be characterized as follows: 1) in terms of position, the subject is the first animate NP to the left of the verb or the NP immediately preceding the verb; 2) the subject always forms some kind of selective relationship with the main verb of the sentence; 3) the subject tends to be specific; 4) the subject plays an important role in the syntactic processes of NP pronominalization, deletion, reflexivization, and imperativization; and 5) the subject is always without a preposition.

Cao Fengfu's discussion of the differences between topic and subject can be summarized in the following two dimensions: topic is weakly related to the predicate verb, while subject is in a selective relationship with the verb; topic is generally not involved in syntactic processes, while subject is in control of syntactic processes.

Yuan Yulin (2010) disagrees with Cao in the following respects:

1) Like subject, topic can also be indefinite, as in "一棵树苗,分枝长得太多就会影响树干的发育" (Yī kē shùmiáo, fēnzhī zhǎng de tài duō jiùhuì yǐngxiǎng shùgàn de fǎyù, 'A sapling, if there are too many branches, the growth of the trunk will be affected.').
2) The so-called topic may not necessarily occur at the very beginning of the sentence, nor is it always the case that topic has no selective relation with the verb predicate. In "这本书,内容比那本书好" (Zhè běn shū, nèiróng bǐ nà běn shū hǎo, 'This book, the content is better than that book's.') and "内容,这本书比那本好" (Nèiróng, zhè běn shū bǐ nà běn hǎo, '(In terms of) content, this book is better than that book.'], both sentence-initial constituents have a selective relationship with the predicate verb.
3) The Chinese topic, like the subject, can also control the pronominalization or deletion of the coreferential NP, as in "小王呢,眼睛不好;所以,(他)只能报考文科" (Xiǎo Wáng ne, yǎnjīng bù hǎo; suǒ yǐ, [tā] zhǐnéng bàokǎo wénkē, '[As for] Little Wang, [his] eyes are not good; therefore, [he] can only apply for arts.'].
4) Chinese topics, like subjects again, can play an important role in grammatical processes such as imperativization, reflexivization, the deletion of identical NPs and passivization, such as "(早饭)你上我家吃吧!" ([Zǎofàn]) nǐ shàng wǒ jiā chī ba!, '[For breakfast], come up to my house!), which is a case of imperativized topic sentence, and "我呢,成绩不好只能埋怨自己不用功" (Wǒ ne, chéngjī bùhǎo zhǐnéng máiyuàn zìjǐ bú yònggōng, 'I, for my poor grades, can only blame myself for not working hard.')

Thus, to Yuan Yulin, there is no reliable way to differentiate subject and topic in Chinese sentences.

According to Xu Liejiong (2002), Chinese is a discourse-configurational language which has subtopics in addition to the main topic. The sentence-initial position is the topic position; on top of that, the position between the subject and the verb is also the topic position. For example, in "他聪明是聪明，但做事情太粗心" (Tā cōngmíng shì cōng míng, dàn zuò shìqíng tài cūxīn, 'He is smart, but he is too careless in doing things.'), "聪明" ('smart') does not occur sentence initially; instead, it occurs in between the subject and the copula verb, making up a "copy topic" in Xu Liejiong and Liu Danqing's (1998/2007) terminology.

The analysis of two positions for topic and subtopic, respectively, is ultimately because the subject of Chinese is also the topic. If the subjects of the so-called double-subject sentences are both person indicating nouns or pronouns, the nominal constituent that occurs sentence initially will still be understood as topic in preference. See (12) and (13).

(12) 伤员老同志为多。

Shāngyuán lǎo   tóngzhì   wéi   duō.
the.wounded old   comrades   be   many
'The wounded, old comrades make up the majority.'

In (12), the primary subject (i.e. "the wounded") and secondary subject ("old comrades") are in a whole–part relation.

(13) 你我接管了。

Nǐ   wǒ   jiēguǎn le.
you   I   take.over PFV
'You, I take over.'

Unlike in (12), the primary subject "you" and secondary subject "I" in (13) are not in a whole–part relation.

Regardless of the whole–part relation between the primary and secondary subjects, the two examples above show that the primary subject can only be understood as a relevant entity, rather than the agent subject. In other words, this contrast demonstrates that the sentence-initial position is the preferred topic position.

6.1.2.2 Topicality

Topicality refers to the property of a constituent to be topical. Topicality is not a property that a referent gets from the clause; instead, it is a property endowed by discourse (Givón, 1984/1990). As the topic of discourse, a concept tends to appear many a time and to be tracked in different ways, which attests to its topicality.

Our observation suggests that the verb-copying construction is of high accessibility and that it is very frequently used to track an action that is stated in the preceding discourse context.

(14) 严师母无限感慨地说:"要说**做人**₁,最是体现在穿衣上的,它是**做人**₂的兴趣和精神,是最要紧的。"萨沙就问:"那么吃呢?"严师母摇了一下头,说:"**吃**是**做人**₃的里子,虽也是重要,却不是像面子那样,支撑起全局,作宣言一般,让人信服和器重的。当然,里子有它实惠的一面,**做人**₄**做给自己看**。可是,假如完全不为别人看的**做人**₅,又有多少味道呢?"(Wang Anyi, *The Song of Everlasting Sorrow*)

Yán shīmǔ wúxiàn gǎnkǎi de shuō: "Yàoshuō **zuòrén**₁, zuì shì tǐxiàn zài chuānyī shàng de, tā shì **zuòrén**₂ de xìngqù hé jīngshén, shì zuì yàojǐn de." Sàshā jiù wèn: "Nàme chī ne?" Yán shīmǔ yáole yīxià tou, shuō: "Chī shì **zuòrén**₃ de lǐzi, suī yěshì zhòngyào, què búshì xiàng miànzi nàyàng, zhīchēng qǐ quánjú, zuò xuānyán yībān, ràng rén xìnfú hé qìzhòng de. Dāngrán, lǐzi yǒu tā shíhuì de yīmiàn, **zuòrén**₄ **zuò gěi zìjǐ kàn**. Kěshì, jiǎrú wánquán bú wèi biérén kàn de **zuòrén**₅, yòu yǒu duōshǎo wèidào ne?"

'Ms. Yan said with infinite emotion, "Speaking of **being human**₁, the most is reflected in dressing, which is the interest and spirit of **being human**₂, thus the most important." Sasha then asked, "What about eating?" Ms. Yan shook her head a little and said, "Eating is the lining of **being human**₃. Although it is also important, it is not like face, which supports the whole picture and makes a declaration to convince people and make yourself valued. Of course, the lining has its own tangible benefits; you can **be human**₄ **for your own sake**. But how much flavor is there in **being human**₅ regardless of all others' view at all?"'

In the above example, "做人" ('being human') appears five times in total. Its first appearance is introduced through the preceding phrase "要说" ('speaking of'). In the subsequent discourse, "做人₂" and "做人₃" are used as modifiers, which are then followed by the verb-copying construction. In its final use, it is the head of the NP "完全不为别人看的做人" ('being human regardless of all others' view at all'). That a concept appears several times in discourse and is tracked in different ways is in itself a sign of topicality.

We know that a topic chain is formed when the same entity appears repeatedly in the process of discourse development. The topic chain is an important aspect of discourse coherence, and the strength of topicality is manifested in the syntactic coding of the topic. The discourse topic has a very strong power in ushering in ensuing discourse (see Liu Anchun and Zhang Bojiang, 2004; Fang Mei, 2005a; Xu Yulong, 2004, p. 147; 2007), as shown by the fact that the zero-subjects of the subsequent sentences will be coreferential with it, forming a complete topic chain.[2]

To recapitulate, topics in Chinese on the one hand can be directly coded in verbal phrases without undergoing the syntactic operation of nominalization, so that the topic identity of a syntactic constituent is more dependent on the topic chain in discourse. And, on the other, the discourse topic can in turn verify its expressive function in individual clauses.

6.1.3 Continuity of action

Xu Liejiong and Liu Danqing (1998/2007) have established the notion of copy topics, illustrated by the sentence "说话都说不出来了" (Shuōhuà dōu shuō-bù-chūlái le, '(One) can't even speak.'). This sentence is actually an instantiation of type (I) verb-copying construction as introduced in Section 6.1.1.1 According to the analysis of Xu Liejiong and Liu Danqing (1998/2007, 2003), the person indicating constituent that takes the sentence-initial position (i.e., our types (II) and (III) of verb-copying construction) is the subject and the main topic, and the verb–object phrase (VP1) in the verb-copying construction is the subtopic.

Their study, however, basically takes the sentence as the unit of analysis. We would argue that, as a very characteristic syntactic structure in Chinese, the verb-copying construction deserves further exploration with regard to its functional motivation. As pointed out in earlier studies, it is indisputable that the subject of Chinese has topic properties from the perspective of syntactic constraints. The key question is how to prove the topic status of the verb–object component part of the verb-copying construction.

As mentioned above, topic is, on the one hand, a concept proposed in opposition to subject on the basis of syntactic differences; and, on the other hand, all constituents with topicality exhibit topic continuity with regard to their referents. As far as NP constituents are concerned, there have been numerous studies on the linguistic realizations of their topic chains, but how verbal referents serve as topics remains to be more adequately investigated. The coding form of the verb-copying construction provides a syntactic possibility for expressing topic continuity. That is, in discourse, the verb-copying construction can be used to establish an action-indicating event as the topic, as illustrated in examples (2) to (5) above.

In (14) above, we see that an action is established as topic by way of "要说" ('speaking of'), and the topic thus marked enjoys the status of the discourse topic. To put it differently, the action thus coded is the topic of the entire discourse.

Previous attention to topic continuity has focused on how an NP concept is tracked and represented in discourse. In fact, the continuity of an action also makes up a key aspect of topic continuity[3] in discourse (Givón, 1983). An action can be considered to have action continuity if it is repeatedly referred to in discourse in different coding forms.

In the following example, the main discourse character is He Qiang, and the main event is looking for a job. The first recurrence of the event is found in the modifier position of the phrase "找工作的历程", and its second recurrence is in the subject position of the clause "找工作屡屡失利." There then follows the verb-copying construction "找工作找了半年多", which functions as an adverbial clause of time.

(15) 何强36岁从某国有机械厂下岗,本想着凭自己的好手艺,**不愁找不到活干**。从去年9月份起,何强就开始了**找工作**的历程。开始他看到报纸上招工信息上的年龄限制时,还没太放在心上,以为能力是第一位的,年龄只是小问题。可是当他一次次走进人才市场后,才发现现实比他原先想的要残酷得多。**找工作**屡屡失利,而且还都是栽在他以前不以为然的年龄上。……

……

"**找工作找了半年多了**,还是这么个状态,成天像无业游民一样。刚下岗时还没有太多顾虑,但现实已经教会了我太多东西。我的要求不高,只希望有一份工作做就可以。"何强说。(Xinhua Net, April 14, 2003, "I don't want to retire at the age of 37" – An analysis of the "35-year-old phenomenon" in the talent market')

Hé Qiáng 36 suì cóng mǒu guóyǒu jīxièchǎng xiàgǎng, běnxiǎngzhe píng zìjǐ de hǎo shǒuyì, **bù chóu zhǎo-bú-dào huó gàn**. Cóng qùnián 9 yuèfèn qǐ, Hé Qiáng jiù kāishǐle **zhǎo gōngzuò** de lìchéng. Kāishǐ tā kàndào bàozhǐ shàng zhāogōng xìnxī shàng de niánlíng xiànzhì shí, hái méi tài fàngzàixīnshàng, yǐwéi nénglì shì dìyīwèi de, niánlíng zhǐshì xiǎo wèntí. Kěshì dāng tā yīcìcì zǒu jìn réncái shìchǎng hòu, cái fāxiàn xiànshí bǐ tā yuánxiān xiǎng de yāo cánkù de duō. **Zhǎo gōngzuò** lǚlǚ shīlì, érqiě hái dōu shì zāi zài tā yǐqián bùyǐwéirán de niánlíng shàng…

…

"**Zhǎo gōngzuò zhǎole bànnián duō le**, háishì zhème gè zhuàngtài, chéngtiān xiàng wúyè yóumín yīyàng. Gāng xiàgǎng shí hái méiyǒu tài duō gùlǜ, dàn xiànshí yǐjīng jiāohuìle wǒ tài duō dōngxī. Wǒ de yāoqiú bù gāo, zhǐ xīwàng yǒu yī fèn gōngzuò zuò jiù kěyǐ." Hé Qiáng shuō.

'He Qiang was laid off from a state-owned machinery factory at the age of 36, thinking that with his good skills he would **have no worry about securing a job**. From September last year, he began the journey of **looking for a job**. At the beginning, when he saw the age limit on the recruitment information in the newspaper, he didn't take it too seriously, thinking that ability was the most important while age was only a minor concern. However, when he walked into the job market again and again, he realized that the reality was much harsher than what he originally thought. He failed repeatedly in **securing a job**, each time because of his age, a factor he did not take seriously earlier on….

…

"(I)'ve **been looking for a job for more than half a year**, but I'm still in such a state, like a hobo all day long. When I was first laid off, I didn't have too much to worry, but reality has taught me a whole lot. My expectation is not high. I just want to have a job to do." He Qiang said.'

136 *Discourse functions of verb-copying constructions*

It is not difficult to see that the verb-copying construction is an important coding form to continue the main event-line. In the next example, the event narrated is Li Delin, the main character of the discourse, looking for the leaders.

(16) ……李德林心中暗暗叫苦，直埋怨自己实在是太迟钝了太迟钝了！<u>扭头出去连忙去各局找头头</u>。可哪那么容易**说找就找着**，都年根了，头头们事多了去啦，慰问啦开座谈会啦看离退休老干部啦还有抓时间跟关系单位和重要人物喝酒打麻将啊，反正是忙得一塌糊涂。**在机关找不着**，李德林**就往这几个局头头的家里去找**。

找了两家人没找着不说，心里还挺别扭，有的连大门都没开，说声不在家就拉倒了。…… (He Shen, "Before and after the New Year's Day" [《年前年后》])

… Lǐ Délín xīnzhōng àn'àn jiàokǔ, zhí mányuàn zìjǐ shízài shì tài chídùn le tài chídùn le! <u>Niǔtóu chūqù liánmáng</u> **qù gèjú zhǎo tóutou**. Kě nǎ nàme róngyì **shuō zhǎo jiù zhǎozháo**, dōu niángēn le, tóutou men shì duō-le-qù la, wèiwèn la kāi zuòtánhuì la kàn lí-tuìxiū lǎo gànbù la háiyǒu zhuā shíjiān gēn guānxì dānwèi hé zhòngyào rénwù hējiǔ dǎmájiàng a, fǎnzhèng shì máng de yītāhútú. **Zài jīguān zhǎo-bù-zháo**, Lǐ Délín **jiù wǎng zhè jǐ gè jú tóutou de jiāli qù zhǎo**.

Zhǎole liǎng jiā rén méi zhǎozháo bùshuō, xīnlǐ hái tǐng bièniu, yǒu de lián dàmén dōu méi kāi, shuō shēng bú zàijiā jiù lādǎo le…

'… Li Delin complained secretly in his heart, blaming himself for being far too slow. He <u>turned round and hurriedly</u> **went to each bureau to find the head**. But it was **no easy job to find them**. It was already the end of the year, and the heads had tons of work to busy themselves with, conveying greetings, attending symposiums, visiting the retired old cadres, grabbing time to drink and play mahjong with the relevant units and important people, to name but a few. In one word, they were incredibly busy. Since the heads **could not be found in their offices**, Li Delin decided **to find them at their homes**.

Not to mention that he failed to find the person at a couple of households, he felt awkward as well. Some did not even answer the door, just slurring "he's not in" at him….'

In the first paragraph of this cited example, the central action of looking for heads occurs four times (see the parts in bold fonts). The verb-copying construction "找了两家人没找着" appears as a subordinate clause, and VP1 in the construction "找了两家人" is also contextualized, expressing anything but new information.

In summary, topic continuity can be achieved in different ways. In one way, it can be achieved through coreference between the person-indicating subject and the protagonist in the preceding context; and alternatively, an event already stated in the preceding context can be coded in the verb-copying construction, i.e., types (II) and (III) as delineated in the introductory part of this chapter, so that the event can be the topic for ensuing discourse. Irrespective of the subtype of the construction, the verb–object component part, although presented in the verbal form, does not have the typical syntactic functions of a declarative predicate. For instance, the verb cannot be reduplicated; neither can the verb–object be followed by tense-aspect markers such as "过" (guò). Therefore, VP1 in the verb-copying construction is a reduced declarative predicate, and its function is equivalent to that of a non-finite VP in morphological languages.

Since topic is referential by nature, this basic property makes the verb in VP1 behave very differently from when it is used as a typical predicate. And this is the underlying reason for the various syntactic constraints on verb-copying constructions.

6.2 Summary

The two successive verb phrases in the verb-copying construction have different information statuses, and the verbal topic generally refers to an act that has already been stated in discourse or is the shared knowledge of the two communicative parties. In terms of information status, the verbal information provided by VP1 is old information or accessible information with fairly high accessibility, while new information is imparted by the subsequent verb-complement component part. When it comes to syntactic representation, VP1 fulfills the expressive function of non-finite VPs in morphological languages.

Topic continuity involves three aspects: 1) thematic continuity, 2) action continuity, and 3) topic/participant continuity. The verb-copying construction is a syntactic configuration that reflects action continuity, constituting an important means of maintaining topic continuity in discourse. Type (I) of the verb-copying construction described in Section 6.1 (zero agent as subject) is a coding form that introduces an action concept as the topic, as illustrated in (16) and (17). Topic continuity can also be achieved by way of double-track operation, i.e., types (II) and (III) of the verb-copying construction. In other words, topic chain is formed through anaphoric reference to the subject on the one hand, and on the other action continuity, which is realized by way of the syntactic means of the verb-copying construction.

In Chinese, the subject is usually the topic. Not only can verbs function as subject or topic without being morphosyntactically marked, non-predicate VPs can do so in the same manner as well. Descriptions and interpretations that take discourse function as the entry point can link the corresponding syntactic forms of specific expressive functions across languages and reveal the interlingual similarities and differences.

7 S-adverbs and their discourse functions

Adverbs are a class of words that typically occur as adverbials. Some adverbs, however, modify the entire sentence or even function at the discourse level beyond the sentence. These adverbs are known as S-adverbs, mostly used at the beginning or the end of a sentence, rather than in the post-subject position immediately preceding the predicate. Semantically, most S-adverbs are time adverbs, followed by evaluative adverbs. In discourse, S-adverbs have a topic chain-blocking effect, and prosodically independent S-adverbs can function to mark the course of events. Sentence-initial time S-adverbs are often used for scene transition, marking plot points.

7.1 Introduction

Adverbs are a class of words that can only be used as adverbials (Zhu Dexi, 1982, p. 192). Dragunov, an early analyst of Chinese adverbs in terms of syntactic position, points out that "the adverb category can be divided into two subcategories: the first subcategory is adjunctive to the whole sentence, and the second belongs directly to the predicate" (1958, p. 189), which is also a classification of general descriptive grammar. If defined in terms of function, the former, whose semantic scope is larger than the clause, can be called S-adverbs, and the latter, whose semantic scope is within the clause, are called VP-adverbs.

When functioning as adverbials, some adverbs modify primarily predicates while others do compound sentences, which renders them most likely to be "entangled" with conjunctions. In *A Grammar of Spoken Chinese*, Chao observes,

> There is a difference between (a) adverbial conjunctions, or words which are at the same time adverbs and conjunctions, and (b) words which are sometimes adverbs and sometimes conjunctions by class overlap… Most of the correlative adverbial conjunctions are of this kind.
>
> (1968, p. 779)

Research on the discourse function of Chinese adverbs mainly focuses on the expression of subjective attitudes and discourse cohesion. Chinese studies published in the 1980s have fully noticed that some adverbs have the discourse cohesive function. For example, Liao Qiuzhong (1986b), when discussing the elements in modern Chinese discourse, has pointed out that these connective elements are not syntactic constituents. The adverbs he classifies as discourse connectives include modal adverbs (e.g. 真的, zhēnde, 'really'), evaluative adverbs (e.g. 其实, qíshí, 'actually'), and time adverbs (e.g. 然后, ránhòu, 'then'). According to Chu (1991), adverbs, occurring either before or after the subject or topic, are not part of sentence structure; instead, they closely concern discourse structure, their position of occurrence related to discourse or text organization. Peng Xiaochuan (1999) emphasizes the discourse function of the adverb 倒 (dào, 'contrary to what is expected or thought') when discussing its grammatical meaning. Zhang Yisheng (2000a) notes the discourse function of adverbs and discusses the grammatical functions and meanings of correlative adverbial conjunctions, which later on developed into a monograph entitled *Discourse Linking Function of Adverbs* (《副词的篇章连接功能》). Shi Jinsheng (2003) suggests that, besides being used mainly for propositions, adverbs also express the subjective attitudes of speakers toward propositions, embodying interpersonal and textual functions.

7.1.1 *Distribution and semantics of S-adverbs*

Qi Huyang (2003) has found that modal adverbs exhibit considerable flexibility in terms of syntactic distribution, for they are not always located in front of verbs or adjectives as other adverbs, but can also precede subjects. And, unlike other subcategories of adverbs, modal adverbs can only be combined at the dynamic sentence level. Yang Defeng (2009) takes the 93 modal adverbs listed in *Chinese Proficiency Vocabulary and Graded Syllabus of Chinese Characters* (《汉语水平词汇与汉字等级大纲》) as the subject of study, the corpus statistics showing that some modal adverbs appear only before or after the subject, while others can appear both before and after the subject. Yang argues that the distribution of modal adverbs is the manifestation of adverb subcategorization. Modal adverbs cannot be freely placed before or after the subject simply according to the needs of expression; instead, their distribution is subject to syntactic conditioning.

It has been shown that a large proportion of S-adverbs are used to express the speaker's attitude or evaluation, including 本来 (běnlái, 'originally'), 大概 (dàgài, 'probably'), 当然 (dāngrán, 'certainly'), 倒是 (dǎoshì, 'rather'), 万一 (wànyī, 'in case'), 的确 (díquè, 'indeed'), 难怪 (nánguài, 'no wonder'), 敢情 (gǎnqing, 'indeed'), 怪不得 (guàibùdé, 'no wonder'), 居然 (jūrán, 'unexpectedly'), 确实 (quèshí, 'actually'), 压根儿 (yàgēn·er, 'at all'), 幸亏 (xìngkuī, 'fortunately'), etc. (Li Quan, 2002; Shi Jinsheng, 2003; Yuan Yulin, 2002a; Zhang Yisheng, 1996, 2000a, 2000b; Liu Xiaohui, 2012). These adverbs can precede or follow the subject.

We believe that the S-adverb is primarily marked by its syntactic position: when it co-occurs with a conjunction that indicates subordination, it must precede the conjunction. In (1), "大概" is outside the proposition proper of the sentence, and its mandatory distribution reflects the correlation between its form and function.

(1) a. 大概因为我没有同意他的意见,他见到我的时候挺不高兴。(因为 is a subordinate conjunction indicating reason.)

   Dàgài yīnwèi wǒ méiyǒu tóngyì tā de yìjiàn, tā jiàndào wǒ de shíhòu tǐng bù gāoxìng.

   'Probably because I didn't agree to his idea, he was quite upset when he saw me.'

   b. *因为大概我没有同意他的意见,他见到我的时候挺不高兴。

   Yīnwèi dàgài wǒ méiyǒu tóngyì tā de yìjiàn, tā jiàndào wǒ de shíhòu tǐng bù gāoxìng.

Conversely, when an S-adverb co-occurs with a coordinate conjunction, it is not mandatory for the S-adverb to precede the conjunction. In (2), for instance, the S-adverb "毕竟" ('after all') follows the disjunctive conjunction "但" ('but'). This is because what disjunctive conjunctions link are coordinate clauses. As a matter of fact, disjunctive conjunctions can even function as macrosyntactic conjunctions (Chao, 1968, p. 791).

(2) 走的走,亡的亡,看来红楼梦里的女人们,虽然都跟怡红院有缘,但毕竟大多数都是有缘无分,有运无命啊。(*This Is Beijing* [《这里是北京》])

   Zǒude zǒu, wángde wáng, kànlái Hónglóumèng lǐ de nǚrénmen, suīrán dōu gēn Yíhóngyuàn yǒuyuán, dàn bìjìng dàduōshù dōushì yǒu yuán wú fèn, yǒu yùn wú mìng a.

   'Some left; some died. It seems that the women in *A Dream of Red Mansions* were all somehow related to the Happy Red Court. Nonetheless, most of them had only the luck to be brought there, but not the fate to stay there all along.'

Of course, not all adverbs that occur before the subject are S-adverbs. For instance, a quantifier adverb can also be used at the beginning of a sentence, but its function is to qualify the number of the nominal constituent in the sentence, as in (3), where 只 is a quantifier adverb meaning 'only'.

(3) a. 我只买了三本书。

   Wǒ zhǐ mǎile sān běn shū.

   'I bought only three books'

   b. 只我买了三本书。

   Zhǐ wǒ mǎile sān běn shū.

   'Only I bought three books.'

Quantifier adverbs are semantically exclusive: (3a) excludes other items than "书" ('book'), while (3b) excludes other people than "我" ('I'). Regardless of its position, the exclusive meaning of 只 remains the same. Moreover, its semantic restriction is on a specific syntactic constituent, not on the whole sentence. A similar case is the use of 就 ('just').

(4) A: 买什么了?
    B: 就三本书。
    A: Mǎi shénme le?
    B: Jiù sān běn shū.
    'A: What did you buy?
    B: Just three books.'

(5) A: 谁上午逛街去了?
    B: 就我,没别人。
    A: Shéi shàngwǔ guàngjiē qù le?
    B: Jiù wǒ, méi biérén.
    'A: Who went shopping in the morning?
    B: Just me, no one else.'

To reiterate, the scope of a quantifier adverb is a syntactic constituent, rather than the whole sentence. Regardless of its distribution, before the verb or at the beginning of the sentence, a quantifier adverb is never an S-adverb.

Scholars have already noted that modal and time adverbs are commonly used sentence initially, while other subcategories are sparingly thus used. For example, Li Quan (1996) has investigated a list of 217 manner adverbs, 33% of the total number of adverbs, finding that there are only two cases in written Chinese where the adverb occurs at the beginning of the sentence, with no use at the end of the sentence at all. Yang Defeng's (2006) exhaustive survey of 62 time adverbs listed in the *Chinese Language Proficiency Vocabulary and Chinese Character Rating Syllabus* in a literary corpus of over ten million words shows that the default slot for time adverbs to occur as adverbials is the post-subject position. When a time adverb is put in front of the subject, it has a wider scope, qualifying the whole event; when it is used post the subject, it has a narrower scope, qualifying only the action by indicating its time. The distribution of time adverbs is constrained not only by syllable structure, but also by the pragmatic motive to highlight the temporal dimension.

Pan Guoying (2010) represents a quantitative statistical approach to adverb research. The 470-million-word Peking University Modern Chinese Corpus demonstrates that the syntactic distribution of modal adverbs and time adverbs is subject to a variety of factors such as syllable structure, semantic meaning, discourse function, and stylistic features.

Here we would argue that the sentence-initial use of adverbs as revealed by these studies is mainly prompted by their discourse function. The narrative discourse takes the course of events as the main line, and the chronology of events and the behavior of event participants make up the progression pattern of this type of discourse. The information on the main line of narration is foreground information, and the layouts outside the main line are background information. Chafe (1980, p. 54) proposes that English narrators pay more attention to time clues, and that plot switch is achieved by means of time-denoting expressions. In fact, the situation is similar in Chinese, where the sentence-initial time words in narrative discourse are also plot demarcation points, and the evaluative adverbs that occur sentence initially are markers of discourse organization in political discourse. Liao Qiuzhong (1987) has sorted out the elements that mark discourse boundaries in Chinese, pointing out that some adverbials, usually located at the beginning of the sentence, can sometimes expand the scope beyond the boundary of the hosting sentence, constituting discourse boundary markers. Semantically, such adverbials can be divided into nine categories, including those of time, place, and evaluation.[1]

We are concerned with the question of how the meaning of the same adverb varies with the position of occurrence, sometimes at the beginning of the sentence and other times post the subject. Two issues seem to be particularly important here.

First, evaluative adverbs, especially prosodically independent ones, indicate different degrees of speaker commitment to the reliability of the propositional information when they occur sentence initially vis-à-vis sentence internally.

Second, the semantics of polysemous adverbs varies with their position of occurrence, prosodically independent ones in particular. When they occur sentence initially, they are more liable for temporal or evaluative reading.

(I) Speaker commitment varies with the syntactic position that modal adverbs take. When they occur sentence initially, a high degree of commitment comes forth.

(6) a. 他真的想领养一个孩子。
   Tā zhēnde xiǎng lǐngyǎng yī gè háizi.
   'He really wants to adopt a child.'
   b. 真的,他想领养一个孩子。
   Zhēnde, tā xiǎng lǐngyǎng yī gè háizi.
   'Really, he wants to adopt a child.'

(7) a. 他真的想领养一个孩子,我相信/猜。
   Tā zhēnde xiǎng lǐngyǎng yī gè háizi, wǒ xiāngxìn/cāi.
   'He really wants to adopt a child, I believe/guess.'
   b. 真的,他想领养一个孩子,我相信。
   Zhēnde, tā xiǎng lǐngyǎng yī gè háizi, wǒ xiāngxìn.
   'Really, he wants to adopt a child, I believe.'

c. ?真的, 他想领养一个孩子, 我猜。
Zhēnde, tā xiǎng lǐngyǎng yī gè háizi, wǒ cāi.
'Really, he wants to adopt a child, I guess.'

(8) a. 我怀疑他是否真的想领养一个孩子。
Wǒ huáiyí tā shìfǒu zhēnde xiǎng lǐngyǎng yī gè háizi.
'I doubt if he really wants to adopt a child.'

b. *真的, 他想领养一个孩子, 我怀疑。
*Zhēnde, tā xiǎng lǐngyǎng yī gè háizi, wǒ huáiyí.
'Really, he wants to adopt a child, I doubt it.'

The difference between (6a) and (6b) above lies in the position of the adverb "真的" ('really'). In (6b), it is put at the beginning of the sentence, which emphasizes the commitment of the speaker. This difference can be attested by examples (7) and (8). When "真的" follows the subject, the original sentence can be followed by "我相信" ('I believe') or "我猜" ('I guess'), as shown in (7a); when it occurs at the beginning of the sentence, it can still be followed by "我相信", but it would sound awkward when followed by "我猜", as illustrated in (7b) and (7c). When it comes to (8), the clause where "真的" occurs as the post-subject adverbial can be the object clause of "怀疑" ('doubt'), but when it takes the sentence-initial position, it is barely acceptable to follow the clause with "我怀疑" ('I doubt'). This phenomenon is difficult to explain by the fact that S-adverbs defy embedding on account of their independent prosody. Parallel to the above phenomenon, modal auxiliary verbs, such as 可能 (kěnéng, 'may') and 应该 (yīnggāi, 'should'), can also occur in different syntactic slots in spoken Chinese, and there is also a difference in commitment level between the sentence initial position and the sentence final position (for details, see Fang Mei, 2013a).

(II) The same adverb, when used after the subject, is a VP-adverb, indicating the manner; when used at the beginning of the sentence, it is an S-adverb, conveying temporal meaning. Compare the use of "渐渐的" ('gradually') in example (9).

(9) a. 亲友渐渐的往外溜, 尤其妇女们脑筋明敏, 全一拐一拐的往外挪小脚。只剩下李山东和孙八至近的几个朋友依旧按着王德不放手。(Lao She, *The Philosophy of Old Zhang* [《老张的哲学》])

Qīnyǒu jiànjiànde wǎngwài liū, yóuqí fùnǚmen nǎojīn míngmǐn, quán yīguǎi~yīguǎi de wǎngwài nuó xiǎojiǎo. Zhǐ shèngxià Lǐ Shāndōng hé Sūn Bā zhìjìn de jǐ gè péngyǒu yījiù ànzhe Wáng Dé bù fàngshǒu.

'Friends and relatives gradually slipped out. The women were especially quick-witted, all limping outward on their small feet. Only a few friends really close to Li Shandong and Sun Ba were still holding Wang De tightly.'

b. 瑞宣呆呆的立在那里，看着，看着，<u>渐渐的</u>他只能看到几个黑影在马路边上慢慢的动，在晴美的阳光下，钱先生的头上闪动着一些白光。
(Lao She, *The Yellow Storm* [《四世同堂》])

Ruìxuān dāidāide lì zài nàlǐ, kànzhe, kànzhe, <u>jiànjiànde</u> tā zhǐnéng kàndào jǐ gè hēiyǐng zài mǎlù biān shàng mànmande dòng, zài qíngměi de yángguāng xià, Qián xiānsheng de tóu shàng shǎndòngzhe yīxiē báiguāng.

'Ruixuan stood there dumbfounded, watching and watching. <u>Gradually</u> he could only see a few dark shadows moving slowly on the roadside. In the clear beautiful sunlight, Mr. Qian's head flashed some white light.'

c. 载涛对自行车的喜爱也影响了他的侄子——末代皇帝溥仪，也就出现了故宫骑车和锯门槛的那一幕。但是没过几年，大清朝灭亡了，载涛的日子也随之难过起来。<u>渐渐的</u>，连房子都修不起了，曾经名噪京城的涛贝勒府变得破败不堪。(*This Is Beijing*)

Zàitāo duì zìxíngchē de xǐ'ài yě yǐngxiǎngle tā de zhízi – mòdài huángdì Pǔyí, yě jiù chūxiànle Gùgōng qíchē hé jù ménkǎn de nà yī mù. Dànshì méi guò jǐ nián, dàqīngcháo mièwángle, Zàitāo de rìzi yě suí zhī nánguò qǐlái. <u>Jiànjiànde</u>, lián fángzi dōu xiū-bù-qǐ le, céngjīng míngzào jīngchéng de Tāo bèilè fǔ biànde pòbàibùkān.

'Zaitao's love of bicycles also influenced his nephew – the last emperor Puyi. That was also why there was the scene of bicycle riding and threshold sawing in the Forbidden City. But a few years later, with the fall of the Qing Dynasty, Zaitao's days got ever harder. <u>Gradually</u>, he couldn't even afford to repair his house. The once famous residence of Prince Zaitao became dilapidated.'

d. 瑞宣呆呆的立在那里，看着，看着，他<u>渐渐的</u>只能看到几个黑影在马路边上慢慢的动，在晴美的阳光下，钱先生的头上闪动着一些白光。
(Lao She, *The Yellow Storm*)

Ruìxuān dāidāide lì zài nàlǐ, kànzhe, kànzhe, tā <u>jiànjiànde</u> zhǐnéng kàndào jǐ gè hēiyǐng zài mǎlù biān shàng mànmande dòng, zài qíngměi de yángguāng xià, Qián xiānsheng de tóu shàng shǎndòngzhe yīxiē báiguāng.

In this example, "渐渐的" in (9a) can be replaced with 陆陆续续 (lùlùxùxù, 'one after another'), while (9b) does not allow this change. The prosodically independent "渐渐的" has an obvious function of dividing up the plot, as in (9c), where the part preceding "渐渐的" expresses the process and the part following it states the result. It is exactly for this reason that it, when put to follow the subject, shifts from expressing the course of event to the expression of the change of state, as in (9d).

(III) The time adverb, when used post the subject, is a VP-adverb, indicating the frequency of a specific action in a specific timeline. Although such an adverb also expresses frequency when occurring sentence initially, it primarily reflects the "whole-part" relationship of its hosting clause with the preceding one, to refine and explain the proposition made in the preceding clause, as illustrated in (10b) and (11b) below.

(10) a. 马林生完全想象得出，马锐的那一眼是怎么看的，他的那双眼睛<u>有时</u>比说出话来还气人。但不管怎么说，这也不能成为暴打人家一顿的理由。(Wang Shuo, *I'm Your Father* [《我是你爸爸》])

    Mǎ Línshēng wánquán xiǎngxiàng-de-chū, Mǎ Ruì de nà yī yǎn shì zěnme kàn de, tā de nà shuāng yǎnjīng <u>yǒushí</u> bǐ shuōchū huà lái hái qìrén. Dàn bùguǎn zěnme shuō, zhè yě bùnéng chéngwéi bàodǎ rénjiā yī dùn de lǐyóu.

    'Ma Linsheng could fully imagine how that glance from Ma Rui looked, and those eyes of his were <u>sometimes</u> more exasperating than the words that he uttered. But in any case, this could not be a reason to beat him up.'

  b. 他变得对马锐不闻不问，<u>有时</u>马锐主动向他请示或汇报些学校和家务方面的问题，他大都置若罔闻，最多嗯哼几句语焉不详地敷衍了事。(Wang Shuo, *I'm Your Father*)

    Tā biànde duì Mǎ Ruì bùwénbùwèn, <u>yǒushí</u> Mǎ Ruì zhǔdòng xiàng tā qǐngshì huò huìbào xiē xuéxiào hé jiāwù fāngmiàn de wèntí, tā dàdōu zhìruòwǎngwén, zuìduō ńhēng jǐ jù yǔyānbùxiáng de fūyǎnliǎoshì.

    'He became indifferent to Ma Rui, and <u>sometimes</u> when Ma Rui asked him for advice or reported on school and household affairs, he mostly ignored them, or at most, grunted a few incoherent words to have them dismissed.'

(11) a. 这时，他从镜子里看到躺在屋床上的儿子<u>偶尔</u>起身歪头往外看，由于里屋很明亮，他能清楚地看到儿子的一举一动。(Wang Shuo, *I'm Your Father*)

    Zhèshí, tā cóng jìngzi lǐ kàndào tǎng zài wū chuángshàng de érzi <u>ǒu'ěr</u> qǐshēn wāi tóu wǎng wài kàn, yóuyú lǐwū hěn míngliàng, tā néng qīngchǔ de kàndào érzi de yījǔyīdòng.

    'At this time, he saw in the mirror that his son, who was lying on the bed in the inner room, <u>occasionally</u> got up and looked out with his head tilted. Because the inner room was very bright, he could see every move of his son clearly.'

  b. 凡是被他们冠以这一评价者他们谈起来都使用最轻蔑的口气。<u>偶尔</u>他们对某个人某件事看法也会发生分歧，但更多的是一个人对另一个人的随声附和。(Wang Shuo, *I'm Your Father*)

    Fánshì bèi tāmen guān yǐ zhè yī píngjià zhě tāmen tán qǐlái dōu shǐyòng zuì qīngmiè de kǒuqì. <u>Ǒu'ěr</u> tāmen duì mǒugèrén mǒujiànshì kànfǎ yě huì fāshēng fēnqí, dàn gèng duō de shì yī gè rén duì lìng yī gè rén de suíshēngfùhè.

'They talk about all those who are given this evaluation in the most contemptuous tone. <u>Occasionally</u> they may disagree about someone or something, but more often than not, one would echo the other.'

The post-subject "有时" ('sometimes') and "偶尔" ('occasionally') are adverbs of frequency, as shown by the fact that their hosting clauses are still grammatically acceptable when they are replaced with other adverbs of frequency. For example, both "有时" in (10a) and "偶尔" in (11a) can be replaced with 经常 (jīngcháng, 'often'), without syntactic consequences. The sentence initial 有时 and 偶尔, however, do not allow such replacement.

(IV) The scope of manner adverbs is usually the predicate, and when such an adverb is fronted to the sentence-initial position, it can be interpreted as expressing either manner or time, both in the course of events.

(12) 炉上的水壶盖轻轻吱叫,缕缕水蒸汽从壶嘴里袅袅冒出,蓦地水壶尖叫, 马林生如梦方醒,忙起身把水壶自炉上拎下。(Wang Shuo, *I'm Your Father*)

Lú shàng de shuǐhú gài qīng~qīng zhījiào, lǚ~lǚ shuǐzhēngqì cóng húzuǐ lǐ niǎo~niǎo màochū, <u>mòde</u> shuǐhú jiānjiào, Mǎ Línshēng rúmèngfāngxǐng, máng qǐshēn bǎ shuǐhú zì lú shàng līn xià.

'The lid of the kettle on the stove squeaked softly, wisps of vapor curling out from the spout. <u>Suddenly</u> the kettle screamed, which awakened Ma Linsheng as if from a dream. He hurried up to carry the kettle off the stove.'

We find that the sentence-initial adverbials listed in Zhang Li (1997) which cannot be moved backward into the sentence are mainly those expressing time. See (13) and (14) for illustration.

(13) <u>往后</u>,你们过你们的日子,孩子过孩子的日子,两下里都要好好的。(*Novel Monthly* [《小说月刊》], Oct. 1998)

<u>Wǎnghòu</u>, nǐmen guò nǐmen de rìzi, háizi guò háizi de rìzi, liǎngxiàlǐ dōu yào hǎo~hǎo de.

'<u>From now on</u>, you live your lives and your children live theirs, and both need be good. '
(14) <u>不知不觉的</u>,树林稀了,土地薄了。(*Novel Monthly*, Oct. 1998)

<u>Bùzhībùjué de</u>, shùlín xīle, tǔdì báole.

'<u>Imperceptibly</u>, the forest has become thin and the land infertile.'

It is interesting to note that the so-called "cannot be moved backward" actually means that the movement will deprive the sentence of the function to express the course of events.

7.1.2 Topic chain-blocking effect of S-adverbs

In Chinese narratives, zero-subject is the default choice for consecutive clauses when they share the same subject referent (Li & Thompson, 1981; Chen Ping, 1987c), which is also called subject omission.

Zero-subject is the coding form for high-continuity topics (Fang Mei, 2005a, 2008). However, topic chains will be blocked when an evaluative adverb that expresses the speaker's attitude appears sentence-initially. This topic chain-blocking effect is manifested in the need for an explicit subject in the hosting clause of the evaluative adverb.

(15) a. 据天赐看,四虎子既有黄天霸这样的朋友,<u>想必</u>他也是条好汉,很有能力,很有主意。(Lao She, *Biography of Niu Tianchi* [《牛天赐传》])

   Jù Tiāncì kàn, Sìhǔzi jì yǒu Huáng Tiānbà zhèyàng de péngyǒu, <u>xiǎngbì</u> tā yěshì tiáo hǎohàn, hěn yǒu nénglì, hěn yǒu zhǔyì.

   'To Tianzhi, since Sihuzi had a friend like Huang Tianba, <u>presumably</u> he was also a good man, very capable, and very resourceful.'

   b. 可是,他刚坐下,就翻脸不认人,要把我赶走!那金贞凤<u>想必</u>也是叫黄家赶了出来,还假充千金小姐!呸!呸!呸!(Lao She, *The Hezhu Match* [《荷珠配》])

   Kěshì, tā gāng zuòxià, jiù fānliǎn bú rèn rén, yào bǎ wǒ gǎnzǒu! Nà Jīn Zhēnfèng <u>xiǎngbì</u> yěshì jiào Huáng jiā gǎnle chūlái, hái jiǎchōng qiānjīn xiǎojiě! Pēi! Pēi! Pēi!

   'But as soon as he sat down, he turned his back on me and tried to drive me away! That Jin Zhenfeng <u>must</u> have been driven out by the Huangs as well, but she still pretended to be a young lady! Ugh! Ugh! Ugh!'

In (15a), the antecedent of "他" ('he') in the third clause is Sihuzi, and the zero-subjects of the two subsequent clauses "很有能力,很有主意" ('very capable and very resourceful') also refer to Sihuzi. If the S-adverb "想必" ('presumably') in the third clause is deleted, "他" in this clause may very well be elliptical. In (15b), "想必" comes after the subject Jin Zhenfeng, and the subsequent clause "还假充千金小姐" ('still pretended to be a young lady') has a zero-subject coreferential with Jin Zhenfeng. The clause would be difficult to accept if the zero-subject is replaced with the pronoun subject "她" ('she').

Also see (16) and (17).

(16) 康有为也遭到通缉,幸亏他及时登上了英国客轮"重庆"号,逃亡日本,总算是躲过一劫。"中华民国"成立以后,1913 年,康有为才从日本回到祖国。(*This Is Beijing*)

   Kāng Yǒuwéi yě zāodào tōngjī, <u>xìngkuī</u> tā jíshí dēngshàngle Yīngguó kèlún "Chóngqìng" hào, táowáng Rìběn, zǒngsuànshì duǒguò yī jié.

"Zhōnghuá Mínguó" chénglì yǐhòu, 1913 nián, Kāng Yǒuwéi cái cóng Rìběn huídào zǔguó.

'Kang Youwei was also wanted, but <u>fortunately</u> he boarded the British passenger ship "Chungking" in time and fled to Japan, escaping a disaster. After the founding of the Republic of China, Kang Youwei returned to his homeland from Japan in 1913.'

(17) 都说,慈禧一辈子要啥有啥,<u>其实</u>她一日三餐都得听人安排,不由自主。想吃点可口的,得提前预订,还不一定能吃得上。(This Is Beijing)

Dōu shuō, Cíxǐ yībèizi yào shà yǒu shà, <u>qíshí</u> tā yī rì sān cān dōu děi tīng rén ānpái, bùyóuzìzhǔ. Xiǎng chī diǎn kěkǒu de, děi tíqián yùdìng, hái bù yīdìng néng chī-de-shàng.

'It is said that Cixi had everything she wanted in her life, but <u>actually</u>, she had to listen to the arrangements even for the three meals of the day. She was not at liberty to decide. If she wanted to eat something delicious, she had to make a reservation in advance, and it was not always possible to get it.'

In example (16), both sentences are about Kang Youwei. The segment "'中华民国'成立以后" ('after the founding of the Republic of China') is a temporal component that marks the boundary of discourse, which necessitates the recurrence of "Kang Youwei" as a nominal subject even though its referent is the same as the topic in the previous sentence, and in the first sentence, the topic noun "Kang Youwei" already appears as the subject in the first clause, and, syntactically speaking, the subsequent coreferential subjects can be made implicit. However, what we see in (16) is an explicit pronoun subject "他" ('he'). In example (17), the topic "Cixi" appears as the subject in the first clause, and the subject of the subsequent clause is not omitted, either; instead, "她" ('she') is used for anaphoric reference. The reason for the occurrence of anaphoric pronoun subjects in these two cases is the use of S-adverbs, "幸亏" ('fortunately') in example (16) and "其实" ('actually') in example (17), whose scope is not limited to the hosting clause itself. Only the presence of the topic can make it possible to define a scope that is larger than a single clause.

The topic chain-blocking effect[2] can explain why some S-adverbs can only be used post the subject but not sentence-initially in specific contexts, though they can occur in both slots.

7.1.3 Prosodically independent S-adverbs

Prosodic independence of sentence-initial adverbs has been noted for long. When discussing the difference between adverbs and conjunctions in his *Problems of Grammatical Analysis in Chinese* (《汉语语法分析问题》), Lü Shuxiang (1979) suggests that those that can appear before or after the subject are conjunctions while those that cannot appear before the subject without a pause are adverbs. In other words, the presence or absence of a pause, to Lü, is an important formal marker in determining whether a word is a conjunction or an adverb.

Prosodically independent as they are, S-adverbs show distributional variation. Some occur only sentence initially while others can also occur sentence finally or in the middle of the sentence as insertions. Li and Thompson (1981) classify adverbs into "movable adverbs" and "immovable adverbs" according to their syntactic distribution: the former can appear either before or after the subject or topic, and the latter can only appear after.

Typical S-adverbs have prosodic independence and are often marked off by punctuation in written Chinese. In terms of scope, they tend to claim a greater one when prosodically independent than when prosodically dependent. Some examples of evaluative S-adverbs are presented below for illustration.

(18) a. 直到多尔衮去世,福临才接受了正规教育。毕竟家庭环境、学习环境都挺好,估计当年孝庄的胎教做得也不错,福临很快就文治武功样样精通了,成为了一个快餐教育的重大成果。(*This Is Beijing*)

Zhídào Duōěrgǔn qùshì, Fúlín cái jiēshòule zhèngguī jiàoyù. Bìjìng jiātíng huánjìng(,) xuéxí huánjìng dōu tǐng hǎo, gūjì dāngnián Xiàozhuāng de tāijiào zuò de yě búcuò, Fúlín hěn kuài jiù wénzhì wǔgōng yàng~yàng jīngtōngle, chéngwéile yī gè kuàicān jiàoyù de zhòngdà chéngguǒ.

'It was not until the death of Dorgon that Fulin began to receive a formal education. <u>After all</u>, the family environment and the learning environment were both quite good, and I guess Xiaozhuang had done a good job in prenatal education as well. Fulin soon became proficient in all aspects of literature and martial arts, representing a major achievement of fast food education.'

b. 更有意思的是,张之洞吃饭的时候,有椅子不坐,喜欢蹲在椅子上吃。其实这点儿倒是可以理解。毕竟,他在山西工作过很长一段时间,习惯了咱西北乡亲们蹲着吃饭的招牌动作,倒也不足为奇了。(*This Is Beijing*)

Gèng yǒuyìsi de shì, Zhāng Zhīdòng chīfàn de shíhòu, yǒu yǐzi bú zuò, xǐhuān dūn zài yǐzi shàng chī. Qíshí zhèi diǎn·er dǎoshì kěyǐ lǐjiě. Bìjìng, tā zài Shānxī gōngzuòguò hěn cháng yī duàn shíjiān, xíguànle zán xīběi xiāngqīnmen dūnzhe chīfàn de zhāopái dòngzuò, dào yě bùzúwéiqí le.

'What is more interesting is that when Zhang Zhidong ate, he did not sit on a chair, but squatted on it. This is actually understandable. <u>After all</u>, he had worked in Shanxi for a long time and was accustomed to the defining posture of our folks in the northwest, squatting to eat. So it is not surprising.'

In this example, "毕竟" ('after all') in (18a) occurs at the beginning of the clause, its scope extending only one clause. The subjects of the second and third subsequent clauses are different from that of the clause hosting "毕竟". In (18b), the S-adverb is prosodically independent, and there are several subsequent clauses, with the subjects all co-referential with "他" ('he') (i.e., Zhang Zhidong). See also (19).

(19) a. 北京南城有座陶然亭公园,<u>想必</u>大伙儿都不陌生。(*This Is Beijing*)

Běijīng nánchéng yǒu zuò Táorántíng gōngyuán, <u>xiǎngbì</u> dàhuǒ·er dōu bú mòshēng.

'There is a Taoranting Park in the south of Beijing, which <u>must</u> be familiar to you all.'

b. 在咱北京城西北角,就是西直门、白石桥那一片儿啊,有一个北京动物园儿。<u>想必啊</u>,甭管您是北京人,还是外地人,再熟悉不过了。谁小时候都去过。(*This Is Beijing*)

Zài zán Běijīng chéng xīběi jiǎo, jiùshì Xīzhímén(,) Báishíqiáo nà yī piān·er a, yǒu yī gè Běijīng Dòngwùyuán·er. <u>Xiǎngbì a</u>, béngguǎn nín shì Běijīngrén, háishì wàidìrén, zài shúxī búguò le. Shéi xiǎoshíhòu dōu qùguò.

'In the northwest corner of Beijing, i.e., in the area of Xizhimen and Baishiqiao, there is Beijing Zoo. <u>I'm pretty sure</u> it is very familiar to you, whether you're from Beijing or from outside Beijing. Everyone went there when young.'

"想必" in (19a) precedes the subject of the closing clause; in (19b) it is prosodically independent and pause-marked with particle 啊, and it is followed by a complex sentence conjoined by "甭管…还是…" ('whether… or…').

Example (20b) is another case to illustrate that prosodically independent adverbs can be marked off with mood particles in spoken Chinese.[3]

(20) a. 几百年过去了,法海寺,依旧那样的深邃、迷人。它背后,一个个未解之谜,也依旧那样的牵动人心。<u>也许</u>,只有寺院中的那些苍松翠柏和大殿里带有神话色彩的壁画能为我们讲述这里更多的、不为人知的传奇故事。(*This Is Beijing*)

Jǐ bǎi nián guòqùle, Fǎhǎi Sì, yījiù nàyàng de shēnsuì(,) mírén. Tā bèihòu, yīgègè wèijiězhīmí, yě yījiù nàyàng de qiāndòngrénxīn. <u>Yěxǔ</u>, zhǐyǒu sìyuàn zhōng de nàxiē cāngsōngcuìbǎi hé dàdiàn lǐ dàiyǒu shénhuà sècǎi de bìhuà néng wèi wǒmen jiǎngshù zhèlǐ gèng duō de(,) bùwéirénzhī de chuánqí gùshì.

'Hundreds of years have passed, but Fahai Temple is still as abstruse and fascinating as ever. Behind it, a number of unsolved mysteries are still as touching as ever. <u>Perhaps</u>, only the pines and cypresses in the temple and the mythical frescoes in the main hall can tell us more of the unknown legends of this place.'

b. 有人说啊,她是历史上最睿智的一个母亲,被封为是大清国的开国女王。在电视剧里头,美若天仙。一看画像,大失所望。<u>也许啊</u>,我这口头表达能力再强,也没法一口气把她故事讲完。(*This Is Beijing*)

Yǒurén shuō a, tā shì lìshǐshàng zuì ruìzhì de yī gè mǔqīn, bèi fēng wéi shì Dàqīngguó de kāiguó nǚwáng. Zài diànshìjù lǐtou, měiruòtiānxiān. Yī kàn huàxiàng, dàshīsuǒwàng. <u>Yěxǔ a</u>, wǒ zhè kǒutóu biǎodá nénglì zài qiáng, yě méifǎ yīkǒuqì bǎ tā gùshi jiǎng wán.

'It is said that she was the wisest mother in history and was named the founding queen of the Qing Dynasty. In the TV series, she was as beautiful as a fairy. But when I saw her portrait, I was greatly disappointed. <u>Perhaps</u>, I can't finish her story in one breath, however strong I am in verbal expression.'

With the mood particle, there can be more than one clause after the S-adverb, and the subsequent clauses can make up a complex sentence. That is to say, the use of the particle can enhance the independence of the S-adverb and make its characteristics more salient.

The modal adverbs that are flexible in distribution roughly fall into two types:

Type 1 can be used independently, and semantically they mostly express judgment (affirmative or negative) and can answer questions alone: a. commentary adverbs, such as 当然 (dāngrán, 'of course'), 也许 (yěxǔ, 'perhaps'), 大概 (dàgài, 'probably'), 的确 (díquè, 'indeed'), 确实 (quèshí, 'indeed'), 本来 (běnlái, 'originally'), 敢情 (gǎnqing, 'indeed'), 不必 (bùbì, 'unnecessarily'), etc.; b. prohibitive adverbs, including 不 (bù), 没 (méi), and 别 (bié).

Type 2 cannot be used independently, even in reply to a question. Semantically, this type of modal adverb is closely related to the expression of result or inference, and thus more likely to develop the function of discourse connection.

Another major category of prosodically independent adverbs is time adverbs. See (21) to (23) for illustration.

(21) 这时,他从镜子里看到躺在屋床上的儿子<u>偶尔</u>起身歪头往外看,由于里屋很明亮,他能清楚地看到儿子的一举一动。(Wang Shuo, *I'm Your Father*)

Zhèshí, tā cóng jìngzi lǐ kàndào tǎng zài wū chuángshàng de érzi <u>ǒu'ěr</u> qǐshēn wāi tóu wǎng wài kàn, yóuyú lǐwū hěn mingliàng, tā néng qīngchǔ de kàndào érzi de yījǔyīdòng.

'At this time, he saw in the mirror that his son, who was lying on the bed in the inner room, <u>occasionally</u> got up and looked out with his head tilted. Because the inner room was very bright, he could clearly see every move of his son.'

(22) 正在大伙儿纳闷的时候,<u>突然</u>,有人发现了断虹桥上有一只石猴子,左手举着这个水瓢,右手撩着自己的衣服,在那儿美呢。(*This Is Beijing*)

Zhèngzài dàhuǒ·er nàmèn de shíhòu, tūrán, yǒurén fāxiànle Duànhóngqiáo shàng yǒu yī zhī shí hóuzi, zuǒshǒu jǔzhe zhège shuǐpiáo, yòushǒu liàozhe zìjǐ de yīfú, zài nà·er měi ne.

'While the group was wondering, <u>suddenly</u> someone spotted a stone monkey on the Broken Rainbow Bridge, holding a ladle in his left hand and his own clothes in his right hand, feeling very pleased.'

(23) 这姿势很别扭,妨碍了他那流畅的遐想。终于,他立起身,跟谁赌气似地大步走向里屋。里屋明亮的灯光下,马锐躺在铺着凉席因而十分平整的大床上睡着了。(Wang Shuo, *I'm Your Father*)

Zhè zīshì hěn bièniu, fáng'àile tā nà liúchàng de xiáxiǎng. <u>Zhōngyú</u>, tā lì qǐ shēn, gēn shéi dǔqì shìde dà bù zǒu xiàng lǐwū. Lǐwū míngliàng de dēngguāng xià, Mǎ Ruì tǎng zài pūzhe liángxí yīn'ér shífēn píngzhěng de dà chuángshàng shuìzháole.

'The pose was awkward and hindered his fluid reverie. <u>Finally</u>, he stood up and strode towards the inner room as if in a fit of pique. In the bright light of the inner room, Ma Rui was lying asleep on the big bed covered with a cool mat and thus very flat.'

It is particularly noteworthy that some adverbs have different meanings and functions when their prosodic feature changes. Compare (24) and (25).

(24) "八虎"是谁呢?就是包括刘瑾在内的八个最受宠幸的太监。当然,也是当时的八个最大的祸害。起初这八虎挺抱团儿,一致对外,跟文武百官形成了对抗势力。但是面对功名利禄,荣华富贵,这八个人,也都不是省油的灯。于是内讧开始了。(*This Is Beijing*)

"Bāhǔ" shì shéi ne? Jiùshì bāokuò Liú Jǐn zàinèi de bā gè zuì shòu chǒngxìng de tàijiàn. Dāngrán, yěshì dāngshí de bā gè zuìdà de huòhài. <u>Qǐchū</u> zhè Bāhǔ tǐng bàotuán·er, yīzhì duìwài, gēn wénwǔbǎiguān xíngchéngle duìkàng shìlì. Dànshì miànduì gōngmínglìlù, rónghuáfùguì, zhè bā gè rén, yě dōu búshì shěngyóu de dēng. Yúshì nèihòng kāishǐle.

'Who were the "Eight Tigers"? They were the eight most favored eunuchs, including Liu Jin. Of course, they were also the eight biggest scourges of the time. <u>At first</u>, the Eight Tigers were quite united, and formed a confrontational force with the civil and military officials. But in the face of fame and fortune, glory and wealth, none of these eight people was easy to deal with. So the internal strife began.'

(25) 话说,天有不测风云,人有旦夕祸福。随着明熹宗朱由校的突然驾崩,魏忠贤的死期也到了。崇祯皇帝登基之后,做的第一件事情,就是铲除魏忠贤党羽。起初,他以为魏忠贤势力强大,坚不可摧,只能让他引咎辞职,回家养老而已。随即,崇祯发现,魏忠贤的亲信,纷纷倒戈,主动供述他的罪状。这会儿,崇祯皇帝才决定斩草除根,杀掉魏忠贤。(*This Is Beijing*)

Huàshuō, tiān yǒu bùcè fēngyún, rén yǒu dànxì huòfú. Suízhe Míng Xīzōng Zhū Yóuxiào de tūrán jiàbēng, Wèi Zhōngxián de sǐqī yě dàole.

Chóngzhēn huángdì dēngjī zhīhòu, zuò de dìyī jiàn shìqíng, jiùshì chǎnchú Wèi Zhōngxián dǎngyǔ. Qǐchū, tā yǐwéi Wèi Zhōngxián shìlì qiángdà, jiānbùkěcuī, zhǐnéng ràng tā yǐnjiùcízhí, huíjiā yǎnglǎo éryǐ. Suíjí, Chóngzhēn fāxiàn, Wèi Zhōngxián de qīnxìn, fēnfēn dǎogē, zhǔdòng gòngshù tā de zuìzhuàng. Zhèihuì·er, Chóngzhēn huángdì cái juédìng zhǎncǎochúgēn, shādiào Wèi Zhōngxián.

'As the saying goes, there are unexpected events in the sky, and misfortunes and blessings in people. With the sudden death of Zhu Youxiao, Xizong of the Ming Dynasty, Wei Zhongxian's death also arrived. The first thing Emperor Chongzhen did after ascending to the throne was to eliminate Wei Zhongxian's party. <u>At first,</u> thinking Wei Zhongxian powerful and indestructible, the Emperor only wanted him to resign and go home. Then he found that Wei Zhongxian's cronies had turned their backs one after another, taking the initiative to confess his guilt. It was then that Emperor Chongzhen decided to pluck up the evil by the root and kill Wei Zhongxian.'

Prosodically independent S-adverbs can play the role of marking plot points. Liu Xiaohui (2012) proposes that sentence-initial time adverbs are found only in the narrative parts of novels and spoken Beijing dialect, with narrative sentences being the norm, and that there is a clear shift in subject or topic when time adverbs occur sentence initially. We argue here that this distribution pattern of time adverbs is a manifestation of their discourse function, given that time S-adverbs have the function of marking plot points.

Another phenomenon related to prosodic independence is the division of labor between adverbs of the "monosyllabic reduplication+*de* (的)" configuration and those without *de*: the former can be prosodically independent when used as S-adverbs, while the latter cannot. Moreover, the former group tends to have a larger scope, thus is more oriented to expressing the course of events and marking the different stages of event development.

(26) a. 说到这儿,您先别害怕,坐稳了,听我跟您<u>慢慢</u>解释。(*This Is Beijing*)

Shuōdào zhè·er, nín xiān bié hàipà, zuò wěn le, tīng wǒ gēn nín <u>màn~màn</u> jiěshì.

'Speaking of this, don't be scared. Sit tight and let me explain to you <u>slowly</u>.'

b. 哥哥死了,哪能让嫂子跟太监这么鬼混呢。所以,<u>慢慢的</u>,恭亲王就对安德海看不惯了。(*This Is Beijing*)

Gēge sǐle, nǎ néng ràng sǎozi gēn tàijiàn zhème guǐhùn ne. Suǒyǐ, <u>màn-màn de</u>, Gōng qīnwáng jiù duì Ān Déhǎi kàn-bù-guàn le.

'His brother died, but how could he let his sister-in-law fool around with a eunuch like that? So, <u>slowly</u>, Prince Gong became uncomfortable with An Dehai.'

In example (26), "慢慢" ('slowly') is used as a VP-adverb to describe the explaining behavior, whereas the prosodically independent "慢慢的" ('slowly') refers to time, denoting an important point in the development of events. In (27), likewise, "渐渐的" ('gradually') also reflects the course of events, describing the different event stages together with "最后" ('eventually') that occurs in later discourse.

(27) 新的睿亲王府,规模十分宏大。……就这样传了十二世,到末代睿亲王中铨,已是民国年间。王爷爵位形同虚设,取消了俸禄。可末代睿亲王中铨的生活习惯依然没变,挥金如土,修房子,修花园,安电话,买汽车。<u>渐渐的</u>,就把祖上留下的财产全给花光了。<u>最后</u>,连王府也被法院查封,作为学院。府中建筑,屡经拆改,渐失原貌。府中神库,改为礼堂,也就是今天的,北京第二十四中学。(*This Is Beijing*)

Xīnde Ruì qīnwáng fǔ, guīmó shífēn hóngdà.... Jiù zhèyàng chuánle shí'èr shì, dào mòdài Ruì qīnwáng Zhōngquán, yǐ shì Mínguó niánjiān. Wángyé juéwèi xíngtóngxūshè, qǔxiāole fēnglù. Kě mòdài Ruì qīnwáng Zhōngquán de shēnghuó xíguàn yīrán méi biàn, huījīnrútǔ, xiū fángzi, xiū huāyuán, ān diànhuà, mǎi qìchē. <u>Jiànjiàn de</u>, jiù bǎ zǔshàng liúxià de cáichǎn quán gěi huā guāng le. <u>Zuìhòu</u>, lián wángfǔ yě bèi fǎyuàn cháfēng, zuòwéi xuéyuàn. Fǔzhōng jiànzhù, lǚ jīng chāi gǎi, jiàn shī yuánmào. Fǔ zhōng shénkù, gǎi wèi lǐtáng, yějiùshì jīntiān de, Běijīng Dì Èrshísì Zhōngxué.

'The new residence of Prince Rui was grand in scale... Thus it was passed on for twelve generations to the last Prince Rui Zhongquan, when it was already the Republic of China. The title of prince existed in name only, and the salary had been abolished. But the last Prince Rui's habits remained unchanged, still squandering money like dirt – renovating houses, laying out gardens, installing telephones, and buying cars. <u>Gradually</u>, he spent all the property left by his ancestors. <u>Eventually</u>, even the royal residence was seized by the court and used as a college. The buildings in the residence were repeatedly torn down and changed, and gradually lost their original appearance. The sacred vault in it was changed into an auditorium, which is today's Twenty-fourth High School of Beijing.'

In addition to "渐渐的" above, another case is 常常的 (chángchángde, 'often'). When functioning as a VP-adverb, it must take the form of 常常, without 的. When prosodically independent, 常常的 is an S-adverb, which belongs to what Liao Qiuzhong (1987) calls the "situation" category.

(28) a. <u>常常的</u>,我站在暴雨滂沱或大雪纷飞的窗前,不无安慰地想,即使被困上十天半个月的,我也一定不会饿死了。(Shu Ting, Berlin Diet [《柏林饮食》])

<u>Chángcháng de</u>, wǒ zhànzài bàoyǔ pāngtuó huò dàxuě fēnfēi de chuāng qián, bù wú ānwèi de xiǎng, jíshǐ bèi kùn shàng shí tiān bàn gè yuè de, wǒ yě yīdìng búhuì èsǐ le.

'Often, I stand in front of the window in a rainstorm or a snowstorm, thinking not without comfort that even if I am trapped for ten days or half a month, I will not die from hunger.'

b. *我常常的站在暴雨滂沱或大雪纷飞的窗前，不无安慰地想，即使被困上十天半个月的，我也一定不会饿死了。

*Wǒ chángcháng de zhànzài bàoyǔ pāngtuó huò dàxuě fēnfēi de chuāng qián, bù wú ānwèi de xiǎng, jíshǐ bèi kùn shàng shí tiān bàn gè yuè de, wǒ yě yīdìng búhuì èsǐ le.

Then it can be argued that the emergence of the adverbial "monosyllabic reduplication+*de*" is closely related to the need for prosodic independence of discourse boundary-marking adverbs: prosodically independent S-adverbs have a stronger discourse function than prosodically dependent ones. Prosodic independence may be the trigger for the addition of 的 to adverbs of reduplication configuration.

7.2 Summary

In terms of distribution, S-adverbs are used sentence-initially, rather than post the subject to immediately precede the predicate. In terms of semantic meaning, most S-adverbs are time adverbs, followed by evaluative adverbs. When used to modify the whole sentence, time adverbs tend to occur where scene transitions are to be effected, marking plot points. S-adverbs have a topic chain-blocking effect and the prosodically independent ones can function to mark the course of events. According to Liao Qiuzhong (1987), there are nine categories of elements that can form discourse boundaries. We believe that prosocially independent S-adverbs can constitute another means to this end.

Notes

1 The nine categories of elements that can form discourse boundaries as proposed by Liao Qiuzhong (1987) are as follows: 1) time and location words or phrases; 2) situation phrases; 3) process phrases; 4) purpose phrases; 5) phrases of information source; 6) perspective phrases; 7) assessment phrases; 8) topic phrases; and 9) aspect phrases. As the category names indicate, categories 1) and 2) indicate the setting of the event, categories 3) and 4) denote the context in which the event occurs, category 5) expresses the information source of the reported event, category 6) identifies the perspective from which things are observed, category 7) reveals the speaker's assessment of the truthfulness of what is said, and categories 8) and 9) express respectively the topic or an aspect of the topic.
2 When the zero-subject in the following clause refers to a constituent other than the subject of the preceding clause, it is not taken as an instance of topic continuation. In the example below, the zero-subject of the clause "大概也就相当于现在的责任编辑" ('is probably equivalent to today's editor-in-charge') is "故宫武英殿的纂修" ('the codifier of the Imperial Palace's Wuying Hall') in the preceding clause.
纪晓岚就曾经在这里工作和战斗过。他当时担任的是故宫武英殿的纂修，大概也就相当于现在的责任编辑。

Jì Xiǎolán jiù céngjīng zài zhèlǐ gōngzuò hé zhàndòuguò. Tā dāngshí dānrèn de shì Gùgōng Wǔyīngdiàn de zuǎnxiū, dàgài yějiù xiāngdāngyú xiànzài de zérèn biānjí.

'Ji Xiaolan used to work and fight here. He was the codifier of the Imperial Palace's Wuying Hall, (a title which) is probably equivalent to today's editor-in-charge.'

3 See also Fang Mei (1994) for examples of adverbs followed by modal particles.

8 From quoting to hedging

In colloquial Beijing dialect, the speech verb 说 (shuō, 'say') has a high-frequency combination 说是, which can be used as a quotation marker. But unlike 说, 说是 can also indicate the speaker's attitude. Specifically, it can express the speaker's uncertainty, weaken the illocutionary force of negative evaluation, and suggest the speaker's disagreement with the reported speech. When used as a hedge, 说是 is phonetically weakened; when used as an attitude marker, it is phonetically intensified. Hence 说是 has become a compound word distinct from 说.

8.1 Introduction

It has been widely noted that "X *shi* (X是)" is a highly productive means of generating compound words in spoken modern Chinese (Dong Xiufang, 2004a; Piao Huijing, 2011; Zhang Yisheng, 2003b), and 说是 (shuōshì, 'it is said'), a high-frequency combination containing 说 ('say'), is found to be able to function as a quotation marker (Chen Ying and Chen Yi, 2010; Yue Yao, 2011a, 2011b), introducing both direct and indirect speech. The question for this chapter then is how 说是 differs from 说 when used as a quotation marker.

We note that the main function of 说是 is metadiscourse expression. The so-called metadiscourse is usually defined as linguistic expressions about discourse. According to Hyland (2005), there are two major categories of metadiscourse resources: 1) the interactive, including transitions, frame markers, endophoric markers, evidentials, code glosses, etc.; and 2) the interactional, including hedges, attitude markers, self-mentions, engagement markers, etc. (see Hyland, 2005, p. 49).

While 说 as a quotation marker has only the evidential function, 说是 has a threefold function: evidential, hedge, and attitude marker.

Our examination of the usage of 说是 is based on the following types of materials: 1) transcriptions of spontaneous dialogue (labeled "Survey Corpus" or "Interview Corpus"); 2) transcriptions of the Beijing TV feature film *This Is Beijing*; 3) transcriptions of the simultaneously recorded TV sitcom *I Love My Family*; and 4) novels by Beijing-based writers.

DOI: 10.4324/9781032700656-8

8.2 Evidential marker

Both 说 and 说是 are used to indicate that the speaker only has indirect access to information, instead of witnessing the event in person. Nonetheless, they differ in participant engagement. 说 as a quotation marker usually gives an account of who the speaker is; that is, the source of information is definite.[1] But 说是 is often used without giving the information source, showing only the evidential characteristic of the information – reported information. See (1) to (3) for illustration.

(1) 和平:哎,得了,说说吧,那卡迪拉克打算一月给你多少钱呢?
 志国:<u>说是</u>除奖金之外每月两千五。(*I Love My Family*)

 Hépíng: Āi, déle, shuō~shuō ba, nà Kǎdílākè dǎsuàn yī yuè gěi nǐ duōshǎo qián ne? Zhìguó: <u>Shuōshì</u> chú jiǎngjīn zhīwài měi yuè liǎng-qiān-wǔ.

 'Heping: Hey, come on, tell me, how much is that Cadillac going to pay you each month?
 Zhiguo: <u>It is said</u> to be 2,500 yuan per month plus bonus.'

(2) 缇香的房子一直卖得火热火热的,不过却一直没有商铺的动静。今天出于好奇,特意打电话去问了一下。没想到,<u>说是</u>这周商铺就要开盘了。(Survey Corpus)

 Tíxiāng de fángzi yīzhí mài de huǒrè~huǒrè de, búguò què yīzhí méiyǒu shāngpù de dòngjìng. Jīntiān chūyú hàoqí, tèyì dǎdiànhuà qù wènle yīxià. Méixiǎngdào, <u>shuōshì</u> zhè zhōu shāngpù jiù yào kāipán le.

 'The houses in Tixiang has been selling like hot cakes, but there has been no news about the stores. Today, out of curiosity, I called to ask about it. Unexpectedly, <u>it was said</u> that the stores would be on sale this week.'

(3) 傅老:吃完饭不在家好好待着,到外面串什么门儿嘛。
 圆圆:<u>说是</u>于奶奶家有喜事。(*I Love My Family*)

 Fù Lǎo: Chī wán fàn bú zàijiā hǎohǎo dàizhe, dào wàimiàn chuān shénme mén·er ma.
 Yuányuán: <u>Shuōshì</u> Yú nǎinai jiā yǒu xǐshì.

 'Old Fu: Why should you go and visit others instead of staying home after dinner?
 Yuanyuan: <u>It is said</u> that there is a happy event at Grandma Yu's house.'

In example (1), "除奖金之外每月两千五" ('2,500 yuan per month plus bonus') is said by "Cadillac", metonymically used to refer to the owner of the vehicle, and this source of information is provided by the speech context; the information source of "这周商铺就要开盘了" ('the stores would be on sale this week') in (2) and "于奶奶家有喜事" ('there is a happy event at Grandma Yu's house') in (3), conversely, can only be inferred from the context through knowledge of relevance.

It should be noted that the construction "说是 NP" has a double reading: it can be analyzed either as "说是+clause" or as "说+是+NP". In the latter reading, 是 remains a link verb of judgment.

(4) 小孩嗓子发炎, 做了血常规, <u>说是</u>病毒性感冒引起的发烧。(Survey Corpus)

Xiǎohái sǎngzi fāyán, zuòle xiē chángguī, <u>shuōshì</u> bìngdú xìng gǎnmào yǐnqǐ de fāshāo.

'The child had a throat infection. When a blood test was done, it was said that the fever was caused by a viral flu.'

(5) 就小五儿那孩子, 还上了一个什么二十一中, <u>说是</u>不好的学校, 三流的, 还交了两万多呢。(Survey Corpus)

Jiù Xiǎowǔ·er nà háizi, hái shàngle yī gè shénme Èrshíyī Zhōng, <u>shuōshì</u> bù hǎo de xuéxiào, sānliú de, hái jiāole liǎng wàn duō ne.

'As for the child Xiaowu, he goes to the so-called the 21st Middle School. <u>It is said</u> to be a bad school, third-rate, but more than 20,000 yuan was charged.'

(6) 老二是那个学校的校队儿。反正踢得还可以, <u>说是</u>踢的后卫。(Survey Corpus)

Lǎo'èr shì nàgè xuéxiào de xiào duì·er. Fǎnzhèng tī de hái kěyǐ, <u>shuōshì</u> tī de hòuwèi.

'The second child is a player of his school team. Anyway, he plays okay and <u>is said</u> to play fullback.'

However, there is a phonological difference between the two different readings: in the "说是+clause" reading, 是 is pronounced lightly while in the "说+是+NP" reading, 是 cannot be pronounced lightly. This critical phenomenon in the synchronic system indicates that the new usage of 说是 is still in the process of development.

According to the evolution of "say" in world languages as outlined in Heine and Kuteva's *World Lexicon of Grammaticalization*, it is a language universal for "say" to evolve from a quotation marker to an evidential (2002, p. 265). 说 in colloquial Beijing dialect has not yet developed into an evidential (Fang Mei, 2006),[2] with the evidential function being fulfilled by its compound form 说是 for the time being.[3] In other words, it is at a stage of transition to a hedge.

8.3 Hedge

The so-called hedges are linguistic devices to show uncertainty or withhold commitment to the truth of an assertion. There are two basic categories: namely, approximators and shields.

Approximators can be further divided into adaptors (such as "sort of" and "more or less") and rounders (such as "roughly" and "approximately"). In communication, to avoid face threat caused by negative expressions, speakers often use hedges to reduce the forces of language and produce roundabout expressions. For example, 不情愿 (bù qíngyuàn, 'unwilling') is rephrased as 不太情愿 (bù tài qíngyuàn, 'not very willing') or 不怎么情愿 (bù zěnme qíngyuàn, 'not quite willing'), 不可口 (bù kěkǒu, 'unpalatable') or 难吃 (nánchī, 'unpalatable') is rephrased as 不太可口 (bù tài kěkǒu, 'not very tasty'), and 不聪明 (bù cōngmíng, 'not smart') or 笨 (bèn, 'stupid') as 不怎么聪明 (bù zěnme cōngmíng, 'not very smart'), so on and so forth. These are all examples of adaptors.

Shields are composed of plausibility shields, such as "I think", "I am afraid", "hard to say", etc., and attribution shields, such as "someone says that", "according to one's estimates", etc., which do not directly express the speaker's uncertainty or hesitation, but quote a third party to indirectly express the speaker's attitude toward something.

说是 as an evidential marker is used for indirect speech, which is equivalent in meaning to 据说 (jùshuō, 'it is said'). Like 据说,[4] 说是 does not co-occur with the subject (especially the agent subject); unlike 据说, 说是 reflects the speaker's reservation about the truthfulness or correctness of the information he or she is reporting, an attitude that can be detected in the speaker's ensuing utterances.

(7) 紫禁城玄武门内的这口珍妃井，在葬送了珍妃性命的同时，也葬送了不少人的名声。……<u>有书记载</u>，当年是珍妃在慈禧西逃的紧要关头，不识大体，以死相逼，自己跳井而死。崔玉贵上前没能拉住。也正是这一举动，使他成为了这一事件的最大嫌疑人。<u>但又有崔玉贵口述记载</u>，<u>说是</u>他手下的一个小太监，奉慈禧之命，把珍妃扔进了井里。结果慈禧为了逃脱干系，怪罪崔玉贵管理不力，纵容手下害死珍妃。<u>不管真相如何</u>，反正崔玉贵最后是背上了这个黑锅。(This Is Beijing)

Zǐjìnchéng Xuánwǔmén nèi de zhè kǒu Zhēnfēijǐng, zài zàngsòngle Zhēnfēi xìngmìng de tóngshí, yě zàngsòngle bùshǎo rén de míngshēng. … <u>Yǒu shū jìzǎi</u>, dāngnián shì Zhēnfēi zài Cíxǐ xī táo de jǐnyào guāntóu, bù shí dàtǐ, yǐsǐxiāngbī, zìjǐ tiàojǐng ér sǐ. Cuī Yùguì shàngqián méi néng lāzhù. Yě zhèngshì zhè yī jǔdòng, shǐ tā chéngwéile zhè yī shìjiàn de zuìdà xiányírén. <u>Dàn yòu yǒu Cuī Yùguì kǒushù jìzǎi</u>, <u>shuōshì</u> tā shǒuxià de yī gè xiǎo tàijiàn, fèng Cíxǐ zhī mìng, bǎ Zhēnfēi rēngjìnle jǐnglǐ. Jiéguǒ Cíxǐ wèile táotuō gānxì, guàizuì Cuī Yùguì guǎnlǐ búlì, zòngróng shǒuxià hàisǐ Zhēnfēi. <u>Bùguǎn zhēnxiàng rúhé</u>, fǎnzhèng Cuī Yùguì zuìhòu shì bèishàngle zhège hēiguō.

'The Well of Consort Zhen inside the Xuanwu Gate of the Forbidden City claimed not only Consort Zhen's life, but also a lot of people's reputation… <u>As recorded in writing</u>, at the critical moment of Cixi fleeing west, Consort Zhen failed to see the general interest, but jumped into the well to threaten Cixi and drowned herself. Cui Yugui went up but failed to pull her back. It was exactly this account that made him the biggest suspect in this incident. But there are also Cui Yugui oral records, saying that it was a small eunuch under him that threw Consort Zhen into the well on the orders of Cixi. In order to get away with it, Cixi blamed Cui Yugui for ineffective management, conniving the eunuch under him to kill Consort Zhen. Whatever the truth is, Cui Yugui ended up taking the blame anyway.'

(8) 碧云寺里菩萨殿,最值得琢磨的,不是菩萨,而是他们的宠物,人家管那叫坐骑。老百姓有句话说,什么人玩什么鸟。咱就来看看这几位菩萨,都养了什么样的宠物。地藏菩萨的宠物,叫"谛听"。《西游记》,想必大家都看过。其中有一集,叫真假美猴王,说是有人冒充孙悟空,结果,谁都辨不出真假来,最后闹到阎王殿,阎王爷请出一位神仙,就叫谛听,说是能听出万物谛来。其实,真正的谛听,并不在地府里,而是在地藏菩萨的屁股底下,更不是什么神仙,只是一只瑞兽。但它耳朵好,能倾听万物却是真的。(*This Is Beijing*)

Bìyúnsì lǐ Púsàdiàn, zuì zhídé zhuómó de, búshì púsà, érshì tāmen de chǒngwù, rénjiā guǎn nà jiào zuòjì. Lǎobǎixìng yǒu jù huà shuō, shénme rén wán shénme niǎo. Zán jiù lái kàn~kàn zhè jǐ wèi púsà, dōu yǎngle shénme yàng de chǒngwù. Dìzàng púsà de chǒngwù, jiào "Dìtīng". "Xīyóujì", xiǎngbì dàjiā dōu kànguò. Qízhōng yǒu yī jí, jiào Zhēnjiǎ Měihóuwáng, shuōshi yǒurén màochōng Sūn Wùkōng, jiéguǒ, shéi dōu biànbù-chū zhēnjiǎ lái, zuìhòu nào dào Yánwángdiàn, Yánwángyé qǐng chū yī wèi shénxiān, jiù jiào Dìtīng, shuōshi néng tīng chū wànwù dì lái. Qíshí, zhēnzhèng de dìtīng, bìng bú zài dìfǔ lǐ, ér shì zài Dìzàng púsà de pìgu dǐxia, gèng búshì shénme shénxiān, zhǐshì yī zhǐ ruì shòu. Dàn tā ěrduǒ hǎo, néng qīngtīng wànwù què shì zhēn de.

'What is the most puzzling about the Bodhisattva Hall of Biyun Temple is not the Bodhisattvas, but their pets, generally called their mounts. As the saying goes, people keep pets of their like. Let's take a look at what pets these Bodhisattvas have. The pet of the Ksitigarbha Bodhisattva is called Diting, meaning "listen attentively". *Journey to the West*, I think we have all read it. One of the episodes, called the Real or Fake Monkey King, goes like this: someone impersonates the Monkey King so well that nobody can identify the real one, and finally they go to the Palace of Hades, where the King of Hades calls out a fairy, called Diting, who is said to be able to listen to the truth of everything. In fact, the real Diting does not live in the Palace of Hades, but under the buttocks of the Ksitigarbha Bodhisattva. And it is not a fairy, but an auspicious animal. In any case, it is true that it has good ears and can listen to all things.'

The speaker's uncertainty about the content of his or her report can be confirmed by the context. In example (7), "说是" introduces the oral accounts, which are indirect speech, and the subsequent "不管真相如何,反正..." indicates that the speaker does not consider the records credible. In (8), "说是" also heads the reported proposition, which is negated immediately by the speaker with the transition marker "其实" and the ensuing discourse.

The speaker's reservations about the stated proposition are sometimes expressed directly in the subsequent discourse. For example, in (9), the follow-up sentence is explicitly coded as "我不太同意".

(9) [那个]我觉得刚才有一个球迷说, 说是那个, 沈祥福给队员的那个压力太大了, 我不太同意这种说法。(Survey Corpus)

[Nèige] wǒ juéde gāngcái yǒu yī gè qiúmí shuō, shuōshi nèige, Shén Xiángfú gěi duìyuán de nèige yālì tài dà le, wǒ bú tài tóngyì zhèzhǒng shuōfǎ.

'[Well] I think, a fan just said, it was said, that Shen Xiangfu gave the players too much pressure. I don't quite agree with that.'

It is because of this evidential use that 说是 is commonly used in folk tales, folk legends and other autobiographical narratives. See (10).

(10) 以前说起这窝头来啊, 以前还有这么个, 呃, 也不知道是真事儿啊还是笑话儿是怎么着。就是这个, 讽刺慈禧太后的事儿。这慈禧太后啊, 这个, 清朝末年的时候儿, 这人民的生活也是越来越苦了是不是?就有很多倡兴革新的大臣呢, 在朝廷里说, 说是, 这个, 这老百姓啊生活真是苦极了, 这个, 一天到晚就吃这个棒子面儿窝头, 这个没什么别的东西可以吃。这慈禧太后就说, "呵, 吃棒子面窝头, 棒子面儿窝头是什么东西啊?给我吃一吃, 我看看这老百姓生活到底是怎么样。"就下令啊, 说是₂得吃一顿啊棒子面儿窝头。就跟这御厨说啊, 做、做窝头。这御厨一想啊, 呦, 这老佛爷要吃这个窝头啊, 这可得小心点儿, 不能乱做。就啊把棒子面儿磨得很细很细, 做出来, 丁不点儿大的小窝头, 很小的小窝头。里边还放上蜂蜜啊, 这个糖啊什么等等的, 做得精制的, 给她端了一盘儿来了。端了一盘来呢, 这慈禧太后来了, 说是₂我这得跟老百姓共甘苦是吧, 吃窝头。(Survey Corpus)

Yǐqián shuōqǐ zhè wōtóu lái a, yǐqián háiyǒu zhème gè, e, yě bù zhīdào shì zhēnshì·er a háishì xiàohuà·er shì zěnmezhe. Jiùshì zhège, fěngcì Cíxǐ tàihòu de shì·er. Zhè Cíxǐ tàihòu a, zhège, Qīngcháo mònián de shíhòu·er, zhè rénmín de shēnghuó yěshì yuèláiyuè kǔ le shì-búshì? Jiù yǒu hěnduō chàngxīng géxīn de dàchén ne, zài cháotíng lǐ shuō, shuōshì, zhège, zhè lǎobǎixìng a shēnghuó zhēnshi kǔ jí le, zhège, yītiāndàowǎn jiù chī zhège bàngzimiàn·er wōtóu, zhège méi shénme bié de dōngxī kěyǐ chī. Zhè Cíxǐ tàihòu jiù shuō, "He, chī bàngzimiàn wōtóu, bàngzimiàn·er wōtóu shì shénme dōngxī a? Gěi wǒ chī-yī-chī, wǒ kàn~kàn zhè lǎobǎixìng shēnghuó dàodǐ shì zěnme yàng." Jiù xiàlìng a, shuōshi₂ děi chī yī dùn a bàngzimiàn·er wōtóu. Jiù gēn zhè yùchú shuō a, zuò(,) zuò wōtóu. Zhè yùchú yī xiǎng a, yōu, zhè lǎofóyé yào chī zhège wōtóu a, zhè kě děi xiǎoxīndiǎn·er, bùnéng luàn zuò. Jiù a bǎ bàngzimiàn·er mò de hěn xì hěn xì, zuò chūlái, dīngbudiǎn·er dà de xiǎo wōtóu, hěn xiǎo de xiǎo wōtóu. Lǐbian hái fàngshàng fēngmì a, zhège táng a shénme děngděng de, zuò de jīngzhì de, gěi tā duānle yī pán·er lái le. Duānle yī pán lái ne, zhè Cíxǐ tàihòu láile, <u>shuōshi</u>, wǒ zhè děi gēn lǎobǎixìng gòng gānkǔ shì ba, chī wōtóu.

'When it comes to the steamed corn bun, there used to be this, uh, I don't know whether it's a real thing or a joke. It is, well, a satire of the Empress Dowager Cixi. At the end of the Qing Dynasty, the people's life got more and more miserable, right? Many ministers who advocated innovation, <u>it was said</u>, stated in the court that the people's life was so hard that they had nothing else but steamed corn buns to eat day in and day out. The Empress Dowager Cixi said, "Oh, steamed corn buns, what are they? Give me a taste, and let me see what on earth the people's life is like." Then it was ordered, <u>it was said</u>, that a meal of steamed corn buns be prepared. When informed of the order, the imperial chef thought, oh, the Old Buddha wants to eat steamed corn buns, and I have to be careful and can't make them indiscriminately. So he grounded the flour extremely fine and made the buns very small, seasoned with honey, sugar and so on, so that they were made very much refined. Then a plate was served to Cixi. The Empress Dowager came, and <u>it was said</u> that she claimed that she had to share the hardships with her people, eating steamed corn buns.

Since 说是, as a quotation marker, has the above-mentioned expressive function, we consider it a hedge. The speaker uses the particular lexical form of 说是 to show the quotative character, reflecting the speaker's uncertainty about the content of the quotation, which makes it a shield, specifically an attribution shield.

In addition to its usage as a shield, 说是 can also be used as an approximator, an adaptor to be exact. When the speaker makes comments, he or she also performs evaluative acts by way of quoting others to express something negative. Examine (11) to (13).

(11) 有些人虽说不是说差之千里吧,也有点儿说是不太相符,是吧,从这思想上也有差距。所以我的主要目标儿也就是找一个思想水平接近,文化程度相当,比较有共同语言的,就是。另外就是比较善良的,心地比较老成的。(Survey Corpus)

Yǒuxiē rén suīshuō búshì shuō chàzhīqiānlǐ ba, yě yǒudiǎn·er <u>shuōshi</u> bú tài xiāngfú, shì ba, cóng zhè sīxiǎng shàng yě yǒu chājù. Suǒyǐ wǒ de zhǔyào mùbiāo·er yějiùshì zhǎo yī gè sīxiǎng shuǐpíng jiējìn, wénhuà chéngdù xiāngdāng, bǐjiào yǒu gòngtóng yǔyán de, jiùshì. Lìngwài jiùshì bǐjiào shànliáng de, xīndì bǐjiào lǎochéng de.

'Some people are not that different from each other, but they are not quite, <u>as people put it</u>, compatible, right, and there is a gap in their ideas. So my main goal is to find a person with a similar level of thinking, a comparable level of education, and a common ground to share, that is it. In addition, he should be kind-hearted, and mature enough.'

(12) 对,反正我是挺反感女孩子抽烟。我要是看一看女的买烟吧,我从心眼儿里,不能说是讨厌吧,反正特别扭。(Survey Corpus)

Duì, fǎnzhèng wǒ shì tǐng fǎngǎn nǚ háizi chōuyān. Wǒ yàoshi kàn yīkàn nǚde mǎi yān ba, wǒ cóng xīnyǎn·er lǐ, bùnéng shuōshi tǎoyàn ba, fǎnzhèng tè bièniu.

'Yes, in any case, I'm quite disgusted with girls smoking. If I see a woman buying cigarettes, it can't be said that I hate it, but I indeed feel very uncomfortable from the bottom of my heart.'

(13) 我参加过,参加过我们同学的婚礼。我觉着像那个婚礼方面吧,关键是根据本人的条件什么的哈。如果条件允许的话呢,就大办。条件不允许呢,最好还是旅行一次。嗯,又开了眼界呢,完了还可以那什么,嗯,办了终身大事儿。我觉得没什么必要。那只是好像说是图虚荣似的。为什么呀?本身呢,你玩儿一趟就属于是蜜月旅行了。(Survey Corpus)

Wǒ cānjiāguò, cānjiāguò wǒmen tóngxué de hūnlǐ. Wǒ juézhe xiàng nàgè hūnlǐ fāngmiàn ba, guānjiàn shì gēnjù běnrén de tiáojiàn shénmede ha. Rúguǒ tiáojiàn yǔnxǔ dehuà ne, jiù dà bàn. Tiáojiàn bù yǔnxǔ ne, zuìhǎo háishì lǚxíng yī cì. En, yòu kāile yǎnjiè ne, wánliǎo hái kěyǐ nèishénme, en, bànle zhōngshēn dàshì·er. Wǒ juéde méishénme biyào. Nà zhǐshì hǎoxiàng shuōshi tú xūróng shìde. Wèishénme ya? Běnshēn ne, nǐ wán·er yī tàng jiù shǔyú shì mìyuè lǚxíng le.

'I have attended, attended the weddings of our classmates. To me, the key to a wedding is the conditions or something like that. If the conditions allow, it could be a big event. If conditions don't allow, it would be best to make a trip, which not only broadens the horizon, but also marks this lifetime event. I don't think it's necessarily for the sake of vanity, as said by some. Why? In itself, it makes your honeymoon trip.'

In the three cases above, 说是 is immediately followed by words of evaluative meaning, "不太相符" ('not quite compatible'), "讨厌" ('hate'), and "图虚荣" ('for the sake of vanity'), respectively. Here we see that the speakers were using the roundabout strategy when making negative evaluations, with the help of 说是, a typical coding device for indirect speech.

The following example is a boundary case where 说是 is not used for quotation, but to indicate the speaker's reservation because there is no exact source of information in the context.

(14) A: 说说这个,说说这个。说一两个中国特别的菜吧。啊,有一些个特别的,好像西方人不大容易,听见过,或者是吃到过的菜。

B: 可能这种菜,中国人也不大容易吃到,只是一种奇闻,奇闻。

A: 是,有很多,就是传说了。听人家说,广东人啊,特别的这个,是吧,没有文化,还是怎么着。说是吃猴子脑子,猴脑。那个,你听说过这种事吗?

B: 听说过。而且好像,那个,故事讲得还挺邪门儿的。(Survey Corpus)

A: Shuō~shuō zhèige, shuō~shuō zhèige. Shuō yī-liǎng-gè Zhōngguó tèbié de cài ba. A, yǒu yīxiēge tèbié de, hǎoxiàng Xīfāngrén búdà róngyì, tīngjiànguò, huòzhě shì chīdàoguò de cài.

B: Kěnéng zhèzhòng cài, Zhōngguórén yě búdà róngyì chīdào, zhǐshì yī zhǒng qíwén, qíwén.

A: Shì, yǒu hěnduō, jiùshì chuánshuō le. Tīng rénjiā shuō, Guǎngdōngrén a, tèbié de zhèige, shì ba, <u>méiyǒu wénhuà, háishì zěnmezhe</u>. <u>Shuōshi</u> chī hóuzi nǎozi, hóu nǎo. Nèige, nǐ tīngshuō guò zhèizhǒng shì ma?

B: Tīngshuō guò. Érqiě hǎoxiàng, nèige, gùshì jiǎngde hái tǐng xiémén·er de.

'A: Tell me about this, tell me about this. Tell me about one or two special Chinese dishes. Ah, there are some special ones, it seems, that Westerners are not very easy to hear of or taste.

B: Maybe this kind of dish is not easy even for the Chinese to taste, either. It's just an anecdote, an anecdote.

A: Yes, there are many that are simply legendary. <u>It is said</u> that the Cantonese, ah, in particular, right, eat monkey brains, monkey brains, <u>due to lack of education, or what</u>. Well, have you heard of such things?

B: Yes, I have. And it's like, uh, the story goes pretty weird.'

In this example, the speaker first shows the source of the information by making explicit use of "听人家说" ('hear people say'), and before saying "没有文化" ('lack of education'), hesitates and uses a filler[5] "是吧" ('right') to materialize a short pause, which is then followed by the hedge "还是怎么着" ('or what') before "说是吃猴子脑子, 猴脑" ('be said to eat monkey brains, monkey brains'). The post-说是 expression "吃猴子脑子" ('eat monkey brains') is not a quote, but a legendary dietary preference of the Cantonese people. If 说是 is replaced with 说, only the quotative function can be fulfilled, with the negative attitude of the speaker being sacrificed.

It is known that the same propositional meaning, if expressed differently, will have different illocutionary forces.[6] The so-called illocutionary force refers to the act performed by the speaker through an utterance. For example, "Open the door!" and "Can you open the door?" are two utterances performing different speech acts (the former is a command and the latter a request), and thus of different illocutionary forces. Relatively speaking, it is more polite to use a question than a plain imperative when you want others to do something for you. This is also the reason for using 说是 in the above example. Specifically, the negative evaluation of the speaker is not expressed directly; the quotative coding form weakens the illocutionary force of the statement.

8.4 Attitude marker

Attitude markers are expressions that reflect the author's or speaker's attitude toward the propositional content. Unlike the two types of usage discussed above, the propositional content introduced by the attitude marker 说是 is not limited to quotative or negative expressions; the meaning conveyed can be paraphrased as "said to be X, but may not be".

In other words, 说是 performs an evaluative act by way of a quotative coding form. In this evolutionary process, along with the emergence of its evaluative function, the two component parts of 说是 have undergone the process of reanalysis, ending up with a stressed "说" to modify "是".

(15) 小桂:胡爷爷,胡奶奶是不是上大连走亲戚去啦?
老胡:是啊,去就去吧,还非把小于也带去。说是路上照顾她,摆什么谱啊,把我一人儿撂家里谁照顾我啊。(I Love My Family)

Xiǎo Guì: Hú yéyé, Hú nǎinai shì-bú-shì shàng Dàlián zǒu qīnqī qù la?

Lǎo Hú: Shì a, qù jiù qù ba, hái fēi bǎ Xiǎo Yú yě dàiqù. <u>Shuōshi</u> lùshàng zhàogù tā, bǎi shénme pǔ a, bǎ wǒ yī rén·er liào jiāli shéi zhàogù wǒ a.

'Little Gui: Grandpa Hu, has Grandma Hu gone to Dalian to visit her relatives?

Old Hu: Yes. She may very well go, but she has insisted taking Little Yu with her. <u>It is said</u> that Yu will take care of her on the way. But what's the point? I'm left home all alone. Who will take care of me?'

(16) 甲:我也奇怪,好像,吃辣的容易让人发热。我倒是觉得好像应该是北方人爱吃辣的似的,好像不是南方人。那么热的地方,还吃那么多辣椒。
乙:啊,可是有人说是,说是以毒攻毒。是不是,天气热的时候,把辣椒一吃下去,就凉快了。说是好像是你身体体温增高,与外界体温相和了,你就不感觉那么热了。
甲:哦,还有这么一说儿?(Survey Corpus)

Jiǎ: Wǒ yě qíguài, hǎoxiàng, chī là de róngyì ràng rén fārè. Wǒ dǎoshì juéde hǎoxiàng yīnggāi shì běifāngrén ài chī là de shìde, hǎoxiàng búshì nánfāng rén. Nàme rè dì dìfāng, hái chī nàme duō làjiāo.

Yǐ: A, kěshì yǒurén <u>shuōshi</u>, <u>shuōshi</u> yǐdúgōngdú. Shì-bú-shì, tiānqì rè de shíhòu, bǎ làjiāo yī chī xiàqù, jiù liángkuai le. <u>Shuōshi</u> hǎoxiàng shì nǐ shēntǐ tǐwēn zēnggāo, yǔ wàijiè tǐwēn xiānghé le, nǐ jiù bù gǎnjué nàme rè le.

Jiǎ: Ó, háiyǒu zhème yīshuō·er?

'A: I just wonder, it seems that eating spicy food is likely to make people hot. I do feel that it should be northerners who love to eat spicy food, instead of southerners. They live in hot places, but still eat so much chilli.

B: Ah, but some people <u>say</u>, <u>say</u> that it is called "fight poison with poison". When the weather is hot, you would feel cooler once you eat chilli. <u>It is said</u> that your body temperature, once increased, would be the same with the environment temperature, and you will not feel so hot.

A: Oh, is there such a thing?'

In (16), the clause after 说是 is neither direct nor indirect speech, but simply a common saying or convention, which conveys the speaker's negative attitude towards the truth or correctness of the information he or she is quoting.

The following is a boundary case where 说是 is used differently from an evidential marker as discussed above. The manifestations are twofold: first, the subsequent constituent is not a quotation of the speaker; second, 说是 reflects the speaker's evaluation. In the case of the evidential marker, the speaker informs the addressee that he or she "does not take a position" on the content of the message being quoted, while 说是 in (17) indicates the speaker's position.

(17) 咱们说,你城市孩子长大了,一下子让你上内蒙,<u>说是</u>一下儿让你上黑龙江,他也琢磨琢磨,他也不敢那么去胡来了。(Survey Corpus)

Zánmen shuō, nǐ chéngshì háizi zhǎngdàle, yīxiàzi ràng nǐ shàng Nèiměng, <u>shuōshi</u> yīxià·er ràng nǐ shàng Hēilóngjiāng, tā yě zhuómó~zhuómó, tā yě bù gǎn nàme qù húlái le.

'Let's say, the city children have grown up. All of a sudden they are told to go to Inner Mongolia, or to go to Heilongjiang, <u>as is said</u>, they will also mull it over. They wouldn't dare to go so nonsense.'

In this example, "to go to Inner Mongolia" and "to go to Heilongjiang" are virtual events, but in the speaker's view, they are negative. Thus 说是 is used to reflect this position on the part of the speaker.

In colloquial Beijing dialect, 说 can be used to introduce a hypothetical conditional clause (Fang Mei, 2006). See (18) and (19) for illustration.

(18) 你自己得有主意。<u>说</u>你父母什么的家里人都不在你身边儿,你怎么办哪? (Interview Corpus)

Nǐ zìjǐ děi yǒu zhǔyì. <u>Shuō</u> nǐ fùmǔ shénme de jiālǐrén dōu bù zài nǐ shēnbiān·er, nǐ zěnme bàn na?

'You have to have your own ideas. <u>Say</u> your parents or other family members are not with you, what would you do?'

(19) 整天的犯困,开车开车能睡着了,走路走路能睡着了。除了<u>说</u>吃饭,随时都可能睡过去。(Interview Corpus)

Zhěngtiān de fànkùn, kāichē kāichē néng shuìzháo le, zǒulù zǒulù néng shuìzháo le. Chúle <u>shuō</u> chīfàn, suíshí dōu kěnéng shuì guòqù.

'I'm sleepy all day long. I can fall asleep while driving; I can also fall asleep while walking. Except for <u>say</u> eating, I can fall asleep at any time.'

说 cannot be replaced by 说是 when used to introduce conditional clauses as illustrated in (18) and (19).

8.5 Lexicalization

The shift from quotative 说 to evaluative 说 is accomplished by compounding with 是, in the process of which the judgmental meaning of 是 plays a key role. This inference can be attested by the synchronic usage of the compound.

In contemporary colloquial Beijing dialect, 说 can be used as a marker of appositive clauses, as in example (20),[7] where (20a) to (20d) all use 说 to introduce the clauses specifying respectively the nouns "谣言" ('rumor'), "预期" ('expectation'), "机会" ('opportunity'), and "时间" ('time').

(20) a. 而且社会上还会传出谣言,说这几个人都跟吴士宏谈过恋爱。(Interview Corpus)

Érqiě shèhuìshàng hái huì chuánchū yáoyán, shuō zhè jǐ gè rén dōu gēn Wú Shìhóng tángguò liàn'ài.

'And rumors would spread in the community that all these guys used to be in a relationship with Wu Shihong.'

b. 在你刚下海的时候,有没有一个预期,说我要赚到多少钱。(Interview Corpus)

Zài nǐ gāng xiàhǎi de shíhòu, yǒu-méi-yǒu yī gè yùqí, shuō wǒ yào zhuàndào duōshǎo qián.

'When you first went into the business, was there an expectation of how much money you wanted to make?'

c. 好容易有个机会,说上电视演戏,结果她还不让去。(Interview Corpus)

Hǎoróngyì yǒu gè jīhuì, shuō shàng diànshì yǎnxì, jiéguǒ tā hái bù ràng qù.

'It was not easy to have an opportunity to act on TV, but it turned out that she wouldn't let him go.'

d. 而且现在这种现代节奏呀,根本容不得你有时间,说你回家住在家里跟妈妈说话呀,没有。

Érqiě xiànzài zhèzhǒng xiàndài jiézòu ya, gēnběn róng-bù-de nǐ yǒu shíjiān, shuō nǐ huíjiā zhù zài jiālǐ gēn māmā shuōhuà ya, méiyǒu.

'And now this modern tempo (of life) simply does not allow you the time to go and live at home to talk with your mother, nope.'

说是 has a similar usage, but it is nonetheless different from 说. In (21), the sentence introduced by 说是$_1$ elaborates the content of the noun "佐证" ('supporting evidence') and the sentence introduced by 说是$_2$ explains what "another version of Li's entry into the capital" is.

From quoting to hedging 169

(21) 有书记载:当年李自成的主力军,是从昌平居庸关进的京。虽然居庸关号称"天险",但李自成的部队,势如破竹,兵不血刃,就夺了关。可见当时,明朝官兵,早已人心涣散,没什么人愿意给崇祯卖命了。关于这种说法,还有<u>佐证</u>。说。<u>李自成,军队破关之后,烧了明朝皇帝陵的十二座享殿,还把所有守灵的松柏都砍掉了</u>。李自成的农民起义军,烧人家祖坟的嗜好,是出了名的,也是最犯忌讳的。尽管史书一再强调,李自成刚进京的时候,军队纪律严明。但是烧皇陵这一举动,足以让李自成失了民心了。说得这么热闹,我们却得到了<u>另外一个李闯王进京版本</u>。说是<u>当年居庸关将领,死守关口,李自成根本就没闯过去,迫不得已绕到了延庆县的帮水峪长城一带。这才辗转,进了咱的北京城</u>。(*This is Beijing*)

Yǒu shū jìzǎi: Dāngnián Lǐ Zìchéng de zhǔlì jūn, shì cóng Chāngpíng Jūyōngguān jìn de jīng. Suīrán Jūyōngguān hàochēng "tiānxiǎn", dàn Lǐ Zìchéng de bùduì, shìrúpòzhú, bīngbùxuèrèn, jiù duóle guān. Kějiàn dāngshí, Míngcháo guānbīng, zǎoyǐ rénxīnhuànsàn, méi shénme rén yuànyì gěi Chóngzhēn màimìng le. Guānyú zhèzhǒng shuōfǎ, háiyǒu <u>zuǒzhèng</u>. **Shuōshì**₁ <u>Lǐ Zìchéng, jūnduì pòguān zhīhòu, shāole Míngcháo huángdì líng de shí'èr zuò xiǎngdiàn, hái bǎ suǒyǒu shǒulíng de sōngbǎi dōu kǎndiàole</u>. Lǐ Zìchéng de nóngmín qǐyì jūn, shāo rénjiā zǔfén de shìhào, shì chūle míng de, yěshì zuì fàn jìhuì de. Jǐnguǎn shǐshū yīzài qiángdiào, Lǐ Zìchéng gāng jìn jīng de shíhòu, jūnduì jìlǜ yánmíng. Dànshì shāo huánglíng zhè yī jǔdòng, zúyǐ ràng Lǐ Zìchéng shīle mínxīn le. Shuō de zhème rènào, wǒmen què dédàole <u>lìngwài yī gè Lǐ Chuǎngwáng jìnjīng bǎnběn</u>. **Shuōshì**₂ <u>dāngnián Jūyōngguān jiànglǐng, sǐshǒu guānkǒu, Lǐ Zìchéng gēnběn jiù méi chuǎng guòqù, pòbùdéyǐ ràodàole Yánqìng xiàn de Bāngshuǐyù chángchéng yīdài. Zhè cái zhǎnzhuǎn, jìnle zán de Běijīng chéng</u>.

'It is written that Li Zicheng's main force entered the capital from Juyongguan of Changping County. Although Juyongguan is known as "a natural stronghold", Li Zicheng's troops carried all before them and took the pass without bloodshed. It can be seen that at that time, the Ming Dynasty officers and soldiers had long been disillusioned, not many people willing to sell their lives to Emperor Chongzhen. There is <u>supporting evidence</u> for this statement. **It is said** that <u>Li Zicheng's army broke through the pass, burned the twelve funeral temples of the Ming emperor's mausoleum, and cut down all the pines and cypresses that guarded the spirits</u>. Li Zicheng's peasant rebel army was notorious for the hobby of burning people's ancestral graves, also a most serious taboo. Although history books repeatedly emphasize that Li Zicheng's army was disciplined when they first entered the capital, the act of burning the imperial funeral temples was enough to make Li Zicheng lose the hearts of the people. So lively the story goes, we have got <u>another version of Li Zicheng's entry into the capital</u>. **It is said** that <u>Li Zicheng did not break through the pass at all because of the fierce guard of the Juyongguan general. Li Zicheng had no choice but to go</u>

around to Yanqing County and made his entry into Beijing through a pass along the Bangshuiyu Great Wall.'

It is worth noting that 说 and 说是 differ in the following dimensions:

1) 说 introduces one clause, while 说是, as a metadiscourse device with an evidential function, can introduce multiple clauses.[8]
2) The use of 说 does not involve the speaker's attitude, while the use of 说是 implicates the speaker's "unsure" attitude, which can find support in context.
3) When 说是 is used as an evidential marker, its quotation function is nonetheless retained; when it is used as a hedge, its function is shifted from quoting to modifying.

In short, 说是 not only has the function of quotation; it also functions differently from 说. When used for different purposes, it has different phonological realizations. As an evidential marker, its subsequent expressions are quotative by nature and the source of information is certain, and in this usage both 说 and 是 retain their original tones. When 说是 is used as a hedge, its subsequent expressions are not quotative, and 是 in it is reduced to the neutral tone. When 说是 is used as an attitude marker to express a negative evaluation, its subsequent expressions are quotative but without highlighting the information source, and 说 will take a contrastive stress (indicated by #) and is articulated intensively. The three usages are represented as 说是$_1$, 说是$_2$ and 说是$_3$ respectively in Table 8.1.

The lexicalization of 说是 is internally consistent with the lexicalization pattern of "V+是" in modern Chinese, in that both have the function of reducing the illocutionary force of speech. Therefore, 說是$_3$, which expresses the negative attitude of the speaker, requires the contrastive stress.

We are of the view that 说是 has completed its lexicalization process by compounding two content morphemes 说 ('say') and 是 ('be'). But can this process be regarded as derivation of the configuration "root morpheme+derivational affix"? If we take into account the large number of "X是" emergent in modern Chinese, it is not a bad idea to characterize 说是 as a derivational construction, given the premise that 是 has indeed become a derivational affix in modern Chinese.

是 as a high-frequency morphemic component has received widespread attention from the academic community. Dong Xiufang (2004a) suggests that

Table 8.1 Usage of 说是

	Function	Quotativeness	Phonological realization
说是$_1$	evidential marker	+	shuōshì
说是$_2$	hedge	−	shuōshi
说是$_3$	attitude marker	+	#shuōshi

是 has become such a productive element in modern Chinese, and that it can be placed after some adverbs and conjunctions to form words, such as 尤其是 (yóuqí-shì, 'especially'), 仅仅是 (jǐnjǐn-shì, 'just'), 特别是 (tèbié-shì, 'especially'), 如果是 (rúguǒ-shì, 'if yes'), 不管是 (bùguǎn-shì, 'no matter'), 或者是 (huòzhě-shì, 'or'), etc. Dong Xiufang (2004a) argues that "X是" is yet to be fully lexicalized when "X" is a two-syllable component, though the monosyllable "X" plus 是 has completed the compounding process, as in the cases of 硬是 (yìngshì, 'just'), 光是 (guāngshì, 'just'), 老是 (lǎoshì, 'always'), 越是 (yuèshì, 'the more'), 若是 (ruòshì, 'if'), 要是 (yàoshi, 'if'), etc., where 是 has further grammaticalized from an independent word into an intra-word component.[9]

Zhang Yisheng (2003b) discusses the evolution of "adverb+是", arguing that "adverb+是" gradually evolves from a verbal phrase of modifier-head configuration to a modifier-head adverb, and then to a conjunctive or modal word. Recent studies have revealed that there is indeed such a tendency for "adverb+是" to intensify its subjectivity, and that this tendency is not limited to compounds formed by "adverb+是." "Conjunction+是" shows a similar evolutionary mechanism as well as some commonality in expression function.

For 说是 to be defined as a derivational construction, one more question needs to be addressed: is this 是 identical in terms of function and meaning with that in other "X是" constructions, say "adverb+是"? Actual language data show clear differences. While it is a common phenomenon for adverbs and conjunctions to be suffixed by 是, not many verbs can compound with 是 to form new words. Outside 说是, there are mainly modal auxiliary verbs (Piao Huijing, 2011; Fang Mei, 2013a) and the verb 想 that can form compounds with 是 (想是 expresses speculation).[10] Moreover, with the addition of 是, the word class changes from verb to adverb. Unlike verbs, adverbs and conjunctions, when suffixed with 是, remain unchanged in word class. From this perspective, the analysis of 是 as an affix is somewhat problematic, as its meaning and function lack internal consistency. The compromise is either to treat 是 following different stems (adverb, conjunction, or verb) as different variations, or to treat all types of "X是" as compounds[11] – combinations of two content morphemes, rather than derivational constructions.

8.6 "Verb+是" and reduced expression of illocutionary force

Compared with the form without 是, the compound verb with 是shows a reduced illocutionary force.

First of all, let's look at 想是. According to *The Modern Chinese Dictionary* (6th edition, The Commercial Press, 2012), there are six senses of "想", the second of which is 'speculate, think', with the example "我想他今天不会来" (Wǒ xiǎng tā jīntiān bú huì lái, 'I don't think he will come today.'). In this usage, the grammatical subject performs the act of "想." In contrast, a 想是-sentence is incompatible with an agent subject, as in examples (22) to (26), where the subject in each case takes the speaker orientation, indicative of the speaker's speculation.[12]

(22) 我也不吃潮烟,我就不会吃烟,我也没叫你装烟,<u>想是</u>你听错了。(Wen Kang, *The Legend of the Heroic Children* [《儿女英雄传》])

Wǒ yě bù chī cháo yān, wǒ jiù bú huì chīyān, wǒ yě méi jiào nǐ zhuāng yān, <u>xiǎngshì</u> nǐ tīng cuò le.

'I won't smoke tobacco from Chao'an County, either. I don't smoke at all. I didn't ask you to fill the smoke, either. You <u>must</u> have misheard it.'

(23) 那女子走到跟前,把那块石头端相了端相,见有二尺多高,径圆也不过一尺来往,约莫也有个二百四五十斤重,原是一个碾粮食的碌碡。上面靠边却有个凿通了的关眼儿,<u>想是</u>为拴拴牲口,再不插根杆儿,晾晾衣裳用的。(Wen Kang, *Heroic Sons and Daughters*)

Nà nǚzǐ zǒu dào gēnqián, bǎ nà kuài shítou duānxiāngle duānxiāng, jiàn yǒu èr chǐ duō gāo, jìngyuán yě búguò yī chǐ láiwǎng, yuēmò yě yǒu gè èr bǎi sì-wǔ-shí jīn zhòng, yuán shì yī gè niǎn liángshí de lùdú. Shàngmiàn kàobiān què yǒu gè záo tōng le de guānyǎn·er, <u>xiǎngshì</u> wèi shuān~shuān shēngkǒu, zàibu chā gēn gǎn·er, liàng~liàng yīshang yòng de.

'The woman walked up to the stone to take a look at it. It was more than two feet in height, no more than a foot in diameter, about 250 pounds in weight, which was originally a stone roller. There was a whole at the top, <u>probably</u> used for tethering livestock or holding a rod to dry clothes with.'

(24) 公子便问那老和尚道:"这里到二十八棵红柳树还有多远?"那老和尚说:"你们上二十八棵红柳树,怎的走起这条路来?你们<u>想是</u>从大路来的呀?你们上二十八棵红柳树,自然该从岔道口往南去才是呢。" (Wen Kang, *The Legend of the Heroic Children*)

Gōngzǐ biàn wèn nà lǎo héshàng dào: "Zhèlǐ dào èr-shí-bā kē hóng liǔshù háiyǒu duōyuǎn?" Nà lǎo héshàng shuō: "Nǐmen shàng èr-shí-bā kē hóng liǔshù, zěndi zǒuqǐ zhè tiáo lù lái? Nǐmen <u>xiǎngshì</u> cóng dàlù lái de ya? Nǐmen shàng èr-shí-bā kē hóng liǔshù, zìrán gāi cóng chàdàokǒu wǎng nán qù cái shì ne."

'Then he asked the old monk, "How far is it to the twenty-eight red willow trees?" The old monk said, "Why are you taking this road when you want to go to the twenty-eight red willow trees? <u>I suppose</u> you came from the main road? If you want to go up to the twenty-eight red willow trees, you should naturally go southward from the fork in the road."'

(25) ……太太既是问下来,<u>想是</u>有意给天赐松绑。设若太太问娃娃该在几个月推出斩首,老刘妈必能知道是应登时绑到法场。(Lao She, *Biography of Niu Tianci* [《牛天赐传》])

…Tàitài jìshì wèn xiàlái, <u>xiǎngshì</u> yǒuyì gěi Tiāncì sōngbǎng. Shèruò tàitài wèn wáwá gāi zài jǐ gè yuè tuīchū zhǎnshǒu, lǎo Liú mā bì néng zhīdào shì yīng dēngshí bǎng dào fǎchǎng.

'Since madam was asking, <u>probably</u> she intended to have Tianci untied. If madam asked when the boy should be beheaded, old maidservant Liu would be able to know that Tianci should be tied to the court right away.'

(26) 这正是二十五号打的最激烈的时候，敌人的坦克<u>想是</u>来向二十五号开炮! (Lao She, *The Unknown Height Has a Name* [《无名高地有了名》])

Zhè zhèngshì èr-shí-wǔ hào dǎ de zuì jīliè de shíhòu, dírén de tǎnkè <u>xiǎngshì</u> lái xiàng èr-shí-wǔ hào kāipào!

'It was the time when Height 25 was fighting most fiercely, and the enemy tanks were <u>probably</u> firing at it.'

The word 想是 in declarative sentences can be replaced by 想必 (xiǎngbì, 'most probably'), as in (22), (23), (25) and (26), whereas the replacement would not be allowable in interrogative sentences, such as example (24). In comparison with 想必, 想是 expresses a weakened inference, which explains why they are not interchangeable in questions. From a functional point of view, 想是 cannot be transformed into "V不(bu)V" (where 不 is a negator) as a modal auxiliary verb often does (say 能不能 [néngbùnéng, 'can or cannot]'); that is, we cannot say 想是不想是. Therefore, 想是 can be roughly regarded as a modal adverb.[13]

Now examine "modal auxiliary verb+是", which is rather close to an S-adverb in function.[14] In naturally occurring speech, it can be independent in prosody; that is, it can be pause-marked on both sides. Moreover, it can be used at the beginning of the sentence, inserted in the middle of the sentence as an interjection, or put at the end of the sentence. See (27) and (28).[15]

(27) 其实,你说,他当着我的时候当然抽的烟不多。只是,<u>可能是</u>,实在控制不住了[@]获奖的时候[@]。因为当时我想了,我想,按照中国的观点啊,那个=<u>可能是</u>=就没什么大希望。(Survey Corpus)

Qíshí, nǐ shuō, tā dāngzhe wǒ de shíhòu dāngrán chōu de yān bù duō. Zhǐshì, <u>kěnéng shì</u>, shízài kòngzhì bú zhù le [@] huòjiǎng de shíhòu [@]. Yīnwèi dāngshí wǒ xiǎngle, wǒ xiǎng, ànzhào Zhōngguó de guāndiǎn a, nàgè=<u>kěnéng shì</u>=jiù méi shénme dà xīwàng.

'In fact, you can tell, he certainly doesn't smoke much in front of me. (He smokes) just, <u>probably</u>, when he really can't control, [@] (say) at the time of winning the award [@]. Because at that time I thought, I thought, according to the Chinese point of view, well = <u>maybe</u> = there was not much hope.'

(28) A: 还有窝头没有?
B: 有窝头,对。那窝头就是,黄金塔,啊。
A: 哎呀,黄金塔!是吧,这个,玉棒子面儿,做成一个圆锥形,……
B: 是。
A: 底下,拿大拇指往里穿一个洞,<u>可能是</u>蒸着让它方便一点儿<u>可能是</u>。汽从里面透过去,熟得快。(Survey Corpus)

A: Hái yǒu wōtóu méiyǒu?
B: Yǒu wōtóu, duì. Nà wōtóu jiùshì, huángjīn tǎ, a.

A: Aīyā, huángjīn tǎ! Shì ba, zhèige, yùbàngzimiàn·er, zuòchéng yī gè yuánzhuī xíng, …

B: Shì.

A: Dǐxia, ná dàmǔzhǐ wǎnglǐ chuān yī gè dòng, <u>kěnéng shì</u> zhēngzhe ràng tā fāngbiàn yīdiǎn·er <u>kěnéng shì</u>. Qì cóng lǐmiàn tòu guòqù, shú de kuài.

'A: Are there any more steamed corn buns?

B: Yes, there are. Steamed corn buns are golden towers, ah.

A: Ah, golden towers! Right, corn flour is shaped into a cone, …

B: Right.

A: From the bottom, a hole is made into it with the thumb. Probably this can make steaming a little easier <u>probably</u>. The steam can go through the inside, which can fasten the cooking.'

The deletion of "可能是" in the above examples will not affect the expression of the propositional meaning. In (27), "可能是" is used twice. The first "可能是" follows "只是" as a self-repair,[16] with a pause on both sides, expressing the speaker's inference that he smokes "when he really can't control." And with this "可能是", the degree of certainty of the speaker's inference is weakened. The second "可能是" is bounded by a phonological delay on both sides, which gaps it phonologically from the preceding and following words. In dialog, phonological delay is highly correlated with the speaker's uncertainty. In example (28), "蒸着让它方便点儿" ('make steaming a little easier') is the speaker's understanding and explanation of the making and shaping of the steamed corn bun. The use of "可能是", like in (27), also weakens the certainty of the speaker's inference.

When it comes to 应该是, it also expresses the speaker's weakened inference, especially in comparison with its component part 应该, which is used for inference expression, such as in 他应该到学校了 (Tā yīnggāi dào xuéxiàole, 'He should have arrived at school.'). More often than not 应该是 is found in conjunction with adverbs of estimation. See (29).

(29) 广化寺,大约建于元朝。明清时期,广化寺殿堂廊屋,规模宏大,为北京最有影响的佛刹。现在关于广化寺建寺的因缘,有两种说法。第一种说法是,以前这个地方啊住着一个僧人。他每天都是念诵佛号,而且每念一声佛号呢,都拿着一粒米来计数。当他把这个米啊,积攒到了四十八石的时候,可想而知啊,他念了多少佛号。他觉得这个因缘成熟了,可以建寺了,于是建起了广化寺。那么第二种说法呢,是以前这儿,还住着一个僧人。他呀,发愿二十年不出山门,在这闭关修行。那么过了二十年之后,这个愿望实现了。那么又过了十年,他建立起了广化寺。但是两个记载啊,年代大概都是在元朝。所以说,根据记载,广化寺修建的年代<u>应该是</u>在,大约1342年左右。(*This Is Beijing*)

Guǎnghuàsì, dàyuē jiàn yú Yuáncháo. Míng Qīng shíqī, Guǎnghuàsì diàntáng lángwū, guīmó hóngdà, wéi Běijīng zuì yǒu yǐngxiǎng de fóchà. Xiànzài guānyú Guǎnghuàsì jiàn sì de yīnyuán, yǒu liǎng zhǒng shuōfǎ. Dì yī zhǒng shuōfǎ shì, yǐqián zhège dìfāng a zhùzhe yī gè sēngrén. Tā měitiān dōushì niànsòng fóhào, érqiě měi niàn yī shēng fóhào ne, dōu názhe yī lì mǐ lái jìshù. Dāng tā bǎ zhège mǐ a, jīzǎn dào le sì-shí-bā dàn de shíhòu, kěxiǎngérzhī a, tā niànle duōshǎo fóhào. Tā juéde zhège yīnyuán chéngshúle, kěyǐ jiàn sì le, yúshì jiàn-qǐle Guǎnghuàsì. Nàme dì'èrzhǒng shuōfǎ ne, shì yǐqián zhè·er, hái zhùzhe yī gè sēngrén. Tā ya, fāyuàn èrshí nián bù chū shānmén, zài zhè bìguān xiūxíng. Nàme guòle èrshí nián zhīhòu, zhège yuànwàng shíxiànle. Nàme yòu guòle shí nián, tā jiànlì-qǐle Guǎnghuàsì. Dànshì liǎng gè jìzǎi a, niándài dàgài dōu shì zài Yuáncháo. Suǒyǐ shuō, gēnjù jìzǎi, Guǎnghuàsì xiūjiàn de niándài <u>yīnggāi-shì</u> zài, dàyuē 1342 nián zuǒyòu.

'Guanghua Temple was built around the Yuan Dynasty. During the Ming and Qing dynasties, Guanghua Temple was the most influential Buddhist temple in Beijing with its grand scale of halls and corridors. Nowadays, there are two stories about the cause of Guanghua Temple's foundation. The first one goes like this. There used to be a monk living here, who chanted the Buddha's name every day. And every time he chanted Buddha, he would take a grain of rice to count. When he had accumulated forty-eight dan of rice (you can imagine how much he had chanted), he felt that the cause was there to build a temple. So he built Guanghua Temple. The second story is that there was a monk who lived here in the past. He made a vow to stay in retreat for 20 years. Twenty years later, his wish was fulfilled. Then, after another ten years, he established Guanghua Temple. Anyhow, both stories are dated to the Yuan Dynasty. So according to the records, Guanghwa Temple <u>should have been</u> built, in 1342 circa.'

In this example, the speaker first says "应该是在" ('should have been'), and then after a pause makes a self-repair by using 大约 ('circa'). The use of this self-repair can serve as evidence of the speaker's communicative intention – to weaken the certainty of his inference.

When postpositioned, 应该是 expresses an after-thought, also to weaken the degree of certainty about the proposition, such as in (30).

(30) 这个碑是满汉碑,满汉双文的碑,下面是个王八驮碑,但是现在可能,可能看不了啦。它那个,这个碑是圈在这个院子里边。围起来了哈。门在这边还是那边?从这进去能看见那碑吗?就那块碑,你知道吗,看不见是吧?只能从那边过去才能看见,是吧?哎,你看,这有一块碑。这儿以前是两块,<u>应该是</u>。现在这是其中一块。但是这个方向不对,这个后来可能被人换过方向了。(*This Is Beijing*)

Zhège bēi shì mǎn hàn bēi, mǎn hàn shuāng wén de bēi, xiàmiàn shì gè wángbā tuóbēi, dànshì xiànzài kěnéng, kěnéng kàn-bù-liǎo la. Tā nàgè, zhège bēi shì quān zài zhège yuànzi lǐbian. Wéi qǐlái le ha. Mén zài zhèbiān háishì nàbiān? Cóng zhè jìnqù néng kànjiàn nà bēi ma? Jiù nà kuài bēi, nǐ zhīdào ma, kàn-bú-jiàn shì ba? Zhǐnéng cóng nàbiān guòqù cáinéng kànjiàn, shì ba? Āi, nǐ kàn, zhè yǒu yī kuài bēi. Zhè·er yǐqián shì liǎng kuài, yīnggāi-shì. Xiànzài zhè shì qízhōng yī kuài. Dànshì zhège fāngxiàng bú duì, zhège hòulái kěnéng bèi rén huànguò fāngxiàng le.

'This monument is a Manchu-Chinese monument, a monument in both Manchu and Chinese, and beneath it is a turtle bearing it. But it may not be possible to see it now. It's, this monument is enclosed in the courtyard. It's enclosed. Is the gate this way or that way? Can you see the monument from here? The monument, you know, you can't see it, can you? You can only see it from over there, right? Hey, look, there's a monument here. There used to be two of them, should have been. Now this is one of them. But this one is in the wrong direction. It may have been moved by someone.'

In this example, the speaker first says "这儿以前是两块" ('There used to be two of them') before he uses "应该是" to weaken the judgment already stated. In the next two sentences, this judgment is further elaborated.

In summary, "modal auxiliary verb+是" expresses the weak inference or low reliability on the part of the speaker, which makes it a form of reduced expression.

8.7 Summary

Compounds of "V+是" formation, such as 说是, 想是 and "modal auxiliary verb+是", constitute important means of evaluation expression though they function kind of differently. Table 8.2 broadly summarizes their different functions.

Relatively speaking, compounds containing 是 bring forth the interpersonal function of the speaker's attitude,[17] which may be the motivation for the emergence of new compounds with 是.

Table 8.2 Expression function of "X是"

Weak inference	Uncertainty	Incredibility	Negative evaluation	Hedging
想是 可能是 应该是	说是 应该是	说是	说是	说是

Notes

1 Pause marked 说 can be used to retell a story, and only in this use can the source of information be left out. For example:

说,一个国王做了个梦,梦见自己的牙齿一颗颗地掉光了。国王醒来后,找来一个释梦者......

(quoted from Yue Yao, 2011a)

<u>Shuō</u>, yī gè guówáng zuòle gè mèng, mèngjiàn zìjǐ de yáchǐ yīkēkē de diào guāng le. Guówáng xǐnglái hòu, zhǎolái yī gè shìmèngzhě.

'<u>Say</u> a king had a dream that his teeth fell out one by one. When he woke up, he called in a dream interpreter...'

Thus used 说 has lost some of its syntactic features as the predicate. For instance, it cannot be negated; nor can it be reduplicated.

2 Wang et al. (2003) suggest that in spoken Taiwan Mandarin, 说 can be either a non-personal quotation marker or a generalized evidential marker, meaning "someone said so". The function of 说 is to convey the speaker's attitude. Xuan Yue (2011) has found that 说 can be used at the beginning of a sentence in northeastern Chinese, in which case 说 may be a reduced form of "X说" (such as 话说, huàshuō, 'say').

3 There are a number of insertions containing 说 which have the function of demonstrating evidence, such as 听说 (tīngshuō, 'it is heard'), 据说 (jùshuō, 'it is said'), 俗话说 (súhuà shuō, 'the saying goes'), 常言说 (chángyán shuō, 'the saying goes'), 按理说 (ànlǐ shuō, 'it stands to reason'), 按说 (ànshuō, 'it stands to reason'), 照(理)说 (zhào (lǐ) shuō, 'it stands to reason'), etc.

4 For the usage of 据说, see Yue Yao (2011a).

5 Filler is a term used in Conversation Analysis to refer to forms of expression that mark pauses or hesitations in discourse. The commonly seen fillers in English include *um, uh, er, ah, like, okay, right, you know*, etc. (Amiridze et al., 2010). Although fillers have no or very little lexical meaning, they are important in the extension process of utterances.

6 The term "illocutionary force" refers to the act performed by the speaker when he says something, such as promise, command, request, announcement, etc. (Austin, 1962).

7 For the use of 说 as a subclause marker, see Fang Mei (2006).

8 In the example "说,一个国王做了个梦,梦见自己的牙齿一颗颗地掉光了。国王醒来后,找来一个释梦者..." (see note 1), we do not think that the word 说 introduces multiple clauses. This use of 说 is the same with 据悉 (jùxī, 'it is known') that occurs at the beginning of news reports, which grants thus used 说 the status of a metadiscourse element. This kind of 说 can sometimes take a modifier, but its grammatical subject cannot be recovered (see example [17] in Chapter 7).

9 According to Dong Xiufang (2004a), it is difficult to analyze 是 as an affix, so it is tentatively called an "intra-word component".

10 The word 想是 indicates the speaker's speculation, and the tone is less certain than that of 想必. For details, see note (12).

11 For the definition and designation of compounding and derivation, see Brinton and Traugott (2005, pp. 34–37).

12 According to Wang Canlong (2009), after 想 developed the meaning of "estimate, speculate" in early modern Chinese, its subject (i.e., the speaker) was often made implicit. This use remained active in all dynasties from Western Jin to the end of the Qing Dynasty. An early example of the use of 想是 can be found in *Analects of Zhu Xi* (《朱子语类》):

伊川之语,<u>想是</u>被门人记错了,不可知. (Vol. 36)
Yīchuān zhī yǔ, <u>xiǎngshì</u> bèi ménrén jì cuò le, bù kě zhī.
'The words of Yichuan <u>are thought</u> to have been misremembered by the disciples, no one can tell.'

The word 想是 can be interpreted as reinforcing subjective judgment, and is therefore a "subjectivity marker." However, in the works of contemporary writers, its frequency of use is declining, as evidenced by a decrease in the absolute number of occurrences and in the distribution of writers who indeed use it. The reason for its declined use may be the atypical nature of 想是 as a "word", which subjects its composition to the possible analysis as a syntactic configuration. As a result, 是 in it is not as much reduced in articulation as its counterpart in 可是 (kěshì, 'but'). On top of that, there are also 想来 (xiǎnglái, 'think') and 想必 (xiǎngbì, 'must') that are functionally similar to 想是. In such a context, 想是 is on the verge of extinction. The results of Wang's chronological survey are very enlightening, but, given the fact that the percentage of materials representing colloquial Beijing dialect is not high in his corpus, the statistical results may have been swayed to greater or lesser extent by the sources. So far as the native speaker's language intuition goes, 想是 is still commonly used in spoken Chinese.

13 According to a preliminary investigation, 想是 is more common in old-school colloquial Beijing Mandarin, but is not used much in contemporary colloquial Beijing dialect. Further investigation is needed for more details.
14 According to Long Guofu, adverbs can be divided into two basic subcategories: the first subcategory used as adjuncts to the whole sentence, and the second belonging directly to the predicate. This classification is also typical of general descriptive grammar. Defined in terms of functional categories, the former, whose semantic scope is larger than the clause, is called S-adverbs; the latter, whose semantic scope is within the clause, is called VP-adverbs. See also Fang Mei (2013a).
15 In this example, "[@]" is used before and after a discourse stretch to indicate that this stretch is accompanied by laughter; the symbol "=" is used to indicate that the preceding syllable is accompanied by a phonological delay.
16 Repair as used in Conversation Analysis refers to an attempt by a conversation participant to correct a real or imagined error in the conversation (e.g., mishearing or misunderstanding). Repair can also be divided into self-repair, where the speaker corrects himself, and other-repair, where the listener makes the correction.
17 See Fang Mei (2017a) for the evaluative function of other "X是" adverbs in colloquial Beijing dialect.

9 Discourse function of speech verb metadiscourse

In narratology, the presence of the narrative process and the narrator in the form of discourse is called "metanarrative". The representative form of traditional Chinese narrative is story-telling. As a live form of narration, the metanarrative of story-telling embodies both the discourse structure of the narrative plot and the interaction between the narrator and the audience. The high-frequency metadiscourse expressions include the speech verb 说 (shuō, 'say') and its compounds, such as 单说 ('just say'). The use of speech verbs represented by 说 as discourse connectives reflects the narrative orientation on the part of the narrator, although the narrator may not be made visible in explicit lexical forms.

9.1 Introduction

Narrative discourse differs from expository discourse in cohesive devices. Expository discourse is based on the logical connection between argument and evidence, and its internal structure is mainly supported by the "nucleus–satellite" relation between sentences (Mann and Thompson, 1987). Conversely, narrative discourse is based on the course of events, and the temporal sequence of events and the behavior of the participants constitute the means of discourse progression. The information on the main narrative line is the foreground information, and the layouts outside the main line make up the background information. Accordingly, in narrative discourse, the adverbials of time and place that occur at the beginning of the sentence often mark the nodes of the plot (Chafe, 1980). The switch of the main event participants – the discourse protagonists – plays an equally important role in the description of the course of events.

In *The Grammar of Discourse*, Longacre (1983, pp. 3–5) classifies discourse into the narrative, procedural, behavioral, and expository based on the criteria of temporal succession and agent orientation (see Fang Mei, 2007, 2013c for syntactic manifestations of their stylistic differences in Chinese).

A typical narrative discourse is characterized by temporal succession and agent orientation. Its macro-structure relies on chronological order for support. For example, in (1a), "又" ('again') and "然后" ('then') are used to express the temporal sequence; in (1b), however, there is no use of temporal expressions, whereby the narrative order is assumed to be the sequence of events by default.

(1) a. 扎蝴蝶结的小姑娘找到了目标,把手绢轻轻地放在一个小个子的姑娘身后,<u>又</u>装作若无其事的样子走了几步,<u>然后</u>猛跑起来。

Zhā húdiéjié de xiǎo gūniáng zhǎodàole mùbiāo, bǎ shǒujuàn qīngqīngde fàngzài yī gè xiǎogèzi de gūniáng shēnhòu, <u>yòu</u> zhuāngzuò ruòwúqíshì de yàngzi zǒule jǐ bù, <u>ránhòu</u> měngpǎo qǐlái.

'The little girl wearing a bowknot in the hair found her target. She gently placed the handkerchief behind a little girl, walked on for a few steps as if nothing had happened, then all of a sudden she began to sprint.'

b. 一张对折的钞票躺在人行道上。一个人弯腰去捡钞票。噌——,钞票飞进了一家店铺的门里。一个胖胖的孩子坐在门背后。他把钞票丢在人行道上,钞票上拴了一根黑线……胖孩子满脸是狡猾的笑容。(Wang Zengqi, *The Kid's Entrapment* [《钓人的孩子》], cited from Liu Lening, 2005)

Yī zhāng duìzhé de chāopiào tǎng zài rénxíngdào shàng. Yī gè rén wānyāo qù jiǎn chāopiào. Cēng—, chāopiào fēijìnle yī jiā diànpù de mén li. Yī gè pàng~pàng de háizi zuò zài mén bèihòu. Tā bǎ chāopiào diū zài rénxíngdào shàng, chāopiào shàng shuānle yī gēn hēi xiàn... pàng háizi mǎnliǎn shì jiǎohuá de xiàoróng.

'A banknote folded in half lay on the sidewalk. A man bent over to pick it up. Whoosh, the banknote flew into the door of a shop. A squabby boy was sitting behind the door. He threw the banknote tied with a black thread back on the sidewalk... The boy wore a sly smile on the face.'

In fact, time and place expressions are also used for the scheduling and organization of topics, plots, and scenes, in addition to marking the nodes of plot development. So these expressions can be referred to as discourse-connecting elements.

Such discourse-connecting elements are macro-syntactic conjunctions in Chao's terminology (1968, p. 791). In relevant literature, the most detailed classification of such elements in Chinese discourse is found in Liao Qiuzhong (1986b), where the elements are classified into two basic categories: temporal connection and logical connection. Under these two categories, there are three subcategories in each according to the semantic relationship between the connected statements, 1) successive connection, 2) inverse connection, and 3) trans-connection, which is further divided into trans-topic connection and off-topic connection. The trans-connection element, according to Liao, indicates that the writer/speaker will enter a new topic, which can be independent of or parallel with the ongoing topic in the context. It is not difficult to see that successive connection and inverse connection are in terms of the logico-semantic relations between successive clauses, while trans-connection is actually in terms of discourse relations.

The members of the trans-connection category described by Liao (1986b) are roughly the same with Chao's (1968) superclausal conjunctions, which, to Chao, are reduced main clauses (1968, p. 794) that fall into two groups: (1) 我想 (Wǒ xiǎng, 'I think'), which is phonetically reduced to a proclitic conjunction or an enclitic auxiliary (Chao 1968, p. 134); and (2) conjunctions, such as 总而言之 (zǒng'éryánzhī, 'in a word'), 这就是说 (zhè jiùshì shuō, 'that is to say'), 换言之 (huànyánzhī, 'in other words'), 换句话说 (huànjùhuàshuō, 'in other words'), 据说 (jùshuō, 'it is said'), 回头 (huítóu, 'turning back'), etc. (Chao, 1968, p. 794). In our opinion, 单说 (dān shuō, 'just say') belongs to the second group of reduced main clauses.

There are some discourse-connecting elements that originate from verbs of speech and witness, 却说 (quèshuō, 'now the story goes'), 单说 (dānshuō, 'just say'), and 就说 (jiùshuō, 'just say') containing verb of speech 说, and 却见 (quèjiàn, 'but to see'), 但见 (dànjiàn, 'but to see'), and 只见 (zhǐjiàn, 'only to see') containing verb of witness 见. Among them, 就说 and 只见 are modern words of later origin, which are roughly interchangeable with the other two members of their respective group in terms of usage. We discuss the group originated from verbs of speech first.

9.2 Metadiscourse and narrator orientation

9.2.1 *Metadiscourse*

The so-called metadiscourse is the linguistic expressions used to talk about the discourse. In Hyland's (2005, p. 49) model, metadiscourse is comprised of two dimensions of interaction: the interactive and the interactional.

The interactive dimension includes five subcategories:

1) transitions, which reflect the relationship between clauses, such as *in addition, but, thus*;
2) frame markers, reflecting the sequence of speech acts, such as *finally, to conclude, my purpose is*;
3) endophoric markers, referring to information in other parts of discourse, e.g., *note above*;
4) evidentials, representing information from other sources, e.g., *according to X, Z states*;
5) code glosses, elaborating in detail propositions already made, e.g., *namely, such as, in other words*.

The interactional dimension also includes five subcategories:

1) hedges, such as *might, perhaps, possibly, about*;
2) boosters, such as *in fact, definitely, it is clear that*;
3) attitude markers, expressing the author/speaker's attitude toward the proposition, such as *unfortunately, I agree, surprisingly*;
4) self-mentions, referring to the degree of explicit author presence, e.g. *I, we, me, our*;
5) engagement markers, which explicitly establishes or strengthens the relationship with the reader, e.g. *consider, note, you can see that*.

For an introduction to the various metadiscourse theories, see Xu Jiujiu (2010).

Given that metadiscourse is language use to refers to the discourse itself, such as "Let's change the topic", "We will discuss these in next chapter", etc., Beauvais (1989) suggests that only those illocutionary predicates that have the force of speech acts are metadiscourse, such as "I believe that" or "we demonstrate that".

According to Hyland (2005, pp. 6–19), metadiscourse is a product of reader/narrator orientation or interpersonal strategy, which reflects the speaker's concern for the recipient's need for detail, clarity, guidance, and interaction in discourse.

In general interaction, metadiscourse is expressed in both verbal and nonverbal forms. To Argyle (1972) and Crismore et al. (1993), nonverbal metadiscourse takes both spoken and written forms, the spoken including paralinguistic means, such as intonation, stress, volume, tone quality, body distance, body gesture, etc., and the written, including layout, medium, punctuation, and so on.

Broadly speaking, interactive metadiscourse lies on the informative level, while interactional metadiscourse is on the interactional level. In the metadiscourse research literature, the discussion of Western scholars focuses mainly on evidentials and code glosses as functional extensions of verbs of speech and witness while self-mentions and engagement markers are believed to be chiefly expressed through first-person pronouns and imperative sentences such as "think about it", "notice that", "you can see", etc.

9.2.2 *Narrator orientation*

Monologic story-telling is representative of narrative discourse. Traditional Chinese "story-telling" has an opening sequence, and its patterning has its own stylistic characteristics.

(2) 水调数声持酒听,午醉醒来愁未醒,送春春去几时回,临晚镜,伤流景,往事后期空记省,沙上并禽池上暝,云破月来花弄影,重重帘幕密遮灯。风不定,人初静,明日落红应满径。(Poem to the Tune of Tianxianzi[右调天仙子])
转瞬端阳已过,夏至正是今朝。园林嘒嘒正鸣蜩,高卧北窗寄傲。两眼懒观新世,社会现象难瞧。生活程度又增高,米面竟长不落。幸喜旗饷到手,节前稍免心焦。炖鱼煮肉就烧刀,懊吃懊喝懊吵。倚赖终非善策,自强莫惮勤劳。千万不可信讹谣,敬告八旗父老。

引场辞之外,这段《西江月》,算饶头。闲言不提,即刻开书。

单说直隶永平府,有一家绅士姓范。世代书香,家里众人进士都拿鞭子轰(举人进士属羊的)出仕作官的也很不少。(Sun Gong, *Fresh Flavors* XIV: Zhang Wenbin [《新鲜滋味之十四种:张文斌》])

Shuǐdiào shùshēng chí jiǔ tīng, wǔzuì xǐnglái chóu wèi xǐng, sòngchūn chūnqù jǐshí huí, lín wǎnjìng, shāng liújǐng, wǎngshì hòuqī kōng jixǐng, shāshàng bìngqín chíshàng míng, yúnpò yuèlái huā nòng yǐng, chóng~chóng liánmù mì zhēdēng. Fēng bú dìng, rén chū jìng, míngrì luòhóng yìng mǎnjìng. (Yòudiào tiānxiānzi)

Zhuǎnshùn duānyáng yǐguò, xiàzhì zhèngshì jīnzhāo. Yuánlín huì~huì zhèng míngtiáo, gāowò běichuāng jì'ào. Liǎngyǎn lǎnguān xīnshì, shèhuì xiànxiàng nánqiáo. Shēnghuó chéngdù yòu zēnggāo, mǐmiàn jìng zhǎng búlào. Xìng xǐ qíxiǎng dàoshǒu, jiéqián shāo miǎn xīnjiāo. Dùnyú zhǔròu jiù shāodāo, àochī àohē àochǎo. Yǐlài zhōngfēi shàncè, zìqiáng mòdàn qínláo. Qiānwàn bùkě xìn éyáo, jìnggào bāqí fùlǎo.

Yǐnchǎngcí zhīwài, zhèduàn "Xījiāngyuè", suàn ráotou. Xiányán bùtí, jíkè kāishū.

Dānshuō zhílì Yǒngpíngfǔ, yǒu yī jiā shēnshì xìng Fàn. Shìdài shūxiāng, jiālǐ zhòngrén jìnshì dōu ná biānzi hōng (jǔrén jìnshì shǔyáng de) chūshì zuòguān de yě hěn bùshǎo.

'I am listening to the melody with a cup of wine in my hand, awake from a drunken sleep to find myself still feeling down. Spring is gone and no one knows when it will be back. Sitting in front of the mirror at dusk, I can't help feeling sorry for the fleeting time. It's futile to reflect on the bygones. On the pond stand a couple of sand birds with their eyes closed, the moonlight sheds on the flowers through the clouds, and in the room heavy curtains block out the lights. When the wind rises up, I begin to quiet down, thinking that the path will be covered with fallen flowers tomorrow.

In an instant the Duanyang Festival is gone, and the Summer Solstice is right on today. In the garden cicadas are chirping, and lying under the north window is the proud poet. Reluctant to observe the new world, I find it hard to understand the social phenomena. The living cost has again increased, and prices for rice and flour keep rising. Luckily I have my payment, and thus am relieved of anxiety before the holiday. I have cooked fish and meat and prepared a bottle of wine, eating and drinking to my heart's content. It is not wise to rely on others, to be self-independent one needs to work hard. Don't believe in the rumors, this is what I want to tell all my friends.

In addition to the introductory remarks, this melody can be regarded as an extra. Without further ado, let's begin our story.

(Let me) **speak only of** <u>a household with the surname Fan in Yongping Prefecture</u>. It was a family of scholars, which boasted of a flock of Advanced Scholars that one had to herd them with a whip (all the Advanced Scholars are rams), and many of them became officials.'

The explicit presentation of the narrative process and the narrator in discourse is called "metanarrative" in narratology. Given the fact that "story-telling" is a form of live narrative, its metanarrative should not only reveal the structure of the narrative proper, but also construct interaction with the audience. The expression of the metanarrative is ultimately a reflection of the narrator's care for the audience.

On the one hand, "story-telling" embodies the common features of narrative discourse, and, on the other, its interactional nature makes the coding of the narrator orientation particularly prominent. The construction of the interaction between narrator and audience can be realized by interspersing commentary along narration.

(3) 秦亡无古乐,世降有梨园。旧史多仇忾,新诗半泪痕。几经霜锁径,今日月临轩。只此饶清趣,忘机昼掩门。

因与花为谱,三霜暂假园。地偏人共淡,香去墨留痕。自笑成通隐,秋来爱此轩。正愁无好句,适有客临门。

<u>在下这两天湿气大作,写字都得爬着,你瞧多大罪孽!有人说我是嘴损的。就说我损罢,可损我才损呢,我并没损好人哪!好人我还夸呢。这些个事也不说。这两天病体颓唐,心绪恶劣,简直的不爱动笔。不动笔可又不行,要作首引场辞,居然会作不上来。只得抄录友人两首秋园谱菊的五律,聊以塞责。</u>

<u>散言碎语交待已毕,这就开书。</u>**单说**西城曹老公观后身,住着一个麻花刘。原是山东人,自幼儿父母双亡,受叔叔婶婶的虐待,几乎没把孩子给折磨死。后来有街坊把他带到北京,在某粥铺学徒,随后下街卖烧饼。人缘儿很好,卖货分外比别人卖的多。到了二十多岁上,...... (Sun Gong, Fresh Flavors IV: Doughnut Liu [《新鲜滋味之四种:麻花刘》])

Qínwáng wú gǔyuè, shìjiàng yǒu líyuán. Jiùshǐ duō chóukài, xīnshī bàn lèihén. Jǐjīng shuāng suǒjìng, jīnrì yuè línxuān. Zhǐcǐ ráo qīngqù, wàngjī zhòu ǎnmén.

Yīnyǔ huā wéipǔ, sānshuāng zàn jiàyuán. Dìpiān rén gòngdàn, xiāngqù mò liúhén. Zìxiào chéng tōngyǐn, qiūlái ài cǐxuān. Zhèngchóu wú hǎojù, shìyǒu kè línmén.

<u>Zàixià zhè liǎngtiān shīqì dàzuò, xiězì dōu děi pāzhe, nǐqiáo duōdà zuìniè! Yǒurén shuō wǒ shì zuǐsǔn de. Jiùshuō wǒ sǔn bà, kěsǔn wǒ cái sǔn ne, wǒ bìng méi sǔn hǎorén na! Hǎorén wǒ hái kuā ne. Zhèxiēge shì yě bù shuō. Zhè liǎngtiān bìngtǐ tuítáng, xīnxù èliè, jiǎnzhí de bú ài dòngbǐ. Bù dòngbǐ kě yòu bùxíng, yào zuò shǒu yǐnchǎngcí, jūrán huì zuò-bú-shànglái. Zhǐdé chāolù yǒurén liǎngshǒu qiūyuán pǔjú de wǔlǜ, liáoyǐ sèzé.</u>

Sǎnyánsuìyǔ jiāodài yǐ bì, zhèjiù kāishū. **Dānshuō** xīchéng Cáolǎogōng Guàn hòushēn, zhùzhe yī gè Máhuā Liú. Yuánshì Shāndōng rén, zìyòu·ér fùmǔ shuāngwáng, shòu shūshu shěnshen de nüèdài, jīhū méi bǎ háizi gěi zhémó sǐ. Hòulái yǒu jiēfang bǎ tā dàidào Běijīng, zài mǒu zhōupù xuétú, suíhòu xiàjiē mài shāobǐng. Rényuán·er hěn hǎo, màihuò fènwài bǐ biérén màide duō. Dàole èrshí duō suì shàng, …

'Ancient music is lost with the disappearance of the Qin Dynasty, and in its stead arises traditional opera. History books are all about hatred, and half of the new poems are about tears. After several spells of frost, the moon is now hanging over the pavilion. So much delight I could take in such serenity, aloof from the world I closed the door in broad daylight.

To keep company with flowers, I stay in the garden even in late autumn. In this remote nook one is free of worldly desires, and when the flowers are gone, the ink mark will remain. Regarding myself as a broad-minded hermit, I love the pavilion in autumn. While I am racking my brain for a good line, there comes a visitor at the gate.

<u>In these days, I have been suffering from eczema, and have to lie on my stomach even when writing. How miserable I am! Some say that I deserve it because of my sarcasm. Even though I am sarcastic, I am not as bad as those shabby guys. After all, I have hurt no good people. And those good people all praise me. I won't talk about this anymore. I have been under weather these days and in a very bad mood. As a result, I don't want to write anything at all. Yet I have no choice but to write. I have to write an introductory remark, yet I have a writer's block. All I can do is to copy down two poems by my friends on the chrysanthemums in the autumn garden, just to finish the work.</u>

<u>Enough for the chitchat, now I'll tell you the story.</u> **To begin with**, at the back of the Caolaogong Temple in the West Side of the city, there lived a man known as Doughnut Liu. Originally from Shandong, he lost both his parents in his childhood and was abused by his uncle and aunt who almost tortured him to death. Later a neighbour took him to Beijing and left him at a porridge shop to work as an apprentice. And then he was sent to sell pancakes on the street. He became so popular that he always sold more pancakes than others. When he was in his twenties,…'

The construction of this kind of interactional relationship can also be achieved by way of Q&A with a virtual addressee.

(4) 过了些时，本县南乡，出了一件奇案，每逢到小说上，一提到奇案，不是谋害亲夫，就是无头的案子，这是千人一面的套子。谁知这宗奇案，跟普通的奇案不同，旁的奇案，都是刑事的案子，惟独这个奇案，是民事的案。<u>这位说了，民事的案子，有甚么出奇?这案要是说出来，管保出奇</u>。**单说**南乡尚家村，有一家绅士姓尚，尚家原是财主，尚老头儿又作过一任知州，告老还乡，跟前三个少爷，一位姑娘。大少爷叫秉义，二少爷叫秉崑，三少爷叫秉田,姑娘叫秉贞,嫁与本村李监生为妻,三位少爷也都成了家。 (Sun Gong, *Fresh Flavors* XXII: Repentance [《新鲜滋味第二十二种:回头岸》])

Guòle xiē shí, běn xiàn Nánxiāng, chūle yī jiàn qí'àn, měiféng dào xiǎoshuō shàng, yī tídào qí'àn, búshì móuhài qīnfū, jiùshì wútóu de ànzi, zhèshì qiānrényīmiàn de tàozi. Shéizhī zhèzōng qí'àn, gēn pǔtōng de qí'àn bùtóng, pángde qí'àn, dōushì xíngshì de ànzi, wéidú zhège qí'àn, shì mínshì de àn. <u>Zhèwèi shuōle, mínshì de ànzi, yǒu shénme chūqí? Zhè àn yàoshi shuō chūlái, guǎnbǎo chūqí.</u> **Dānshuō** Nánxiāng Shàngjiācūn, yǒu yī jiā shēnshì xìng Shàng, Shàngjiā yuán shì cáizhǔ, Shàng lǎotóu·er yòu zuòguò yī rèn zhīzhōu, gàolǎohuánxiāng, gēnqián sān gè shàoye, yī wèi gūniang. Dà shàoye jiào Bǐngyì, èr shàoye jiào Bǐngkūn, sān shàoye jiào Bǐngtián, gūniang jiào Bǐngzhēn, jià yǔ běn cūn Lǐ Jiānshēng wéi qī, sān wèi shàoye yě dōu chéngle jiā.

'After a while, something mysterious took place in Nanxiang Town in this county. Whenever a mystery is mentioned in a novel, it was either about the murder of a husband or a case without any clue. That's how a novel develops with no exceptions. However, this one is different. The other mysteries are all criminal cases, while this is a civil one. <u>You might wonder, what is so special about the civil case? If I tell you about it, you will think that it is indeed special.</u> **Let me begin**: in Shangjia Village of Nanxiang Town, there was a gentleman whose surname was Shang. The Shangs were originally a family of wealth. The old man Shang once served as a magistrate and returned to his hometown when he retired. He had three sons and a daughter. The eldest son was named Bingyi, the second Bingkun, and the third Bingtian. And the daughter was named Bingzhen, who was married to a Mr. Li, a student of the Imperial College from the same village. The three sons also had their own families.'

In terms of historical transmission, "story-telling" has a great influence on modern Chinese narration. The following, for example, is the opening of Lao She's *Rickshaw Boy*, where the narrator appears directly as "我们" ('we').

(5) <u>我们</u>所要介绍的祥子,不是骆驼,因为"骆驼"只是个外号;那么,我们就先说祥子,随手儿把骆驼与祥子那点关系说过去,也就算了。 (Lao She, *Rickshaw Boy* [《骆驼祥子》])

<u>Wǒmen</u> suǒyào jièshào de Xiángzi, búshì luòtuo, yīnwèi "luòtuo" zhǐshì gè wàihào; nàme, wǒmen jiù xiān shuō Xiángzi, suíshǒu·er bǎ luòtuo yǔ Xiángzi nà diǎn guānxì shuō guòqù, yě jiù suànle.

'Xiangzi, whom <u>we</u> are to introduce, was not a camel, because "Camel" was only his nickname. So let us start with Xiangzi, just mentioning in passing how he became linked with camels.'

Modern Chinese narrative discourse bears obvious traces of traditional "story-telling", reflecting the narrator orientation and the interaction between the narrator and the narratee in various forms of metadiscourse. We propose that the functional extension of some words in narrative discourse is closely related to the narrative style of "story-telling" since modern times.

In the following, we discuss the usage of 单说 (dānshuō, 'just say') with examples from novels of late Qing and early ROC.

9.3 Discourse functions of 单说

单说 (dānshuō, 'just say') is often used in two types of situations: first, to initiate the plot, specifically when discourse transits from opening remarks to the storyline, and second, to mark a shift in the plot by changing the scene or the topic.

9.3.1 Plot initiation

The plot is often initiated by introducing the main character of the narrative, and the high-frequency syntactic patterns include the existential *you*-sentence, such as "单说直隶永平府,有一家绅士姓范。……" in (2) above, and the presentational sentence, such as "单说西城曹老公观后身,住着一个麻花刘。……" in (3). See (6) for another example.

(6) 浩劫谁开五大洲,无端纷乱扰全球。蜗争蚁战宁天意,斗角钩心运鬼谋。此局真成千古变,浮生空抱百年忧。静观物理殊堪笑,浊酒频浇一遭愁。
拙诗念罢,开场说书。**单说**民国元年,选举议员的时候儿,<u>河南伊阳县,有一个当选的议员,姓周号叫小宋</u>。三十多岁,父母双全,没有弟兄,家里很是丰富。(Sun Gong, *Fresh Flavors III: Neo-Confucianist Zhou* [《新鲜滋味之三种:理学周》])

Hàojié shuí kāi wǔ dàzhōu, wúduān fēnluàn rǎo quánqiú. Wōzhēngyǐzhàn nìng tiānyì, dòujiǎogōuxīn yùn guǐmóu. Cǐjú zhēn chéng qiāngǔbiàn, fúshēng kōng bào bǎiniányōu. Jìngguān wùlǐ shū kānxiào, zhuójiǔ pínjiāo yī qiǎnchóu.

Zhuōshī niànbà, kāichǎng shuōshū. **Dānshuō** Mínguó yuánnián, xuǎnjǔ yìyuán de shíhòu·er, <u>Hénán Yīyáng xiàn, yǒu yī gè dāngxuǎn de yìyuán, xìng Zhōu hào jiào Xiǎosòng</u>. Sānshí duō suì, fùmǔ shuāngquán, méiyǒu dìxiōng, jiālǐ hěnshì fēngfù.

'Catastrophes have separated the five continents; chaos prevail all over the world. Petty squabbling is Heaven's will; schemes and intrigues are all cunning tricks. The situation is truly of eternal change; all my life I can't help feeling worried. The innate laws of things seem absurd to me; I thus drown my worries in wine.

After reading my poem, let's start the story. **Only to speak of** the first year of the Republic of China, when the congressional elections were going on. <u>In Yiyang County, Henan Province, there was an elected congressman with the family name Zhou, who styled himself as Xiaosong</u>.

He was in his thirties, with both parents alive, but without brothers, his family being very rich.'

It is known that existential and presentational sentences are typical syntactic patterns for topic introduction in Chinese (Li and Thompson, 1981, p. 100; Chu, 1998, p. 203). The post-verbal noun in such sentences is often the discourse topic with a fairly strong discourse initiating function (Liu Anchun and Zhang Bojiang, 2004; Fang Mei, 2005a; Xu Yulong, 2004, 2007), which is manifested in the fact that the zero-subject of a series of subsequent clauses will be coreferential with thus introduced topics to form a complete topic chain.[1] In (6), for example, the topic of the clause serial "三十多岁,父母双全,没有弟兄,家里很是丰富" ('[He was] in his thirties, with both parents alive, but without brothers, his family being very rich.') is the elected congressman with the family name Zhou.

9.3.2 Scene shift

The usage of scene shift is different from that of plot initiation, in that scene shift often adopts the sequence of negation followed by affirmation in narration.

(7) 话不烦叙,烟家伙拿到,还拿来一小盒儿烟来,公母俩当时躺在一个床上,仲芝烧了一口才要抽,贺氏说:"你先给我啵!"当时一别气儿把这口抽空,又烧了一口,仲芝才抽。<u>公母俩这里抽烟,暂且不提</u>,**单说**如芝见他们公母俩逅奔东院,叹了一声,向江氏说道:"你瞧他们夫妇两个,面似菠菜,等于活鬼,方才吃完了饭,一个打哈欠,一个流鼻涕,简直的支持不住了,我让他们歇着去,我那是给他们台阶儿,现在你猜他们作甚么呢?" (Sun Gong, *Fresh Flavors* XXII: Repentance [《新鲜滋味第二十二种:回头岸》])

Huà bù fánxù, yān jiāhuo nádào, hái nálái yī xiǎo hé·er yān lái, gōngmuliǎ dāngshí tǎng zài yī gè chuáng shàng, Zhòngzhī shāole yī kǒu cáiyào chōu, Hèshì shuō: "Nǐ xiān gěi wǒ bo!" Dāngshí yībiéqì·er bǎ zhè kǒu chōukōng, yòu shāole yī kǒu, Zhòngzhī cái chōu. <u>Gōngmuliǎ zhèlǐ chōuyān, zànqiě bù tí</u>, **dānshuō** Rúzhī jiàn tāmen gōngmuliǎ hòu bēn dōngyuàn, tànle yī shēng, xiàng Jiāngshì shuōdào: "Nǐ qiáo tāmen fūfù liǎng gè, miàn sì bōcài, děngyú huóguǐ, fāngcái chīwánle fàn, yī gè dǎhāqian, yī gè liúbítì, jiǎnzhí de zhīchí búzhù le, wǒ ràng tāmen xiēzhe qù, wǒ nàshì gěi tāmen táijiē·er, xiànzài nǐ cāi tāmen zuò shénme ne?"

'Without further ado, the couple took the pipe out, and also a small box of opium. The couple immediately laid down on the same bed. Zhongzhi lighted the pipe and was about to smoke when his wife Mrs. He said, "Let me take a puff first!" Right away she took a big puff and finished the opium. She then lighted another pipe of opium for Zhongzhi to smoke. <u>The couple were smoking here, and I won't mention them for the time</u>

being. **Let's turn to** Ruzhi. After seeing the couple, he rushed to the east courtyard. With a sigh, he said to Mrs. Jiang, "Look at the couple, how pale they look, just like ghosts. Right after dinner, one kept yawning, and the other had a runny nose. It seemed that they couldn't hold it any more. I told them to go and have a rest, as I didn't want them to lose face. What do you think they are doing right now?"'

(8) 李二去找吴瘸子, <u>暂且不提</u>。**单说**大春子,由酒铺儿出来走了不远儿,迎头遇见一个人。此人姓张行五,人称天主张。他原信奉希腊教,后来不守教规,被人逐出教外。这个人心地非常之坏,自打出教之后,任落子没有。
(Sun Gong, *Fresh Flavors* XXVI: Five Righteous Men [《新鲜滋味第二十六种:五人义》])

Lǐ Èr qù zhǎo Wú Quézi, <u>zànqiě bù tí</u>. **Dānshuō** Dà Chūnzi, yóu jiǔpù·er chūlái zǒule bùyuǎn·er, yíngtóu yùjiàn yī gè rén. Cǐ rén xìng Zhāng háng wǔ, rén chēng Tiānzhǔ Zhāng. Tā yuán xìnfèng Xīlà Jiào, hòulái bù shǒu jiàoguī, bèi rén zhúchū jiào wài. Zhège rén xīndì fēicháng zhī huài, zìdǎ chū jiào zhīhòu, rèn làozi méiyǒu.

'Li Er went to find Cripple Wu, and <u>I won't mention it for the time being</u>. **Let's speak of** Big Chunzi. Soon after he walked out of the wine shop, he ran into a man head-on. The man was surnamed Zhang and he was the fifth child in his family. He was known as Catholic Zhang. He used to be a member of the Greek Church, but was expelled from it as he violated its doctrines. The man was evil at heart, and since he was expelled, he had no means of living whatsoever.'

9.3.3 *Topic shift*

This usage switches the protagonist of the narrative by contrastive expressions such as "不提…,单说…" ('no more about…, let's just talk about…') and "闲话打住/不提…,单说…" ('without further ado, let's turn to…'). See (9), (10) and (11) for illustration.

(9) <u>闲话不提</u>,单说大春子。破城之后,他有鬼胎,那阵子很提心吊胆,恐怕人家报复。后来听说主教英呢肯提不准报复,他心里感激的了不得。
(Sun Gong, *Fresh Flavors* XXVI: Five Righteous Men)

<u>Xiánhuà bù tí</u>, dānshuō Dà Chūnzi. Pòchéng zhīhòu, tā yǒu guǐtāi, nà zhènzi hěn tíxīndiàodǎn, kǒngpà rénjiā bàofù. Hòulái tīngshuō zhǔjiào Yīngníkěntí bùzhǔn bàofù, tā xīnlǐ gǎnjī de liǎobùdé.

'<u>Without further ado, let's turn to</u> Big Chunzi. When the city was taken, he was fearful with a guilty conscience. And he had been on tenterhooks these days, afraid of retaliation against him. Later, when he heard that Bishop Innocenti forbade retaliation, he was very grateful.'

(10) 春爷听在心里,又要了两壶酒。那天一共吃了八吊几百钱,自然是春爷会账,快嘴吃了个乐不可支。春爷说:你给打听打听,麻花刘有甚么消息,后天咱们还是这儿见。"快嘴说:"你交给我了。后天还得喝你个酒儿(这块骨头)。"春爷说:"那就不用搞了。"快嘴说:"我也不道谢了。"两个人当时出离了茶馆儿。

<u>不提快嘴,单说春爷</u>。回到家中,杨氏一天没吃饭,大奶奶那里直劝,说:又有孩子吃奶,你不吃东西行吗?"春爷安慰了一番,大致把快嘴说的话,略说了一遍,随后说道:...... (Sun Gong, *Fresh Flavors* IV: Doughnut Liu [《新鲜滋味之四种:麻花刘》])

Chūnyé tīng zài xīnlǐ, yòu yàole liǎng hú jiǔ. Nàtiān yīgòng chīle bā diào jǐ bǎi qián, zìrán shì Chūnyé huìzhàng, Kuàizuǐ chīle gè lèbùkězhī. Chūnyé shuō: Nǐ gěi dǎting~dǎting, Máhuā Liú yǒu shénme xiāoxi, hòutiān zánmen háishì zhè·er jiàn." Kuàizuǐ shuō: "Nǐ jiāogěi wǒ le. Hòutiān háiděi hē nǐ gè jiǔ·er (zhè kuài gǔtou)." Chūnyé shuō: "Nàjiù búyòng gǎole." Kuàizuǐ shuō: "Wǒ yě bù dàoxiè le." Liǎng gè rén dāngshí chūlíle cháguǎn·er.

 <u>Bùtí Kuàizuǐ, dānshuō Chūnyé</u>. Huídào jiāzhōng, Yángshì yī tiān méi chīfàn, dà nǎinai nàlǐ zhí quàn, shuō: "Yòu yǒu háizi chīnǎi, nǐ bùchī dōngxi xíng ma?" Chūnyé ānwèile yīfān, dàzhì bǎ Kuàizuǐ shuō de huà, lüè shuōle yī biàn, suíhòu shuōdao: ...

'Master Chun took every word in, and asked for two more pots of wine. That day, the dinner cost more than 80 copper coins. Of course it was Master Chun who paid the bill, and Big Mouth was overwhelmed with joy.

Master Chun said, "I entrust you to make inquiries, to see if you can get any news about Doughnut Liu. I'll meet you here the day after tomorrow."

Big Mouth responded, "Rest assured. You are to treat me with another round of drink the day after then (such a base person)."

Master Chun said, "Then don't do it."

Big Mouth said, "Then I don't have to say thanks."

At this, the two left the teahouse.

<u>No more about Big Mouth, let's just talk about Master Chun</u>. When he returned home, he found that Mrs. Yang hadn't eat anything for a whole day. The elder mistress was trying to comfort her, "You have baby to breastfeed. You cannot do it without eating anything, can you?" To make Mrs. Yang feel better, Master Chun told her briefly what Big Mouth had said, and then he said, ...'

(11) 彼时天已昏黑,这就点灯笼找火把,分途进行。灯笼火把亮子油松照如白昼,王四扯着脖子,满街上直喊姑爷,招的狗是直咬,这分儿乱就不用说啦。一直绕了多半夜,哪里有姜登朝的影儿。偏巧有个街坊是近视眼,跟着也这们一瞎扑,没留神耍在粪坑子里啦,大喊救人。好容易才把他揪上来,这分儿臭就不用提啦。天光已然大亮,这位臭爷,好在离家近,<u>自己爬回家中不提</u>。

单说王四,见寻不着姑爷,急的也要跳河,大家把他劝回家中。妈妈儿也很着急。(Sun Gong, *Fresh Flavors* VI: Commander Liu [《新鲜滋味第六种:刘军门》])

Bǐshí tiān yǐ hūnhēi, zhè jiù diǎn dēnglóng zhǎo huǒbǎ, fēntú jìnxíng. Dēnglóng huǒbǎ liàngzi yóusōng zhào rú báizhòu, Wáng Sì chēzhe bózi, mǎnjiē shàng zhíhǎn gūye, zhāo de gǒu shì zhíyǎo, zhè fēn·er luàn jiù búyòng shuō la. Yīzhí ràole duō bànyè, nǎlǐ yǒu Jiāng Dēngcháo de yǐng·er. Piānqiǎo yǒu gè jiēfang shì jìnshìyǎn, gēnzhe yě zhèmen yī xiāpū, méi liúshén shuǎ zài fènkēngzi lǐ la, dàhǎn jiùrén. Hǎoróngyì cái bǎ tā jiūshànglái, zhè fēn·er chòu jiù búyòng tí la. Tiānguāng yǐrán dàliàng, zhè wèi chòuyé, hǎozài lí jiā jìn, <u>zìjǐ páhuí jiāzhōng bùtí</u>.

<u>Dānshuō Wáng Sì</u>, jiàn xún-bù-zháo gūye, jíde yě yào tiàohé, dàjiā bǎ tā quàn huí jiāzhōng. Māma·er yě hěn zhāojí.

'It was already dark then. Having lighted up lanterns and torches, they proceeded to search for the man. The light of the lanterns and torches were so bright that it seemed as if they were searching in broad daylight. Wang Si shouted at the top of his voice the name of his son-in-law, only to provoke the dogs to bark. Needless to say, it was all chaotic. The search went on till past midnight, and Jiang Dengchao was still nowhere to be found. It happened that one of the neighbors who was short-sighted was also searching with the crowd for Jiang. Accidentally, he fell into the dung hole and yelled for help. With some difficulty, he was pulled out of the hole. You can imagine how he stank. Now it was already dawn, and this stinky man <u>went back to his home</u>. Fortunately, it was not far off.

<u>As for Wang Si</u>, since he couldn't find his son-in-law, he was so worried that he wanted to jump into the river himself. When he took other's advice and went back home, he found that his wife was also very anxious.'

In this category of usage, although the topic is not introduced by way of the existential or presentational sentence, it has as strong an initiating power as the previous category. The topic introduced by 单说 is by default the referent of the zero-subject in the subsequent clause(s).

If the topic introduced by 单说 involves no contrast with a different entity, it is marked in writing by a separate paragraph.

(12) 大家走后,秀氏痛哭流涕,又苦劝了一回,大春子向来最听秀氏的话,今天有点邪神附体,跟秀氏瞪着眼睛这们一嚷,怒发冲冠,双眥欲裂,要玩儿命的神气。秀氏见他这宗状况,也就不敢再劝了。

单说这个李二,外号儿叫画眉李(足见素日能聊)向来捉风捕影,平地起孤丁,有造谣言学校最优等毕业文凭。(Sun Gong, *Fresh Flavors* XXVI: Five Righteous Men)

Dàjiā zǒu hòu, Xiùshì tòngkūliútì, yòu kǔquànle yī huí, Dà Chūnzi xiànglái zuì tīng Xiùshì de huà, jīntiān yǒudiǎn xiéshén fùtǐ, gēn Xùshì dèngzhe yǎnjīng zhèmen yīrǎng, nùfàchōngguān, shuāngzìyùliè, yào wán·ermìng de shénqì. Xiùshì jiàn tā zhè zǒng zhuàngkuàng, yějiù bùgǎn zàiquàn le.

Dānshuō zhège Lǐ Èr, wàihào·er jiào Huàméi Lǐ (zújiàn sùrì néng liáo) xiànglái zhuōfēngbǔyǐng, píngdì qǐ gūdīng, yǒu zào yáoyán xuéxiào zuì yōuděng bìyè wénpíng.

'After everyone left, Mrs. Xiu cried her heart out and tried hard to persuade him. Big Chunzi had always been obedient to her, but today he behaved as if he were possessed by an evil spirit. He glared and screamed at her, his hair standing on end with anger, and his eyes almost popping out. He seemed like a desperate animal. Seeing him like this, Mrs. Xiu did not dare to say anything more.

<u>Speaking of</u> Li Er, whose nickname was Magpie Li (so we can see how talkative he was), he would always make accusation on hearsay and was good at making up stories. He was one of the most outstanding graduates from the rumor school.'

(13) ......在那个年月,当奶子的,混着这样事,总算是不错了。

单说这个奶妈子,娘家姓魏婆家姓赵,今年二十六岁,高身量白胖子,是个旗装,为人端庄正派,忠厚老实,...... (Sun Gong, *Fresh Flavors* XV: The Search and Rescue of an Orphan [《新鲜滋味第十五种:搜救孤》])

......Zài nàgè niányuè, dāng nǎizi de, hùnzhe zhèyàng shì, zǒngsuàn shì bùcuò le.

Dānshuō zhège nǎimāzi, niángjiā xìng Wèi pójiā xìng Zhào, jīnnián èrshíliù suì, gāo shēnliang bái pàngzi, shì gè qízhuāng, wéirén duānzhuāng zhèngpài, zhōnghòu lǎoshí, ...

'…At that time, if one could manage to find a job as a wet nurse, she would be considered fortunate.

<u>Speaking of</u> this wet nurse, her surname was Wei and she married a man with the surname Zhao. She was 26 years old this year, tall and plump; she was of Manchu nationality, demure and decent in manner, loyal and honest in personality,…'

Whether it is used for plot initiation or plot transition, 单说 is an expression that shows the narrator orientation and reflects the organization of the narrative discourse on the part of the narrator.

According to Liao Qiuzhong (1986b), the trans-connection element is used to indicate that the author/speaker is going to enter a new topic, which can be independent of or parallel to a topic in the context. There are two types of trans-connections: transitional and off-topic. The "transitional trans-connection" element (e.g., 至于 [zhìyú, 'as to']) means that the writer/speaker will leave the main plotline and say something about it). In recent years, 至于 has been analyzed as a topic marker, in that it has the function of shifting the topic.

Here we would argue that 单说 is different from 至于 in their respective usage to shift the topic.

First, the new topic introduced by 至于 is not what the narrator's focus of narration; instead, only incidental comments will be made of such a topic. See (14) for example.

(14) 如果多数人都同意，那就这么定了。至于个别同志有不同意见，在下面再做做思想工作。

Rúguǒ duōshù rén dōu tóngyì, nà jiù zhème dìngle. Zhìyú gèbié tóngzhì yǒu bùtóng yìjiàn, zài xiàmiàn zài zuò~zuò sīxiǎng gōngzuò.

'If the majority of people agree, then it is settled. As for individual comrades who have different ideas, some ideological work can be done on individual basis.'

Second, 单说 is used to shift the topic in narrative discourse while 至于 tends to be thus used in expository texts, which predetermines that 单说 cannot be replaced by 至于 in the examples cited above.

9.4 Metadiscourse functions of *shuo*-compounds

Metadiscourse expressions containing the word 说 'say/speak' are of the following semantic categories:

Source: 听说 (tīngshuō, 'it's heard'), 据说 (jùshuō, 'it's said'), 俗话说 (súhuà shuō, 'as the saying goes'), 常言说 (chángyán shuō, 'as the saying goes')

Explanation: 比如说 (bǐrú shuō, 'for example'), 譬如说 (pìrú shuō, 'for example'), 换言之 (huànyánzhī, 'in other words'), 换句话说 (huànjùhuàshuō, in other words), 简而言之 (jiǎn'éryánzhī, 'in short'), 就是说 (jiùshìshuō, 'that is to say'), 反过来说 (fǎnguòláishuō, 'conversely'), 按理说 (ànlǐshuō, 'by reason'), 按说 (ànshuō, 'by reason'), 照说 (zhàoshuō, 'by reason'), 再(者)说 (zài [zhě] shuō, 'furthermore'), 不管怎么说 (bùguǎn zěnme shuō, 'in any case'), 具体说 (jùtǐ shuō, 'specifically speaking'),

Summarization: 总起来说 (zǒngqǐláishuō, 'all in all'), 总体上说 (zǒngtǐshàngshuō, 'generally speaking'), 一般来说(yībān láishuō, 'generally speaking'), 这么说 (zhèmeshuō, 'in this way'), 说来 (shuōlái, 'speaking of')

Attitude: 不用说 (bùyòng shuō, 'no need to say,'), 老实说 (lǎoshí shuō, 'honestly speaking'), 不瞒你说 (bù mán nǐ shuō, 'to be frank with you'), 说实在的 (shuō shízài de, 'to be frank with you'), 说真的 (shuō zhēn de, 'to tell you the truth'), 说到底 (shuō dàodǐ, 'when all is said'), 说心里话 (shuō xīnlǐ huà, 'speaking from the heart'), 相对来说 (xiāngduì láishuō, 'relatively speaking'), 应当说 (yīngdāng shuō, 'should say'), 可以说 (kěyǐ shuō, 'it can be said'), 不消说 (bùxiāo shuō, 'no need to say')Two high-frequency *shuo*-compounds 话说 (huàshuō, 'as the story goes') and 再说 (zàishuō, 'as for') are elaborated below.

9.4.1 话说 ('as the story goes')

话说 (huàshuō, 'as the story goes') is similar in function to 单说, in that it is a discourse opener on the speaker's own initiative. In the following are three examples from *The Scholars* (《儒林外史》), where 话说 occurs at the beginning of the first sentence of each chapter.

(15) 第二回 王孝廉村学识同科 周蒙师暮年登上第

话说山东兖州府汶上县有个乡村,叫做薛家集。这集上有百十来人家,都是务农为业。村口一个观音庵,殿宇三间之外,另还有十几间空房子,后门临著水次。这庵是十方的香火,只得一个和尚住。集上人家,凡有公事,就在这庵里来同议。

Dì'èrhuí Wáng Xiàolián cūnxué shí tóngkē, Zhōu Méngshī mùnián dēng shàngdì

Huàshuō Shāndōng Yǎnzhōu Fǔ Wènshàng Xiàn yǒu gè xiāngcūn, jiàozuò Xuējiā Jí. Zhè jíshàng yǒu bǎi-shí-lái rénjiā, dōushì wùnóng wéiyè. Cūnkǒu yī gè Guānyīn Ān, diànyǔ sān jiān zhīwài, lìng háiyǒu shíjǐ jiān kōng fángzi, hòumén línzhe shuǐcì. Zhè ān shì shífāng de xiānghuǒ, zhǐdé yī gè héshang zhù. Jíshàng rénjiā, fányǒu gōngshì, jiù zài zhè ānlǐ lái tóngyì.

'Chapter 2 Provincial Graduate Wang meets a fellow candidate in a village school, Zhou Jin passes the examination in his old age

As the story goes, in Xue Market, a village of Wenshang County, Shandong, there lived over a hundred families, all of whom worked on the land. At the entrance to the village was a Guanyin Temple with three halls and a dozen empty rooms. Its back door overlooked the river. Peasants from all around contributed to the upkeep of this temple, and only one monk lived there. The villagers would come whenever they had public business to discuss.'

(16) 第三回 周学道校士拔真才 胡屠户行凶闹捷报 开篇

话说周进在省城要看贡院,金有余见他真切,只得用几个小钱同他去看。不想才到'天'字号,就撞死在地下。

Dìsānhuí Zhōu Xuédào xiàoshì bá zhēncái Hú Túhù xíngxiōng nào jiébào kāipiān

Huàshuō Zhōu Jìn zài shěngchéng yào kàn gòngyuàn, Jīn Yǒuyú jiàn tā zhēnqiè, zhǐdé yòng jǐ gè xiǎoqián tóng tā qù kàn. Bùxiǎng cáidào 'tiān' zìhào, jiù zhuàngsǐ zài dìxià.

'Chapter 3 Examiner Zhou picks out true talent, Butcher Hu cuts up rough after good news The Opening

As the story goes, Zhou Jin wanted to look over the examination school in the provincial capital, and Jin Youyu, seeing him so eager, had to tip the gateman to get him in. However, when they came to Cell No. 1, Zhou Jin fell senseless to the ground.'

(17)   第四回 荐亡斋和尚吃官司 打秋风乡绅遭横事 开篇
<u>话说</u>老太太见这些家伙什物都是自己的，不觉欢喜，痰迷心窍，昏绝于地。

Dìsìhuí Jiànwáng Zhāi héshang chī guānsī, Dǎqiūfēng xiāngshēn zāo hèngshì Kaipian

<u>Huàshuō</u> lǎotàitai jiàn zhèxiē jiāhuo shíwù dōushì zìjǐ de, bùjué huānxǐ, tán mí xīnqiào, hūnjué yú dì.

'Chapter 4 A monk invited to say masses is involved in a lawsuit, a country gentleman out to raise money runs into trouble The Opening

<u>As the story goes</u>, when Fan Jin's mother realized that everything in the house was hers, she fell senseless to the ground, overwhelmed with joy.'

According to Xuan Yue's (2011) statistics on several traditional Chinese novels (each chapter headed by a couplet giving the gist of its content), 102 of the 120 chapters of Outlaws of the Marsh (《水浒传》) begin with 话说; in the case of Journey to the West (《西游记》), 21 chapters start with 话说 and 43 chapters with 却说 (quèshuō, 'but say'); in *The Legend of the Heroic Children* (《儿女英雄传》), there is no use of 话说 for the purpose of topic introduction, but there are 189 instances of 却说 for that purpose; and in *The Scholars* (《儒林外史》), there are three instances of 话说, all occurring at the very beginning of their respective hosting chapter.

9.4.2 再说 ('as for')

Similar to 单说 in structure, 再说 has also undergone a process from a declarative clause to a macro-syntactic conjunction (Zheng Guiyou, 2001; Luo Yaohua and Niu Li, 2009).

(18)   武松把那大虫的本事，<u>再说</u>了一遍。(*Outlaws of the Marsh*, Chapter 23)
Wǔsōng bǎ nà dàchóng de běnshì, <u>zàishuō</u>le yī biàn.
'Wu Song <u>told</u> them <u>once again</u> the whole story of the tiger.'

In (18) above, 再说 is a predicative verb phrase, where 说 is marked by the perfective 了, with 再 being an adverb, meaning 'again'.

In (19), by contrast, 说 can no longer be understood as an action performed by the character in the story. 再说 has actually become a means for the storyteller to introduce the topic of the narrative.

(19)   <u>再说</u>金老，得了这一十五两银子，回到店中……(*Outlaws of the Marsh*, Chapter 3)
<u>Zàishuō</u> Jīn Lǎo, déle zhè yī-bǎi-wǔ-shí liǎng yínzi, huídào diànzhōng…
'<u>As for</u> Old Jin, he returned to his inn with the fifteen ounces of silver…'

"金老" ('Old Jin') introduced by 再说 in (19) is a character in the story. Usually, a thus-introduced character has already appeared in the previous narrative, and its reintroduction with 再说 indicates that the narrative returns to this character. In other words, 再说 is used to reinstate a topic that has already occurred in previous discourse.

9.5 Summary

Verbal phrases such as 单说 are different from verbs of speech and witness: when 单说 is used as the predicate of a clause, the subject by default is the narrator, not the agentive subject of the speaking action, if it is made implicit.

Verbal phrases represented by 单说, when occurring clause initially, are incompatible with the subject of the clause, as well as other syntactic properties of the verb, such as *-le*, *-zhe*, *-guo* and other tense-aspect markers, because their predicative function has been reduced. Along with the decategorization of their status as verbs, their discourse and metadiscourse functions emerge.

Note

1 Chu (1998, p. 3) characterizes Chinese topic chains as having three stages: introduction, pick-up, and continuation. In the example below, the word "有" ('have') introduces two nouns, Luoyang the city and Yang Ningluo the songstress. The latter, nonetheless, is more likely to be chosen as the topic in subsequent clauses, and accordingly the subjects of the next three consecutive clauses are all in zero form, coreferential with the songstress.

> 洛阳有个名歌女, 叫杨苧罗, 聪慧过人, 以语言尖巧冠于一时。
> Luòyáng yǒu gè míng gēnǚ, jiào Yáng Níngluó, cōnghuìguòrén, yǐ yǔyán jiānqiǎo guànyúyīshí.
> 'There was a famous songstress in Luoyang named Yang Ningluo, who was extremely intelligent and best known for her eloquence.'

10 Discourse cohesion and orientation expression

In terms of discourse function, grammaticalized speech and witness verbs show metadiscourse properties by indicating the narrator orientation, but there are differences between the two verb types. Specifically, speech verbs represented by 单说 (dānshuō, 'just say') only reflect the narrator orientation, serving as discourse frame markers to open the plot or establish the discourse topic. Conversely, witness verbs, yet to be fully grammaticalized, can still be used as verbs to denote intra-plot character orientation as well as omniscient orientation, as is the case with 但见 (dànjiàn, 'only see') and 只见 (zhǐjiàn, 'only see'). When a witness verb is used in a context where its subject cannot be restored, it is a sign to show that the verb has been transformed from a predicator to a discourse connective.

10.1 Introduction

Chapter 9 focuses on the discourse organization function of 单说 (dānshuō, 'just say') arguing that macro-syntactic conjunctions originated from verbs or clauses are of important status in Chinese. In terms of discourse function, both speech and witness verbs have metadiscourse properties when grammaticalized, indicating the narrator orientation beyond the plot proper. But there are differences between the two subcategories: 单说 is an expression denoting purely the narrator orientation, which is used to open the plot or establish the discourse topic, thus a frame marker; conversely, witness verbs, yet to be fully grammaticalized, can be used to reflect either the intra-plot character orientation or the "omniscient" orientation, as is the case with 但见 (dànjiàn, 'only see').

When 但见 is used to indicate the orientation of an intra-plot character, it allows the zero-subject reading (that is, the zero-subject is coreferential with the topic), though, like 单说, it is incompatible with an explicit subject. When 但见 denotes the omniscient orientation, the hosting clause defies the zero-subject reading; thus used 但见 functions as a cue for the narratee to pay attention to the subsequent narrative, giving it the status of foreground information. Therefore, it is an engagement marker, and the overlap between the narrator orientation and that of the character is the critical context for its grammaticalization into a metadiscourse element. The syntax of the Chinese zero-subject clause has led to the reduction of low-control matrix-clause verbs (e.g., 说 [shuō, 'say'], 见 [jiàn, 'see']) into discourse cohesive devices.

In contemporary Chinese discourse, the more often used is 只见 (zhǐjiàn, 'only see'). Liu Anchun and Zhang Bojiang (2004) have discussed its discourse function; Dong Xiufang (2007) unambiguously regards it in written Chinese as a discourse marker, maintaining that 只见 is instantiated in some cases to indicate the narrator or author orientation because thus used 只见 is not preceded by a definite subject. Its use is to introduce an emerging situation and advance the foreground narrative, which gives 只见 the status of a discourse marker. Examples (1) and (2) are cited from Dong (2007).

(1) 乌拉圭球员本戈切亚主罚任意球,<u>只见</u>他拔脚怒射,球飞过巴西队人墙,从球门左上角入网。

Wūlāguī qiúyuán Běngēqièyà zhǔfá rènyìqiú, <u>zhǐjiàn</u> tā bá jiǎo nù shè, qiú fēi guò Bāxī duì rén qiáng, cóng qiúmén zuǒshàngjiǎo rùwǎng.

'Uruguayan player Bengoechea took the free kick, <u>only to see</u> him fly his foot for a fierce drive. The ball flew over the Brazilian human wall and went into the net from the upper left corner of the goal.'

(2) 4名小伙子上阵了,化伟第一个滑下来,<u>只见</u>他凌空一跃,平稳地滑落在雪道上,获得108分的好成绩。

Sì míng xiǎohuǒzi shàngzhènle, Huà Wěi dìyīgè huá xiàlái, <u>zhǐjiàn</u> tā língkōng yī yuè, píngwěn de huáluò zài xuědào shàng, huòdé 108 fēn de hǎo chéngjī.

'Four boys took the field. Hua Wei was the first to slide down, <u>only to see</u> him leap into the air and slide smoothly down the piste, gaining 108 points.'

This use of 只见 can also be seen in the news media. See (3) and (4).

(3) 9日上午9时04分,美国俄克拉何马城中心,"轰"的一声巨响,<u>只见</u>火光冲天,浓烟滚滚,响声和震动波及数十英里之外。

Jiǔ rì shàngwǔ jiǔ shí língsì fēn, Měiguó Ékèlāhémǎ chéng zhōngxīn, "hōng" de yī shēng jù xiǎng, <u>zhǐjiàn</u> huǒguāngchōngtiān, nóngyāngǔngǔn, xiǎngshēng hé zhèndòng bōjí shù shí yīnglǐ zhīwài.

'At 9:04 a.m. on the 9th, there came a loud "bang" at the center of Oklahoma City, the United States, <u>only to see</u> fires soaring into the sky, thick smoke billowing, noise and vibration spreading dozens of miles away.'

(4) 5时15分,护卫队长一声令下,军乐队高奏国歌,<u>只见</u>升旗手一挥手,五星红旗在千万双眼睛的注目礼中冉冉上升。

Wǔ shí shíwǔ fēn, hùwèi duìzhǎng yīshēnglìngxià, jūnyuèduì gāo zòu guógē, <u>zhǐjiàn</u> shēngqí shǒu yī huīshǒu, wǔxīnghóngqí zài qiānwàn shuāng yǎnjīng de zhùmùlǐ zhōng rǎnrǎn shàngshēng.

'At 5:15 a.m., the escort captain gave the order for the military band to play the national anthem, <u>only to see</u> the flag raiser swing his hand, and the five-star red flag rise slowly in the attention of millions of eyes.'

Dong Xiufang (2007) points out that this type of usage is already seen in Song Dynasty works, such as (5).

(5) 话说那先生撒帐未完,<u>只见</u>翠莲跳起身来,摸着一条面杖,将先生夹腰两面杖,便骂道:……(*Story of Quick Talker Li Cuilian* [《快嘴李翠莲记》])

Huàshuō nà xiānshēng sāzhàng wèiwán, <u>zhǐjiàn</u> Cuìlián tiàoqǐshēnlái, mōzhe yītiáo miànzhàng, jiāng xiānshēng jiāyāo liǎng miànzhàng, biàn mà dào: …

'It is said that the gentleman was still spreading the tent, <u>only to see</u> Cuilian jump up, reach for a rolling pin, and beat the gentleman on the waist twice before she scolded,…'

We are of the view that this type of 只见 is a discourse cohesive device, and its usage is in line with the earlier form 但见 (dànjiàn). To understand its modern usage, it is necessary to examine its predecessor 但见.

More importantly, 但见 can be used to express both the orientation of the character within the plot and that of the "omniscient" narrator, which differentiates it from 单说 as well as 只见.

10.2 Intra-plot character orientation

In this use, the implicit actor of 见 can be recovered to precede 但见. Take (6) for example.

(6) 大春子正挨着英主教坐着。他偷眼观看,**但见**英主教有四十多岁,站起来是个高身量,四方脸,白胖子,高鼻子(欧洲人没有扁鼻子的)连鬓黑胡子,足有一尺多长,很是个样子。(Sun Gong, *Fresh Flavors* XXVI: Five Men's Righteousness [《新鲜滋味第二十六种:五人义》])

Dà Chūnzi zhèng āizhe Yīng zhǔjiào zuòzhe. Tā tōuyǎn guānkàn, **dànjiàn** Yīng zhǔjiào yǒu sìshí duō suì, zhàn qǐlái shì gè gāo shēnliang, sìfāng liǎn, bái pàngzi, gāo bízi (Ōuzhōurén méiyǒu biǎn bízi de), lián bìn hēi húzi, zú yǒu yī chǐ duō cháng, hěn shìgè yàngzi.

'Big Chunzi was sitting next to the English Bishop. He peeped out, **only to see** <u>that the Bishop was over forty years old, stood tall, a fat white man with a square face, a tall nose (the Europeans don't have flat noses) and a black beard of a full foot long, looking very handsome.</u>'

(7) 在庙里绕了个湾子,喝了会儿茶,二反出来,走在灶温饭铺门口儿,忽听后头有人直叫:曹先生曹老爷,你可怜可怜我啵!"曹立泉回头一瞧,不由

200 *Discourse cohesion and orientation expression*

的一楞儿。**但见**一个五十多岁的穷老太太,挽着个旗阄儿,穿着个破蓝布衫儿,愁眉泪眼,一脸的菜色,原来不是别人,正是他师娘富二太太。曹立泉知道没有什么好事,……(Sun Gong, *Fresh Flavors* XVIII: Cao the Second Watch [《新鲜滋味第十八种:曹二更》])

Zài miàolǐ ràole gè wānzi, hēle huì·er chá, èrfǎn chūlái, zǒu zài Zàowēn fànpù ménkǒu·er, hū tīng hòutou yǒurén zhí jiào: Cáo xiānshēng Cáo lǎoyé, nǐ kělián~kělián wǒ bo!" Cáo Lìquán huítóu yī qiáo, bùyóude yī lèng·er. **Dànjiàn** yī gè wǔshí duō suì de qióng lǎo tàitai, wǎnzhe gè qíjiū·er, chuānzhe gè pò lán bù shān·er, chóuméi lèiyǎn, yī liǎn de càisè, yuánlái bú shì biérén, zhèngshì tā shīniáng Fù èr tàitai. Cáo Lìquán zhīdào méiyǒu shénme hǎoshì, ...

'After a walk and some tea in the temple, he came out. When walking past Zaowen restaurant, he heard someone calling from behind, Mr. Cao, Master Cao, have mercy on me! Turning around, Cao Liquan could not help but flinch. (**He**) **saw** a poor old lady in her fifties, wearing a Manchu style hair knot and a ragged blue cloth shirt, with knitted brows, teary eyes, and a pale face due to hunger. She was none other than his master's second wife, Mrs. Fu. Cao Liquan knew there was nothing good,…'

In (6), 但见 is preceded by the clause "他偷眼观看" ('he peeped out'), and the subject of the action 但见 is obviously the character Big Chunzi. Likewise, the subject of "但见一个五十多岁的穷老太太,…" in (7) is Cao Liquan.

10.3 Omniscient orientation

In addition to the orientations of the character in the plot, 但见 can also express the "omniscient" orientation (also called "God's orientation" or "supernarratorial orientation"; for the supernarratorial orientation, see Shen Dan, 2004: 95; Tan Junqiang, 2014: 56–71). The omniscient orientation is neither the character's nor the narrator's.

(8) …… 老焦说:"事到如今,没有别的法子。得手把孩子给他害了就完了。"这里研究害人,暂且不提。单说春莺,自生产之后,母子皆安,伯英夫妇乐的都闭不上嘴。洗三那天,来了不少亲友,成氏也前来添盆。**但见**这个孩子,又胖又大,啼声洪亮,实在是个英物。(Sun Gong, *Fresh Flavors* XV: The Search and Rescue of an Orphan [《新鲜滋味第十五种:搜救孤》])

Lǎo Jiāo shuō: "Shìdàorújīn, méiyǒu bié de fǎzi. Déshǒu bǎ háizi gěi tā hàile jiù wánle." Zhèlǐ yánjiū hài rén, zànqiě bù tí. Dānshuō Chūnyīng, zì shēngchǎn zhīhòu, mǔzǐ jiē ān, Bóyīng fūfù lè de dōu bì bú shàng zuǐ. Xǐsān nàtiān, láile bùshǎo qīnyǒu, Chéng shì yě qiánlái tiānpén. **Dànjiàn** zhège háizi, yòu pàng yòu dà, tíshēng hóngliàng, shízài shì gè yīngwù.

'… Old Jiao said, "As things stand, there is no other way. We can get rid of the child when convenient." Here they were negotiating how to harm people, but let's not mention it, but turn to Chunying. She gave birth to a baby boy, both mother and son being safe and sound. Boying and his wife were both smiling from ear to ear. When the baby was bathed on the third day after its birth according to the custom, many friends and relatives came. Mrs. Cheng also came to add her share of blessings to the bath tub. **It was found that** <u>the baby was fat and big, with a loud cry, looking quite extraordinary</u>.'

Unlike the character orientation, there is no implicit actor of 见 that can be restored to precede 但见 in this kind of usage. Thus used 但见 is to draw the reader or the narratee's attention to what is about to be narrated, which makes it an engagement marker. Therefore, this type of 但见 is more a discourse cohesive device than a witness verb functioning as the predicate.

There are some border cases which allow for flexible orientation interpretation. In (9), for example, the orientation could be either the narrator's or the character'.

(9) 夫妻二人研究已定,第二天贺氏挎着瓦罐,仲芝柱着打狗棒,一直来到如芝门前。**但见**<u>门前放着一乘大轿,原来是县长王大令拜会如芝,在书房谈话</u>。仲芝就要回去,贺氏说:……"这正是好机会,这个时候儿不憨蠢他,甚么时候儿憨蠢他?"当时来到门前,大嚷老爷太太。(Sun Gong, *Fresh Flavors* XXII: Repentance [《新鲜滋味第二十二种:回头岸》])

Fūqī èr rén yánjiū yǐ dìng, dì'èrtiān Hè shì kuàzhe wǎ guàn, Zhòngzhī zhùzhe dǎgǒubàng, yīzhí láidào Rúzhī ménqián. **Dànjiàn** <u>ménqián fàngzhe yī chéng dà jiào, yuánlái shì xiànzhǎng Wáng Dàlìng bàihuì Rúzhī, zài shūfáng tánhuà</u>. Zhòngzhī jiùyào huíqù, Hè shì shuō:… "Zhè zhèngshì hǎo jīhuì, zhège shíhòu·er bù hānchǔn tā, shénme shíhòu·er hānchǔn tā?" Dāngshí láidào ménqián, dàrǎng lǎoyé tàitài.

'The couple had made the decision. The next day, they went to Ruzhi's gate, Mrs. He carrying a crock and Zhongzhi holding a dog club. <u>In front of the gate</u> **there was/they saw** <u>a big sedan chair. It turned out to be the county governor Wang Daling, who had come to visit and was talking with Ruzhi in the study</u>. Zhongzhi was about to go back when Mrs. He said, "This is the right moment. When would you fool him around if not now?" At that, she came up to the gate, yelling "Master!" and "Madam!".

The boundary cases suggest that 但见 as a metadiscourse element was still in the process of functional expansion and evolution when in popular use. The overlap between the narrator orientation and the character orientation constituted the critical context in which 但见 grammaticalized into a metadiscourse element. The emergence of its use for omniscient orientation brought its function closer to that of discourse cohesive devices, which, to us, explains why it defies the recovery of the clausal subject. This usage has been carried over to modern Chinese, but the lexical form has changed from 但见 to 只见.

Compared with 但见, 只见 is more grammaticalized, in that it is fully incompatible with agentive subjects and character orientation interpretation. Its discourse cohesive function has thus become more stable.

10.4 Narrator orientation and metadiscourse function

Along with the weakening of the predicate function of 但见, its discourse function and metadiscourse function gradually emerged. In terms of narrative function, there are two important differences between 但见 and 单说.

First, 但见 is an engagement marker of participation, prompting the narratee to pay attention to something newly introduced into discourse. In contrast, 单说 is a frame marker, used for topic management and discourse organization.

Second, with the emergence of the omniscient orientation, 但见 evolves from an in-plot narrative orientation to an out-of-plot narrative orientation whereas 单说 is consistently an expression of the narrator orientation, which is outside the plot.

单说 is used to organize discourse structure, and as a frame marker, its frequency of occurrence is much higher than that of 但见 (Table 10.1).

The syntax of the Chinese zero-subject clause plays an important role in the emergence of the metadiscourse function of 单说 and 但见, in that the zero-subject prompts the speech/witness verb in the main clause to undergo the process of "impersonal perspectivization", which makes it lose its status as the predicate of the main clause so that its "structural" object-complement clause can extend to be interpreted as foreground information.

Table 10.1 Frequency counts of 但见 and 单说 in *Fresh Flavors*

Chapter	但见	单说	Chapter	但见	单说
Neo-Confucianist Zhou (理学周)	1	3	Repentance (回头岸)	1	5
Aunt as mother-in-law (姑作婆)	0	2	Little Scorpion (小蝎子)	3	14
Doughnut Liu (麻花刘)	2	6	Cao the Second Watch (曹二更)	2	10
Eye for palace satin (裤缎眼)	1	9	Dong Xinxin (董心新)	3	7
Commander Liu (刘军门)	0	5	Five men's righteousness (五人义)	4	17
Zhang Wenbin (张文斌)	1	8	Righteousness of a chaste soul (贞魂义)	0	3
Search and rescue of an orphan (搜救孤)	1	10	The evil of alcohol (酒之害)	3	8
Hermit Wang (王遁世)	1	7	Square and round head (方圆头)	3	9

In terms of linguistic coding, this type of usage differs from its counterpart in English in that it shows the narrator's discourse organization intention without making explicit use of personal pronouns. English narrators are more concerned with temporal clues, and plot transition is normally by means of temporal words (Chafe, 1980, p. 4). In Chinese, speech verbs with invisible speakers (rather than imperative sentences such as "Let's talk about…") are often used to open the plot and change the topic, which is perhaps closely related to the story-telling tradition of Chinese novels.

10.5 Summary

It is a language universal for verbs of speech, perception and cognition to grammaticalize (Heine and Kuteva, 2002, pp. 261–9), which is manifested in the syntactic changes of low-control main clause verbs (see Givón, 1980 for "control") from the predicate role to discourse components reflecting the speaker's attitude or intention, such as "I think" and "you know" in English (see Thompson and Mulac, 1991; Thompson, 2002), and 我觉得 (wǒ juéde, 'I think') (see Fang Mei, 2005b, 2018), 不知道 (bù zhīdào, 'not know') (Tao Hongyin, 2003), and 说 (shuō, 'say') (Wang et al., 2003) in Chinese.

A large number of macro-syntactic conjunctions grammaticalized from clauses in Chinese are subjectless and thus can be understood as the grammaticalization of the verbs themselves. Such discourse-connecting components exhibit differences in function and path of emergence.

1) Some consistently express the speaker orientation, e.g., words containing 说 or other morphemes denoting a similar meaning.
2) Others shift from the orientation of the participant in the event (e.g., the agent orientation) to a supra-narratorial orientation (omniscient orientation), e.g., words containing 见 or other witness indicating morphemes.

Macro-syntactic conjunctions have emerged as discourse cohesive devices in the context of live narration, or simulated live narration, mostly from the narrator orientation. Given the live context of story-telling, the narrator does not need to syntactically encode himself as a participant role. The reduced clause then emerges as a discourse cohesive device in the interactional context where the subject is not important in syntactic configuration, which can then be taken as the inevitable result of "my hand records my mouth" and "the words are recorded as they are spoken."

11 Characteristics of traditional narratives and their impacts on Chinese grammar

Traditional Chinese novels are mostly derived from story-telling scripts. As the narrative guideline, the scripts are characterized by a distinctive feature of on-siteness, interlacing story-telling and speaker evaluation and intertwining intra-plot character orientation with speaker orientation. The narrative tradition of such scripts has exerted profound impacts on the organization of modern Chinese narrative discourse. First, there are interactional expressions to construct on-site effects; second, the switch of narrative orientation is explicitly coded; and third, the discourse frame, topic management, and the switch from narration to evaluation are realized in the default form of clauses of first-person or zero-form subjects, with the zero-subject clauses liable to be further reduced to connectives.

11.1 Introduction

A typical representative of modern Chinese narrative texts is story-telling scripts, which consist of two main categories: one is popular stories, which narrate the stories of emperors and generals in plain language; the other is novels, telling the stories of ordinary people in vernacular.

Typical narratives are monologic stories; story-telling scripts are the most representative narratives in Chinese oral literature. The so-called story-telling scripts are the scripts told at venues of story-telling, or texts written to be "said". Traditional story-telling has an opening sequence. Its pattern of beginning and ending has distinctive features, which are manifested as the interlacing of story-telling and narrator evaluation in terms of speech act and the alternating of character orientation and narrator orientation in terms of the orientation taking. This narrative tradition has greatly influenced not only the organization of the narrative discourses of future generations, but also the discourse grammar of modern Chinese. This chapter discusses the two influences in separate sections.[1]

DOI: 10.4324/9781032700656-11

11.2 Narrative features of story-telling novels

In narratology, story refers to the object of presentation. The same story can be presented in different discourses. The telling of a story actually consists of three aspects:

1. story: the event being narrated, i.e., what is narrated, including the event, characters, context, etc.;
2. narrative discourse/text: the oral or written discourse/text of the narrated story, concerning various narrative forms and techniques;
3. narration: the act or process of discourse production

(Shen Dan and Wang Yali, 2010, p. 16)

Stories are independent, and the same story can be presented through different media (e.g., fiction, film, drama, etc.). The narrative discourse in which a story is delivered is an important concern of narratology.

The story-telling script is the story-teller's handy guide. Given such a status, it is characterized by a distinctive on-siteness in terms of narrative patterning and orientation taking, which is to be elaborated below in terms of narrative opening, topic introduction, topic shift, and plot closing.

11.2.1 The opening and closing of the plot

The typical narrative is monologic story-telling. The Chinese "story-telling" has an opening sequence, which distinguishes it from the discourse organization of modern literary novels. Before the formal start of the plot, there is always an introduction, as illustrated in (1).

(1) 词曰：
试看书林隐处，几多俊逸儒流。虚名薄利不关愁，裁冰及剪雪，谈笑看吴钩，评议前王并后帝。分真伪占据中州，七雄扰扰乱春秋。兴亡如脆柳，身世类虚舟。见成名无数，图名无数，更有那逃名无数。霎时新月下长川，江湖变桑田古路。讶求鱼缘木，拟穷猿择木，恐伤弓远之曲木。不如且覆掌中杯，再听取新声曲度。

诗曰：
纷纷五代乱离间，一旦云开复见天。
草木百年新雨露，车书万里旧江山。
寻常巷陌陈罗绮，几处楼台奏管弦。
人乐太平无事日，莺花无限日高眠。
话说这八句诗，乃是故宋神宗天子朝中一个名儒，姓邵讳尧夫，道号康节先生所作。…… (*Outlaws of the Marsh* [《水浒传》])

Cí yuē:
Shìkàn shūlín yǐnchù, jǐduō jùnyì rúliú. Xūmíng bólì bù guān chóu, cáibīng jí jiǎnxuě, tánxiào kàn wúgōu, píngyì qiánwáng bìng hòudì. Fēn

zhēnwěi zhànjù zhōngzhōu, qīxióng rǎorǎo luàn chūnqiū. Xīngwáng rú cuìliǔ, shēnshì lèi xūzhōu. Jiàn chéngmíng wúshù, túmíng wúshù, gèng yǒu nà táomíng wúshù. Shàshí xīnyuè xià chángchuān, jiānghú biàn sāngtián gǔlù. Yà qiúyúyuánmù, nǐ qióngyuánzémù, kǒng shāng gōngyuǎn zhī qūmù. Bùrú qiě fù zhǎngzhōng bēi, zài tīngqǔ xīnshēng qǔdù.

Shī yuē:
Fēnfēn wǔdài luàn líjiān, yīdàn yúnkāi fù jiàntiān.
Cǎomù bǎinián xīn yǔlù, chēshū wànlǐ jiù jiāngshān.
Xúncháng xiàngmò chén luóqǐ, jǐchù lóutái zòu guǎnxián.
Rénlè tàipíng wú shì rì, yīnghuā wúxiàn rì gāo mián.
<u>Huàshuō</u> zhè bā jù shī, nǎishì gù Sòng Shénzōng tiānzǐ cháozhōng yī gè míngrú, xìng Shào huì Yáofū, dàohào Kāngjié xiānshēng suǒzuò. ...

'As the lyric goes:
Withdrawn in mountains of books, so many scholars remain cultured and refined in seclusion. Fame and wealth are not what they worry about, they are keen on writing poems and songs, laughing and talking about the wars past and present, commenting on the rise and fall of kings and emperors. Fights for the throne and strife among warlords are all bygones. History is full of ups and downs, and vicissitudes of life all end up in vain. Countless have risen to fame, countless strive for it, and countless evade it. In no time the new moon is down, and rivers and lakes turn into farmlands and roads. Some toil with no gain, a cornered monkey can't find a branch to rest, and frightened birds were startled at crooked twigs. Why not just drink up the wine, and listen to the new wonderful songs.'

As the poem goes:
After Five Dynasties' turmoil and strife,
The clouds dispersed to reveal the sky.
Refreshing rain brought old trees new life,
Culture and learning once again were high.
Ordinary folk in the lanes wore silk,
Music drifted from mansions and towers.
Under the heaven all was serene,
Men dozed off at noon midst gay birds and flowers.
<u>As the story goes</u>, this eight-line poem was written during the reign of Emperor Shenzong of the Song Dynasty by a famous scholar named Shao Yaofu, also known as Master Kangjie.

The above example is the opening of *Outlaws of the Marsh*, where "词曰:..." ('As the lyric goes,...') and "诗曰:..."('As the poem goes,...') lie outside the

Characteristics of traditional narratives 207

plot. The first discourse topic "一个名m儒"('a famous scholar') is actually introduced with "话说…" ('As the story goes…').

In the following example, the plot begins also with "话说" (the underlined), though the event or the topic of the novel is indicated by the underlined *you*-sentence that occurs in the preceding paragraph.

(2) 人世间事,最屈在不过的,就是冤狱;最苦恼不过的,就是恶婚姻。这两件事,若是凑到一齐,不必你身历其境,自己当局,每听见旁人述说,就能够毛骨悚然,伤心坠泪。<u>在前清末季,京城安定门里,菊儿胡同,有春阿氏谋害亲夫一案</u>,各处的传闻不一。各报纸的新闻,也有记载失实的地方。现经市隐先生把此案的前因后果,调查明确,并嘱余编作小说。余浣蔷读罢,始知这案中真相,实在可惊!可愕!可哭!可泣!兹特稍加点缀,编为说部,公诸社会,想阅者亦必骇愕称奇,伤心坠泪也。

<u>话说</u>东城方中巷,有一著名教育家,姓苏名市隐,性慷慨,好交游,生平不乐仕进。惟以诗酒自娱,好作社会上不平之鸣。这一日,天气清和,[]往地安门外访友。[]走至东西牌楼西马市地方,正欲雇车,忽然身背后有人唤道:"市隐先生,往哪里去?"市隐回头一看,正是至交的朋友原淡然。二人相见行礼,各道契阔。(*Mrs. Chun'a: Husband Murderer*, Chapter 1 [《春阿氏谋害亲夫》第一回])

Rénshì jiān shì, zuì qūzài bùguò de, jiùshì yuānyù; zuì kǔnǎo bùguò de, jiùshì è hūnyīn. Zhè liǎng jiàn shì, ruòshì còudào yīqǐ, bùbì nǐ shēnlìqíjìng, zìjǐ dāngjú, měi tīngjiàn pángrén shùshuō, jiù nénggòu máogǔsǒngrán, shāngxīn zhuìlèi, <u>zài qiánqīng mòjì, jīngchéng Āndìngmén lǐ, Jú·er Hútòng, yǒu Chūn·ā Shì móuhài qīnfū yī àn</u>, gèchù de chuánwén bùyī. Gè bàozhǐ de xīnwén, yěyǒu jìzǎi shīshí de dìfāng. Xiàn jīng Shìyǐn xiānshēng bǎ cǐ àn de qiányīnhòuguǒ, diàochá míngquè, bìng zhǔ yú biānzuò xiǎoshuō. Yú huànqiáng dú bà, shǐzhī zhè ànzhōng zhēnxiàng, shízài kějīng! Kě'è! Kěkū! Kěqì! Zī tè shāojiā diǎnzhuì, biānwéi shuōbù, gōngzhū shèhuì, xiǎng yuèzhě yì bì hài'è chēngqí, shāngxīn zhuìlèi yě.

<u>Huàshuō</u> dōngchéng Fāngzhōng Xiàng, yǒu yī zhùmíng jiàoyùjiā, xìng Sū míng Shìyǐn, xìng kāngkǎi, hào jiāoyóu, shēngpíng bù lè shìjìn. Wéi yǐ shījiǔ zìyú, hào zuò shèhuì shàng bùpíng zhī míng. Zhèyīrì, tiānqì qīnghé, [ ] wǎng Dì'ānmén wài fǎngyǒu. [ ] Zǒuzhì Dōngxī Páilóu Xīmǎshì dìfāng, zhèng yù gùchē, hūrán shēnbèihòu yǒurén huàndào: "Shìyǐn xiānshēng, wǎng nǎlǐ qù?" Shìyǐn huítóu yīkàn, zhèngshì zhìjiāo de péngyǒu Yuán Dànrán. Èr rén xiāngjiàn xínglǐ, gè dào qìkuò.

'In the world, the most aggrieved is nothing but unjust imprisonment; the most distressing is nothing but an unhappy marriage. If these two take place at the same time on one person, without being personally involved, you will be overwhelmed and shed sad tears every time you hear about it. <u>During the late Qing Dynasty, in Juer Hutong located inside the Anding Gate of the capital city, a women known as Chun'a murdered her husband</u>. All kinds of rumors were spread about the case. Even the reports on some newspapers were not accurate. Mr. Su Shiyin, who had investigated into the case and figured out its causes and consequences, asked me to write a novel about it. After reading the major part of his investigation report, I have come to know the truth of the case. It is really shocking, staggering, saddening and depressing! Hereby, with a little embellishment of my own, I have made it a novel and published it to the public. I believe those who read it will be as shocked and saddened as me.

<u>As the story goes</u>, there is a famous educator living in Fangzhong Hutong in the east part of the city, whose surname is Su and first name Shiyin. Mr. Su is generous and sociable, not interested in an official career. Indulged in poetry and wine, he is inclined to speak out his grievance against social injustice. On a fine and peaceful day, [ ] Mr. Su went to Di'anmen to visit a friend. [ ] When he was about to call a rickshaw at Ximashi of the Dongxi Archway, he suddenly heard someone calling behind: "Mr. Su, where are you going?" Shiyin turned around and found that it was his closest friend Yuan Danran. The two greeted and paid respects to each other, both happy after being apart for a long time.'

In example (2), the *you*-sentence post 话说 introduces the main character, the famous educator Su Shiyin. Although no explicit subject appears in the ensuing clauses, the zero-subjects are all coreferential with the topic introduced by "有".

"话说…" is actually a high-frequency discourse opener. In Chapter 9, we have cited examples from *The Scholars* to illustrate that it can occur at the very beginning of a chapter. The examples are reproduced below as (3a) and (3b).

(3) a. <u>话说</u>山东兖州府汶上县有个乡村,叫做薛家集。这集上有百十来人家,都是务农为业。(*The Scholars*, Chapter 2)

<u>Huàshuō</u> Shāndōng Yǎnzhōu Fǔ Wènshàng Xiàn yǒu gè xiāngcūn, jiàozuò Xuējiā Jí. Zhè jí shàng yǒu bǎi-shí-lái rénjiā, dōushì wùnóng wéiyè.

'<u>As the story goes</u>, in Xue Market, a village of Wenshang County, Shandong Province, there lived over a hundred families, all of whom worked on the land.'

b. <u>话说</u>周进在省城要看贡院,金有余见他真切,只得用几个小钱同他去看。不想才到"天"字号,就撞死在地下。(*The Scholars*, Chapter 3)

<u>Huàshuō</u> Zhōu Jìn zài shěngchéng yào kàn gòngyuàn, Jīn Yǒuyú jiàn tā zhēnqiè, zhǐdé yòng jǐ gè xiǎoqián tóng tā qù kàn. Bùxiǎng cáidào 'tiān' zìhào, jiù zhuàngsǐ zài dìxià.

'<u>As the story goes</u>, Zhou Jin wanted to look over the examination school in the provincial capital, and Jin Youyu, seeing him so eager, had to tip the gateman to get him in. However, when they came to Cell No. 1, Zhou Jin fell senseless to the ground.'

Characteristics of traditional narratives 209

To echo such chapter openers, the story-teller commonly uses the closure "且听下回分解" to end the narration. See (4) for example.

(4) a. 毕竟史进与三个头领怎地脱身, 且听下回分解。(*Outlaws of the Marsh* [《水浒传》], Chapter 3)
Bìjìng Shǐ Jìn yǔ sān gè tóulǐng zěndi tuōshēn, qiětīng xiàhuí fēnjiě.
'How did Shi Jin and the three bandit chiefs escape? Listen to the next chapter for explanation.'

b. 毕竟扯住鲁提辖的是甚人, 且听下回分解。(*Outlaws of the Marsh*, Chapter 3)
Bìjìng chězhù Lǔ Tíxiá de shì shèn rén, qiětīng xiàhuí fēnjiě.
'Who was the person that grabbed Lu Da? Listen to the next chapter for explanation.'

Although there is no noun that directly reflects on-siteness, the verb "听" ('listen') brings out the "speaker–listener" relationship between the narrator and the audience. The verb "话说" is the speaker's own way of opening up narration, while "且听…" is an imperative expression directed at the audience.

11.2.2 Topic introduction and topic shift

A commonly seen form of topic introduction is to use 单说 (dānshuō, 'just say'), which can be used to introduce a discourse topic, as illustrated in (5).

(5) 闲话还是不提, 说话这就开书。单说保定府西主人关外, 有一家富户, 家里房产买卖不少, 干脆说很有几个糟钱。姓李行五, ……((Sun Gong, *Fresh Flavors* V: Eye for Palace Satin [《新鲜滋味之五种:库缎眼》])
Xiánhuà háishì bù tí, shuōhuà zhè jiù kāishū. Dānshuō Bǎodìng Fǔ xī Zhǔrén Guān wài, yǒu yī jiā fùhù, jiālǐ fángchǎn mǎimài bù shǎo, gāncuì shuō hěn yǒu jǐ gè zāoqián. Xìng Lǐ háng wǔ, …
'No more of this digression, let me begin the story. Just say a wealthy family outside the Master Pass of Baoding Prefecture, it had many properties and businesses, or simply it had a lot of money. The master was surnamed Li, and he was the fifth child in this family,…'

When not used at the beginning of the host chapter, 单说 can occur when the topic shifts. Sometimes, there are expressions to mark the end of the previous storyline, such as "…不必细说" ('… need not go into details') in (6), "…打住" ('so much for…') in (7), or "…不提" ('… not to be mentioned'), etc.

(6) 一路之上, 也没有多少可叙的。到了南阳, 同城文武如何迎接, 如何接任, 又如何拜同城, 那都是外官场照例的套子, 不必细说。
单说南阳府知府胡太尊, 那天请刘军门吃饭。同席子一共七位, 主人之外, 首席自然是刘军门喽。(Sun Gong, *Fresh Flavors* VI: Commander Liu, [《新鲜滋味之六种:刘军门》])

Yīlù zhī shàng, yě méiyǒu duōshǎo kě xù de. Dàole Nányáng, tóngchéng wénwǔ rúhé yíngjiē, rúhé jiērèn, yòu rúhé bài tóngchéng, nà dōushì wài guānchǎng zhàolì de tàozi, búbì xìshuō.

Dānshuō Nányáng Fǔ zhīfǔ Hú Tàizūn, nàtiān qǐng Liú Jūnmén chīfàn. Tóngxízi yīgòng qī wèi, zhǔrén zhīwài, shǒuxí zìrán shì Liú Jūnmén lou.

'There is not much to say about the journey. When he arrived in Nanyang, he was greeted by the civil and military officials of the city. After taking office, he went to visit his colleagues. All these are the usual routines of the officialdom, so there is no need to go into details.

Just say Magistrate Hu of Nanyang Prefecture, he invited Commander Liu to dinner the other day. A total of seven people were at the dinner table. Besides Magistrate Hu, sitting at the head of the table was naturally Commander Liu.'

(7) 闲话二次打住。单说春爷,第二天又奔往茶馆儿。…… (Sun Gong, *Fresh Flavors* IV: Doughnut Liu, [《新鲜滋味之四种:麻花刘》])

Xiánhuà èrcì dǎzhù. Dānshuō Chūn Yé, dì'èrtiān yòu bēnwǎng cháguǎn·er. …

'Once again, no more of this digression. Just say Master Chun, he rushed to the teahouse the next day. …'

It is easy to see that both the establishment of a new topic and the shift of the topic in discourse are means whereby the narrator reveals himself. The recurring verbs of speech, such as 叙 ('narrate') and 说 ('say'), can only be understood as the story-teller's acts, rather than the characters' in the story.

11.2.3 Interactional expressions

Story-telling is live narration, which needs not only fully reflect the discourse organization of the plot, but also build interpersonal interaction with the audience.

If we look at traditional novels, we can see that the interaction constructed between the narrator and the virtual audience is an important feature of such narrative texts.

(8) 您说这事也真怪,小额自从上上这个药,就瞧疮口里头直长肉珠儿,真是一天比一天浅,四五天的工夫,居然就快长平啦。(*Little E* [《小额》])

Nínshuō zhèshì yě zhēn guài, Xiǎo É zìcóng shàngshang zhège yào, jiù qiáo chuāngkǒu lǐtou zhí zhǎng ròuzhū·er, zhēnshì yītiān bǐ yītiān qiǎn, sì-wǔ-tiān de gōngfu, jūrán jiù kuài zhǎngpíng la.

'Look, this is really weird. Ever since Little E applied this ointment, the wound began to heal. It was becoming smaller and smaller day by day, and in four or five days, it was almost healed.'

Characteristics of traditional narratives   211

(9) 那位瞧书的说啦:"你编的这个小说,简直的没理。你说伊老者素常得人,为甚么青皮连跟他打架,旁边儿的人会不管劝劝呢?眼瞧着让他们打上。世界上岂有此理?"诸位有所不知,他们正要打架的时候儿,正赶上堂官来啦,里里外外一阵的大乱。(Little E)

Nàwèi qiáoshū de shuō la: "Nǐ biān de zhège xiǎoshuō, jiǎnzhí de méilǐ. Nǐshuō Yī Lǎozhě sùcháng dérén, wèishénme qīngpí lián gēn tā dǎjià, pángbiān·er de rén huì bùguǎn quàn~quàn ne? Yǎnqiáozhe ràng tāmen dǎshàng. Shìjiè shàng qǐyǒucǐlǐ?" Zhūwèi yǒusuǒbùzhī, tāmen zhèngyào dǎjià de shíhòu·er, zhèng gǎnshàng tángguān lái la, lǐlǐwàiwài yīzhèn de dàluàn.

'You might say, "This story of yours sounds utterly irrational. You said that Elder Yi usually enjoyed great popularity among people. Then why didn't the standers-by stop it when those rascals came to beat him? They were just standing there and watching them beat. Who ever heard of such a thing?" There is something you don't know. When they were about to beat, the minister came, and it was in a turmoil inside and out.'

(10) 亲侄子吃顿饭都费事,过继更休想了,头一个先得过继内侄。您就瞧罢!过继内侄的,十个里头,有九个糟心的。溯本穷源,为甚么妇人都是这宗毛病呢?就因为没受过好教育,不明白真理,所以一味的私心。唐家的武后,前清的慈禧太后,按说是聪明绝顶啦,就是这地方儿想不开,所以糟心。(Sun Gong, *Fresh Flavors* X: Iron Wang San [《新鲜滋味之第十种:铁王三》])

Qīn zhízi chī dùn fàn dōu fèishì, guòjì gèng xiūxiǎng le, tóuyīgè xiān děi guòjì nèizhí. Nín jiù qiáo ba! Guòjì nèizhí de, shí gè lǐtou, yǒu jiǔ gè zāoxīn de. Sùběnqióngyuán, wéishénme fùrén dōushì zhèzōng máobìng ne? Jiù yīnwèi méi shòuguò hǎo jiàoyù, bù míngbái zhēnlǐ, suǒyǐ yīwèi de sīxīn. Tángjiā de Wǔ Hòu, qián Qīng de Cíxǐ Tàihòu, ànshuō shì cōngmíngjuédǐng la, jiùshì zhè dìfāng·er xiǎngbùkāi, suǒyǐ zāoxīn.

'It took a lot of trouble to have dinner with his nephew, not to mention to adopt him, as he had to adopt the son of his wife's brother first. Just look at it. For those who adopt the son of their wife's brother, nine out of ten would end up in vexation. The root cause is women. How come? Because they are not well-educated and are not reasonable. As a result, they are quite self-centered. The Empress Wu of the Tang Dynasty and the Empress Dowager Cixi of the Qing Dynasty were both supposed to be extremely clever, but they both did something silly in this respect. No wonder they were vexed.'

Here, the use of the second-person pronoun 您 in (8) is a virtual addressee of the narrator, while "那位瞧书的说啦" ('You might say') in (9) is actually a question addressed to the virtual reader, which is to be answered by the author himself. The ensuing "诸位有所不知" ('There is something you don't know.') is also an expression directed at the virtual readership. In (10), "您就瞧吧"

('Just look at it.') is an imperative sentence that directs the reader's attention to the subsequent narrative.

11.2.4 Interlacing narration and evaluation

In addition to the aforementioned construction of interaction between the narrator and the audience, the on-siteness nature of story-telling scripts also manifests itself in the interlacing of the speaker's narration of the story and his personal evaluation of the progression of the narration. The parts in parentheses in (11) to (13) below are the story-teller's comments on what is narrated.

(11) 头道菜一上来,谁也摸不清是甚么,用刀子切也切不动,曹猴儿急了,说:"拿筷子来罢!"(吃大餐要筷子,闻所未闻。)(Sun Gong, *Fresh Flavors* III: Neo-Confucianist Zhou [《新鲜滋味之三种:理学周》])

Tóudào cài yī shànglái, shéi yě mōbùqīng shì shénme, yòng dāozi qiē yě qiē- bú-dòng, Cáo Hóu·er jíle, shuō: "Ná kuàizi lái ba!" (Chī dàcān yào kuàizi, wénsuǒwèiwén.)

'As soon as the first dish was served onto the table, no one could figure out what it was. They tried cutting it up with the knife but failed. Monkey Cao lost his patience and said, "Bring me the chopsticks!" (It's unheard of for anyone who eats Western food with chopsticks.)'

(12) 赵大好喝两盅儿,又好戴高帽子(全都是糟心的毛病)。狗爷知道他妹丈这宗脾气,所以极力的狗事。要按亲戚说,他是大舅子,赵大是妹丈,得管他叫大哥。(Sun Gong, *Fresh Flavors* III: Neo-Confucianist Zhou)

Zhào Dà hào hē liǎngzhōng·er, yòu hào dài gāomàozi (quán dōushì zāoxīn de máobìng). Gǒu Yé zhīdào tā mèizhàng zhè zōng píqì, suǒyǐ jílì de gǒushì. Yào àn qīnqī shuō, tā shì dàjiùzi, Zhào Dà shì mèizhàng, děi guǎn tā jiào dàgē.

'Big Zhao liked drinking and receiving flattery (both are annoying habits). Master Dog knew his brother-in-law's temper, so he tried his best to flatter him. In terms of kinship, he was the elder brother of Zhao's wife, and Big Zhao was his brother-in-law, so he was also Zhao's elder brother.'

(13) 单说保定府西主人关外,有一家富户,家里房产买卖不少,干脆说很有几个糟钱。姓李行五,因为他身量高,都管他叫大李五(号可不叫顺亭),五十多岁,夫人儿苗氏。跟前一儿两女,儿子叫李拴头,十一、二岁。大女儿叫金姐儿,已然出阁,给的是本处财主丁老虎的儿子,叫作丁狗儿(虎父生犬子,可称半语子养哑吧,一辈不如一辈)。(Sun Gong, *Fresh Flavors* V: Eye for Palace Satin)

Dānshuō Bǎodìng Fǔ xi Zhǔrén Guān wài, yǒu yī jiā fùhù, jiālǐ fángchǎn mǎimài bùshǎo, gāncuì shuō hěnyǒu jǐgè zāoqián. Xìng Lǐ háng wǔ, yīnwèi tā shēnliang gāo, dōu guǎn tā jiào Dà Lǐ Wǔ (hào kě bù jiào Shùntíng), wǔshí duō suì, fūrén·er Miáo Shì. Gēnqián yī ér liǎng nǚ, érzi jiào Lǐ Shuāntóu, shíyī(,), èr suì. Dà nǚ'ér jiào Jīnjiě·er, yǐrán chūgé, gěi de shì běnchù cáizhǔ Dīng Lǎohǔ de érzi, jiàozuò Dīng Gǒu'er (hǔfù shēng quǎnzǐ, kě chēng bànyǔzi yǎng yǎba, yī bèi bùrú yī bèi).

'Just say a wealthy family outside the Master Pass of Baoding Prefecture, it had many properties and businesses, or simply it had a lot of money. The master was surnamed Li, and he was the fifth child in this family. Since he was tall, he was also called Big Li the Fifth (his alternative name is not Shunting). He was in his fifties and his wife was of the surname Miao. He had one son and two daughters. His son, named Li Shuantou, was eleven or twelve years old. His eldest daughter, Jinjie, was already married to Doggie Ding, the son of a rich man named Tiger Ding. (Tiger father begets doggie son, which suits the saying: a mute father begets a deaf-mute son – each generation is less worthy than the previous one.)'

In example (11), "吃大餐要筷子,闻所未闻" ('It's unheard of for anyone who eats Western food with chopsticks.') is an evaluation of the character's behavior in the story; "全都是糟心的毛病" ('both are annoying habits') in (12) is an evaluation of the character's habits (love of drinking and being flattered); and in example (13), "号可不叫顺亭" ('his alternative name is not Shunting') is equivalent to a footnote, and "虎父生犬子,可称半语子养哑吧,一辈不如一辈" ('Tiger father begets doggie son, which suits the saying: a mute father begets a deaf-mute son – each generation is less worthy than the previous one.') is again the story-teller's comment.

From story narration to evaluation of the narrated content, the shift of different speech acts is represented in the form of accompanying notes.

11.3 Narration orientation

Narrative discourse varies along a variety of dimensions: 1) order: whether to break the natural chronological order; 2) temporal spacing: how much ink is used to describe what happens in a certain period of time; 3) frequency: the relationship between the number of narratives and the number of events; 4) discourse mode: regulation of the narrative information by distance control or orientation choice; 5) discourse form: levels and types of narration (Shen Dan and Wang Liya, 2010, p. 25). Among the above dimensions, both the orientation and level of narration are closely related to the choice of discourse form.

The so-called narration orientation refers to the perspective from which the story is observed during the course of narration. In both written narratives and narratives in other media such as film, the same story can have very different effects if it is narrated from different orientations. Traditional narratology studies orientation with the focus on the way events are presented in fiction. When it comes to the level of narration, there are differences between written and oral narratives. In oral narratives, the narrator and the addressee face each other, and the addressee can directly observe the narration process, the narrator's voice, facial expressions and gestures playing an important role in achieving the narrative effect (Shen Dan and Wang Liya, 2010, p. 19). Therefore, evaluative expressions such as the bracketed parts in examples (11), (12) and (13) above are also reflections of the on-siteness feature of story-telling.[2] When it comes to the linguistic perspective, we are more concerned with the impact of different expressions on the basic linguistic categories, or, rather, what linguistic devices can distinguish and convey different orientations.

11.3.1 Orientation markers

Some words are used to indicate narration orientation, such as "在……看来" ('in the view of…').

(14) 杨继盛在监狱里,溜溜关了三年,满朝文武百官,却死活找不出,这位大好人的任何罪状来。最后呢,杨继盛还是被杀了。为什么呢?没有理由。在当时看来,得罪严嵩的人,就该死。杨继盛死后,松筠庵,就改成了祠堂。因为杨继盛号椒山,所以,达智桥胡同里的这座,杨继盛故居,又叫杨椒山祠了。(*This is Beijing* [《这里是北京》])

Yáng Jìshèng zài jiānyù lǐ, liūliū guānle sān nián, mǎncháo wén-wǔbǎiguān, què sǐhuó zhǎobùchū, zhèwèi dà hǎorén de rènhé zuìzhuàng lái. Zuìhòu ne, Yáng Jìshèng háishì bèi shāle. Wèishéme ne? Méiyǒu lǐyóu. <u>Zài dāngshí kànlái</u>, dézuì Yán Sōng de rén, jiù gāi sǐ. Yáng Jìshèng sǐ hòu, Sōngyún Ān, jiù gǎichéngle cítáng. Yīnwèi Yáng Jìshèng hào Jiāoshān, suǒyǐ, Dázhìqiáo Hútòng lǐ de zhè zuò, Yáng Jìshèng gùjū, yòu jiào Yáng Jiāoshān Cí le.

'Yang Jisheng had been detained in prison for three long years. None of the officials, civil and military, could find any evidence that might prove this good man guilty. Yet in the end, Yang Jisheng was killed any way. Why? For no reason. <u>In the eyes (of people) at that time</u>, anyone who offended Yan Song was doomed to die. After Yang Jisheng's death, Temple Songyun was transformed into an ancestral hall. As Yang Jisheng was also known as Jiaoshan, his former residence in Dazhiqiao Hutong is also called Temple of Yang Jiaoshan.'

(15) 他对朱由校的忠诚,在外人看来,有点得不偿失,甚至有点多余。难怪他这么多年,都混不出个头来。(*This is Beijing*)

Tā duì Zhū Yóuxiào de zhōngchéng, <u>zài wàirén kànlái</u>, yǒudiǎn débùchángshī, shènzhì yǒudiǎn duōyú. Nánguài tā zhème duō nián, dōu hùn-bù-chū gè tóu lái.

'His loyalty to Zhu Youxiao, <u>in the eyes of others</u>, was not worth the gain, or even seemed redundant. No wonder he hadn't made his mark for so many years.'

In (14) and (15) above, both "在当时看来" ('in the eyes [of people] at that time') and "在外人看来" ('in the eyes of others') take the syntactic configuration of "在......看来", a phenomenon that has been noticed in metadiscourse research.

We would argue here that the linguistic forms that indicate narration orientations are of two main categories, metadiscourse and sentence pattern, which are discussed separately below.

11.3.2 *Metadiscourse*

Hyland (2005, p. 49) classifies metadiscourse into two categories according to its function: one is interactive metadiscourse, which reflects the relationship within the discourse and serves to guide the reader's understanding of the discourse; the other is interactional metadiscourse, which reflects the interaction between the author and the reader and serves to engage the reader in the process of communication. Roughly speaking, interactive metadiscourse lies on the informative level, while interpersonal metadiscourse is on the interactional level.[3]

Person choice is an important manifestation of metadiscourse as well as an important way of orientation taking. The speaker's choice of pronouns predetermines whether it is first-person narration or third-party narration. The use of first-person narration is a direct manifestation of speaker narration, such as the opening of *Little E* as illustrated in (16), where "听我慢慢儿的道来" ('Please hear me out.') is in the first person.

(16)　庚子以前，北京城的现象，除了黑暗，就是顽固，除了腐败，就是野蛮，千奇百怪，称得起甚么德行都有。老实角儿是甘受其苦，能抓钱的道儿，反正没有光明正大的事情。顶可恶的三样儿，就是仓、库、局。要说这三样儿害处，诸位也都知道，如今说一个故事儿，就是库界的事情，这可是真事。诸位别忙，<u>听我慢慢儿的道来</u>。(*Little E*)

　　Gēngzǐ yǐqián, Běijīng chéng de xiànxiàng, chúle hēi'àn, jiùshì wángù, chúle fǔbài, jiùshì yěmán, qiānqíbǎiguài, chēngdeqǐ shénme déxíng dōuyǒu. Lǎoshíjué·er shì gānshòuqíkǔ, néng zhuāqián de dào·er, fǎnzhèng méiyǒu guāngmíngzhèngdà de shìqíng. Dǐng kěwù de sānyàng·er, jiùshì cāng(,) kù(,) jú. Yàoshuō zhè sānyàng·er hàichu, zhūwèi yě dōu zhīdào, rújīn shuō yī gè gùshì·er, jiùshì kùjiè de shìqíng, zhè kěshì zhēnshì. Zhūwèi bié máng, <u>tīng wǒ mànman·er de dàolái</u>.

　　'Before 1900, the city of Beijing, permeated with barbarism and corruption, was shrouded in darkness and obstinacy. It could be said that the city was a bizarre motley of grotesques. Upright and honest people were those who suffered. In the businesses that could make money, there was nothing fair or honest. The three most hateful ones were the storehouse, warehouse, and bureau. As for the harms that these three had done, I believe you all know. The story I am now going to tell you is about the warehouse. This is a true story. Be patient, <u>please hear me out</u>.'

However, there are discrepancies in first-person narratives. The first-person narrator can also be a participant within the event, in which case the narrative is a personal recount. See (17).

(17) "冷吗？"我问，手不知道放在哪里。
柳青没回答，面无表情。(Feng Tang, *Beijing, Beijing* [《北京北京》])
"Lěng ma?" Wǒ wèn, shǒu bù zhīdào fàngzài nǎlǐ.
Liǔ Qīng méi huídá, miànwúbiǎoqíng.
'"Are you cold?" I asked, not knowing where to put my hand.
Liu Qing didn't answer, her face expressionless.'

The first-person narrator may also be outside the event, as is the case in example (16). Another example is from Lao She's *Rickshaw Boy* (《骆驼祥子》), where the narrator appears in the first person in the opening of the narrative discourse.

(18) 我们所要介绍的祥子，不是骆驼，因为"骆驼"只是个外号；那么，我们就先说祥子，随手儿把骆驼与祥子那点关系说过去，也就算了。(Lao She, *Rickshaw Boy*)
Wǒmen suǒyào jièshào de Xiángzi, bú shì luòtuo, yīnwèi "luòtuo" zhǐshì gè wàihào; nàme, wǒmen jiù xiān shuō Xiángzi, suíshǒu·er bǎ luòtuo yǔ Xiángzi nàdiǎn guānxì shuō guòqù, yě jiù suànle.
'The story is about Xiangzi, not a camel, because "Camel" was only his nickname. So, let us start with Xiangzi, just mentioning in passing how he became linked with camels.'

As we know, *Rickshaw Boy* is not the story of the writer himself. This narrative style of direct appearance on the part of the narrator is nothing but a technique commonly seen in traditional Chinese chapter novels, when different chapters are also related by way of such discourse organizers as 话说 (huàshuō, 'speaking of'), 单说 (dānshuō, 'just say'), etc.

11.3.3 Character orientation

In addition to personal pronouns, visual verbs such as 看 (kàn, 'look/see'), 见 (jiàn, 'see'), or 瞧 (qiáo, 'look/see') are often used to express orientation.

When expressing the orientation of a character within a plot in the course of narration, the visual verb clause either has an overt actor, or the covert actor can be recovered, such as in (19).

(19) 曹立泉回头一瞧，不由的一楞儿。[]但见一个五十多岁的穷老太太，挽着个旗阄儿，穿着个破蓝布衫儿，愁眉泪眼一脸的菜色，原来不是别人，正是他师娘富二太太。(Sun Gong, *Fresh Flavors* XXVIII: Cao the Second Watch [《新鲜滋味第二十八种:曹二更》])

Cáo Lìquán huítóu yī qiáo, bùyóude yīlèng·er. [] Dànjiàn <u>yī gè wǔshí duō suì de qióng lǎotàitai, wǎnzhe gè qíjiū·er, chuānzhe gè pò lán bù shān·er, chóuméi lèiyǎn yī liǎn de càisè</u>, yuánlái bú shì biérén, zhèngshì tā shīmiáng Fù Ěr Tàitai.

'Turning around, Cao Liquan could not help but flinch. [He] saw <u>a poor old lady in her fifties, wearing a Manchu-style hair knot and a ragged blue cloth shirt, with knitted brows, teary eyes, and a pale face due to hunger</u>. She was none other than his master's second wife, Mrs. Fu.'

In the example above, the underlined part can be interpreted as what Cao Liquan saw.

11.3.4 *Omnipotent orientation*

In the following example, it is difficult to interpret the content after "但见" as what the characters saw.

(20) 单说春莺,自生产之后,母子皆安,伯英夫妇乐的都闭不上嘴。洗三那天,来了不少亲友,成氏也前来添盆。[ ]但见这个孩子,又胖又大,啼声洪亮,实在是个英物。(Sun Gong, *Fresh Flavors* XV: The Search and Rescue of an Orphan [《新鲜滋味第十五种:搜救孤》])

Dānshuō Chūnyīng, zì shēngchǎn zhīhòu, mǔzǐ jiē ān, Bóyīng fūfù lède dōu bì-bú-shàng zuǐ. Xǐsān nàtiān, láile bùshǎo qīnyǒu, Chéng Shì yě qiánlái tiānpén.? [ ] Dànjiàn zhège háizi, yòu pàng yòu dà, tíshēng hóngliàng, shízài shì gè yīngwù.

'Just say Chunying. She gave birth to a baby boy, both mother and son being safe and sound. Boying and his wife were both smiling from ear to ear. When the baby was bathed on the third day after its birth according to the custom, many friends and relatives came. Mrs. Cheng also came to add her share of blessings to the bath tub. [It was] found that the baby was fat and big, with a loud cry, looking quite extraordinary.'

This type of usage is characterized by the fact that the agent of the visual verb cannot be recovered. The function of 但见 is to prompt the reader or listener to pay attention to what is about to be narrated. In other words, 但见 is a way for the narrator to put himself inside the story, thus giving the reader or listener the feeling of being personally on the scene.

11.3.5 *Switching orientation*

In narration, the same visual verb can be used to indicate different orientations, sometimes the character's and sometimes the narrator's. Compare (21), (22) and (23).

(21) 有一天晚晌，记者跟随先祖母在门外纳凉，曹二更的木厂子已然关门，<u>就瞧</u>由东边来了一个人行步匆匆，打着一个纸灯笼，一下坡儿，差点儿没栽了一个跟头。(Sun Gong, *Fresh Flavors* XXVIII: Cao the Second Watch)

Yǒu yītiān wǎnshǎng, jìzhě gēnsuí xiān zǔmǔ zài ménwài nàliáng, Cáo Èrgēng de mùchǎngzi yǐrán guānmén, <u>jiù qiáo</u> yóu dōngbian láile yī gè rén xíngbù cōngcōng, dǎzhe yī gè zhǐ dēnglóng, yīxiàpō·er, chàdiǎn·er méi zāile yī gè gēntou.

'One evening, the reporter was sitting outside the door with his now-late grandmother, enjoying the cool of summer. At that time, Cao the Second Watch's timber mill was already closed. Then a man was seen coming in haste from the east, holding a paper lantern in his hand. When he came down the slope, he stumbled and almost fell down.'

(22) 大拴子刚走，这当儿底下人回禀说，酒醋局希四老爷来啦。额大奶奶说："快请。"底下人出去，功夫不大，<u>就瞧</u>希四爷摇摇摆摆踱了进来。(*Little E*)

Dà Shuānzi gāngzǒu, zhèdāng·er dǐxiàrén huíbǐng shuō, Jiǔcù Jú Xīsì lǎoyé lái la. É Dà Nǎinai shuō: "Kuàiqǐng." Dǐxiàrén chūqù, gōngfū bú dà, <u>jiù qiáo</u> Xī Sì yé yáoyáobǎibǎi duóle jìnlái.

'As soon as Big Shuanzi left, the servant came and reported that Master Xi Si from the Vinegar and Wine Bureau had arrived. The Elder Madam E said, "Bring him in." The servant went out, and in a while, Master Xi Si swaggered in.'

(23) 正这儿说着，<u>就瞧</u>起外边慌慌张张的跑进一个人来。大家伙儿一瞧，都吓了一跳。您猜进来的这个人是谁？正是伊老者的二少爷善全。(*Little E*)

Zhèng zhè·er shuōzhe, <u>jiù qiáo</u> qǐ wàibian huānghuāngzhāngzhāng de pǎojìn yī gè rén lái. Dàjiāhuǒ·er yī qiáo, dōu xiàle yī tiào. Nín cāi jìnlái de zhège rén shì shéi? Zhèngshì Yī lǎozhě de èr shàoyé Shànquán.

'As he was talking, he saw someone rush in from outside in a flurry. Everybody was taken aback when they saw him clearly. Guess who this person was? It was Shanquan, the second son of Old Man Yi.'

In example (21), "瞧" ('see') can be interpreted as from the orientation of a character in the story. But the agent of the seeing action in example (22) or (23) can by no means be the character that has been presented in the previous discourse; that is, it is not a character in the storyline. In these two cases, "就瞧" ('just see') is used as a guide to an episode that, in the narrator's opinion, requires special attention. To put it differently, "就瞧" is used to focus on a new development. In modern written Chinese, the function is performed by 只见 ('just see').

The switch in narrative orientation can also be achieved by epistemic verbs. See (24) for example.

(24) 李鸿章,跟荣禄关系挺铁,有利益裙带关系。也知道,他跟慈禧之间,高于君臣的默契。于是求荣禄,帮忙疏通疏通。碍于面子,荣禄只好向慈禧说情。<u>不知慈禧是为了避嫌,还是真生气了</u>。先是当场勃然大怒,但结果呢,在荣禄的一番劝解之后,慈禧还是心一软,把徐致靖的死刑,改判了终身监禁。(This is Beijing)

Lǐ Hóngzhāng, gēn Róng Lù guānxì tǐng tiě, yǒu lìyì qúndài guānxì. Yě zhīdào, tā gēn Cíxǐ zhījiān, gāoyú jūnchén de mòqì. Yúshì qiú Róng Lù, bāngmáng shūtōng~shūtōng. Àiyú miànzi, Róng Lù zhǐhǎo xiàng Cíxǐ shuōqíng. <u>Bùzhī Cíxǐ shì wèile bìxián, háishì zhēn shēngqìle</u>. Xiānshì dāngchǎng bórándànù, dàn jiéguǒ ne, zài Róng Lù de yīfān quànjiě zhīhòu, Cíxǐ háishì xīn yī ruǎn, bǎ Xú Zhìjìng de sǐxíng, gǎipànle zhōngshēn jiānjìn.

'Li Hongzhang was on intimate terms with Rong Lu. And these two had a relationship of interest connected through marriage. Li also knew that Rong had a rapport with Empress Dowager Cixi, which was beyond the relationship between a monarch and his subject. So Li asked Rong to help grease the wheels. Out of fear of hurting Li's feelings, Rong had to plead with Cixi. <u>Whether she was to avoid rousing suspicion or she was really angry, nobody knew</u>. Anyway, Cixi flew into a rage on the spot. However, under Rong Lu's persuasion, Cixi eventually relented and changed Xu Zhijing's capital punishment to life imprisonment.'

In this excerpt, the underlined sentence is the narrator's comment on what has been narrated, which makes it lie outside the plot. Accordingly, the epistemic verb phrase "不知" ('not know') indicates not the cognitive state of the characters in the plot, but that of the narrator's.

11.4 Narratives in colloquial Beijing dialect

Story-telling is live narration, which needs to fully reflect the discourse organization of the plot itself and at the same time construct interaction with the audience. The representation of on-siteness characterizes the narration of chapter novels, and this way of narration in which the speaker reveals himself is not only inherited in the novel, but also has an important influence on the organization of narrative discourse in future generations and, consequently, on the discourse grammar of modern Chinese. The influence is mainly manifested in the following two aspects:

1) The narrative discourse has a large number of interactional expressions for the purpose of building the onsite effect;
2) The linguistic forms reflecting the narration orientation include not only the choice of person and metadiscourse, but also some sentence patterns with the function of interactional expression.

Since there is no threshold of cultural class in story-telling, its diction is then required to be the closest to the high-frequency spoken forms of that time, which makes such texts representative documentation of the spoken language of its era, with the possibility of truly reflecting the conditions for grammatical evolution.

11.4.1 Constructing on-site effect

We note that the narrative style of the narrator manifesting himself in the traditional chapter novel is not only inherited in the modern novel, but is also a common paradigm of modern narrative discourse. In the following narrative, for example, the narrator constructs an interactional relationship with the listener by way of the inclusive first-person pronoun "咱".

(25) 说起康熙爷,绝对属于男人里挑出来的精英。就算在皇帝堆儿里,也是个数一数二的佼佼者。<u>咱常说</u>,成功男人的背后,一定有一个支持他的女人。康熙爷也不例外。只不过,他背后这个女人,不是皇后,而是她的皇祖母,孝庄皇太后。<u>话说当年在武英殿</u>,康熙跟他的几个小兄弟,智擒了鳌拜。这事儿,至今令人谈论起来津津乐道。殊不知,整个事件的幕后策划,就是咱们的孝庄皇太后。<u>一日</u>,在孝庄的指点下,玄烨以下棋为名,召见了他的岳父索额图。老中青三代人,连夜拟定了,擒鳌拜的整体方略,才有了武英殿里,初生牛犊不怕虎的那一幕。(This is Beijing)

Shuōqǐ Kāngxī Yé, juéduì shǔyú nánrén lǐ tiāo chūlái de jīngyīng. Jiùsuàn zài huángdì duī·er lǐ, yěshì gè shǔyīshǔ'èr de jiǎojiǎozhě. <u>Zán chángshuō</u>, chénggōng nánrén de bèihòu, yīdìng yǒu yī gè zhīchí tā de nǚrén. Kāngxī Yé yě bú lìwài. Zhǐbúguò, tā bèihòu zhège nǚrén, búshì huánghòu, érshì tā de huáng zǔmǔ, Xiàozhuāng Huángtàihòu. <u>Huàshuō dāngnián zài Wǔyīng Diàn</u>, Kāngxī gēn tā de jǐ gè xiǎo xiōngdì, zhìqínle Áobài. Zhèshì·er, zhìjīn lìngrén tánlùn qǐlái jīnjīnlèdào. Shūbùzhī, zhěnggè shìjiàn de mùhòu cèhuà, jiùshì zánmen de Xiàozhuāng Huángtàihòu. <u>Yīrì</u>, zài Xiàozhuāng de zhǐdiǎn xià, Xuányè yǐ xiàqí wéimíng, zhàojiànle tā de yuèfù Suǒ'étú. Lǎo zhōng qīng sān dài rén, liányè nǐdìngle, qín Áobài de zhěngtǐ fānglüè, cái yǒule Wǔyīng Diàn lǐ, chūshēng niúdú bú pà hǔ de nà yī mù.

'<u>Speaking of</u> Emperor Kangxi, he was definitely a man of men. Even among emperors, he could be considered as one of the best. <u>As we often say</u>, behind a successful man, there must be a woman who supports him. Emperor Kangxi was no exception. However, the woman behind Kangxi was not his empress, but his grandmother, Empress Dowager Xiaozhuang. <u>It is said that in Wuying Hall</u>, Kangxi maneuvered and captured Aobai with his young brothers. This event has been talked about a lot till now. You can hardly imagine that the one who made the ploy behind the scenes was Empress Dowager Xiaozhuang. <u>One day</u>, under the guidance of Xiaozhuang, Kangxi summoned his father-in-law Suo'etu in the name of playing chess. The three generations of the royal family worked out overnight the overall strategy of capturing Aobai. This was how the capture in the Wuying Hall came to happen. Just as the saying goes, new-born calves make little of tigers.'

In (25), "咱常说" ('As we often say,...') is chosen over "俗话说" (súhuà shuō, 'As the saying goes,...') to construct interaction between the speaker and the addressee, in that "咱" is the inclusive first-person pronoun, which refers to both the speaker and the addressee. The main character "Emperor Kangxi" is introduced by "说起" ('speaking of'); the specific event is then opened with "话说当年在武英殿……" ('It is said that in Wuying Hall,...'), and the temporal expression "一日" ('one day') is used to mark a node in the storyline.

In addition to interactional expressions (such as the inclusive first-person pronouns 咱 and 咱们), some sentence patterns are also used in narrative discourse to construct interactional relationship between the narrator and the audience.

(i) Imperative sentences

The typical function of imperative sentences is to ask someone to do something. In the process of narration, the use of imperative sentences helps construct interaction between the narrator and the audience.

(26) 轮到汉菜上桌,洪承畴,也只能随着太后皇帝的节奏,喝酒夹菜。您想想,一个五大三粗的男人,怎么能跟女人孩子的饭量相比。洪承畴这饭吃不饱,是一定的了。(*This is Beijing*)

Lúndào hàncài shàngzhuō, Hóng Chéngchóu, yě zhǐnéng suízhe tàihòu huángdì de jiézòu, hējiǔ jiācài. <u>Nín xiǎngxiǎng</u>, yī gè wǔdàsāncū de nánrén, zěnme néng gēn nǚrén háizi de fànliàng xiāngbǐ. Hóng Chéngchóu zhè fàn chī-bù-bǎo, shì yīdìng de le.

'When the Han dishes were served onto the table, Hong Chengchou could only drink and eat in accordance with the rhythm of the Emperor and Empress Dowager. <u>Think about it</u>, how could such a big and tall man eat as little as a woman or a child? It is certain that Hong Chengchou would not have enough food to satisfy his hunger.'

(27) 据《清稗类钞》的另一种记载,说慈禧跟慈安俩人原本相安无事。后来慈禧病了,慈安独揽大权。您听清楚喽,是东太后慈安独揽大权。(*This is Beijing*)

Jù "Qīng Bài Lèi Chāo" de lìngyīzhǒng jìzǎi, shuō Cíxǐ gēn Cí'ān liǎ rén yuánběn xiāng'ānwúshì. Hòulái Cíxǐ bìngle, Cí'ān dúlǎn dàquán. <u>Nín tīng qīngchǔ lou</u>, shì Dōng Tàihòu Cí'ān dúlǎn dàquán.

'According to another record in *Collections of Anecdotes in Qing Dynasty*, Cixi was said to get along well enough with Ci'an. Later, when Cixi fell ill, Ci'an took over the power. <u>Take heed</u>, it is the East Empress Dowager Ci'an who seized the power.'

(28) 一提到这个皇上啊,感情生活啊,都说什么,后宫佳丽三千,三宫六院七十二嫔妃啊。这皇上的感情生活,真的这么随心所欲吗?我看不一定。<u>也请您琢磨琢磨</u>,就那光绪皇帝,那感情生活就挺苦的。大老婆,是慈禧太后硬塞给他的。您看那长相,那脾气,就够光绪一呛。(*This is Beijing*)

Yī tídào zhège huángshàng a, gǎnqíng shēnghuó a, dōu shuō shénme, hòugōng jiālì sānqiān, sāngōngliùyuàn qīshí'èr pínfēi a. Zhè huángshàng de gǎnqíng shēnghuó, zhēnde zhème suíxīnsuǒyù ma? Wǒ kàn bùyīdìng. <u>Yě qǐng nín zhuómo~zhuómo</u>, jiù nà Guāngxù Huángdì, nà gǎnqíng shēnghuó jiù tǐng kǔ de. Dà lǎopó, shì Cíxǐ Tàihòu yìng sāi gěi tā de. Nín kàn nà zhǎngxiàng, nà píqì, jiù gòu Guāngxù yī qiàng.

'When it comes to the love life of emperors, what do we say? They are said to have three thousand beauties in the harem and seventy-two concubines in the six courts of the palace. Yet could the emperors really get their own way and take any woman they love? I don't think so. <u>Please think about it</u>. Take Emperor Guangxu for example, his love life was full of bitterness and hardship. His eldest wife was forced on him by Empress Dowager Cixi. Her look and temper alone were enough to make his life unbearable.'

In terms of speech act, an imperative sentence performs the act of request, i.e., a communicative act that requires the participation of the audience. Narration, on the other hand, performs the act of story-telling, which does not depend on the audience's participation.

(ii) Rhetorical questions

A rhetorical question is a question to be answered by the speaker or author self, such as "您猜进来的这个人是谁" ('Guess who this person was?') in example (23) above. For more examples see (29) and (30).

(29) 东厂,咱们都知道,就在王府井的东厂胡同里。但<u>您知道西厂在哪儿吗</u>?我告诉您,在西单一带。(*This is Beijing*)

Dōngchǎng, zánmen dōu zhīdào, jiù zài Wángfǔjǐng de Dōngchǎng Hútòng lǐ. Dàn <u>nín zhīdào Xīchǎng zài nǎ·er ma</u>? Wǒ gàosù nín, zài Xīdān yīdài.

'Dongchang, as we all know, is in Dongchang Hutong in Wangfujing. But <u>do you know</u> where Xichang is? Now I'll tell you, it is somewhere in Xidan.'

(30) 司礼监,现北京市东城区,景山东街吉安所右巷10号,从黄化门街到景山后街一带。刘瑾的主要工作地点,就在现在(的)东城区,景山东街的吉安所右巷10号。明朝那会儿,这是司礼监的所在地。司礼监,是明朝的一个特殊部门,由太监组成。<u>这些太监都干什么呢?</u>这么说吧,小到叫皇上起床,大到代皇帝写口谕,都是司礼监的职责。(*This is Beijing*)

Sīlǐjiān, xiàn Běijīng Shì Dōngchéng Qū, Jǐngshān Dōngjiē Jí'ānsuǒ Yòuxiàng Shíhào, cóng Huánghuàmén Jiē dào Jǐngshān Hòujiē yīdài. Liú Jǐn de zhǔyào gōngzuò dìdiǎn, jiù zài xiànzài (de) Dōngchéng Qū, Jǐngshān Dōngjiē de Jí'ānsuǒ Yòuxiàng Shíhào. Míngcháo nàhuì·er, zhè shì Sīlǐjiān de suǒzàidì. Sīlǐjiān, shì Míngcháo de yī gè tèshū bùmén, yóu tàijiān zǔchéng. <u>Zhèxiē tàijiān dōu gànshénme ne?</u> Zhème shuō ba, xiǎo dào jiào huángshàng qǐchuáng, dà dào dài huángdì xiě kǒuyù, dōushì Sīlǐjiān de zhízé.

'The Emperial Etiquette Office was located at today's No. 10, Ji'ansuo Right Hutong, Jingshan East Street, Dongcheng District, Beijing, covering the area from Huanghua Gate Street to Jingshan Back Street. Liu Jin mainly worked here. In the Ming Dynasty, the Emperial Etiquette Office was located here. The Office, a special organization of the Ming Dynasty, was composed of eunuchs. <u>What did the eunuchs do?</u> Let's put it this way, they were responsible for a wide range of duties, from waking up the emperor to writing dictates on behalf of the emperor.'

In (31) below, there is an imperative sentence "您可别小看这一万块钱。" ('Don't underestimate the value of 10,000 yuan.'), which is followed by a rhetorical question (the underlined) to engage the audience.

(31) 张自忠重视教育,是出了名的。他在天津当市长的时候,不但建立了教育局,还每年给因经费短缺,而面临危机的南开中学拨款1万元。您可别小看这一万块钱。<u>您知道当时的一万元相当于咱们今天多少钱吗?</u>我们大概其算了一下,差不多相当于今天的80万元人民币。由此可见,张自忠将军对教育事业的重视了吧。(*This is Beijing*)

Zhāng Zìzhōng zhòngshì jiàoyù, shì chūle míng de. Tā zài Tiānjīn dāng shìzhǎng de shíhòu, búdàn jiànlìle jiàoyùjú, hái měinián gěi yīn jīngfèi duǎnquē, ér miànlín wēijī de Nánkāi Zhōngxué bōkuǎn yī wàn yuán. Nín kě bié xiǎokàn zhè yī wàn kuài qián. <u>Nín zhīdào dāngshí de yī wàn yuán xiāngdāngyú zánmen jīntiān duōshǎo qián ma?</u> Wǒmen dàgàiqí suànle yīxià, chàbùduō xiāngdāngyú jīntiān de bāshíwàn yuán rénmínbì. Yóucǐkějiàn, Zhāng Zìzhōng jiāngjūn duì jiàoyù shìyè de zhòngshì le ba.

'Zhang Zizhong always attached great importance to education, which is known to all. When he was the mayor of Tianjin, he not only established the Education Bureau, but also allocated 10,000 yuan each year to Nankai Middle School, which was faced with a crisis due to funding shortages. Don't underestimate the value of 10,000 yuan. <u>Do you have any idea how much the 10,000 yuan at that time equals today?</u> A rough calculation tells us that it is worth about 800,000 yuan today. This shows that General Zhang Zizhong did attach great importance to education.'

11.4.2 *Alternating between narration and evaluation*

The interactionality of narrative discourse relies on the frequent alternation between narration and evaluation. The means used in modern spoken narratives are in line with the paradigm of story-telling scripts discussed above, which include the use of verbs of saying to introduce the discourse topic, use of the first person to reveal the speaker, and the choice of second-person pronouns, imperative sentences, and rhetorical sentences to construct interaction with the audience.

There are also some special expressions to alternate between story-telling and evaluation, such as "您想啊" ('Think about it,…') in the following example.

(32) 咱们分析乾隆和和珅的关系，有人呢，得出这么一个结论。说这和珅啊，一辈子光顾着算计别人了，反过头来，被乾隆皇上给算计了。乾隆生前的时候呢，借着和珅的手敛财。等他一死，这财产啊，留给儿子嘉庆了。**您想啊**，<u>一抄家一灭门，这和珅一辈子积的钱，全归嘉庆了，相当于好几个国库啊</u>。这嘉庆，至少少奋斗十年。这正应了那句话啊，红楼梦里，形容王熙凤的，机关算尽太聪明，反断了卿卿性命。(This is Beijing)

Zánmen fēnxī Qiánlóng hé Hé Shēn de guānxì, yǒurén ne, déchū zhème yī gè jiélùn. Shuō zhè Hé Shēn a, yībèizi guāng gùzhe suànjì biérén le, fǎnguòtóulái, bèi Qiánlóng huángshàng gěi suànjì le. Qiánlóng shēngqián de shíhòu ne, jièzhe Hé Shēn de shǒu liǎncái. Děng tā yī sǐ, zhè cáichǎn a, liúgěi érzi Jiāqìng le. **Nín xiǎng a**, <u>yī chāojiā yī mièmén, zhè Hé Shēn yībèizi jī de qián, quán guī Jiāqìng le, xiāngdāngyú hǎo-jǐ-gè guókù a</u>. Zhè Jiāqìng, zhìshǎo shǎo fèndòu shí nián. Zhè zhèng yìngle nà jù huà a, Hónglóumèng lǐ, xíngróng Wáng Xīfèng de, jīguān suànjìn tài cōngmíng, fǎn duànle qīngqīng xìngmìng.

'Let's analyze the relationship between Qianlong and He Shen. Someone has come to such a conclusion: He Shen, who had been scheming against others all his life, fell victim at last to Emperor Qianlong's plot. When Qianlong was alive, he raked in money through the hand of He Shen. As soon as he died, the money was left to his son Jiaqing. **Think about it**, <u>He Shen's properties were confiscated and his entire family were exterminated. The wealth he had accumulated throughout his life went to Jiaqing, which amounted to the wealth of several treasuries</u>. It saved Jiaqing at least ten years' efforts. Just as what is said about Wang Xifeng in the classic **A Dream of Red Mansions**, too much plotting and scheming is the cause of her own undoing.'

In (32), "您想啊" introduces the speaker's comments (the underlined part) on the event he is describing. The use of the imperative sentence with the verb "想" ('think') has made the transition from the narration of the event to the speaker's comments. Example (33) illustrates another special expression.

(33) ……先是当场勃然大怒,但结果呢,在荣禄的一番劝解之后,慈禧还是心一软,把徐致靖的死刑,改判了终身监禁。**您看出来了吧**,<u>这荣禄和慈禧两个人啊,互相扶持,互相帮忙,给足了对方面子,还避了嫌。其中的默契,真是非常人可以理解</u>。(*This is Beijing*)

… Xiānshì dāngchǎng bórándànù, dàn jiéguǒ ne, zài Róng Lù de yīfān quànjiě zhīhòu, Cíxǐ háishì xīn yī ruǎn, bǎ Xú Zhìjìng de sǐxíng, gǎipànle zhōngshēn jiānjìn. **Nín kànchūlái le ba**, <u>zhè Róng Lù hé Cíxǐ liǎng gè rén a, hùxiāng fúchí, hùxiāng bāngmáng, gěizúle duìfāng miànzi, hái bìle xián. Qízhōng de mòqì, zhēnshì fēi chángrén kěyǐ lǐjiě.</u>

'… Cixi flew into a rage on the spot. However, under Rong Lu's persuasion, Cixi eventually relented and changed Xu Zhijing's capital punishment to life imprisonment. **Now you can see**, <u>Rong Lu and Cixi supported and helped each other, showing due respect to the other's feelings and avoiding rousing suspicion at the same time. Such a rapport would seem incomprehensible to ordinary people.</u>'

The expression "您看出来了吧" here means "可见" (kějiàn, 'It can be seen that…'), which leads to the evaluative conclusion on the part of the speaker. While "可见" is a direct means to initiate the speaker's evaluative conclusion, "您看出来了吧" is a pattern expressing inquiry, which renders it more interactional.

Evaluation is different from event narration in that the reference is usually generic (Fang Mei, 2019a). See (34).

(34) 五次来北京,康有为一共七次上书,请求变法。起初根本没人搭理他。俗话说"人微言轻",<u>一个老百姓想跟皇上说上话</u>,太难了。更何况那会儿主事儿的,是光绪皇帝的大姨妈,慈禧太后。(*This is Beijing*)

Wǔ cì lái Běijīng, Kāng Yǒuwéi yīgòng qī cì shàngshū, qǐngqiú biànfǎ. Qǐchū gēnběn méirén dāli tā. Súhuà shuō "rénwēiyánqīng", <u>yī gè lǎobǎixìng xiǎng gēn huángshàng shuō shàng huà</u>, tài nán le. Gènghékuàng nàhuì·er zhǔshì·er de, shì Guāngxù Huángdì de dà yímā, Cíxǐ Tàihòu.

'Kang Youwei had been to Beijing five times, and submitted seven pleas for reformation altogether. At first, he was ignored. As the saying goes, "in one's humble position, one's word does not carry much weight". <u>It is too difficult for a common man to have any chance to speak to the emperor.</u> What's more, it was Emperor Guangxu's aunt, Empress Dowager Cixi, who was in charge at that time.'

226 *Characteristics of traditional narratives*

In (34) above, the referent of "一个老百姓" ('a common man') is not a definite entity in the context, but any person with the status of commoner. Grammatical subjects of "*yi* ('one')+CL+noun" configuration can be replaced by bare nouns, but sentences with such subjects, unlike sentences with "indefinite NP subjects", cannot be rewritten as *you*-sentences (Fan Jiyan, 1985).

(35) 只可惜,此次承德消暑游,对于咸丰来说,只能用四个字概括,叫作"有去无回"。咸丰十一年七月十七,慈安、慈禧成了寡妇了。<u>一个男人倒下去,两个女人站起来</u>。从此以后,慈安、慈禧手拉手,肩并肩,联合恭亲王,灭了八大辅臣。怀揣"同道堂""御赏"两枚大印,抱着孩子,走上了清末政治舞台。(*This is Beijing*)

Zhǐ kěxī, cǐ cì Chéngdé xiāoshǔ yóu, duìyú Xiánfēng láishuō, zhǐnéng yòng sì gè zì gàikuò, jiàozuò "yǒuqùwúhuí". Xiánfēng shíyī nián qīyuè shíqī, Cí'ān(,) Cíxǐ chéngle guǎfù le. <u>Yī gè nánrén dǎo-xiàqù, liǎng gè nǚrén zhàn-qǐlái</u>. Cóngcǐ yǐhòu, Cí'ān(,) Cíxǐ shǒulāshǒu, jiānbìngjiān, liánhé Gōng Qīnwáng, mièle bā dà fǔchén. Huáichuāi "Tóngdàotáng" "Yùshǎng" liǎng méi dàyìn, bàozhe háizi, zǒushàngle Qīng mò zhèngzhì wǔtái.

'It is a pity that for Xianfeng, this summer tour to Chengde can only be summarized as "a one-way trip". On July 17, 1861, Ci'an and Cixi were widowed. <u>As one man fell, two women stood up</u>. From then on, Ci'an and Cixi, hand in hand and shoulder to shoulder, wiped out the eight ministers with the help of Prince Gong. With the two imperial seals of "Tongdao Hall" and "Imperial Appreciation" in hand and a child in their arms, the two empresses stepped onto the political stage of the late Qing Dynasty.'

Although in isolation "一个男人倒下去" ('a man fell') can be rewritten as a *you*-sentence (i.e., "有一个男人倒下去"), the above context does not license this rewriting.

Sentences with "*yi* ('one')+CL+noun" subjects have the function of cutting off the topic chain, which enables them to occur when comments are to be made on a known entity. See (36) and (37) for illustration.

(36) 清史稿上说,张廷玉,仗着自己是三朝元老,要这要那,患得患失。却也有人说,乾隆心胸狭窄,嫉贤妒能。**君臣的事情**,自古就没有对错。张廷玉为大清朝贡献了一辈子,不可能因为乾隆朝的官方评价,就葬送了他一世的清白。即便如史书记载,真是倚老卖老,患得患失了,转过头来想一想,<u>一个年近古稀之人</u>,奉献了一辈子,也谨慎了一辈子。好不容易鼓起勇气,想为自己争取点什么,又有何罪过呢。(*This is Beijing*)

Qīngshǐ gǎo shàng shuō, Zhāng Tíngyù, zhàngzhe zìjǐ shì sāncháo yuánlǎo, yào zhè yào nà, huàndéhuànshī. Què yě yǒurén shuō, Qiánlóng xīnxiōngxiázhǎi, jíxiándùnéng. **Jūnchén de shìqíng**, zìgǔ jiù méiyǒu duìcuò. Zhāng Tíngyù wèi dà Qīngcháo gòngxiànle yībèizi, bù kěnéng yīnwèi Qiánlóng cháo de guānfāng píngjià, jiù zàngsòngle tā yī shì de qīngbái. Jíbiàn rú shǐshū jìzǎi, zhēnshì yǐlǎomàilǎo, huàndéhuànshī le, zhuǎnguòtóulái xiǎng-yī-xiǎng, **yī gè nián jìn gǔxī zhī rén**, fèngxiànle yībèizi, yě jǐnshènle yībèizi. Hǎo-bù-róngyì gǔqǐ yǒngqì, xiǎng wèi zìjǐ zhēngqǔ diǎn shénme, yòu yǒu hé zuìguò ne.

'According to the records in Qing History, Zhang Tingyu, a minister to three emperors, was determined to have his own way, mindful of his own gains and losses. However, some people also thought that Qianlong was narrow-minded and jealous of talents. There has been no right or wrong in matters **concerning the emperors and their ministers** since ancient times. Zhang Tingyu had devoted his entire life to the Qing monarchy, and it is impossible for the official evaluation of the Qianlong monarchy to smear his innocence and reputation. Even if as recorded in the history books, he became self-conceited because of his seniority, only worrying about his own gains and losses, so what? Come to think of it, **an almost-seventy-year-old man, dedicated his whole life to the monarchy and being prudent for a lifetime, finally mustered up courage to grab something for himself, what's wrong with it?**'

In the above example, when the first evaluation appears, the noun phrase "君臣的事情" ('matters concerning the emperors and their ministers') is used, which is generic in reference, and accordingly the subsequent predicate "自古就没有对错" ('there is no right or wrong since ancient times') is in the simple present tense. Later on in (36), the "*yi* ('one')+CL+noun" phrase "一个年近古稀之人" ('an almost-seventy-year-old man') occurs. Although it can be understood as Zhang Tingyu, the topic entity of the previous stretch of discourse, here the speaker is no longer narrating the person and his behavior, but is ready to make comments on him. The speaker is using a marked syntactic form "*yi* ('one')+CL+noun" to differentiate in his own speech two distinct speech acts, narration and evaluation (see Fang Mei, 2019a).

(37) 说起宣武区的菜市口,给人印象最深的,就得数清朝时候的刑场了。但今天,我们要给您叨的,是菜市口另外一个身份,奸相严嵩的户口所在地,丞相胡同。菜市口菜市口,指的就是这个路口。路口南边的菜市口胡同,便是明朝大奸臣,严嵩住的地方。过去,这儿叫丞相胡同。……严嵩住的宅子,**究竟有多大呢?您琢磨琢磨吧**。现在的菜市口南大街,就是过去的丞相胡同。就算当年的胡同没有现在的大马路这么宽,那咱就按照单向车道的宽窄算。甭管是占地面积,还是使用面积,也都不算小了吧。**一个丞相住在半条菜市口大街上**,倒也是无可厚非的事儿。所以咱也没有必要,追究人家不明财产的来历。(*This is Beijing*)

Shuōqǐ Xuānwǔ Qū de Càishìkǒu, gěi rén yìnxiàng zuìshēn de, jiù děi shǔ Qīngcháo shíhòu de xíngchǎng le. Dàn jīntiān, wǒmen yào gěi nín niàndao de, shì Càishìkǒu lìngwài yī gè shēnfèn, jiānxiàng Yán Sōng de hùkǒu suǒzàidì, Chéngxiàng Hútòng. Càishìkǒu Càishìkǒu, zhǐ de

228 *Characteristics of traditional narratives*

jiùshì zhège lùkǒu. Lùkǒu nánbian de Càishìkǒu Hútòng, biànshì Míng-cháo dà jiānchén, Yán Sōng zhù de dìfāng. Guòqù, zhè·er jiào Chéngxiàng Hútòng. ... Yán Sōng zhù de zháizi, **jiūjìng yǒu duōdà ne? Nín zuómo~zuómo ba**. Xiànzài de Càishìkǒu Nándàjiē, jiùshì guòqù de Chéngxiàng Hútòng. Jiùsuàn dāngnián de hútòng méiyǒu xiànzài de dàmǎlù zhème kuān, nà **zán** jiù ànzhào dānxiàng chēdào de kuānzhǎi suàn. Béngguǎn shì zhàndì miànjī, háishì shǐyòng miànjī, yě dōu bú suàn xiǎo le ba. **Yī gè chéngxiàng** zhù zài bàntiáo Càishìkǒu Dàjiē shàng, dào yě shì wúkěhòufēi de shì·er. Suǒyǐ **zán** yě méiyǒu bìyào, zhuī-jiū rénjiā bùmíng cáichǎn de láilì.

'**Speaking of** Caishikou in Xuanwu District, the most interesting part of it is the execution ground of the Qing Dynasty. But today, what we want to tell you is another identity of Caishikou, the Prime Minister Hutong, the former residence of the treacherous minister Yan Song. Caishikou, literally "crossing at the food market", refers to this intersection. Caishikou Hutong on the south side of the intersection was where Yan Song, the treacherous minister of the Ming Dynasty, lived. In the past, this place was called Prime Minister Hutong. ... **How big is the residence** where Yan Song used to live? **Think about it**. The current Caishikou South Street is the former Prime Minister Hutong. It is true that the hutongs back then were not as wide as the current main roads. Yet even if **we** measure it according to the width of a one-way lane, the minister's residence is big enough, no matter in terms of its coverage area or its net size. There is nothing wrong with a Prime Minister taking up half of the Caishikou street as his residence. And there is no need for **us** to investigate the unidentified sources of his property.'

In this example, the paragraph initial "说起" ('speaking of') introduces the topic Caishikou, which is followed by a rhetorical question ("究竟有多大呢？"), an imperative sentence ("您琢磨琢磨吧。"), and the inclusive first-person pronoun "咱", to establish interaction with the audience. Then the excerpt uses an indefinite-subject sentence ("一个丞相住在半条菜市口大街上，倒也是无可厚非的事儿") to end narration and in the meanwhile initiate evaluation. Such commentary sentences that are embedded in narration do not reflect the course of events, which explains why they are usually in the simple present tense (see Fang Mei, 2019a).

11.5 Narrator orientation and lexical grammaticalization

11.5.1 *Macrosyntactic conjunctions*

A large number of macrosyntactic conjunctions (see Chao, 1968) are derived from zero-subject clauses, which can even be understood as the grammaticalization of the predicate verb itself. In discussing conjunctions,

Chao (1968, p. 794) makes the point that there is a class of macrosyntactic conjunctions that overlap with reduced main clauses.

There have been a variety of studies in this line. Timewise, Dong Xiufang (2007) discusses lexicalization and the formation of discourse markers; Luo Yaohua and Niu Li (2009) elaborate the grammaticalization of "再说" (zàishuō, 'what's more', literally 'say again'); Dong Xiufang (2010) argues that the discourse marker "我告诉你" (wǒ gàosù nǐ, 'I tell you') is derived from a complete clause; and Cao Xiuling (2010) delineates the evolution process from subject-predicate structures to discourse markers.

The "reduced main clause" more often than not is a metadiscourse expression containing 说 (shuō, 'say'), such as 听说 (tīngshuō, 'it's heard'), 据说 (jùshuō, 'it's said'), 俗话说 (súhuàshuō, 'as the saying goes'), 常言说 (chángyán shuō, 'as the saying goes'), 按理说 (ànlǐ shuō, 'as the reason goes'), 按说 (ànshuō, 'as the reason goes'), 照说 (zhào shuō, 'as the reason goes'), 依我说 (yī wǒ shuō, 'in my opinion'), 照我说 (zhào wǒ shuō, 'in my opinion'), 比如说 (bǐrú shuō, 'for example'), 譬如说 (pìrú shuō, 'for example'), 换言之 (huànyánzhī, 'in other words'), 换句话说 (huàn jù huà shuō, 'to put it differently'), 简单地说 (jiǎndān de shuō, 'to put it simply'), 就是说 (jiùshì shuō, 'that is to say'), 相对来说 (xiāngduì lái shuō, 'relatively speaking'), 反过来说 (fǎn guòlái shuō, 'to put it the other way around'), 顺便说一下 (shùnbiàn shuō yīxià, 'by the way/in passing'), 总的来说 (zǒng de lái shuō, 'in general'), 总起来说 (zǒng qǐlái shuō, 'in general'), 总体上说 (zǒngtǐshàng shuō, 'in general'), 一般来说 (yībān láishuō, 'in general'), 一般说来 (yībān shuō lái, 'generally speaking'), 不用说 (bùyòng shuō, 'needless to say'), 老实说 (lǎoshí shuō, 'honestly speaking'), 不瞒你说 (bù mán nǐ shuō, 'to be frank with you'), 说实在的 (shuō shízài de, 'to be frank with you'), 说真的 (shuō zhēnde, 'to tell you the truth'), 说到底 (shuō dàodǐ, 'ultimately'), 说心里话 (shuō xīnlǐ huà, 'to speak from the heart'), 再(者)说 (zài (zhě) shuō, 'what's more'), 应当说 (yīngdāng shuō, 'should say'), 可以说 (kěyǐ shuō, 'it can be said'), 不消说 (bùxiāo shuō, 'needless to say'), 不管怎么说 (bùguǎn zěnme shuō, 'in any case'), 具体说 (jùtǐ shuō, 'specifically speaking'), 这么说 (zhème shuō, 'in this way'), 说来 (shuō lái, 'speaking of'), etc. The verb of speech in the above-mentioned expressions occurs as a lexical component, having lost its basic grammatical functions as a verb. For example, it cannot be followed by tense-aspect markers such as *-le*, *-zhe*, *-guo*, *-laizhe*, etc.; nor can it co-occur with verbal classifiers (e.g., 一次 [yīcì, 'once']). In terms of their grammatical performance, these metadiscourse expressions can be understood as the grammaticalization of the verb itself. Cross-linguistically, the grammaticalization of "say" evolves towards the evidential category (Heine and Kuteva, 2002, p. 256; Rett and Murray, 2013), which renders the functional extension of Chinese speech verbs to metadiscourse particularly important.

Another group of macrosyntactic conjunctions consists of the expressions with visual verbs, such as 却见 (quèjiàn, 'only to see'), 但见 (dànjiàn, 'only to see'), 只见 (zhǐjiàn, 'only see'), 可见 (kějiàn, 'it can be seen'), etc.

Examine 可见 first. In modern spoken Chinese, 可见 is used to elicit a general assessment on the part of the narrator. It can be prosodically independent or even followed by a mood particle. See the following examples for illustration.

(38) 这座门是乾隆在修完圆明园之后，顺手儿，在这儿建的。其实圆明园里，有很多中西结合的建筑。**可见**乾隆是一个思想比较开放、审美比较时尚的皇帝。这样的西洋门，在北京只有两座。(*This is Beijing*)

Zhè zuò mén shì Qiánlóng zài xiūwán Yuánmíngyuán zhīhòu, shùnshǒu·er, zài zhè·er jiàn de. Qíshí Yuánmíngyuán lǐ, yǒu hěnduō zhōngxī jiéhé de jiànzhù. **Kějiàn** Qiánlóng shì yī gè sīxiǎng bǐjiào kāifàng(,) shěnměi bǐjiào shíshàng de huángdì. Zhèyàng de xīyáng mén, zài Běijīng zhǐyǒu liǎng zuò.

'This gate was built by Qianlong right after the construction of the Winter Palace without much further trouble. In fact, there are many buildings of both Chinese and Western styles in the Winter Palace, **from which it can be seen** that Qianlong was an emperor with an open mind and a fashionable aesthetic perception. There are only two Western-style gates in Beijing.'

(39) 在旧社会，西服革履者，与拉车卖浆的同桌共饮，并无贵贱之分。由此**可见**，豆汁儿，确实是贫富相宜，雅俗共赏，普通得不能再普通的食品了。(*This is Beijing*)

Zài jiùshèhuì, xīfúgélǚ zhě, yǔ lāchē màijiāng de tóngzhuō gòngyǐn, bìng wú guìjiàn zhī fēn. Yóucǐ **kějiàn**, dòuzhī·er, quèshí shì pínfù xiāngyí, yǎsúgòngshǎng, pǔtōng de bùnéng zài pǔtōng de shípǐn le.

'In the old society, people in suits and leather shoes would drink and eat at the same table with rickshaw boys and peddlers, disregarding the distinction between high and low classes. **It can be seen** that soybean juice is indeed a common food, suitable for both the rich and the poor, appealing to both refined and popular taste.'

(40) 康有为第一次来北京，是在25岁那年，来参加乡试。到1898年戊戌变法失败，他在北京与外地之间，一共打了五个来回儿。但住的地方，只有一个，就是宣武区，米市胡同43号的南海会馆。咱以前介绍过不少北漂的名人，刚来北京的时候，都住会馆。但人家到最后，多少都能，再置办上一两套房子。康有为在北京，却只有南海会馆这么一个落脚之处。**可见**，这么多年，康先生混得不咋地。(*This is Beijing*)

Kāng Yǒuwéi dìyīcì lái Běijīng, shì zài 25 suì nànián, lái cānjiā xiāngshì. Dào 1898 nián Wùxū Biànfǎ shībài, tā zài Běijīng yǔ wàidì zhījiān, yīgòng dǎle wǔgè láihuí·er. Dàn zhù de dìfang, zhǐyǒu yī gè, jiùshì Xuānwǔ Qū, Mǐshì Hútòng 43 hào de Nánhǎi Huìguǎn. Zán yǐqián jièshàoguò bùshǎo běipiāo de míngrén, gānglái Běijīng de shíhòu, dōu zhù huìguǎn. Dàn rénjiā dào zuìhòu, duōshǎo dōu néng, zài zhìbàn shàng yī-liǎngtào fángzi. Kāng Yǒuwéi zài Běijīng, què zhǐyǒu Nánhǎi Huìguǎn zhème yī gè luòjiǎo zhī chù. **Kějiàn**, zhème duō nián, Kāng xiānsheng hùnde bùzǎdì.

'Kang Youwei came to Beijing for the first time, when he was 25 years old to take the provincial examination. By 1898, when the Reform Movement failed, he had made five round trips to and from Beijing. But each time he stayed at the same place, the Nanhai Guild Hall at No. 43 Mishi Hutong, Xuanwu District. As we have mentioned before, many celebrities would stay at the guild hall when they came to Beijing for the first time. But in the end, they could manage to buy one or two houses of their own. Yet Kang Youwei had nowhere else but the Hall to live in. **It can be seen** that for so many years, Mr. Kang had not been doing very well.'

(41) 很多人认为这四扇石屏风啊，是圆明园的遗物。因为大家看到夹镜和垂虹两个字，就会想到圆明园四景之一，叫作夹镜鸣琴。它呢是出自李白的两句诗，叫作"两湖夹明镜，双桥落彩虹"。所以很多书，想当然把它列为到圆明园的遗物当中了。您看完前两句后，就应该能想到，它是描写舒春园石舫周围的景色的。那么它的建造年代，应该是乾隆年间，由和珅建造的。可是圆明园呢是雍正时期建造的，**可见啊**，它不是圆明园的遗物。(*This is Beijing*)

Hěnduō rén rènwéi zhè sì shàn shí píngfēng a, shì Yuánmíngyuán de yíwù. Yīnwèi dàjiā kàndào jiájìng hé chuíhóng liǎng gè zì, jiùhuì xiǎngdào Yuánmíngyuán sìjǐng zhīyī, jiàozuò Jiájìng Míngqín. Tā ne shì chūzì Lǐ Bái de liǎng jù shī, jiàozuò "liǎnghú jiá míngjìng, shuāngqiáo luò cǎihóng". Suǒyǐ hěnduō shū, xiǎngdāngrán bǎ tā lièwéi dào Yuánmíngyuán de yíwù dāngzhōng le. Nín kànwán qián liǎng jù hòu, jiù yīnggāi néng xiǎngdào, tā shì miáoxiě Shūchūnyuán Shífǎng zhōuwéi de jǐngsè de. Nàme tā de jiànzào niándài, yīnggāi shì Qiánlóng niánjiān, yóu Hé Shēn jiànzào de. Kěshì Yuánmíngyuán ne shì Yōngzhèng shíqī jiànzào de, **kějiàn a**, tā búshì Yuánmíngyuán de yíwù.

'Many people think that these four stone screens are relics of the Winter Palace. Because whenever we see the words "jiajing" ('mirror-in-between') and "chuihong" ('falling rainbow'), we will think of one of the four sceneries in the Winter Palace, which is called "Jianjing Mingqin" ('Mirror-in-between and Gurgling Waterfall'). It is from two lines of Li Bai's poem, "A lake like a mirror lying in between two rivers, the two bridges like rainbows falling down from heaven." So in many books, the stone screens are listed as the relics of the Winter Palace without much thinking. After reading the two lines of the poem, you should be able to realize that the scenery described is around the Marble Boat in Shuchun Garden, which means that it was built by He Shen during the Qianlong period. But the Winter Palace was built during the Yongzheng period. So **it can be seen** that the screens are not relics of the Winter Palace.'

In modern Chinese, 只见 has replaced 但见 to introduce a new situation and at the same time draw the reader's attention to it (see Dong Xiufang, 2007).

(42) 9日上午9时04分,美国俄克拉何马城中心,"轰"的一声巨响,**只见**火光冲天,浓烟滚滚,响声和震动波及数十英里之外。

Jiǔ rì shàngwǔ jiǔ shí língsì fēn, Měiguó Ékèlāhémǎ chéng zhōngxīn, "hōng" de yī shēng jùxiǎng, **zhǐjiàn** huǒguāngchōngtiān, nóngyān gǔngǔn, xiǎngshēng hé zhèndòng bōjí shù shí yīnglǐ zhī wài.

'At 9:04 a.m. on the 9th, there came a loud "bang" at the center of Oklahoma City, the United States, **only to see** fires soaring into the sky, thick smoke billowing, noise and vibration spreading dozens of miles away.'

(43) 5时15分,护卫队长一声令下,军乐队高奏国歌,**只见**升旗手一挥手,五星红旗在千万双眼睛的注目礼中冉冉上升。

Wǔ shí shíwǔ fēn, hùwèi duìzhǎng yīshēnglìngxià, jūnyuèduì gāozòu guógē, **zhǐjiàn** shēngqíshǒu yī huīshǒu, wǔxīnghóngqí zài qiānwàn shuāng yǎnjīng de zhùmùlǐ zhōng rǎnrǎn shàngshēng.

'At 5:15, on the words of command from the captain of the National Flag Guards, the military band began to play the national anthem. **One could see** the flag-raiser waved his hand, and the five-star red flag rose slowly in thousands of people's gaze of salute.'

From the above analysis, it is not difficult to see that there are functional differences in the expressions that are derived from verb clauses, even though they contain the same verb. Thus used 只见 is an engagement marker, which is utilized in discourse to direct the attention of the addressee to something newly introduced into the discourse.

11.5.2 Functional differences

The macrosyntactic conjunctions that originate from reduced main clauses subject their emergence to live or simulated live narration, which is manifested in: (a) the discourse frame in which the speaker is made visible, (b) the alternation between narration and evaluation, and (c) high-frequency interaction.

In terms of discourse frame marking, the macrosyntactic conjunctions can be broadly divided into three different functional categories: 1) plot marking: opening, transition; 2) topic marking: establishment, continuation, shift; and 3) speech act marking: narration (inside the event), evaluation (outside the event).

Examine some of the expressions described above:

"单说" (dānshuō, 'just say'): frame marker, used to open plot or establish discourse topic;

"只见" (zhǐjiàn, 'only see'): engagement marker, prompting the addressee or the reader to pay attention to the important episode that follows;

"可见" (kějiàn, 'it can be seen'): frame marker, to mark the transition from narration to evaluation and to lead in the speaker's summary of what has been narrated; used as inter-clausal as well as macrosyntactic conjunction;

"看来" (kànlái, 'it seems'): frame marker, to mark the transition from narration to evaluation and to lead in the speaker's comments on what he or she has said; used as macrosyntactic conjunction only.

The "say" category of metadiscourse, i.e., words and expressions containing 说 or morphemes of a similar meaning, such as 话说 (huàshuō, 'speaking of'), 单说 (dānshuō, 'just say'), and 再说 (zàishuō, 'say again), always maintains the function of denoting the narrator orientation.

The "see" category of metadiscourse performs two functions: 1) to express the development from the participant orientation to the omniscient orientation, such as 只见 (zhǐjiàn, 'only see'); 2) to express the narrator orientation and in turn function as a conjunction to indicate summarization.

Story-telling is an important form of oral folk literature, and its narrative style represents a typical pattern of Chinese narrative discourse. The interactional nature of story-telling scripts provides an important basis for examining the influence of interactional communication on the evolution of the Chinese language.

11.6 Summary

Traditional novels are mostly derived from story-telling scripts. As the handy guide of narration, the scripts have the distinctive feature of on-siteness in both narrative patterning and orientation taking. In terms of speech act, the telling of the story is intertwined with the narrator's evaluation; in terms of narrative orientation, the character orientation is interlaced with the narrator orientation. This narrative tradition has exerted an important influence on the organization of the narrative discourse of future generations, which is mainly manifested in three aspects.

First, the narrative discourse contains a large number of interactional expressions to achieve the on-site effect.

Second, the narrative orientation is reflected through the choice of person, metadiscourse, and some sentence patterns with interactional functions.

Third, a variety of discourse frame markers are derived from zero-subject clauses with verbal, visual, and epistemic verbs as the predicates. They are used to open and transit the plot; to establish, continue, or shift the topic; or to mark the alternation between the act of story-telling and the act of evaluating.

Since story-telling is conducted in a live context, the narrator does not need to syntactically encode his role as a participant, which, we argue, results in a lack of syntactic encoding of the narrator role. The interactional context is then a precondition for the emergence of reduced clauses serving as discourse-connecting elements.

In story-telling, the script is no more than a record of the interactional scene; that is, "I write what I say" and "I write as I say". Thus the syntactic encoding of the grammatical subject seems not so important, which actually has long been taken as a feature of Chinese grammar. Here we would argue that it is a grammatical feature predetermined by the communicative scene and the communicative mode; that is, it is a manifestation of how syntax is shaped by communicative needs.

Notes

1 The late-Qing corpus of Beijing dialect cited in this chapter is based on *A Collection of Rare Documents of Early Beijing Dialect* (《早期北京话珍稀文献集成》) edited by Liu Yun, a volume in the book serial *Rare Books and Classics of Early Beijing Dialect: Annotations and Studies* (《早期北京话珍本典籍校释与研究》) edited by Wang Hongjun, Guo Rui and Liu Yun (Peking University Press, 2018). The modern Beijing dialect corpus consists of Lao She's novels and plays. The contemporary Beijing dialect corpus is composed of: 1) the narration of the television series *This Is Beijing*, and 2) novels and essays by Beijing writers.
2 In today's cross-talk narration, it is normally the case for the leading role to tell the story and the supporting role to make comments on the side, i.e., saying the commentary as bracketed in examples (11) to (13).
3 Hyland's model recognizes that metadiscourse is comprised of two dimensions of interaction: the interactive, which helps to guide the reader through the text; and the interactional, which involves the reader in the text.

The sources of the interactive dimension include:

Transitions: express relations between main clauses, e.g., *in addition, but, thus, and*
Frame markers: refer to discourse acts, sequences or stages, e.g., *finally, to conclude, my purpose is*
Endophoric markers: refer to information in other parts of the text, e.g., *noted above*
Evidential: refer to information from other texts, e.g., *according to X, Z states*
Code glosses: elaborate propositional meanings, e.g., *namely, such as, in other words*

The sources of the interactional dimension include:

Hedges: withhold commitment and open dialogue, e.g., *might, perhaps, possible, about*
Boosters: emphasize certainty or close dialogue, e.g., *in fact, definitely, it is clear that*
Attitude markers: express writer's attitude to proposition, e.g., *unfortunately, I agree, surprisingly*
Self-mentions: explicit reference to author(s), e.g., *I, we, my, me, our*
Engagement markers: explicitly build relationship with reader, e.g., *consider, note, you can see that*

(adapted from Hyland, 2005, p. 49)

Concluding remarks

As a non-morphological language, Chinese has its own syntactic integration rules, which are mostly reflected in discourse grammar. This book ends up with the following major findings.

Firstly, a considerable number of subject omissions in Chinese discourse are not only devices for discourse coherence, but also means of syntactic reduction, cataphoric zero-subject clauses being a typical case.

Secondly, Chinese has very limited syntactic constraints on the syntactic composition of the subject as well as the relationship between the subject and its predicate. The subject is also the topic in Chinese, and it can occur in the verb form directly, unlike morphological languages that allow only noun phrases or subject clauses to occur in this syntactic slot. Nonetheless, verbal expressions need to undergo the process of desentientialization to gain the topic status in Chinese discourse. In writing, it may occur in the "N *de* V" structure. In speech, the addition of the indicative 这 (zhè, 'this') to the left margin of a clause can make it lose self-sufficiency; another option is to place the verb in the verb-reduplication construction.

Thirdly, some seemingly unusual syntactic phenomena can be more accurately explained if one looks beyond the individual sentence to the actual context in which the syntactic phenomena appear. For example, the NP of "*yi* ('one') + CL + noun" in Chinese has long been regarded as parallel to the English "indefinite article + noun" in reference, but an examination of Chinese discourse shows that it is actually no equivalent to its English "counterpart". Instead, it plays a unique role in the topic chain. The same is also true for the "N *de* V" structure and verb reduplication.

Fourthly, Chinese discourse conjunctives are mainly derived from verbs of saying, going through a clear process of grammaticalization from content words to macro-syntactic conjunctions, which is closely related to the tradition of Chinese oral literature.

Taking functional linguistics as the theoretical orientation and combining functional linguistic theories with Chinese language facts, this book explores a number of issues: discourse phenomena and syntactic integration, the information status and discourse function of some special syntactic structures, the emergence of the discourse function of metadiscourse, to name but a few. The book endeavors to link discourse functions with syntactico-semantic laws to reveal their inner relationship; it also unveils the law of information packaging that underlies different structural forms. In a nutshell, it explores the functional motives behind grammatical phenomena.

The book observes Chinese grammatical patterns in their discourse use. It is anticipated that this usage-based approach can further deepen the understanding of Chinese grammatical laws.

Afterword to the Chinese Edition

This research is supported by the Innovation Project of the Chinese Academy of Social Sciences, and is a phased achievement of "Syntax and Semantics of Modern Chinese", a key discipline construction project of the Chinese Academy of Social Sciences.

The contents of the book have been presented as academic conference papers and have received comments and suggestions from a number of conference participants. Special thanks to the following scholars: Wei-Tien Dylan Tsai, Chen Ping, Chen Yi, Feng Shengli, Guo Rui, Jin Lixin, Li Wei, Lee Hun Tak Thomas, Li Zongjiang, Li Xianyin, Liu Dawei, Liu Lening, Meichun Liu, Lu Bingfu, Kang Kwong Luke, Lu Jianming, Pan Haihua, Ren Ying, Shao Jingmin, Shen Jiaxuan, Shi Chunhong, Shi Dingxu, Shi Jinsheng, Tao Hongyin, Wan Quan, Wang Canlong, Wang Xiuli, Zhang Bojiang, Zhang Li, Zhang Wangxi, Zhang Yisheng, Zhu Qingzhi, Zhu Keyi, Xing Xin, Xu Liejiong, and Xu Yangchun.

Thanks are also due to my postdoctoral fellows Tian Ting and Wang Wenying, and my PhD students Fang Di and Guan Yue, for their reading and proofreading the full text of the manuscript.

Appendix

Chart of Chinese Pinyin and International Phonetic Alphabet (IPA)

Consonants

Pinyin	IPA	Pinyin	IPA	Pinyin	IPA
b	[p]	g	[k]	s	[s]
p	[pʰ]	k	[kʰ]	zh	[tʂ]
m	[m]	h	[x]	ch	[tʂʰ]
f	[f]	j	[tɕ]	sh	[ʂ]
d	[t]	q	[tɕʰ]	r	[ʐ] or [ɻ]
t	[tʰ]	x	[ɕ]	y	[j]
n	[n]	z	[ts]	w	[w]
l	[l]	c	[tsʰ]	ng	[ŋ]

Monophthong vowels

Pinyin	IPA	Pinyin	IPA	Pinyin	IPA
a	[A]	e	[ɤ]	u	[u]
o	[o]	i	[i]	ü	[y]

Vowel glides

Pinyin	IPA	Pinyin	IPA	Pinyin	IPA
ai	[ai]	ing	[iŋ]	uai	[uai]
ei	[ei]	ia	[ia]	ui (uei)	[uei]
ao	[au]	iao	[iau]	uan	[uan]
ou	[ou]	ian	[iæn]	uang	[uaŋ]
an	[an]	iang	[iaŋ]	un (uen)	[uən]
en	[ən]	ie	[iɛ]	ueng	[uəŋ]
in	[in]	iong	[yŋ]	üe	[yɛ]
ang	[aŋ]	iou	[iou]	üan	[yæn]
eng	[əŋ]	ua	[ua]	ün	[yn]
ong	[uŋ]	uo	[uo]	ng	[ŋ]

References

Sources in Chinese

Bao, Huaiqiao & Lin, Maocan (鲍怀翘, 林茂灿) (eds.). (2014). *An introduction to experimental phonetics* (《实验语音学概要》) (revised edition, first edition edited by Wu Zongji & Lin Maocan). Beijing: Peking University Press.

Cao, Fengfu (曹逢甫). (1990/2005). *Sentence and clause structure in Chinese: A functional perspective* (《汉语的句子与子句结构》). Translated by Wang Jing. Beijing: Beijing Language and Culture University Press.

Cao, Xiuling (曹秀玲). (2010). From subject-predicate structure to discourse marker – Grammaticalization of "*wo/ni* V" (从主谓结构到话语标记——"我/你V"的语法化及相关问题). *Chinese Language Learning* (《汉语学习》), No. 5: 38–50.

Chen, Guohua, & Wang, Jianguo (陈国华, 王建国). (2010). Unmarked non-subject topics in Chinese (汉语的无标记非主语话题). *Chinese Teaching in the World* (《世界汉语教学》), No. 3: 310–24.

Chen, Jing, & Gao, Yuan (陈静, 高远). (2000). Is Chinese a topic-prominent language? (汉语是主题突出型语言吗?). *Foreign Languages and Their Teaching* (《外语与外语教学》), No. 5: 11–4.

Chen, Manhua (陈满华). (2010). The non-cataphoric zero subject clause motivated by background information packaging (由背景化触发的非反指零形主语小句). *Studies of the Chinese Language* (《中国语文》), No. 5: 413–25+479-80.

Chen, Peiling, & Tao, Hongyin (陈佩玲, 陶红印). (1998). Grammatical and prosodic patterns in Taiwan Mandarin narrative discourse (台湾官话叙事体中韵律单位的语法构成及其规律初探). *Studies in Language and Linguistics* (《语言研究》), No. 1: 1–22.

Chen, Ping (陈平). (1987a). Four dichotomies concerning nominal elements in Chinese (释汉语中与名词性成分相关的四组概念). *Studies of the Chinese Language* (《中国语文》), No. 2: 81–92.

Chen, Ping (陈平). (1987b). On discourse analysis (话语分析说略). *Language Teaching and Research* (《语言教学与研究》), No. 3: 4–20.

Chen, Ping (陈平). (1987c). A discourse analysis of zero anaphora in Chinese (汉语零形回指的话语分析). *Studies of the Chinese Language* (《中国语文》), No. 5: 363–378. (Also seen in Chen Ping [1991/2017])

Chen, Ping (陈平). (1991/2017). *Modern linguistic studies-Theories, methods and facts* (《现代语言学研究——理论·方法与事实》). Chongqing: Chongqing Publishing House. (Republished in 2017 by the Commercial Press with the title *The form, meaning and function of Chinese* 《[汉语的形式、意义与功能]》)

Chen, Ping (陈平). (2004a). Double NP constructions and topic-comment articulation in Chinese (《汉语双项名词句与话题陈述结构》). *Studies of the Chinese Language* (《中国语文》), No. 6: 493–507.

Chen, Qinghan (陈庆汉). (2002). Review of the research on the grammatical quality of the headword "V" in the "N-de-V" phrase ("N的V"短语中心语"V"语法性质研究述评). *Chinese Language Learning* (《汉语学习》), No. 5: 53–7.

Chen, Yi (陈一). (2008). Reclassification of antithetic expressions and its significance (对举表达式的再分类及其意义). *Journal of Chinese Linguistics* (《中国语言学报》), No. 13, 19–31. Beijing: The Commerical Press.

Chen, Ying, & Chen, Yi (陈颖, 陈一). (2010). The evolution mechanisms and pragmatic functions of the fixed phrase *shuō shì* (固化结构"说是"的演化机制及其语用功能). *Chinese Teaching in the World* (《世界汉语教学》), No. 4: 505–13.

Chen, Yudong, & Ma, Renfeng (陈玉东, 马仁凤). (2016). An analysis of the prosodic features of turn-Taking in talk show discourse – A case study of A Date with Luyu (谈话节目话轮转换的韵律特征分析——以〈鲁豫有约〉为例). In Fang Mei (ed.), *Interactional Linguistics and Chinese language studies I* (《互动语言学与汉语研究第》一辑). Beijing: World Publishing Corporation.

Chu, Chauncey (屈承熹). (1991). The discourse function of Chinese Adverbs (汉语副词的篇章功能). *Language Teaching and Research* (《语言教学与研究》), No. 2: 64–78.

Chu, Chauncey (屈承熹). (2000). Representation of topic and pragmatic relations (话题的表达形式与语用关系). *Studies of Modern Chinese* (《现代中国语研究》) (Japan), No. 1.

Deng, Lingyun (邓凌云). (2005). The analysis of the connective measurement between the clauses in a running sentence (简析流水句的小句间联结手段). *Journal of Hunan University of Science and Engineering* (《湖南科技学院学报》), No. 8: 116–18.

Dong, Xiufang (董秀芳). (2003a). On the lexicalization of "X *shuo*" ("X说"的词汇化). *Linguistic Sciences* (《语言科学》), No. 2: 46–57.

Dong, Xiufang (董秀芳). (2003b). The grammaticalization tendency of the pre-NP rising tone *yi* in Beijing Mandarin (北京话名词短语前阳平"一"的语法化倾向). In Wu Fuxiang & Hong Bo (eds.), *Grammaticalization and grammar studies (I)* (《语法化与语法研究[》一]). Beijing: The Commercial Press.

Dong, Xiufang (董秀芳). (2004a). Further grammaticalization of "shi": From functional word to word-internal element ("是"的进一步语法化:由虚词到词内成分). *Contemporary Linguistics* (《当代语言学》), No. 1: 35–44+94.

Dong, Xiufang (董秀芳). (2004b). *Lexicon and morphology of Chinese* (《汉语的词库与词法》). Beijing: Peking University Press.

Dong, Xiufang (董秀芳). (2005). Empathy strategies and the unconventional use of pronouns in verbal communication (移情策略与言语交际中代词的非常规用法). In Qi Huyang (ed.), *Research on Chinese function words and teaching Chinese as a foreign language* (《现代汉语虚词研究与对外汉语教学》). Shanghai: Fudan University Press.

Dong, Xiufang (董秀芳). (2007). Discourse marker *zhijian* in Written Mandarin (汉语书面语中的话语标记"只见"). *Nankai Linguistics* (《南开语言学刊》), No. 2: 74–8+155.

Dong, Xiufang (董秀芳). (2010). A discourse marker derived from clausal form: wo gaosu ni (来源于完整小句的话语标记"我告诉你"). *Linguistic Sciences* (《语言科学》), No. 5: 279–86.

Dragunov, Aleksandr (龙果夫). (1958). *Modern Chinese grammar research* (《现代汉语语法研究》). Beijing: Science Press.

Fan, Fanglian (范方莲). (1963). Existential sentences (存在句). *Studies of the Chinese Language* (《中国语文》). No. 5:386–95.

Fan, Jiyan (范继淹). (1985). Indefinite-subject sentences (无定NP主语句). *Studies of the Chinese Language* (《中国语文》), No. 5.

Fang, Di (方迪). (2018a). *A study of assessment expressions in spoken Chinese – An interactional perspective* 《(汉语口语中的评价表达研究——基于互动视角)》. PhD Dissertation of Graduate School of Chinese Academy of Social Sciences.

Fang, Di & Xie, Xinyang (方迪, 谢心阳). (2018). An introduction to *Interactional Linguistics: Studying Language in Social Interaction* (《互动语言学:社会互动中的语言研究介》绍). In Fang Mei & Cao Xiuling (eds.), *Interactional Linguistics and Chinese language studies II* (《互动语言学与汉语研究第》二辑). Beijing: Social Science Literature Press.

Fang, Mei (方梅). (1985). On the omission of clausal subjects in compound sentences (关于复句中分句主语省略的问题). *Journal of Yanbian University* (《延边大学学报》) (Social Science Edition), No. 1: 44–54. Also seen in *Chinese Linguistics and Literature* 《(汉语言文字学)》, copy material of Renmin University of China, No. 1, 1986.

Fang, Mei (方梅). (1991). Prompting *shi*-sentences (具有提示作用的"是"字句). *Studies of the Chinese Language* (《中国语文》), No. 5: 342–47.

Fang, Mei (方梅). (1994). A functional study of modal particles in Beijing Mandarin (北京话句中语气词的功能研究). *Studies of the Chinese Language* (《中国语文》), No. 5: 129–38.

Fang, Mei (方梅). (2000a). Functional properties of the imperfective as seen from "V*zhe*" (从"V着"看汉语不完全体的功能特征). *Grammar Study and Exploration* (《语法研究和探索》) (IX). Beijing: The Commercial Press.

Fang, Mei (方梅). (2000b). Reduced conjunctions as discourse markers (自然口语中弱化连词的话语标记功能). *Studies of the Chinese Language* (《中国语文》), No. 5: 459–70+480.

Fang, Mei (方梅). (2002). On the gramaticalization of *zhe* in Beijing Mandarin: From demonstrative to definite article (指示词"这"和"那"在北京话中的语法化). *Studies of the Chinese Language* (《中国语文》), No. 4: 343–56+382–83.

Fang, Mei (方梅). (2004). A study of postposed relative clauses in spoken Chinese (汉语口语后置关系从句研究). *Collection of academic papers for the celebration of the 50th anniversary of the founding of Studies of the Chinese Language* (《庆祝〈中国语文〉创刊五十周年学术论文集》). Beijing: The Commercial Press.

Fang, Mei (方梅). (2005a). Discourse grammar and studies on Chinese discourse grammar (篇章语法与汉语篇章语法研究). *Journal of Chinese Social Sciences* (《中国社会科学》), No. 6: 165–72.

Fang, Mei (方梅). (2005b). On grammatical bleaching of evidential and epistemic verbs: From complement-taking predicates to pragmatic markers (认证义谓宾动词的虚化——从谓宾动词到语用标记). *Studies of the Chinese Language* (《中国语文》), No. 6: 495–507+575.

Fang, Mei (方梅). (2006). Garmmaticalization of *shuo* (说, 'say') in Beijing Mandarin: From lexical verb to subordinator (北京话里"说"的语法化——从言说动词到从句标记). *Journal of Chinese Dialects* (《中国方言学报》), No. 1. Beijing: The Commercial Press.

Fang, Mei (方梅). (2007). Stylistic motivations for syntax shaping (语体动因对句法的塑造). *Contemporary Rhetoric* (《当代修辞学》), No. 6: 1–7.

Fang, Mei (方梅). (2008). Two emergent grammatical structures motivated by background information packaging – A case study on the cataphoric zero subject clause and the descriptive relative clause (由背景化触发的两种句法结构——主语零形反指和描写性关系从句). *Studies of the Chinese Language* (《中国语文》), No. 4: 291–303+383.

Fang, Mei (方梅). (2009). Grammaticalization of personal pronouns in Beijing Mandarin (北京话人称代词的虚化). In Wu Fuxiang & Cui Xiliang (eds.), *Grammaticalization and grammar study (IV)* (《语法化与语法研究(》四)). Beijing: The Commercial Press.

Fang, Mei (方梅). (2011). Two patterns of action reference in colloquial Beijing Mandarin (北京话的两种行为指称形式). *Dialect* (《方言》), No. 4: 368–77.

Fang, Mei (方梅). (2012a). Discourse structure and emergent meaning of conjunctions (会话结构与连词的浮现义). *Studies of the Chinese Language* (《中国语文》), No. 6: 500–8+575.

Fang, Mei (方梅). (2013a). Grammaticalization of auxiliary verbs in spoken Chinese (助动词在汉语口语中的虚化). In *Studies on Chinese Grammar: In honor of the 60th Birthday of Kimura Hideki* (《木村英树还历记念–中国语文法论丛》). Japan: Haku-teisha (白帝社).

Fang, Mei (方梅). (2013b). On *haishi* – the emergence of the optative mood (说"还是"——祈愿情态的浮现). In Academia Sinica (ed.), *Language and Linguistics* (《语言暨语言学》). Taiwan: Academia Sinica.

Fang, Mei (方梅). (2013c). Syntactic manifestations of stylistic features (谈语体特征的句法表现). *Contemporary Rhetoric* (《当代修辞学》), No. 2: 9–16.

Fang, Mei (方梅). (2015). The grammatical implications of tone 1 sandhi in retroflexed words in Beijing Mandarin (北京话儿化词语阴平变调的语法意义). *Anthology on Linguistics* (《语言学论丛》), Vol. 51, 33–51. Beijing: The Commercial Press.

Fang, Mei (方梅). (2016a). Interactional functions of the sentence final particle variants in Beijing Mandarin: A case study on *ya*, *na*, and *la* (北京话语气词变异形式的互动功能——以"呀、哪、啦"为例). *Language Teaching and Research* (《语言教学与研究》), No. 2: 67–79.

Fang, Mei (方梅). (2016b). Modes of dependent clause correlation and syntactic integration (依附小句的关联模式与句法整合). In *Exploring Chinese sentence patterns – Proceedings of the International Symposium on Chinese Syntax* (《汉语句式问题探索——汉语句式国际学术研讨会论文集》). Beijing: China Social Sciences Press.

Fang, Mei (方梅) (ed.). (2016). *Interactional Linguistics and Chinese language studies* (《互动语言学与汉语研究》) Vol. 1. Beijing: World Publishing Corporation.

Fang, Mei (方梅). (2017a). On conventionalization of negative assessment expressions (负面评价表达的规约化). *Studies of the Chinese Language* (《中国语文》), No. 2: 131–47+254.

Fang, Mei (方梅). (2017b). Narrative discourse cohesion and orientation representation: A case study of *danshuo* and *danjian* (叙事语篇的衔接与视角表达——以"单说、但见"为例). *Language Teaching and Research* (《语言教学与研究》), No. 5: 59–69.

Fang, Mei (方梅). (2017c). S-adverb and relevant discourse issues (饰句副词及相关篇章问题). *Chinese Language Learning* (《汉语学习》), No. 6: 3–11.

Fang, Mei (方梅). (2018). *Emergent grammar: Studies based on spoken and written Chinese* (《浮现语法——基于汉语口语和书面语的分析》). Beijing: The Commerical Press.

Fang, Mei (方梅). (2019a). The tradition of Chinese storyteller script and its inheritance in contemporary Chinese narration and grammar (话本小说的叙事传统对现代汉语语法的影响). *Contemporary Rhetoric* (《当代修辞学》), No. 1: 1–13.

Fang, Mei (方梅). (2019b). On the discourse function of the so-called "indefinite-subject" sentence (从话语功能看所谓"无定NP主语句"). *Chinese Teaching in the World* (《世界汉语教学》), No. 2: 189–200.

Fang, Mei & Song, Zhenhua (方梅, 宋贞花). (2004). Impacts of genre on frequency of occurrence – A statistic analysis of relative clauses in Chinese conversation (语体差异对使用频率的影响——汉语对话语体关系从句的统计分析). *Journal of Chinese Language and Computing*, 14(2): 113–24.

Fang, Mei & Yue, Yao (方梅, 乐耀). (2017). *Conventionalization and stance representation* (《规约化与立场表达》). Beijing: Peking University Press.

Fang, Mei & Zhu, Qingxiang (方梅, 朱庆祥). (2015). *The essence of Chinese and Western academic masterpieces – Volume of Lü Shuxiang – Chinese grammatical analysis* (《中西学术名篇精读·吕叔湘卷·汉语语法分析问题》). Shanghai: Zhongxi Book Company.

Fu, Shuling (傅书灵). (2010). On the "NP *er* (而) VP" construction in ancient Chinese (关于古汉语"名而动"的一点思考). *Studies of the Chinese Language* (《中国语文》), No. 5: 461–68+480.

Gao, Zengxia (高增霞). (2003). Review of studies on the serial verb construction (《连动式研究评述》). *Journal of Liaocheng University* (《聊城大学学报》) (Philosophy and Social Sciences Edition), No. 6: 75–9.

Gao, Zengxia (高增霞). (2005). Chinese clausal integration from the perspective of desententialization (《从非句化角度看汉语的小句整合》). *Studies of the Chinese Language* (《中国语文》), No. 1, 29–38. Also seen in *Chinese Linguistics and Literature* 《(语言文字学)》, copy material of Renmin University of China, No. 6, 2005.

Gao, Zengxia (高增霞). (2006). *A grammaticalization perspective to serial verb constructions in modern Chinese* (《现代汉语连动式的语法化视角》). Beijing: China Archives Publishing House.

He, Yang (贺阳). (1994). An exploration into Chinese sentence-completing elements (汉语完句成分试探). *Language Teaching and Research* (《语言教学与研究》), No. 4: 26–38.

He, Ziran (何自然). (1988). *Introduction to pragmatics* (《语用学概论》). Changsha: Hunan Education Press.

Hong, Bo (洪波). (2008). The accessibility of *zhi* (之)-clause and some relevant issues in pre-Qin Chinese (周秦汉语"之s"的可及性及相关问题). *Studies of the Chinese Language* (《中国语文》), No. 4: 304–16+383.

Hu, Mingyang & Jin, Song (胡明扬, 劲松). (1989). An exploration into flowing sentences (流水句初探). *Language Teaching and Research* (《语言教学与研究》), No. 4: 42–54.

Huang, He (黄河). (1990). Sequencing of co-occurring common adverbs (常见副词共现时的顺序). In *Collection of prized papers* (《缀玉集》). Beijing: Peking University Press.

Huang, Nansong (黄南松). (1994). On the grammatical categories for phrases to be self-sufficient clauses (试论短语自主成句所应具备的若干语法范畴). *Studies of the Chinese Language* (《中国语文》), No. 6: 441–7.

Huang, Nansong (黄南松). (1996a). On existential sentences (论存在句). *Chinese Learning* (《汉语学习》), No. 4: 8–32.

Huang, Yueyuan (黄月圆). (1996b). On the complementary distribution of *ba*/*bei*-construction and verb copying construction (把/被结构与动词重复结构的互补分布现象). *Studies of the Chinese Language* (《中国语文》), No. 2: 92–100.

Jin, Ting'en (金廷恩). (1999). Brief analysis of Chinese sentence-completing elements (汉语完句成分说略). *Chinese Learning* (《汉语学习》), No. 6: 8–13.

Kong, Lingda (孔令达). (1994). Linguistic forms that impact the self sufficiency of Chinese sentences (影响汉语句子自足的语言形式). *Studies of the Chinese Language* (《中国语文》), No. 6: 434–40.

Lai, Xiangang (赖先刚). (1994). On the consecutive use of adverbs (副词的连用问题). *Chinese Learning* (《汉语学习》), No. 2: 25–31.

Li, Aijun (李爱军). (2005a). Acoustic analysis on friendly speech (友好语音的声学分析). *Studies of the Chinese Language* (《中国语文》), No. 5: 418–31+479–80.

Li, Aijun (李爱军). (2008). Research on emotional stress (情感重音研究). *Chinese Journal of Phonetics* (《中国语音学报》), Vol. 1. Beijing: The Commercial Press.

Li, Jinrong (李劲荣). (2016). "Indefinite form taking the end position" and "indefinite form taking the start position" – Two types of Chinese existential constructions ("无定居后"与"无定居首"——汉语存在句的两种形式). *Chinese Teaching in the World* (《世界汉语教学》), No. 2: 183–96.

Li, Jinxi (黎锦熙). (1924). *New Chinese Grammar* (《新著国语文法》). Beijing: The Commercial Press.

Li, Jinxia, & Liu, Yun (李晋霞，刘云). (2003). The evidential meaning of "*shuo*" from the perspective of differences between "*ruguo*" and "*ruguoshuo*" (从"如果"与"如果说"的差异看"说"的传信义). *Linguistic Sciences* (《语言科学》), No. 4: 59–70.

Li, Linding (李临定). (1986). *Sentence patterns in Modern Chinese* (《现代汉语句型》). Beijing: The Commercial Press.

Li, Min (李敏). (2005b). Event referencing "N *de* V" ("N的V"指称事件). *Journal of Henan University* (《河南大学学报》) (Social Science Edition), No. 3: 91–5.

Li, C.N., S.A. Thompson & R.M. Thompson. (1994). The discourse motivation for the perfective aspect: The Mandarin particle *le* (已然体的话语理据:汉语助词"了"). In James Tai & Xue Fengsheng (eds.), *Functionalism and Chinese grammar* (《功能主义与汉语语法》). Beijing: Beijing Language Institute Press.

Li, Quan (李泉). (1996). Adverbs and adverb reclassification (副词和副词的再分类). In Hu Mingyang (ed.), *Exploring word class issues* (《词类问题考察》). Beijing: Beijing Language Institute Press.

Li, Quan (李泉). (2002). Adverb reclassification in terms of distribution (从分布上看副词的再分类). *Studies in Language and Linguistics* (《语言研究》), No. 2: 85–91.

Li, Xianju (李咸菊). (2004). Exploring the pragmatic functions of verb copying sentences (重动句几种语用功能探微). *Journal of Sichuan Education Institute* (《四川教育学院学报》), No. 7: 65–8.

Li, Xianyin (李先银). (2016b). Discourse negation and discourse negation marker *nikanni* (话语否定与话语否定标记"你看你"). *Naikai Linguistics Journal* (《南开语言学刊》), Vol. 1, 94–105. Beijing: The Commercial Press.

Li, Xianyin (李先银). (2017). *Conventional expressions of negative attitude in modern Chinese discourse* (《现代汉语话语否定标记研究》). Beijing: World Publishing Corporation.

Li, Zuofeng (李佐丰). (1994). *Content words in classical Chinese* (《文言实词》). Beijing: Language & Culture Press.

Liao, Qiuzhong (廖秋忠). (1984). Omission of verb-dominated constituents in modern Chinese (现代汉语中动词支配成分的省略). *Studies of the Chinese Language* (《中国语文》), No. 4. Also seen in *Collected works of Liao Qiuzhong* 《(廖秋忠文集)》. Beijing: Beijing Language Institute Press, 1992.

Liao, Qiuzhong (廖秋忠). (1986a). Correference expression in modern Chinese discourse (现代汉语篇章中的指同表达). *Studies of the Chinese Language* (《中国语文》), No. 2. Also seen in *Collected works of Liao Qiuzhong* 《(廖秋忠文集)》. Beijing: Beijing Language Institute Press, 1992.

Liao, Qiuzhong (廖秋忠). (1986b). Connecting elements in modern Chinese discourse (现代汉语篇章中的连接成分). *Studies of the Chinese Language* (《中国语文》), No. 6: 62–91.

Liao, Qiuzhong (廖秋忠). (1986c). Frame-pane relation in discourse and reference identification (篇章中的框—棂关系与所指的确定). *Grammar Study and Exploration* (《语法研究和探索》) (III). Beijing: Peking University Press. Also seen in *Collected works of Liao Qiuzhong*《(廖秋忠文集)》. Beijing: Beijing Language Institute Press, 1992.

Liao, Qiuzhong (廖秋忠). (1987). Scope of governance in discourse (篇章中的管界问题). *Studies of the Chinese Language* (《中国语文》), No. 4:250–61.

Liao, Qiuzhong (廖秋忠). (1991). Discourse, pragmatics and syntactic study (篇章与语用和句法研究). *Language Teaching and Research* (《语言教学与研究》), No. 4: 16–44.

Lin, Dajin & Xie, Chaoqun (林大津, 谢朝群). (2003). Interactional Linguistics: Developments and prospects (互动语言学的发展历程及其前景). *Modern Foreign Languages* (《现代外语》), No. 4: 410–18.

Lin, Yuwen (林裕文). (1984). *Endocentric complex sentences* (《偏正复句》). Shanghai: Shanghai Education Press.

Lin, Zhong (林忠). (2010). A syntactico-semantic investigation into verb-copying sentences from the perspective of functional grammar (功能语法视角下的重动句句法语义考察). *Journal of Chongqing University of Technology (Social Sciences)* (《重庆理工大学学报(社会科学)》), No. 5: 99–103.

Liu, Anchun, & Zhang, Bojiang (刘安春, 张伯江). (2004). "Indefinite-subject sentences" and related sentence patterns in discourse (篇章中的不定名词主语句及相关句式). *Journal of Chinese Language and Computing*, 14(2): 97–105.

Liu, Danqing (刘丹青). (2002). Semantic and syntactic properties of kind-denoting elements in Chinese (汉语类指成分的语义属性和句法属性). *Studies of the Chinese Language* (《中国语文》), No. 5: 411–22+478–9.

Liu, Lening (刘乐宁). (2005). Style, stylistic features and discourse connection (文体、风格与语篇连接). In Feng Shengli & Hu Wenze (eds.), *New developments in written Chinese teaching and research* (《对外汉语书面语教学与研究的最新发展》) (*Proceedings of the Symposium on Teaching Chinese as a Foreign Language to Senior Students at Harvard University* [哈佛大学高年级对外汉语教学研讨会论文集]). Beijing: Beijing Language & Culture Press.

Liu, Xiaohui (刘小辉). (2012). Distribution of adverbs and their semantico-functional analysis across text types (副词的分布及其跨语体的语义—功能分析). Master's thesis of Graduate School of Chinese Academy of Social Sciences.

Liu, Xueqin (刘雪芹). (2000). Types of verb-copying sentences (重动句的类别). *Journal of Yangzhou University* (《扬州大学学报》) (Philosophy and Social Sciences Edition), No. 5: 48–51.

Liu, Xueqin (刘雪芹). (2011). A study on the referential meaning of objects in verb-copying sentences (现代汉语重动句宾语指称意义研究). *Chinese Learning* (《汉语学习》), No. 5: 35–42.

Liu, Yaqiong & Tao, Hongyin (刘娅琼, 陶红印). (2011). Indexing evaluative stances with negative rhetorical interrogatives in Mandarin conversation (汉语谈话中否定反问句的事理立场功能及类型). *Studies of the Chinese Language* (《中国语文》), No. 2: 110–20+191.

Liu, Yuehua (刘月华). (1983). Distribution of adverbials and sequencing of multiple adverbials (状语的分布和多项状语的顺序). *Grammar Study and Exploration* (《语法研究和探索》) (I). Beijing: The Commercial Press.

Lu, Jianming (陆俭明). (1980). Transposition in the grammar of spoken Chinese (汉语口语句法里的易位现象). *Studies of the Chinese Language* (《中国语文》), No. 1:28–41.

Lu, Jianming (陆俭明). (1982a). A tentative investigation into the independent use of adverbs in modern Chinese (现代汉语副词独用刍议). *Language Teaching and Research* (《语言教学与研究》), No. 2: 27–41+49.

Lu, Jianming (陆俭明). (1982b). On dislocated attributives (关于定语易位的问题). *Studies of the Chinese Language* (《中国语文》), No. 3:179–81.

Lu, Jianming (陆俭明). (1983). A study on the independent use of adverbs (副词独用考察). *Studies in Language and Linguistics* (《语言研究》), No. 2: 168–183.

Luke, Kang Kong (陆镜光). (2000). Postposed sentential constituents as post-completion devices in conversational turn-taking (句子成分的后置与话轮交替机制中的话轮后续手段). *Studies of the Chinese Language* (《中国语文》), No. 4: 303–10+381.

Luke, Kang Kong (陆镜光). (2002). Identifying the end of sentences in progress (在进行中的句子中辨识句末). In Shao Jingmin & Xu Liejiong (eds.), *New developments in Chinese grammar studies (1)* (《汉语语法研究的新拓展(》一)). Hangzhou: Zhejiang Education Press.

Luke, Kang Kong (陆镜光). (2004a). On incremental sentences (说延伸句). In *A collection of academic papers celebrating the 50th anniversary of the founding of Studies of the Chinese Language* (《庆祝<中国语文>创刊50周年学术论文集》). Beijing: The Commercial Press.

Luke, Kang Kong (陆镜光). (2004b). A Cross-linguistic study of incremental sentences (延伸句的跨语言对比). *Language Teaching and Research* (《语言教学与研究》), No. 6: 1–9.

Luo, Yaohua (罗耀华). (2007). A research on the sentence-making issue of the adverbial non-subject-predicate sentence (副词性非主谓句成句问题研究). Doctoral Dissertation of Central China Normal University.

Luo, Yaohua & Niu, Li (罗耀华, 牛利). (2009). On the grammaticalization of *zaishuo* ("再说"的语法化). *Language Teaching and Research* (《语言教学与研究》), No. 1: 73–80.

Lü, Jining (吕吉宁). (2004). An Investigation into the grammaticalization of "*you*"-sentences ("有"字句语法化考察). MA Thesis of Beijing Language and Culture University.

Lü, Shuxiang (吕叔湘). (1940[1990]). On auxiliary words *zai* and *zhe* in The Record of the Transmission of the Lamp (《释景德传灯录中》在、著二助词). In *The Collected Works of Lü Shuxiang (Volume 2)* (《吕叔湘文集(第二卷)》), *Chinese Grammar Essays* (《汉语语法论文集》). Beijing: The Commercial Press, 1990.

Lü, Shuxiang (吕叔湘). (1944a). The scope of application of *ge* with a discussion on the dropping of *yi* in front of unit words (个字的应用范围，附论单位词前一字的脱落). In *The Collected Works of Lü Shuxiang (Volume 2)* (《吕叔湘文集(第二卷)》), *Chinese Grammar Essays* 《(汉语语法论文集)》. Beijing: The Commercial Press, 1990.

Lü, Shuxiang (吕叔湘). (1944b[1982]). *Essentials of Chinese grammar* (《中国文法要略》). Beijing: The Commercial Press.

Lü, Shuxiang (吕叔湘). (1979). *Chinese grammatical analysis* (《汉语语法分析问题》). Beijing: The Commercial Press.

Lü, Shuxiang (吕叔湘) (ed.). (1982). *800 words in modern Chinese* (《现代汉语八百词》) (revised edition). Beijing: The Commercial Press.

Lü, Shuxiang (吕叔湘). (1985). *Demonstratives in Modern Chinese* (《近代汉语指代词》) (supplemented by Jiang Lansheng). Shanghai: Academia Press; Beijing: The Commercial Press, 2017.

Ma, Jianzhong (马建忠). (1898[1983]). *Ma's grammar* (《马氏文通》). Beijing: The Commercial Press.

Myhill, John, & Hibiya, Junko. (1988). The discourse function of clause-chaining. In John Haiman & Sandra Thompson (Eds.), *Clause combining in grammar and discourse*. Amsterdam: John Benjamins, 361–98.

Nie, Renfa (聂仁发). (2001). Discourse analysis of verb-copying sentences (重动句的语篇分析). *Journal of Social Sciences of Hunan Normal University* (《湖南师范大学社会科学学报》), No. 1: 114–118.

Oota, Tatsuo (太田辰夫). (1958). *A historical grammar of the Chinese language* (《中国语历史文法》). (As translated by Jiang Shaoyu (蒋绍愚) & Xu Changhua (徐昌华), Peking University Press, 1987.)

Oota, Tatsuo (太田辰夫). (1988). *A general examination of the history of the Chinese language* (《汉语史通考》). (As translated by Jiang Lansheng (江蓝生) & Bai Weiguo (白维国), Chongqing Publishing House, 1991.)

Pan, Guoying (潘国英). (2010). A study on word order of adverbials in modern Mandarin Chinese (现代汉语状语语序研究). Doctoral Dissertation of East China Normal University.

Peng, Xiaochuan (彭小川). (1999). On the contextual function of the Chinese adverb "dao" (论副词"倒"的语篇功能——兼论对外汉语语篇教学). *Journal of Peking University* (《北京大学学报》) (Philosophy and Social Sciences Edition), No. 5: 132–37.

Piao, Huijing (朴惠京). (2011). On the lexicalization form of "high-frequency disyllabic optative verb + *shuo*/*shi*" (词汇化形式"高频双音节能愿动词+说/是"). *Chinese Teaching in the World* (《世界汉语教学》), No. 4: 470–78.

Qi, Huyang (齐沪扬). (1987). On the reduplication of monosyllabic adverbs (浅谈单音副词的重叠). *Studies of the Chinese Language* (《中国语文》), No. 4:262–7.

Qi, Huyang (齐沪扬). (2002). Analysis of the function of modal particles in the modal category (情态语气范畴中语气词的功能分析). *Journal of the School of Literature, Nanjing Normal University* (《南京师范大学文学院学报》), No. 3: 141–52.

Qi, Huyang (齐沪扬). (2003). An analysis of the pragmatic functions of modal adverbs (语气副词的语用功能分析). *Language Teaching and Research* (《语言教学与研究》), No. 1: 62–71.

Sanui, Tadayoshi (讃井唯允). (1993). Pragmatic concretization and generalization—Beginning with the so-called "indefinite-subject sentence" and "existential sentence" (语用上的具体化与一般化——从所谓"无定NP主语句"与"存现句"说起).   *Journal of Humanities 234*, Literature Department of Tokyo Metropolitan University. For the Chinese version, see *Selected Papers on Japanese Modern and Contemporary Chinese Studies* 《(日本近、现代汉语研究论文选)》. Beijing: Beijing Language Institute Press, 1993.

Shen, Dan (申丹). (2004). *Narratology and research on novel stylistics* (《叙述学与小说文体学研究》) (3rd edition). Beijing: Peking University Press.

Shen, Dan, & Wang, Liya (申丹, 王丽亚). (2010). *Western narratology: Classics and post-classics* (《西方叙事学:经典与后经典》). Beijing: Peking University Press.

Shen, Jiaxuan (沈家煊). (1989). Topics without comments – An analysis of topic-comment in terms of Q&A (不加说明的话题——从"对答"看"话题—说明"). *Studies of the Chinese Language* (《中国语文》), No. 5: 326–33.

Shen, Jiaxuan (沈家煊). (1990). Boundary between pragmatics and semantics (语用学和语义学的分界). *Foreign Language Teaching and Research* (《外语教学与研究》), No. 2: 26–35+80.

Shen, Jiaxuan (沈家煊). (1994a). A survey of studies on grammarization ("语法化"研究综观). *Foreign Language Teaching and Research* (《外语教学与研究》), No. 4: 17–24+80.

Shen, Jiaxuan (沈家煊). (1998). On the grammaticalization of pragmatic usage (语用法的语法化). *Fujian Foreign Languages* (《福建外语》), No. 2, 1–8+14.

Shen, Jiaxuan (沈家煊). (1999). Grammaticalization and the distorted relationship between form and meaning (语法化和形义间的扭曲关系). In Shi Feng & Pan Wuyun (eds.), *New Developments of Chinese Linguistics* (《中国语言学的新拓展》), 217–30. Hong Kong: City University of Hong Kong Press.

Shen, Jiaxuan (沈家煊). (2001). "Subjectivity" and "subjectivization" of language (语言的"主观性"和"主观化"). *Foreign Language Teaching and Research* (《外语教学与研究》), No. 4: 268–75+320.

Shen, Jiaxuan (沈家煊). (2003a). Compound sentences in three conceptual domains: acting, knowing, and uttering (复句三域"行、知、言"). *Studies of the Chinese Language* (《中国语文》), No. 3: 483–93.

Shen, Jiaxuan (沈家煊). (2003b). Can the disposal construction be disposed of? – On the subjectivity of *Ba* construction in Mandarin Chinese (如何处置"处置式"——论把字句的主观性). *Studies of the Chinese Language* (《中国语文》), No. 5: 387–99+478.

Shen, Jiaxuan (沈家煊). (2012). On minor sentences and flowing sentences in Chinese: In commemoration of the 120th birthday of Yuen Ren Chao ("零句"和"流水句"—为赵元任先生诞辰120周年而作). *Studies of the Chinese Language* (《中国语文》), No. 5: 403–15+479.

Shen, Jiaxuan (沈家煊). (2016). Preface (序). In Fang Mei (ed.), *International linguistics and Chinese study I* (《互动语言学与汉语研究第》一辑). Beijing: World Publishing Corporation.

Shen, Jiaxuan, & Wan, Quan (沈家煊, 完权). (2009). A further study on the *zhi*-construction and the function of *zhi* (之) in pre-Qin (也谈"之字结构"和"之"字的功能). *Studies in Language and Linguistics* (《语言研究》), No. 4: 1–12.

Shen, Jiaxuan, & Wang, Dongmei (沈家煊, 王冬梅). (2000). "N *de* V" and "reference-target" constructions ("N的V"和"参照体—目标"构式). *Chinese Teaching in the World* (《世界汉语教学》), No. 4: 25–32.

Shen, Jiong (沈炯). (1992). On Chinese tone patterns (汉语语调模型刍议). *Language Studies* (《语文研究》), No. 4: 16–24.

Shen, Jiong (沈炯). (1994b). Chinese intonation structure and intonation type (汉语语调构造和语调类型). *Dialect* (《方言》), No. 3: 221–8.

Shi, Chunhong (施春宏). (2010). Interactions between the form and the meaning of the verb-copying construction (动词拷贝句句式构造和句式意义的互动关系). *Studies of the Chinese Language* (《中国语文》), No. 2: 99–113.

Shi, Dingxu (石定栩). (1999). On topic sentences (主题句研究). In Xu Liejiong (ed.), *Commonality and individuality: Controversies in Chinese linguistics* (《共性与个性——汉语语言学中的争议》), 1–36. Beijing: Beijing Language and Culture University.

Shi, Jinsheng (史金生). (2003). On the scope, types, and order of sequential use of modal adverbs (语气副词的范围、类别和共现顺序). *Studies of the Chinese Language* (《中国语文》), No. 1: 17–31+95.

Shi, Youwei (史有为). (1995). Post-subject pause and topic (主语后停顿与话题). *Journal of Chinese Linguistics* (《中国语言学报》), No. 5: 97–123.

Shi, Youwei (史有为). (1997). Sentence completing and sentence-completing markers (完句和完句标志), as seen in *A new perspective of Chinese* (《汉语如是观》). Beijing: Beijing Language and Culture University.

Si, Hongxia (司红霞). (2003). How to practise sentence-completing elements in Chinese teaching as a second language (完句成分在对外汉语教学中的运用). *Chinese Learning* (《汉语学习》), No. 5: 63–8.

Song, Rou (宋柔). (2013). Stream model of Generalized Topic Structure in Chinese text (汉语篇章话题广义话题结构的流水句模型). *Studies of the Chinese Language* (《中国语文》), No. 6: 483–94+575.

Song, Shaonian, & Zhang, Yan (宋绍年, 张雁). (1997). Referentialization and nominalization of predicate elements in ancient Chinese (古汉语谓词性成分的指称化与名词化). In *Proceedings of the Second International Symposium on Ancient Chinese Grammar* (《第二届国际古汉语语法研讨会论文集》). Beijing: Language & Culture Press.

Song, Zuoyan, & Tao, Hongyin (宋作艳, 陶红印). (2008). A comparative study of Chinese and English causal clause sequences in discourse (汉英因果复句顺序的话语分析与比较). *Journal of Chinese* (《汉语学报》), No. 4: 61–71+96.

Sun, Chaofen (孙朝奋). (1988). The discourse function of numeral classifiers in Mandarin Chinese (汉语数量词在话语中的功能). *Journal of Chinese Linguistics* 16 (2): 298–323. Also seen in Dai Haoyi & Xue Fengsheng (eds.), *Functionalism and Chinese grammar*《功能主义与汉语语法》》. Beijing: Beijing Language Institute Press, 1994.

Sun, Chaofen (孙朝奋). (1994). A review of *Grammaticalization* (《虚化论评》介). *Foreign Linguistics* (《国外语言学》), No. 4: 19–25+18.

Sun, Xixin (孙锡信). (1999). *Modal words in modern Chinese – A diachronic study of Chinese modal words* (《近代汉语语气词——汉语语气词的历时考察》). Beijing: Language & Culture Press.

Tan, Junqiang (谭君强). (2014). *Introduction to narratology: From classical narratology to postclassical narratology* (《叙事学导论——从经典叙事学到后经典叙事学》) (2nd Edition). Beijing: Higher Education Press.

Tao, Hongyin (陶红印). (1994). Conversation Analysis, functionalism, and their application in Chinese grammar studies (言谈分析、功能主义及其在汉语语法研究中的应用). In Shi Feng (ed.), *Overseas Chinese linguistics research* (《海外中国语言学研究》). Beijing: Language & Culture Press.

Tao, Hongyin (陶红印). (1999). Discourse taxonomies and their grammatico-theoretical implications (试论语体分类的语法学意义). *Contemporary Linguistics* (《当代语言学》), No. 3: 15–24+61.

Tao, Hongyin (陶红印). (2000). "Eating" and emergent argument structure (从"吃"看动词论元结构的动态特征). *Studies in Language and Linguistics* (《语言研究》), No. 3: 21–38.

Tao, Hongyin (陶红印). (2002). The semantics and pragmatics of relative clause constructions in Mandarin narrative discourse (汉语口语叙事体关系从句结构的语义和篇章属性). *Contemporary Research on Modern-Chinese* (《现代中国语研究》) (Japan), No. 4: 47–57.

Tao, Hongyin (陶红印). (2003). Phonological, grammatical, and discourse evidence for the emergence of *zhidao* constructions in Mandarin conversation (《从语音、语法和话语特征看"知道"格式在谈话中的演化》). *Studies of the Chinese Language* (《中国语文》), No. 4: 291–302.

Tao, Hongyin (陶红印). (2007). The pragmatics of argument structure in Chinese procedural discourse (操作语体中动词论元结构的实现及语用原则). *Studies of the Chinese Language* (《中国语文》), No. 1: 3–13.

Tao, Hongyin, & Liu, Yaqiong (陶红印, 刘娅琼). (2010). From register differences to grammatical structural differences: Grammatical constructions in natural speech and the media (I & II) (《从语体差异到语法差异(上、下)——以自然会话与影视对白中的把字句、被动结构、光杆动词句、否定反问句为例》). *Contemporary Rhetoric* (《当代修辞学》), No. 1: 37–44, & No. 2: 22–7.

Tao, Hongyin, & Zhang, Bojiang (陶红印，张伯江). (2000). The status of indefinite Ba-constructions in modern and contemporary Chinese and its implications (无定式把字句在近现代汉语中的地位问题及其理论意义). *Studies of the Chinese Language* (《中国语文》), No. 5: 433–46+479–80.

Tao, Jianhua, & Xu, Xiaoying (陶建华，许晓颖). (2003). Emotion-oriented speech synthesis system (面向情感的语音合成系统). *Proceedings of the First China Affective Computing and Intelligent Interaction Academic Conference* (《第一届中国情感计算及智能交互学术会议论文集》), 191–8.

Uchida, Keiichi (内田庆市). (1989). "Indefinite-subject sentences" in Chinese – Another type of "existential sentence" (汉语的"无定名词主语句"——另外一种"存现句"). Originally published in *Minutes of the Faculty of Education, Fukui University* (37). For the Chinese version, see *Selected papers on Japanese modern and contemporary Chinese studies* 《(日本近、现代汉语研究论文选)》. Beijing: Beijing Language Institute Press, 1993.

Wan, Quan (完权). (2018). Minor sentences are at the root of the interaction between grammar and society in Chinese (零句是汉语中语法与社会互动的根本所在). In Fang Mei & Cao Xiuling (eds.), *International linguistics and Chinese study II* (《互动语言学与汉语研究第》二辑). Beijing: Social Science Academic Press (China).

Wang, Ailu (王艾录). (1990). Reflections on sentence-completing criteria in Chinese (汉语成句标准思考). *Journal of Shanxi University* (《山西大学学报》), No. 4: 80–84.

Wang, Canlong (王灿龙). (1999). Supplementary comments on verb-copying constructions (重动式补议). *Studies of the Chinese Language* (《中国语文》), No. 2: 122–25.

Wang, Canlong (王灿龙). (2000). On the anaphoric function of the personal pronoun *ta* (人称代词"他"的照应功能研究). *Studies of the Chinese Language* (《中国语文》), No. 3: 228–37+287.

Wang, Canlong (王灿龙). (2003). Factors constraining the use of "indefinite-subject sentences" (制约无定主语句使用的若干因素). *Grammar Study and Exploration* (《语法研究和探索》) (XII). Beijing: The Commercial Press.

Wang, Canlong (王灿龙). (2009). *Xiangshi* as a subjectivity marker on the brink of disappearance (一个濒于消亡的主观性标记词——想是). *Contemporary Linguistics* (《当代语言学》), No. 1: 35–46+94.

Wang, Dongmei (王冬梅). (2002). The nature of V in "N de V" structure ("N的V"结构中V的性质). *Language Teaching and Research* (《语言教学与研究》), No. 4: 55–64.

Wang, Hongjun (王洪君). (1987). On the disappearance of the Chinese self-referential nominalization marker *zhi* (汉语自指的名词化标记"之"的消失). *Anthology on Linguistics* (《语言学论丛》), Vol. 14. Beijing: The Commercial Press.

Wang, Hongjun, Li, Rong, & Yue, Yao (王洪君，李榕，乐耀). (2009). "*Le$_2$*," and the speaker's appearance in subjective close-range interaction ("了2"与话主显身的主观近距交互式语体). *Anthology on Linguistics* (《语言学论丛》), Vol. 40. Beijing: The Commercial Press.

Wang, Hongqi (王红旗). (2001). *A theory of reference* (指称论). PhD dissertation of Nankai University.

Wang, Hongqi (王红旗). (2014). Definiteness and indefiniteness of Chinese subject and object (汉语主语、宾语的有定与无定). *Anthology on Linguistics* (《语言学论丛》), Vol. 50. Beijing: The Commercial Press.

Wang, Jianci, & Wang, Jiankun (王健慈，王健昆). (2000). Displacement of pre-and post-subject adverbs (主语前后副词的位移). In Lu Jianming (ed.), *Modern Chinese grammar research facing the challenges of the new century – Proceedings of the '98 International Conference on Modern Chinese Grammar* (《面临新世纪挑战的现代汉

语语法研究——'98现代汉语语法学国际会议论文集》). Jinan: Shandong Education Press.

Wang, Jianguo (王建国). (2007). Topic continuity: A contrastive study of topic chains in Chinese and English (论话题的延续:汉英话题链的对比研究). Doctoral dissertation of Beijing Foreign Studies University.

Wang, Li (王力). (1980). *Manuscript on the history of Chinese* (《汉语史稿》) (Vol. 2). Shanghai: Zhonghua Book Company.

Wang, Li (王力). (1989). *A history of Chinese grammar* (《汉语语法学史》). Beijing: The Commercial Press.

Wang, Xiuli (王秀丽). (2008). Introductory expressions in discourse frame: Discourse analysis of existential structures (话语范围导入词——对存现句的语篇分析). *Foreign Language Teaching and Research* (《外语教学与研究》), No. 5: 345–51+400.

Wen, Lian (文炼). (1992). Sentence comprehension strategies (句子的理解策略). *Studies of the Chinese Language* (《中国语文》), No. 4:260–4.

Wu, Fuxiang (吴福祥). (2004). New developments of grammar study in recent years (近年来语法化研究的进展). *Foreign Language Teaching and Research* (《外语教学与研究》), No. 1: 18–24.

Wu, Jingcun, & Liang, Boshu (吴竞存, 梁伯枢). (1992). *Syntactic structure in modern Chinese and its analysis* (《现代汉语句法结构与分析》). Beijing: Language & Culture Press.

Xiang, Kaixi (项开喜). (1997). A functional study of the verb-copying construction in Chinese (汉语重动式的功能研究). *Studies of the Chinese Language* (《中国语文》), No. 4: 260–7.

Xiao, Xiqiang, & Zhang, Jing (肖奚强, 张静). (2004). A review of research on the verb-copying sentence in modern Chinese (现代汉语重动句研究综述). *Journal of Nanjing Radio and Television University* (《南京广播电视大学学报》), No. 1: 27–30.

Xiao, Zhiye, & Shen, Jiaxuan (肖治野, 沈家煊). (2009). Three domains of the sentence-final particle le_2 (了$_2$) in Mandarin Chinese ("了2"的行、知、言三域). *Studies of the Chinese Language* (《中国语文》), No. 6: 518–27+576.

Xie, Xinyang (谢心阳). (2016). Theoretical explorations in Interactional Linguistics: An Introduction to *Grammar Studies for Interactional Linguistics* (互动语言学的理论探索《—面向互动语言学的语法研究介》绍). In Fang Mei (ed.), *International linguistics and Chinese study I* (《互动语言学与汉语研究第》一辑). Beijing: World Publishing Corporation.

Xie, Xinyang, & Fang, Mei (谢心阳, 方梅). (2016). The prosodic expression of weakened conjunctions in naturally occurring spoken Chinese (汉语自然口语中弱化连词的韵律表现). In Fang Mei (ed.), *International linguistics and Chinese study II* (《互动语言学与汉语研究第》一辑). Beijing: World Publishing Corporation.

Xing, Fuyi (邢福义). (1985). *Compound sentences and connective words* (《复句与关系词语》). Ha'erbin: Heilongjiang People's Publishing House.

Xing, Fuyi (邢福义). (2001). *Research on Chinese compound sentences* (《汉语复句研究》). Beijing: The Commercial Press.

Xiong, Zhongru (熊仲儒). (2008). Licensing conditions of "indefinite-subject sentences" in Chinese (汉语中无定主语的允准条件). *Journal of Anhui Normal University* (《安徽师范大学学报》) (Philosophy and Social Sciences), No. 5: 541–48.

Xiong, Ziyu, & Lin, Maocan (熊子瑜, 林茂灿). (2004). Prosodic features of *a* (啊) and their conversational communicative functions ("啊"的韵律特征及其话语交际功能). *Contemporary Linguistics* (《当代语言学》), No. 2: 116–27+189.

Xu, Jie (徐杰). (2005a). Subject as a constituent, topic as a feature and their respective typologies (主语成分、"话题"特征及相应的语言类型). In Xu Jie (ed.), *Studies in Chinese linguistics: A typological perspective* (《汉语研究的类型学视角》), 299–333. Beijing: Beijing Language and Culture University Press.

Xu, Jingnong (徐晶凝). (2009). Tense-aspect study from the integrated discourse-mood perspective (时体研究的语篇、情态整合视角). *Anthology on Linguistics* (《语言学论丛》), Vol. 40. Beijing: The Commercial Press.

Xu, Jingning (徐晶凝). (2012). Choice of le_1/le_2 in past realis event clauses (过去已然事件句对"了1""了2"的选择). *Anthology on Linguistics* (《语言学论丛》), Vol. 45. Beijing: The Commercial Press.

Xu, Jiujiu (徐赳赳). (1990). A discourse analysis of *ta* in narratives (叙述文中"他"的话语分析). *Studies of the Chinese Language* (《中国语文》), No. 5:325–37.

Xu, Jiujiu (徐赳赳). (1995a). Discourse analysis in the past two decades (话语分析二十年). *Foreign Language Teaching and Research* (《外语教学与研究》), No. 1: 14–20+80.

Xu, Jiujiu (徐赳赳). (2001). Introducing *A Discourse Grammar of Mandarin Chinese* (《汉语话语语法》介绍). *Foreign Language Teaching and Research* (《外语教学与研究》), No. 5: 393–96.

Xu, Jiujiu (徐赳赳). (2003a). *Anaphora in Chinese texts* (《现代汉语篇章回指研究》). Beijing: China Social Sciences Press.

Xu, Jiujiu (徐赳赳). (2005b). Associative anaphora in Chinese discourse (现代汉语联想回指分析). *Studies of the Chinese Language* (《中国语文》), No. 3: 195–204+287.

Xu, Jiujiu (徐赳赳). (2010). *Text linguistics of modern Chinese* (《现代汉语篇章语言学》). Beijing: The Commercial Press.

Xu, Liejiong (徐烈炯). (2002). Whether Chinese is a discourse configurational language (汉语是话语概念结构化语言吗?). *Studies of the Chinese Language* (《中国语文》), No. 5: 400–10+478.

Xu, Liejiong, & Liu, Danqing (徐烈炯, 刘丹青). (1998/2007). *Topic structure and function* (《话题的结构与功能》). Shanghai: Shanghai Education Press.

Xu, Liejiong, & Liu, Danqing (eds.) (徐烈炯, 刘丹青). (2003). *New ideas about topic and focus* (《话题与焦点新论》). Shanghai: Shanghai Education Press.

Xu, Yulong (许余龙). (1996). Identification of sentence topic in Chinese and English discourse (汉英篇章中句子主题的识别). *Foreign Language* (《外国语》), No. 3, 3–9.

Xu, Yulong (许余龙). (2003b). Inter-clausal anaphora in Chinese complex sentences (汉语主从句间的回指问题). *Contemporary Linguistics* (《当代语言学》), No. 2: 97–107+189.

Xu, Yulong (许余龙). (2004). *Towards a functional-pragmatic model of discourse anaphora resolution – A study based on a database-driven analysis of Chinese folk stories and newspaper articles* (《篇章回指的功能语用探索——一项基于汉语民间故事和报刊语料的研究》). Shanghai: Shanghai Foreign Language Education Press.

Xu, Yulong (许余龙). (2005c). Topic marking in Chinese narrative discourse: A perspective in discourse anaphora resolution (从回指确认的角度看汉语叙述体篇章中的主题标示). *Contemporary Linguistics* (《当代语言学》), No. 2: 122–31+189–90.

Xu, Yulong (许余龙). (2007). Topic introduction and discourse anaphora in Chinese and English: A corpus-based contrastive study (话题引入与语篇回指——一项基于民间故事语料的英汉对比研究). *Foreign Language Education* (《外语教学》), No. 6: 1–5.

Xuan, Yue (玄玥). (2011). On a new usage of "shuo (说)" ("说"的一种新用法——客观叙述标记词). *Chinese Linguistics* (《汉语学报》), No. 2: 28–35+95.

Yang, Chengkai (杨成凯). (2003). Subject and topic of Chinese sentences (汉语句子的主语和话题). In Xu Liejiong & Liu Danqing (eds.), *New ideas about topic and focus* (《话题与焦点新论》), 51–82. Shanghai: Shanghai Education Press.

Yang, Defeng (杨德峰). (2006). On the location of the adverbs of time in the sentence (时间副词作状语位置的全方位考察). *Applied Linguistics* (《语言文字应用》), No. 2: 69–75.

Yang, Defeng (杨德峰). (2009). On the location of the mood adverb in the sentence (语气副词作状语的位置). *Chinese Learning* (《汉语学习》), No. 5: 28–34.

Yang, Suying (杨素英). (2000). A contrastive study of the semantic functions of quantifier "one" in Chinese and English (数量词"一"在中英文中不同的语义功能). In Lu Jianming (ed.), *Modern Chinese grammar research facing the challenge of the new century—Proceedings of 98' International Conference on Modern Chinese Grammar* (《面临新世纪挑战的现代汉语语法研究——98'现代汉语语法学国际学术会议论文集》). Jinan: Shandong Education Press.

Yang, Yuling (杨玉玲). (2004). Review of studies on verb-copying sentences (重动句研究综述). *Chinese Learning* (《汉语学习》), No. 3: 37–42.

Yuan, Yulin (袁毓林). (2002a). Sequencing principle of multiple adverbs and its cognitive interpretation (多项副词共现的语序原则及其认知解释). *Anthology on Linguistics* (《语言学论丛》), Vol. 26. Beijing: The Commercial Press.

Yuan, Yulin (袁毓林). (2002b). The grammatical status and grammaticalization of Chinese topics: Diachronic and synchronous considerations based on authentic spoken language (汉语话题的语法地位和语法化程度——基于真实口语的历时和共时考量). *Anthology on Linguistics* (《语言学论丛》), Vol. 25, 82–115. Beijing: The Commercial Press. Also seen in Xu Liejiong & Liu Danqing (eds.), *New ideas about topic and focus*《(话题与焦点新论)》, Shanghai: Shanghai Education Press, 2003.

Yuan, Yulin (袁毓林). (2010). The parallelism of the realization relationship between Chinese and English in grammatical categories——Also on noun/verb and reference/statement, subject and topic, sentence and paragraph in Chinese (汉语和英语在语法范畴的实现关系上的平行性——也谈汉语里名词/动词与指称/陈述、主语与话题、句子与话段). *Journal of Sino-Tibetan Languages Study* (《汉藏语学报》), No. 4. Beijing: The Commercial Press.

Yue, Yao (乐耀). (2011a). The differences in the use of quotative evidential *jushuo* and *tingshuo* in modern Chinese (现代汉语引证类传信语"据说"和"听说"的使用差异). *Anthology on Linguistics* (《语言学论丛》), Vol. 43. Beijing: The Commercial Press.

Yue, Yao (乐耀). (2011b). Evidentiality and its interaction with other linguistic categories in Mandarin Chinese (汉语传信的范畴及其与相关语言范畴的互动研究). Doctoral dissertation of Peking University.

Yue, Yao (乐耀). (2011c). The interaction between subjectivity and pragmatic principles in Chinese conversation viewed from the formation of discourse marker: A case study on the phrase "bú shi wǒ shuō nǐ" (从"不是我说你"类话语标记的形成看会话中主观性范畴与语用原则的互动). *Chinese Teaching in the World* (《世界汉语教学》), No. 1: 69–77.

Yue, Yao (乐耀). (2016). Stance-taking of the concessive tautology in Mandarin conversation (从互动交际的视角看让步类同语式评价立场的表达). *Studies of the Chinese Language* (《中国语文》), No. 1: 58–69+127.

Yue, Yao (乐耀). (2017). Turn-constructional unit as an important research topic in Interactional Linguistics (互动语言学研究的重要课题——会话交际的基本单位). *Contemporary Linguistics* (《当代语言学》), No. 2: 246–71.

Yue, Yao (乐耀). (2019). Communicative interaction, social action, and grammar sensitive to conversational sequence – A review of *Grammar in Everyday Talk: Building Responsive Actions* (交际互动·社会行为和对会话序列位置敏感的语法《—日常言谈中的语法:如何构建回应行为述》评). *Anthology on Linguistics* (《语言学论丛》), Vol. 59. Beijing: The Commercial Press.

Yutaka, Furukawa (古川裕). (1989). An investigation into adverbs modifying the word *shi* (副词修饰"是"字情况考察). *Studies of the Chinese Language* (《中国语文》), No. 1.

Zhan, Kaidi (詹开第). (1981). *You*-sentences (有字句). *Studies of the Chinese Language* (《中国语文》), No. 1:27–34.

Zhan, Weidong (詹卫东). (1998). The characteristics of "NP *de* VP" in sentence and discourse organization ("NP+的+VP"偏正结构在组句谋篇中的特点). *Language Studies* (《语文研究》), No. 1: 16–23.

Zhang, Bojiang (张伯江). (1993). The construction of "N *de* V" ("N的V"结构的构成). *Studies of the Chinese Language* (《中国语文》), No. 4:252–9.

Zhang, Bojiang (张伯江). (2000). Transitivity analysis of Chinese serial verb construction (汉语连动式的及物性解释). *Grammar Study and Exploration* (《语法研究和探索》) (IX). Beijing: The Commercial Press.

Zhang, Bojiang, & Fang, Mei (张伯江, 方梅). (1996/2014). *Functional studies of Chinese grammar* (《汉语功能语法研究》). Nanchang: Jiangxi Education Press; Beijing: The Commercial Press, 2014.

Zhang, Jianjun (张健军). (2004a). An investigation into sentence-completing issues in modern Chinese (现代汉语完句问题探讨). MA thesis of Northeast Normal University.

Zhang, Li (张俐). (1997). An analysis of sentence-initial adverbials that cannot be postposed (不能后移的句首状语试析). *Journal of Henan University* (《河南大学学报》) (Social Science Edition), No. 3:28–30+121.

Zhang, Li (张俐). (1999). An analysis of sentence-initial adverbials that can be postposed (可以后移的句首状语试析). *Journal of Henan University* (《河南大学学报》) (Social Science Edition), No. 5:99–102.

Zhang, Meilan, & Chen, Siyu (张美兰, 陈思羽). (2006). Topic markers in Beijing dialect during the period between the end of the Qing Dynasty and the beginning of the Republic of China (清末民初北京口语中的话题标记——以100多年前几部域外汉语教材为例). *Chinese Teaching in the World* (《世界汉语教学》), No. 2: 63–73+3.

Zhang, Min (张敏). (2003a). A typological analysis of the source of grammaticalization of the attributive marker *zhi* in ancient Chinese (从类型学看上古汉语定语标记"之"语法化的来源). In Wu Fuxiang (ed.), *Grammarization and grammar research* (《语法化与语法研究》) (I). Beijing: The Commercial Press.

Zhang, Xinhua (张新华). (2007). On the theoretical considerations of indefinite-subject sentences (与无定名词主语句相关的理论问题). *Journal of Peking University* (《北京大学学报》) (Philosophy and Social Sciences Edition), No. 5: 103–11.

Zhang, Ye, & Ren, Xiaotong (章也, 任晓彤). (2004). Probe into the sentence patterns "N *de* V" and "N *zhi* V" in Chinese (试论汉语中的"N+的+V"结构和"N+之+V"结构). *Journal of Inner Mongolia Normal University* (《内蒙古师范大学学报》) (Philosophy and Social Sciences Edition), No. 1: 76–82.

Zhang, Yisheng (张谊生). (1996). Sequential use of adverbs and order of co-occurrence (副词的连用类别和共现顺序). *Journal of Yantai University* (《烟台大学学报》), No. 2:86–95.

Zhang, Yisheng (张谊生). (2000a). The nature, scope and classification of modern Chinese adverbs (现代汉语副词的性质、范围与分类). *Studies in Language and Linguistics* (《语言研究》), No. 1: 51–63.

Zhang, Yisheng (张谊生). (2000b/2014). *Studies on modern Chinese adverbs* (《现代汉语副词研究》). Shanghai: Xuelin Publishing House; Beijing: The Commercial Press, 2014.

Zhang, Yisheng (张谊生). (2003b). On the connections between diachronic changes and synchronic variations of "adverb+*shi*" in Chinese ("副+是"的历时演化和共时变异——兼论现代汉语"副+是"的表达功用和分布范围). *Linguistic Sciences* (《语言科学》), No. 3: 34–49.

Zhang, Yisheng (张谊生). (2004b). *Exploring modern Chinese adverbs* (《现代汉语副词探索》). Shanghai: Xuelin Publishing House.

Zhang, Yufeng (张豫峰). (2009). An analysis of the completing elements of causative sentences (现代汉语使动句的完句成分考察). *Journal of Fudan University* (《复旦学报》) (Social Sciences Edition), No. 3: 106–11.

Zheng, Guiyou (郑贵友). (2001). Connective *zaishuo* and its discourse function (关联词"再说"及其篇章功能). *Chinese Teaching in the World* (《世界汉语教学》), No. 4: 32–8.

Zheng, Juanman, & Zhang, Xianliang (郑娟曼, 张先亮). (2009). *Nikan ni* as a discourse marker of "blame" (责怪式话语标记"你看你"). *Chinese Teaching in the World* (《世界汉语教学》), No. 4: 202–9.

Zhong, Xiaoyong (钟小勇), (2010). An analysis of the discourse referentiality of the object in verb-copying sentences (重动句宾语话语指称性分析). *Chinese Teaching in the World* (《世界汉语教学》), No. 2: 199–211.

Zhou, Chenlei (周晨磊). (2012). From textual to interpersonal: The development of the meaning and function of *huashuo* (从语篇到人际——"话说"的意义和功能演变). *Chinese Teaching in the World* (《世界汉语教学》), No. 5: 499–508.

Zhou, Shihong, & Shen, Li (周士宏, 申莉). (2017). The sentence with an unidentifiable NP subject and its relevant "you" (有) complex presentative construction (汉语中的"无定名词主语句"及相关的"有"字呈现句). *Journal of School of Literature, Beijing Normal University* (《励耘学刊》), No. 5: 105–20.

Zhu, Dexi (朱德熙). (1982). *Lectures on grammar* (《语法讲义》). Beijing: The Commercial Press.

Zhu, Dexi (朱德熙). (1983). Self reference and transferred reference: The grammatical and semantic functions of the Chinese nominalization markers *de, zhe, suo*, and *zhi* (自指和转指——汉语名词化标记"的、者、所、之"的语法功能和语义功能). *Dialect* (《方言》), No. 1: 16–31.

Zhu, Dexi (朱德熙). (1987). Sentence and subject: An example of Indo-European influence on modern written Chinese and Chinese syntactic analysis (句子和主语——印欧语影响现代书面汉语和汉语句法分析的一个实例). *Chinese Teaching in the World* (《世界汉语教学》), inaugural issue: 31–4.

Zhu, Jun (朱军). (2014). Expressive function of rhetorical question format "X + *shenme* + X" in negative position (反问格式"X什么X"的立场表达功能考察). *Chinese Learning* (《汉语学习》), No. 3: 20–7.

Zhu, Qingxiang (朱庆祥). (2012). The dependency and relevance of clauses in modern Chinese: A study based on corpora of different varieties (现代汉语小句的依存性与关联性——基于分语体语料库的研究). Doctoral dissertation of Graduate School of Chinese Academy of Social Sciences.

Sources in English

Amiridze, Nino, Boyd H. Davis, & Margaret Maclagan (eds.). (2010). *Fillers, pauses and placeholders*. Amsterdam: John Benjamins.

Argyle, Michael. (1972). Non-verbal communication in human social interaction. In Robert A. Hinde (ed.), *Non-verbal Communication*. Cambridge: Cambridge University Press.

Ariel, Mira. (1988) Referring and accessibility. *Journal of Linguistics* 24: 65–87.
Ariel, Mira. (1990). *Accessing noun-phrase antecedents*. London and New York: Routledge.
Ariel, Mira. (1991). The function of accessibility in a theory grammar. *Journal of Pragmatics* 16: 443–463.
Ariel, Mira. (1994). Interpreting anaphoric expressions: A cognitive versus a pragmatic approach. *Journal of Linguistics* 30: 3–42.
Asher, Nicholas. (2004). Discourse Topic. *Theoretical Linguistics* 30(1): 163–201.
Atkinson, J. Maxwell. (1984). Public speaking and audience responses: Some techniques for inviting applause. In J. Maxwell Atkinson and John Heritage (eds.), *Structure of social action: Studies in conversation analysis*. Cambridge: Cambridge University Press, 370–409.
Atkinson, J. Maxwell, & John Heritage (eds.). (1984). *Structures of social action: Studies in conversation analysis*. Cambridge: Cambridge University Press.
Auer, Peter. (1996). On the prosody and syntax of turn-taking. In Elizabeth Couper-Kuhlen and Margret Selting (eds.), *Prosody and conversation*. Cambridge: Cambridge University Press, 57–100.
Auer, Peter, Elizabeth Couper-Kuhlen, & Frank Muller. (1999). *Language in time: The rhythm and tempo of spoken interaction*. Oxford: Oxford University Press.
Austin, L. John. (1962). *How to do things with words*. Oxford: Clarendon Press.
Bakhtin, Mikhail. (1934/1981). *The dialogic imagination: Four essays by Mikhail Bakhtin*. Austin, Texas: University of Texas Press.
Barth-Weingarten, Dagmar, Elisabeth Reber, & Margret Selting (eds.). (2010). *Prosody in interaction*. Amsterdam: John Benjamins.
Beauvais, Paul. (1989). A speech-act theory of metadiscourse. *Written Communication* 6(1): 11–30.
Bergmann, Pia, Jana Brenning, Martin Pfeiffer & Elisabeth Reber (eds.). (2012). *Prosody and embodiment in Interactional Grammar*. Berlin: de Gruyter.
Bernardo, Robert. (1979). The function and content of relative clauses in spontaneous narratives. *Proceedings of Fifth Annual Meeting of the Berkeley Linguistics Society*, 539–51.
Biq, Yung-O. (1990). The Chinese third-person pronoun in spoken discourse. *Proceedings of the 26th Annual Meeting of the Chicago Linguistic Society*, 61–72.
Biq, Yung-O. (1991). The multiple uses of the second person singular pronoun in conversational Mandarin. *Journal of Pragmatics* 16: 307–21.
Biq, Yung-O. (2000). Recent developments in discourse and grammar. *Chinese Studies* 18: 357–94.
Biq, Yung-O., James H.-Y. Tai, & Sandra A. Thompson. (1996). Recent development in functional approaches to Chinese. In James Huang and Audrey Li (eds.), *New horizons in Chinese linguistics*. Dordrecht: Kluwer, 97–140.
Bolinger, Dwight. (1977). *Meaning and form*. London and New York: Longman.
Brazil, David. (1995). *A grammar of speech*. Oxford: Oxford University Press.
Brinton, Laurel J. (1996). *Pragmatic markers in English: Grammaticalization and discourse functions*. Berlin: Mouton de Gruyter.
Brinton, Laurel J. & Elizabeth C. Traugott. (2005). *Lexicalization and language changes*. Cambridge: Cambridge University Press.
Brown, Gillian, & George Yule. (1983). *Discourse analysis*. Cambridge: Cambridge University Press.

Bussmann, Hadumod. (2000). *Routledge dictionary of language and linguistics*. Beijing: Foreign Language Teaching and Research Press.
Chafe, Wallace. (1976). Givenness, contrastiveness, definiteness, subjects, topics, and point of view. In Charles N. Li (ed.), *Subject and topic*. New York: Academic Press, 25–55.
Chafe, Wallace. (1979). The flow of thought and the flow of language. In Talmy Givón (ed.), *Discourse and syntax*. New York: Academic Press, 159–181.
Chafe, Wallace. (1980). *The Pear Story: Cognitive, cultural and linguistic aspects of narrative production*. Norwood, NJ: Ablex Publishing Corporation.
Chafe, Wallace. (1987). Cognitive constraints on information flow. In R. Tomlin (ed.), *Coherence and grounding in discourse*. Amsterdam: John Benjamins, 21–51.
Chafe, Wallace. (1994). *Discourse, consciousness, and time: The flow and displacement of conscious experience in speaking and writing*. Chicago: University of Chicago Press.
Chao, Yuen Ren (1968). *A grammar of spoken Chinese*. Berkeley: University of California Press. For the Chinese version, see 《汉语口语语法》, translated by Lü Shuxiang. Beijing: The Commercial Press, 1979.
Chen, Ping. (1986). Referent introducing and tracking in Chinese narratives. PhD dissertation. Los Angeles: University of California, Los Angeles.
Chen, Ping. (2004b). Identifiability and definiteness in Chinese. *Linguistics* 42(6): 1129–1184.
Chen, Ping. (2009). Aspects of referentiality. *Journal of Pragmatics* 41(8): 1657–1674.
Chu, Chauncey. (1998). *A discourse grammar of Mandarin Chinese*. New York: Peter Lang Publishing. For the Chinese version, see 《汉语篇章语法》, translated by Pan Wenguo, et al. Beijing: Beijing Language and Culture University Press, 2006.
Comrie, Bernard. (1981). *Language universals and linguistic typology*. Chicago: University of Chicago Press.
Couper-Kuhlen, Elizabeth. (2012). Some truths and untruths about final intonation in conversational questions. In Jan P. de Ruiter (ed.), *Questions: Formal, functional and interactional perspectives*. Cambridge: Cambridge University Press, 123–145.
Couper-Kuhlen, Elizabeth. (2014). What does grammar tell us about action? *Pragmatics* 24(3): 623–647.
Couper-Kuhlen, Elizabeth, & Cecilia E. Ford (eds.). (2004). *Sound patterns in interaction*. Amsterdam: John Benjamins.
Couper-Kuhlen, Elizabeth, & Margret Selting (eds.). (1996). *Prosody in conversation*. Cambridge and New York: Cambridge University Press.
Couper-Kuhlen, Elizabeth, & Margret Selting. (2001). Introducing interactional linguistics. In Margret Selting and Elizabeth Couper-Kuhlen (eds.), *Studies in interactional linguistics*. Amsterdam/Philadelphia: John Benjamins, 1–22.
Couper-Kuhlen, Elizabeth, & Margret Selting. (2018). *Interactional linguistics: Studying language in social interaction*. Cambridge: Cambridge University Press.
Couper-Kuhlen, Elizabeth, & Tsuyoshi Ono. (2007). 'Incrementing' in conversation: A comparison of practices in English, German and Japanese. *Pragmatics* 17(4): 513–552.
Couper-Kuhlen, Elizabeth, Barbara A. Fox, & Sandra A. Thompson. (2014). Forms of responsivity: Grammatical formats for responding to two types of request in conversation. In Susanne Günther, Wolfgang Imo, & Jörg Bücker (eds.), *Grammar and dialogism: Sequential, syntactic, and prosodic patterns between emergence and sedimentation*. Berlin: de Gruyter, 109–138.

Crismore, Avon, Raija Markkanen, & Margaret Steffensen. (1993). Metadiscourse in persuasive writing: A study of texts written by American and Finnish university students. *Written Communication* 10 (1): 39–71.

Cristofaro, Sonia. (2005). *Subordination*. Oxford: Oxford University Press.

Croft, William. (1990). *Typology and universals*. Cambridge: Cambridge University Press.

Croft, William. (1995). Intonation units and grammatical structure. *Linguistics* 33(5): 839–882.

Crystal, David. (1997/2008). *A dictionary of linguistics and phonetics*. Hoboken, NJ: Wiley-Blackwell. For the Chinese version, see《现代语言学词典》, translated by Shen Jiaxuan. Beijing: The Commercial Press, 2011.

Diessel, Holger. (1999). *Demonstratives: Form, function and grammaticalization*. Amsterdam: John Benjamins.

Dryer, Matthew S. (1992). The Greenbergian word order correlations. *Language* 68(1): 81–138.

Du Bois, John W. (1980). Beyond definiteness: The trace of identity in discourse. In Wallace L. Chafe (ed.), *The Pear Stories: Cognitive, cultural, and linguistic aspects of narrative production*. Norwood: Ablex Publishing Corporation, 203–74.

Du Bois, John W. (1985). Competing motivations. In John Haiman (ed.), *Iconicity in syntax*. Amsterdam: John Benjamins Publishing Company.

Du Bois, John W. (1987). The discourse basis of ergativity. *Language* 63: 805–55.

Du Bois, John W. (2014). Towards a dialogic syntax. *Cognitive Linguistics* 25(3): 359–410.

Du Bois, John W. & Sandra A. Thompson. (1993). Dimensions of a theory of information flow. University of California, Santa Barbara. MS.

Erbaugh, Mary S. (1987). Psycholinguistic evidence for foregrounding and backgrounding. *Coherence and Grounding in Discourse*. Amsterdam: John Benjamins, 109–30.

Fang, Mei. (2012b). The emergence of a definite article in Beijing Mandarin: The evolution of the proximal demonstrative zhè. In Zhiqun Xing (ed.), *The newest trends in the study of grammaticalization and lexicalization in Chinese*. Berlin: Mouton de Gruyter, 55–86.

Fillmore, Charles J. (1997). *Lectures on deixis*. Stanford: Distributed for Center for the Study of Language and Information Publications.

Finegan, Edward. (1995). Subjectivity and subjectivisation: An introduction. In Stein, Dieter and Susan Wright (eds.), *Subjectivity and subjectivisation: Linguistic perspectives*. Cambridge: Cambridge University Press, 1–15.

Foley, William A. & Robert D. Van Valin. (1984). *Functional syntax and universal grammar*. Cambridge: Cambridge University Press.

Ford, Cecilia E. (1993). *Grammar in interaction: Adverbial clauses in American English conversations*. Cambridge: Cambridge University Press.

Ford, Cecilia E. (2002). Denial and the construction of conversational turns. In Joan Bybee and Michael Noonan (eds.), *Complex sentences in grammar and discourse*. Amsterdam: John Benjamins, 61–78.

Ford, Cecilia E., Barbara A. Fox, & Sandra A. Thompson. (2002). Constituency and the grammar of turn increments. In Cecilia E. Ford, Barbara A. Fox, & Sandra A. Thompson (eds.), *The language of turn and sequence*. Oxford: Oxford University Press, 14–38.

Ford, Cecilia E., Sandra A. Thompson, & Veronika Drake. (2012). Bodily-visual practices and turn continuation. *Discourse Processes* 49(3–4): 192–212.

Fox, Barbara A. (2000). Micro-syntax in conversation. Paper presented at Interactional Linguistics Conference, Spa.
Fox, Barbara A. (2007). Principles shaping grammatical practices: An exploration. *Discourse Studies* 9: 299–318.
Fox, Barbara A. & Robert Jasperson. (1995). The syntactic organization of repair. In Philip Davis (ed.), *Descriptive and theoretical modes in the New Linguistics*. Amsterdam: John Benjamins, 77–134.
Fox, Barbara A. & Sandra A. Thompson. (1990a). A discourse explanation of the grammar of relative clauses in English conversation. *Language* 66: 297–316.
Fox, Barbara A. & Sandra A. Thompson. (1990b). On formulating reference: An interactional approach to relative clauses in English conversation. *Pragmatics* 4: 183–96.
Fox, Barbara A. & Sandra A. Thompson. (2010). Responses to wh-questions in English conversation. *Research on Language and Social Interaction* 43(2): 133–56.
Fox, Barbara A., Makoto Hayashi, & Robert Jasperson. (1996). A cross-linguistic study of syntax and repair. In Elinor Ochs, Emanuel A. Schegloff, & Sandra A. Thompson (eds.), *Interaction and grammar*. Cambridge: Cambridge University Press, 185–237.
Fox, Barbara A., Sandra A. Thompson, Cecilia E. Ford, & Elizabeth Couper-Kuhlen. (2013). Conversation Analysis and linguistics. In Jack Sidnell and Tanya Stivers (eds.), *The handbook of Conversation Analysis*. Chichester: Wiley-Blackwell, 726–40.
Fox, Barbara A., Yael Maschler, & Susanne Uhmann. (2009). Morpho-syntactic resources for the organization of same-turn self-repair: Cross-linguistic variation in English, German and Hebrew. *Gesprächsforschung* 10: 245–91.
Fraser, Bruce. (1996). Pragmatic markers. *Pragmatics* 6: 167–90.
Givón, Talmy. (1971). Historical syntax and synchronic morphology: An archaeologist's field trip. *Chicago Linguistic Society* 7 (1): 394–415.
Givón, Talmy. (1979). *On understanding grammar*. New York: Academic Press.
Givón, Talmy. (1980). The binding hierarchy and the typology of complements. *Studies in Language* 4(3): 333–77.
Givón, Talmy. (1983). Topic continuity in discourse: An introduction. In Talmy Givón (ed.), *Topic continuity in discourse: A quantitative cross-language study*. Amsterdam: John Benjamins, 1–42.
Givón, Talmy. (1984/1990). *Syntax: A functional-typological introduction, Vol. II*. Amsterdam: John Benjamins.
Givón, Talmy. (1987). Beyond foreground and background. In Russell S. Tomlin (ed.), *Coherence and grounding in discourse*. Amsterdam: John Benjamins, 175–88.
Goodwin, Charles. (1979). The interactive construction of a sentence in natural conversation. In George Psathas (ed.), *Everyday language: Studies in Ethnomethodology*. New York: Irvington, 97–121.
Goodwin, Charles. (1981). *Conversational organization: Interaction between speakers and hearers*. New York: Academic Press.
Goodwin, Charles. (1995). Sentence construction within interaction. In Uta M. Quasthoff (ed.), *Aspects of oral communication*. Berlin: Walter de Gruyter, 198–219.
Goodwin, Marjorie H. (1980). Processes of mutual monitoring implicated in the production of description sequences. *Sociological Inquiry* 50: 303–317.
Gumperz, John J. (1982). *Discourse strategies*. Cambridge: Cambridge University Press.
Gundel, Jeanette K. (1988). Universals of topic-comment structure. In Michael Hammond, Edith A. Moravcsik and Jessica Wirth (eds.), *Studies in syntactic typology*. Amsterdam: John Benjamins, 209–39.

Haboud, Marleen. (1997). Grammaticalization, clause union and grammatical relations in Ecuadorian Highland Spanish. In Talmy Givón (ed.), *Grammatical relations: A functionalist perspective*. Amsterdam/Philadelphia: John Benjamins, 199–227.
Haddington, Pentti. (2006). The organization of gaze and assessments as resources for stance taking. *Text and Talk* 26: 281–328.
Halliday, Michael A.K. (2000). *An introduction to functional grammar* (2nd edition). Beijing: Foreign Language Teaching and Research Press.
Hawkins, John A. (1990). A parsing theory of word order universals. *Linguistic Inquiry* 21(2): 223–61.
Heath, Christian. (1984). Talk and recipiency: Sequential organization in speech and body movement. In J. Maxwell Atkinson and John Heritage (eds.), *Structures of social action: Studies in Conversation Analysis*. Cambridge: Cambridge University Press, 247–65.
Heath, Christian. (1986). *Body movement and speech in medical interaction*. Cambridge: Cambridge University Press.
Heine, Bernd, Ulrike Claudi, & Friedrike Hunnemeyer. (1991). *Grammaticalization: A conceptual framework*. Chicago: The University of Chicago.
Heine, Bernd, & Tania Kuteva. (2002). *World lexicon of grammaticalization*. Cambridge: Cambridge University Press.
Heritage, John. (1998). Oh: Prefaced responses to inquiry. *Language in Society* 27: 291–334.
Heritage, John. (2012). Epistemic in action: Action formation and territories of knowledge. *Research on Language and Social Interaction* 45(1): 1–29.
Heritage, John. (2015). Well-prefaced turns in English conversation: A conversation analytic perspective. *Journal of Pragmatics* 88: 88–104.
Himmelmann, Nikolaus P. (1996). Demonstratives in narrative discourse: A taxonomy of universal uses. In Babara A. Fox (ed.), *Studies in anaphora*. Amsterdam: John Benjamins, 205–45.
Hopper, Paul J. (1979). Aspect and foregrounding in discourse. In Talmy Givón (ed.), *Syntax and semantics, Vol. 12: Discourse and syntax*. New York: Academic Press, 213–41.
Hopper, Paul J. (1987). Emergent grammar. *Berkeley Linguistic Society* 13: 139–57.
Hopper, Paul J. (1997). Diachronic and typological implications of foregrounding construction. The International Conference on Historical Linguistics, Hamburg.
Hopper, Paul J. (2011). Emergent grammar and temporality in interactional linguistics. In Peter Auer and Stefan Pfander (eds.), *Constructions: Emerging and emergent*. Berlin: Walter de Gruyter, 22–44.
Hopper, Paul J. & Elizabeth C. Traugott. (1993). *Grammaticalization*. Cambridge: Cambridge University Press.
Hopper, Paul J. & Sandra A. Thompson. (1980). Transitivity in grammar and discourse. *Language* 56(2): 251–99.
Hu, Jianhua, Haihua Pan, & Liejiong Xu. (2001). Is there a finite vs. nonfinite distinction in Chinese? *Linguistics* 39(6): 1117–48.
Huang, C.-T. James. (1989). Pro drop in Chinese: A generalized control approach. In Osvaldo Jaeggli, & Kenneth Safir (eds.), *The null subject parameter*. Dordrecht: Kulwer, 185–214.
Huang, C.-T., James, Y.-H., Audrey Li, & Yafei Li. (2009). *The syntax of Chinese*. Cambridge: Cambridge University Press.
Huang, Shuanfan. (1999). The emergence of a grammatical category definite article in spoken Chinese. *Journal of Pragmatics* 31: 77–94.

Hyland, Ken. (2005). *Metadiscourse: Exploring interaction in writing*. London and New York: Continuum.
Jasperson, Robert. (2002). Some linguistic aspects of closure cut-off. In Cecilia E. Ford, Barbara A. Fox, & Sandra A. Thompson (eds.), *The language of turn and sequence*. Oxford and New York: Oxford University Press, 257–86.
Kärkkäinen, Elise, & Tiina Keisanen. (2012). Linguistic and embodied formats for making (concrete) offers. *Discourse Studies* 14(5): 587–611.
Keenan, Edward L. (1985). Relative clause. In Timothy Shopen (ed.), *Language typology and syntactic description Vol. II: Complex construction*. Cambridge: Cambridge University Press, 141–70.
Keenan, Ochs E. & Bambi Schieffelin. (1976). Topic as a discourse notion: A study of topic in the conversation of children and adults. In Charles N. Li (ed.), *Subject and topic*. New York: Academic Press, 335–84.
Kendrick, Kobin H. & Paul Drew. (2016). Recruitment: Offers, requests, and the organization of assistance in interaction. *Research on Language and Social Interaction* 49(1): 1–19.
Labov, William. (1972). The transformation of experience in narrative syntax. In William Labov (ed.), *Language in the inner city*. Philadelphia: University of Pennsylvania Press, 345–96.
Leech, Geoffrey. (1983). *Principles of pragmatics*. London and New York: Longman.
Lehmann, Christian. (1988). Towards a typology of clause linkage. In John Haiman, & Sandra A. Thompson (eds.), *Clause combining in grammar and discourse*. Amsterdam: John Benjamins, 181–225.
Lerner, Gene H. (1987). Collaborative turn sequences: Sentence construction and social action. PhD dissertation. Irvine: University of California, Irvine.
Lerner, Gene H. (1991). On the syntax of sentences-in-progress. *Language in Society* 20(3): 441–58.
Lerner, Gene H. (2004). On the place of linguistic resource in the organization of talk in interaction: Grammar as action in prompting a speaker to elaborate. *Research on Language and Social Interaction* 37: 151–84.
Li, Charles (ed.). (1976). Subject and topic. New York: Academic Press.
Li, Charles, & Sandra A. Thompson. (1979). Third-person pronouns and zero anaphora in Chinese discourse. In *Syntax and semantics Vol. 12: Discourse and syntax*. New York: Academic Press, 311–35.
Li, Charles, & Sandra A. Thompson. (1981). *Mandarin Chinese: A functional reference grammar*. California: University of California Press.
Li, Charles, Sandra A. Thompson, & R. McMillan Thompson. (1982). The discourse motivation for the perfective aspect: The Mandarin particle *le*. In Paul J. Hopper (ed.), *Tense-aspect: Between semantics and pragmatics*. Amsterdam: John Benjamins: 19–44.
Li, Xiaoting. (2013). Language and the body in the construction of units in Mandarin face-to-face interaction. In Beatrice Szczepek Reed (ed.), *Units of talk-units of action*. Amsterdam/Philadelphia: John Benjamins, 343–75.
Li, Xiaoting. (2014a) Leaning and recipient intervening questions in Mandarin conversation. *Journal of Pragmatics* 67: 34–60.
Li, Xiaoting. (2014b). *Multimodality, interaction, and turn-taking in Mandarin conversation*. Amsterdam: John Benjamins.
Li, Xiaoting. (2016c). Some discourse-interactional uses of *yinwei* 'because' and its multimodal production in Mandarin conversation. *Language Sciences* 58: 51–78.

Li, Yen-Hui Audrey. (1990). *Order and constituency in Madarin Chinese*. Dordrecht: Kluwer.
Linell, Per. (1998). *Approaching dialogue: Talk, interaction and contexts in dialogical perspectives*. Amsterdam: John Benjamins.
Linell, Per. (2005). *The written language bias in linguistics: Its nature, origins, and transformations*. London: Routledge.
Local, John, & Gareth Walker. (2005). 'Mind the gap': Further resources in the production of multi-unit, multi-action turns. *York Papers in Linguistics Series 2*, Issue 1: 133–43.
Local, John, & Gareth Walker. (2012). How phonetic features project more talk. *Journal of the International Phonetic Association* 42(3): 255–80.
Longacre, Robert E. (1983). *The grammar of discourse*. New York: Plenum Press.
Longacre, Robert E. (2007). Sentences as combinations of clauses. In Timothy Shopen (ed.), *Language typology and syntactic description, Vol. II: Complex constructions*. Cambridge: Cambridge University Press, 235–86.
Luke, Kang-Kwong, Tsuyoshi Ono, & Sandra A. Thompson (eds.). (2012). Turns and increments: A comparative perspective. Special issue. *Discourse Processes* 49(3–4): 155–62.
Lyons, John. (1977). *Semantics. Vol. 2*. Cambridge: Cambridge University Press.
Lyons, John. (1982). Deixis and subjectivity: Loquor, ergo sum? In Robert J. Jarvella, & Wolfgang Klein (eds.), *Speech, place, and cction: Studies in deixis and related topics*. Chichester and New York: John Wiley, 101–24.
Lyons, John. (1999). *Definiteness*. Cambridge: Cambridge University Press.
Mann, William C. & Sandra A. Thompson. (1987). Rhetorical structure theory: Description and construction of text structures. *Natural language generation*. Dordrecht: Springer, 85–95.
Maruyama, Akiyo. (2003). Japanese *wa* in conversational discourse: A contrast marker. *Studies in Language* 27(2): 245–85.
Matthiessen, Christian, & Sandra A. Thompson. (1988). The structure of discourse and 'subordination'. In John Haiman and Sandra A. Thompson (eds.), *Clause combining in grammar and discourse*. Amsterdam: John Benjamins, 275–329.
Mazeland, Harrie. (2013). Grammar in conversation. In Jack Sidnell and Tanya Stivers (eds.), *The handbook of Conversation Analysis*. Chichester: Wiley-Blackwell, 475–91.
Miller, Jim, & Regina Weinert. (1998). *Spontaneous spoken language: Syntax and discourse*. Oxford: Clarendon Press.
Mondada, Lorenza. (2006). Participants' online analysis and multimodal practices: Projecting the end of the turn and the closing of the sequence. *Discourse Studies* 8(1): 117–29.
Ochs, Elinor, & Bambi Schieffelin. (1989). Language has a heart. *Text and Talk* (9): 7–26.
Ochs, Elinor, Emanuel A. Schegloff, & Sandra A. Thompson (eds.). (1996). *Interaction and grammar*. Cambridge: Cambridge University Press.
Ogden, Richard A. (2006). Phonetics and social action in agreements and disagreements. *Journal of Pragmatics* 38(10): 1752–75.
Ogden, Richard A. (2013). Clicks and percussives in English conversation. *Journal of the International Phonetic Association* 43(3): 299–320.
Ono, Tsuyoshi, & Sandra A. Thompson. (1994). Unattached NPs in English conversation. *Proceedings of the 20th Annual Meeting of the Berkeley Linguistics Society* 20: 402–419.

Ono, Tsuyoshi, & Sandra A. Thompson. (1995). What can conversation tell us about syntax? In Philip W. Davis (ed.), *Alternative linguistics: Descriptive and theoretical modes*. Amsterdam: John Benjamins, 213–71.
Ono, Tsuyoshi, & Sandra A. Thompson. (2017). Negative scope, temporality, fixedness, and right-and left-branching: Implications for typology and cognitive processing. *Studies in Language* 41(3): 543–76.
Ono, Tsuyoshi, Sandra A. Thompson, & Ryoko Suzuki. (2000). The pragmatic nature of the so-called subject marker *ga* in Japanese: Evidence from conversation. *Discourse Studies* 2(1): 55–84.
Payne, Thomas E. (1997). *Describing morphosyntax: A guide for field linguistics*. Cambridge: Cambridge University Press.
Rauniomaa, Mirka, & Tiina Keisanen. (2012). Two multimodal formats for responding to requests. *Journal of Pragmatics* 44(6–7): 829–42.
Raymond, Geoffrey. (2000). The structure of responding: Conforming and nonconforming responses to yes/no type interrogatives. PhD dissertation. Los Angeles: University of California, Los Angeles.
Raymond, Geoffrey. (2003). Grammar and social organization: Yes/no interrogatives and the structure of responding. *American Sociological Review* 68: 939–67.
Raymond, Geoffrey. (2010). Grammar and social relations: Alternative forms of yes/no-type initiating actions in health visitor interactions. In Alice F. Freed, & Susan Ehrlich (eds.), *'Why do you ask?' The function of questions in institutional discourse*. New York: Oxford University Press, 87–107.
Raymond, Geoffrey. (2013). On the relevance of 'slots' in type-conforming responses to polar interrogatives. In Beatrice S. Reed, & Geoffrey Raymond (eds.), *Units of talk-units of action*. Amsterdam: John Benjamins, 169–206.
Reinhart, Tanya. (1984). Principles of gestalt perception in the temporal organization of narrative texts. *Linguistics* 22: 779–809.
Rett, Jessica, & Sarah E. Murray. (2013). A semantic account of mirative evidentials. *Proceedings of SALT* 23: 453–472.
Richards, Jack C. & Richard W. Schmidt. (2000). *Longman dictionary of language teaching and applied linguistics*. Beijing: Foreign Language Teaching and Research Press.
Sacks, Harvey, Emanuel A. Schegloff, & Gail Jefferson. (1974). A simplest systematics for the organization of turn-taking for conversation. *Language* 50(4): 696–735.
Schegloff, Emanuel A. (1984). On some gestures' relation to talk. In J. Maxwell Atkinson and John Heritage (eds.), *Structures of social action: Studies in conversation analysis*. Cambridge: Cambridge University Press, 266–95.
Schegloff, Emanuel A. (1996). Turn organization: One intersection of grammar and interaction. In Elinor Ochs, Emanuel A. Schegloff, & Sandra A. Thompson (eds.), *Interaction and grammar*. Cambridge: Cambridge University Press, 52–133.
Schegloff, Emanuel A. & Gene H. Lerner. (2009). Beginning to respond: Well-prefaced responses to wh-questions. *Research on Language and Social Interaction* 42: 91–115.
Schiffrin, Deborah. (1987). *Discourse markers*. Cambridge: Cambridge University Press.
Schiffrin, Deborah. (1994). Making a list. *Discourse Processes* 17: 377–406.
Selting, Margret, & Elizabeth Couper-Kuhlen (eds.). (2001). *Studies in Interactional Linguistics*. Amsterdam: John Benjamins.
Shi, Dingxu. (1989). Topic chain as a syntactic category. *Journal of Chinese Linguistics*, 17(2): 223–62.
Shi, Dingxu. (2000). Topic and topic-comment construction in Mandarin Chinese. *Language* 76(2): 383–408.

Shibatani, Masayoshi. (1991). Grammaticalization of topic into subject. In Elizabeth C. Traugott, & Bernd Heine (eds.), *Approaches to grammaticalization*. Amsterdam: John Benjamins, 93–133.

Sorjonen, Marja-Leena. (2001a). Simple answers to yes-no questions: The case of Finnish. In Margret Selting, & Elizabeth Couper-Kuhlen (eds.), *Studies in Interactional Linguistics*. Amsterdam: John Benjamins, 405–32.

Sorjonen, Marja-Leena. (2001b). *Responding in conversation: A study of response particles in Finnish*. Amsterdam: John Benjamins.

Sperber, Dan, & Deirdre Wilson. (1986). *Relevance: Communication and cognition*. London: Basil Blackwell.

Stein, Dieter, & Susan Wright (eds.). (1995). *Subjectivity and subjectivisation in language*. Cambridge: Cambridge University Press.

Stivers, Tanya, & Federico Rossano. (2010). Mobilizing response. *Research on Language and Social Interaction* 43(1): 3–31.

Stivers, Tanya, Nick J. Enfield, & Stephen C. Levinson (eds.). (2010). Question-response sequences in conversation across ten languages. *Journal of Pragmatics* 42(10): 2615–2860.

Sun, Chaofen, & Tamly Givón. (1985). On the so-called SVO word order in Mandarin Chinese: A quantified text study and its implications. *Language* 61 (2): 329–51. Also seen in James H-Y Tai, & Xue Fengsheng (eds.), *Functionalism and Chinese grammar* (《功能主义与汉语语法》). Beijing: Beijing Language Institute Press, 1994.

Tai, James, & Wenze Hu. (1991). Functional motivations for the so-called 'inverted sentences' in Beijing conversational discourse. *Journal of the Chinese Language Teachers' Association* 26(3): 75–104.

Tang, Tingchi. (2000). Finite and nonfinite clauses in Chinese. *Language and Linguistics* 1: 191–214.

Tao, Hongyin. (1996). *Units in Mandarin conversation: Prosody, discourse, and grammar*. Amsterdam: John Benjamins.

Tao, Hongyin. (1999). The grammar of demonstratives in Mandarin conversational discourse: A case study. *Journal of Chinese Linguistics* 27: 69–103.

Tao, Hongyin, & Michael J. McCarthy. (2001). Understanding non-restrictive which-clause in spoken English, which is not an easy thing. *Language Sciences* 23: 651–77.

Tao, Hongyin, & Sandra A. Thompson. (1994). The discourse and grammar interface: Preferred clause structure in Mandarin conversation. *Journal of the Chinese Language Teachers Association* 29(3): 1–34.

Thompson, Sandra A. (1998). A discourse explanation for the cross-linguistic differences in the grammar of interrogation and negation. In Anna Siewierska and Jae Jung Song (eds.), *Case, typology, and grammar*. Amsterdam: John Benjamins, 307–41.

Thompson, Sandra A. (2002). 'Object complements' and conversation: Towards a realistic account. *Studies in Language* 26(1): 125–63.

Thompson, Sandra A. & Anthony Mulac. (1991). A quantitative perspective on the grammaticalization of epistemic parentheticals in English. In Elizabeth Gloss Traugott, & Bernd Heine (eds.), *Approaches to grammaticalization* (Vol. 2). Amsterdam: John Benjamins, 313–29.

Thompson, Sandra A. & Elizabeth Couper-Kuhlen. (2005). The clause as a locus of grammar and interaction. *Discourse Studies* 7(4–5): 481–505.

Thompson, Sandra A., Elizabeth Couper-Kuhlen, & Barbara A. Fox. (2015). *Grammar and everyday talk: Building responsive actions*. Cambridge: Cambridge University Press.

Tomlin, Russell S. (1985). Foreground-background information and the syntax of subordination. *Text* 5(1–2): 85–122.
Trask, Robert Lawrence. (1995). *A dicti-onary of grammatical terms in linguistics*. London: Rutledge.
Traugott, Elizabeth C. (1985). On regularity in semantic change. *Journal of Literary Semantics* 14: 155–73.
Traugott, Elizabeth C. (1988). Pragmatic strengthening and grammaticalization. In Shelley Axmaker, Annie Jaisser, & Helen Singmaster (eds.), *Proceedings of the Fourteenth Annual Meeting of the Berkeley Linguistics Society*. Berkeley: Berkeley Linguistics Society, 406–16.
Traugott, Elizabeth C. (1999). From subjectification to intersubjectification. Paper presented at the Workshop on Historical Pragmatics, Fourteenth International Conference on Historical Linguistics. Vancouver, Canada, July.
Traugott, Elizabeth C. (2000). From etymology to historical pragmatics. Paper presented at the Conference on Studies in English Historical Linguistics, University of California, Los Angeles.
Van Kuppevelt, J. (1996). Inferring from topics: Scalar implicatures as topic-dependent inferences. *Linguistics and Philosophy* 19(4): 393–443.
Wang, Yu-Fang, Aya Katza, & Chih-Hua Chen. (2003). Thinking as saying: *Shuo* ('say') in Taiwan Mandarin conversation and BBS talk. *Language Sciences* 25(5): 457–88.
Whaley, Lindsay J. (1997). *Introduction to typology: The unity and diversity of language*. California: Sage Publications.
Xu, Yulong. (1987). A study of referential functions of demonstratives in Chinese discourse. *Journal of Chinese Linguistics* 15: 132–51.
Xu, Yulong. (1995b). Resolving third-person anaphora in Chinese text: Toward a functional-pragmatic model. PhD dissertation. Hong Kong: Hong Kong Polytechnic University.
Xu, Liejiong, & D. Terence Langendoen. (1985). Topic structures in Chinese, Sections 4.3–7. *Language* 61: 11–27.
Zhang, Wei. (1998). Repair in Chinese conversation. PhD dissertation of University of Hong Kong.

Index

accessibility 15, 55, 105, 106, 119, 124, 127, 130, 133, 138, 140, 143, 147
accessible information 14, 15, 87, 133, 138, 147
active 14, 133
after-thought 28, 29, 185
agent orientation 12, 189, 213
ambiguity 22
anaphora 13, 21, 22, 24, 38, 64, 65, 67, 87, 91, 134, 136–8
aspect marking 13
assessment 96–8, 103, 240
attitude marker 167, 176, 180, 192

background information 24, 26, 27, 38, 54, 61, 70, 74, 76, 79, 81, 89, 92, 94, 103, 152, 189
behavioral discourse 12
booster 192

cataphora 49, 79
clause 12–4, 16–20, 23–7, 30, 31, 38, 40–63, 65–79, 81, 86, 87, 89, 90, 92–8, 101–3, 106, 110, 111, 114, 115, 122, 123, 126, 127, 131, 134, 135, 142, 144–6, 148, 150, 153, 155–61, 169, 177, 178, 180, 191, 198, 201, 205–8, 210, 212–4, 218, 226, 238, 239, 242–5
clause-chaining language 45, 46
cleft/focus constructions 24
code gloss 167, 191, 192
comment 20, 62, 63, 66, 68, 115, 126, 127, 140, 161, 173, 203, 223, 229, 235–7, 243
context-dependency 110
continuation 54, 65, 67, 79, 85, 116, 242
Conversation Analysis 12, 27, 29, 34, 38
conversation 11, 12, 14, 23, 27–30, 33, 34, 38, 109, 111, 114, 117

coordination 41, 48, 55, 61, 79
co-referential 160
cosubordination 41

de-categorization 35, 37
decay 22
dependency 40, 41, 49, 53, 110
dependent clause 40–53, 56
deranked verb 42, 43
desententialization 50–2, 245
discontinuous/inaccessible topics 24
Discourse Analysis/Text Grammar 13
Discourse Grammar 11–3, 29, 34, 38, 214, 229, 245
discourse topic 20–2, 54, 58, 63, 64, 67, 79, 81, 93, 94, 96, 98, 99, 103, 106, 110, 143, 144, 198, 207, 217, 219, 234, 242
discourse universe 27
discourse 11–3, 15, 18, 20–2, 24, 27, 28, 30, 33–5, 38, 41, 46, 50, 51, 53–5, 58, 61–8, 74, 76, 79, 81–3, 85–94, 96–8, 99, 103, 105, 106, 110–2, 114, 116, 117, 119, 120, 122, 124–8, 130–4, 136, 138–40, 142–4, 146–9, 151, 152, 158, 161, 163–5, 167, 172, 180, 189–92, 194, 196, 197, 198, 202–4, 206–9, 211–20, 223, 225–7, 229–31, 234, 237, 239, 242–6
ditransitive construction 76, 77, 79

embeddedness 41
enclitic 191
endophoric marker 167, 191
engagement marker 167, 192, 207, 211, 212, 242, 243
evaluative 81, 94, 103, 148, 149, 152, 157, 159, 165, 173, 174, 176, 178, 224, 235
event-line 27, 74, 103, 146

evidential marker 168, 170, 177, 180
evidential 70, 71, 167–70, 172, 177, 180, 191, 192, 239
expository 12
extensional increment 28

filler 175
final clause 45, 46
finite clause 40–3
finite verb 41, 42, 58, 131
finite 40–3, 46
focus of consciousness 14
foreground information 24, 26, 27, 70, 79, 89, 103, 122, 152, 189, 207, 212
frame marker 167, 191, 207, 212, 242, 243
fully inflected 41

generic reference 16, 81, 85, 86, 88, 89, 103, 105, 107, 108, 110, 116, 117

habitual aspect 81, 94, 96, 101–3
hedge 167, 169, 170, 173, 175, 180, 192
high accessibility marker 15

illocutionary force 44, 50, 51, 167, 175, 180, 181
impersonal perspectivization 212
increment-by-increment 28
indefinite 16, 17, 24, 67, 81–7, 89, 90, 92–4, 96, 98, 101–3, 141, 236, 238, 245
independent clause 41, 43, 45–7, 49, 50, 56
individual reference 81, 86, 105, 108, 109, 110, 117
individual 11, 25, 81, 86, 101, 105, 107–10, 117, 144, 203, 245
information flow 14
information status 14, 15, 27, 38, 89, 103, 113, 114, 147, 245
information structure 11, 15, 30, 38, 113
informative 17, 31, 192, 225
integrate 28, 51, 53
interaction 12, 14, 34, 63, 189, 191, 192, 194, 196, 220, 222, 225, 229, 231, 234, 238, 242
interactional 11–3, 18, 27, 33, 34, 167, 191, 192, 194, 195, 213, 214, 220, 225, 229–31, 234, 235, 243, 244
interactive 27, 167, 191, 192, 225
interpersonal strategy 192
interpersonal 11, 149, 186, 192, 220, 225
inter-subjectivity 33
intonation unit 12, 18–20
inverted sentence 28, 29

L-dislocated DEF-NP 24
linear grammar 28, 29
look back 22
low accessibility marker 15

macrosyntactic conjunction 150, 190, 205, 207, 213, 238, 239, 242, 243, 245
medial clause 45, 46
meta-discourse 38, 167, 180, 189, 191, 192, 203, 206, 207, 211, 212, 225, 229, 239, 243, 246
meta-narrative 189, 194
mood 41, 49–53, 59, 160, 161, 195, 240
most continuous/accessible topic 24
motivation 11, 144, 186
movable adverbs 159

narration 30, 81, 83, 89, 92, 97, 98, 103, 113, 126, 152, 189, 194, 196, 198, 203, 213–5, 219, 220, 222–7, 229, 231, 232, 234, 235, 237, 238, 242, 243
narrative action 96
narratives 12, 15, 20, 30, 34, 94, 103, 157, 172, 214, 223, 229, 234
narratology 189, 194, 215, 223
narrator 25, 84, 86, 97, 152, 189, 191, 192, 194, 196, 197, 202, 203, 206–14, 219–24, 227–31, 238, 240, 243
narrator orientation 191, 192, 194, 196, 202, 207, 211–4, 238, 243
nominality verbal noun 50, 51, 53
non-final clause 45
non-finite clause 40, 41, 42
non-finite 40–2, 46, 53, 147
non-informative 17, 31
nonverbal 192

one-new-concept constraint 12, 18, 19
on-line processing 27

preferred argument structure 18, 19
proclitic 191
pronominalization 13, 141
pronoun 13–6, 18, 19, 22–4, 33, 34, 37, 54, 67, 71, 78, 91, 95, 97, 101, 102, 106, 110, 117, 133, 140, 142, 157, 158, 192, 213, 221, 225, 226, 230, 231, 234, 238

R-dislocated DEF-NP's 24
reader 14, 15, 139, 192, 211, 222, 225, 227, 242, 243
reduced main clause 191

referent 14–7, 22, 54–6, 58, 62, 63, 68, 71, 73, 74, 77, 79, 82, 83, 86–8, 91–4, 114, 120, 123, 125, 126, 131, 138, 142, 144, 157, 158, 201, 236
referential indefinite NP 24
reflexivization 13, 141
repair 154
Rhetorical Structure Theory 11

S-adverb 148–51, 153, 157–9, 161, 163–5
scene-setting 27, 83
Self-mention 167, 192
self-repair 184, 185
semi-active 14, 133
sentence topic 20, 63, 68, 106
speaker-oriented 34
specific 20, 33, 52, 66, 72, 81, 85, 88, 98, 103, 108, 109, 130, 136, 141, 147, 151, 154, 158, 231
story-telling 96, 189, 192, 194, 196, 197, 213–5, 220, 222, 224, 229, 230, 232, 234, 243, 244
stressed 24, 86, 176
subjectivity 33, 38, 181
subjectivization 33
subordination 13, 27, 41, 48, 55, 61, 149
syntacticization 35

telling 36, 107, 111, 215, 243
temporal structure 95, 96, 99, 101, 103
temporal succession 12, 189
tense 35, 41, 42, 49–53, 59, 237, 238
the syntax of sentences-in-progress 12, 27, 32
thematic structure 12, 127

theme 24, 65, 66, 119
topic chain 12, 13, 38, 58, 67–9, 92, 94, 101, 141, 143, 144, 147, 148, 157, 158, 165, 198, 236, 245
topic continuity 22, 23, 54, 55, 62, 63, 67, 71, 75, 78, 79, 91, 98, 99, 101, 107, 110, 112, 116, 124, 130, 144, 146, 147
topic 12, 13, 20–4, 38, 54, 55, 58, 62–9, 71, 75, 78, 79, 81, 87, 88, 91–4, 96–9, 101, 103, 105–7, 110–2, 114–20, 123–6, 130, 133, 140–3, 144, 146–9, 157–9, 163, 165, 190–2, 197–9, 201–3, 205–7, 212–5, 217–20, 234, 236–8, 242–5
topicality 12, 13, 21, 55, 63, 65, 92, 98, 99, 114, 142–4
tracking 30
transition 28, 30, 85, 103, 148, 165, 167, 169, 172, 191, 202, 213, 235, 242, 243
transitivity 27, 40, 68–76, 79, 122, 123
trivial information 21, 24, 65, 87, 90, 92, 93, 117
turn 27, 28, 35, 56, 61, 64, 90, 94, 103, 127, 139, 144, 146, 157, 163, 178, 191, 199, 210, 211, 216, 218, 227, 243

unplanned sentences 28

verb-coping construction 130
VP-adverb 148, 153, 154, 164

weight-reduction 27

zero anaphora 24, 65
zero cataphora 49, 79

For Product Safety Concerns and Information please contact our EU
representative GPSR@taylorandfrancis.com
Taylor & Francis Verlag GmbH, Kaufingerstraße 24, 80331 München, Germany

www.ingramcontent.com/pod-product-compliance
Lightning Source LLC
Chambersburg PA
CBHW070747020526
44116CB00032B/2004